Dedication

To Perry Whittle, whose support, both moral and technical, helps me keep it all in perspective, and who downplays my failings and promotes my successes shamelessly.

Thank You:

Special thanks to the editor of this edition, Wendy Sharp, Senior Acquisitions Editor, for her helpful editorial direction and words of encouragement. A huge thank you to Andreas Heim, Director of Technology, Smashing Ideas, for doing an incredibly thorough and thoughtful technical edit, answering questions, and offering tips and advice along the way. Kudos to copy editor Tiffany Taylor, for rooting out my unnecessary words and lapses of grammar and style, and to production coordinators Pat Christenson and Lupe Edgar, and Owen Wolfson for making these pages clean and clear.

A tip of the hat to those whose various forms of assistance in past editions still echo in this one: Brad Bechtel, Lisa Brazieal, Erika Burback, Jeremy Clark, Cliff Colby, Peter Alan Davy, Jane DeKoven, Jonathan Duran, Victor Gavenda, Suki Gear, Becky Morgan, Erica Norton, Christi Payne, Janice Pearce, Nancy Reinhardt, Sharon Selden, Kathy Simpson, James Talbot, Bentley Wolfe, and Lisa Young.

And finally, heartfelt thanks to Marjorie Baer, Executive Acquisitions and Development Editor, Peachpit Press, for her supportive friendship and for bringing me to this project in the first place.

VISUAL QUICKSTART GUIDE

MACROMEDIA

FLASH 8

FOR WINDOWS AND MACINTOSH

Katherine Ulrich

 Peachpit Press

Visual QuickStart Guide
Macromedia Flash 8 for Windows and Macintosh
Katherine Ulrich

Peachpit Press

1249 Eighth Street
Berkeley, CA 94710
510/524-2178
800/283-9444
510/524-2221 (fax)

Find us on the Web at: www.peachpit.com
To report errors, please send a note to errata@peachpit.com
Peachpit Press is a division of Pearson Education

Publishedby Peachpit Press, in association with Macromedia Press
Copyright © 2006 by Katherine Ulrich

Editor: Wendy Sharp
Production Coordinators: Pat Christensen, Lupe Edgar
Copyeditor: Tiffany Taylor
Technical Editor: Andreas Heim
Compositors: WolfsonDesign
Indexer: Julie Bess
Cover design: Peachpit Press, Aren Howell
Cover production: Andreas Schueller

ISBN 0-321-34963-6

9 8 7 6 5 4

Printed and bound in the United States of America

CONTENTS AT A GLANCE

TABLE OF CONTENTS

INTRODUCTION

Vectors on the Web! That was the early promise and excitement of Flash, back when the Internet was expanding exponentially and suddenly everybody wanted a "Web presence, filled with color and motion." Macromedia Flash gave Web designers an efficient way to send artwork and animation over the limited-bandwidth connections that most viewers had. Plus it offered a full set of natural-style drawing tools for creating graphic content and animating it. Another Flash advantage was its easy scripting for adding interactivity.

Ultimately, Flash's efficiency at feeding graphics through the Internet's bandwidth constrictions attracted Web-content developers seeking to create complex interactive and data-driven sites, developers who were more knowledgeable about complex coding and scripting. With each new generation of the product, as Web developers push the boundaries of Flash's interactive capabilities, Macromedia has responded by increasingly exposing the inner workings of Flash through ActionScript and the JavaScript API. Today, ActionScript is a full-fledged scripting language, and Flash is a tool designed to address the needs not only of designers who want to create beautiful, low-bandwidth artwork and animation, but also of developers who want to create robust multimedia Internet applications quickly.

About Flash

Flash began life as Future Splash Animator, a nifty little program for creating and animating vector art. In 1997, Macromedia acquired Future Splash, changed the name to Flash, and promoted the program as a tool for creating graphic content for the World Wide Web. The early Flash excelled as a tool for Web-site design providing everything needed to create visually interesting (as opposed to a text-only) Web sites: tools for creating graphic elements, for animating those elements, for creating interface elements and interactivity, and for writing the HTML necessary to display all those elements as a Web page via a browser. In addition to those tools, Flash 8 also includes ActionScript 2.0 for scripting complex interactivity, video-import tools, and data-handling components.

Each new generation of Flash adds features and functions that expand the program's capabilities. Originally centered on creating vector artwork, animation, and basic interactivity, Flash is now a toolkit for creating what have come to be called Rich Internet Applications (RIAs). An RIA might be anything from an online store to a corporate training module to a snazzy promotional piece describing this year's hottest new car, complete with customizable virtual test-drives. Yet the program preserves the easy-to-use drawing and animation tools that made it so popular to begin with. And Flash continues to assist authors with differing skill levels and different objectives to create the interactivity their projects require. The most recent version, Flash 8, comes in two flavors: Flash Basic 8 and Flash Professional 8. Both versions include design tools and scripting tools. Flash Professional 8 has extra features that will appeal particularly to people creating complex interactive sites or developing Flash Lite content (a stream-lined version of Flash content that's delivered over mobile devices, such as phones).

Vectors vs. Bitmaps

The data that creates vector graphics and the data that creates bitmapped graphics are similar, in that they're mathematical instructions to the computer about how to create images onscreen. Bitmaps, however, are often lengthier and result in a less versatile graphic; vector graphics are compact and scaleable. Bitmap instructions break a whole graphic into dots and describe each one; vector instructions describe the graphic mathematically as a series of lines and arcs (**Figure i.1**). Picture a 1-inch black horizontal line on a field of white. For a bitmap, the instructions would go something like this: Make a white dot, make a white dot, make a black dot, make a black dot, make a black dot, repeating until there are enough black dots to make a 1-inch line. Then the white-dot instructions start again and continue to fill the rest of the screen with white dots. The vector instructions would be a formula for a straight line, plus the coordinates that define the line's position onscreen.

Figure i.1 For a computer to draw a bitmapped graphic, it must receive a set of instructions for each dot (each bit of data) that makes up the image. Instructions for a vector graphic describe the lines and curves that make up the image mathematically. The bitmapped line (left) appears much rougher than the vector line (right). You can't enlarge the bitmapped line without losing quality. But you can make the vector line as big as you like; it retains its solid appearance.

What Makes Flash a Special Web-Design Tool?

Flash's early claim to fame was its ability to deliver vector images over the Web. What's the advantage of using vector graphics? Vectors keep file sizes down, and they're scaleable: This means you can maintain control of what a Web site looks like when your viewer resizes the browser window, for example, making the whole thing stay in proportion as the window grows or shrinks.

Another advantage that Flash provides is progressive download capability. Progressive download allows some elements of a Web site to display immediately upon download while more information continues to arrive over the Internet. Both the use of vector images and the use of progressive download enhance the viewer's experience.

Other facets of Flash's appeal include its ability to create original artwork with both Bézier and natural-style drawing tools; its ability to handle imported artwork, sound, and video; and its ability to assist designers and developers in creating animation and interactivity. Over time, Macromedia has enhanced Flash's tools for creating interactivity. Now, Flash contains a full-fledged object-oriented scripting language. ActionScript 2.0 is compliant with the ECMA-262 specification, making it much more like JavaScript. ActionScript 2.0 supports inheritance, strong typing, and the event model.

How Flash Animates

Flash uses standard animation techniques to create the illusion of movement. You create a series of still images, each slightly different from the next. By displaying the images rapidly, one after another, you simulate continuous movement. Flash's animation tools help you create, organize, and synchronize the animation of multiple graphic elements, sounds, and video clips.

Flash File Formats

Flash is both an authoring environment for creating content and a playback system for making that content viewable on a local computer or in a Web browser. You create artwork, animation, and interactivity in Flash-format files. These files have the extension .fla and are often referred to as *FLAs*. To make that content viewable on the Web, you convert the FLA files to Flash Player format; Flash Player files have the extension .swf. Another name for the playable format is *SWF* (pronounced *swif*).

How Flash Delivers

Flash's publishing feature creates the necessary HTML code to display your Flash content in a Web browser. You can also choose alternate methods of delivering Flash content—as animated GIF images, for example, or as a QuickTime movie. Flash creates those alternate files during the publishing process.

About Flash Player

In Flash's early days, the need to use a player to view Flash content was considered a drawback to creating Web content with Flash. Designers feared that users would be reluctant to spend time downloading another helper application for their browsers. But Flash has become the de facto standard for delivering Web rich-media content—especially interactive vector art and animation on the Web—and Flash Player is now widely distributed. Macromedia estimates that more than 97 percent of machines that are being used to access the Internet already have some version of Flash Player installed.

Flash 8: What's New?

Although Macromedia uses the names Basic and Professional to distinguish the two versions of Flash 8, the division of features may not match everyone's idea of what those words mean. The breakdown of features doesn't directly correlate to the divisions that are often made about who uses Flash: designer versus developer, artist versus programmer, or beginner/amateur versus experienced/professional. Flash Basic is a tool for creating artistic, interactive Web content, and so is Flash Professional. The Professional version adds features that will be of particular help to those who use Flash to develop Web applications, but the Professional version adds advanced graphics, animation, and video features as well.

The goal of *Flash 8 Visual Quickstart Guide* is to bring beginning-to-intermediate Flash users quickly up to speed using Flash's design, animation, and basic interactivity tools. Unfortunately, that means we can't spend time on some of Flash's other impressive tools, such as video and complex ActionScripting. Many excellent resources can help you learn more about Flash's advanced features once you've finished this book.

The following headings highlight some of the new features of Flash 8.

What Is Progressive Downloading?

Most viewers lack the patience to wait for an entire site to download, especially one that includes big bitmaps, sounds, or video. Flash breaks the content of your Web site into chunks that can be sent over the Internet a little bit at a time. Progressive download (which is also sometimes referred to as *streaming* in Flash) means that once some of the art of your site has downloaded, Flash can display it while the rest of your data continues to download. As Flash plays the first pieces of your movie, subsequent pieces keep coming into your viewer's computer, and Flash feeds them out at the specified rate. If you plan your movie right, the images coming in never catch up to the images being displayed, and your viewer sees only a continuous flow of images.

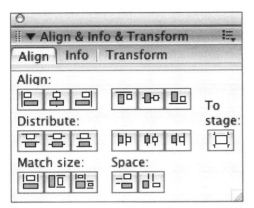

Figure i.2 Flash 8 offers tabbed panel groups. To view a different panel, click its name.

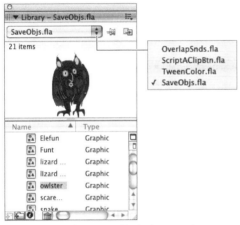

Figure i.3 The Library panel in Flash 8 contains information for all the Flash documents currently open. To view the contents of a different library, choose it from the menu of open documents.

Interface Improvements

Pasteboard. Flash's authoring environment contains the *Stage*, where you place the artwork that appears in your final Flash creation, and the *Pasteboard* (formerly called the *work area*), a storage area surrounding the Stage. The Pasteboard gives you more storage space for objects that need to stay behind the scenes than the work area used to. The Pasteboard grows to meet your needs. If you place graphic elements that are larger than the current Pasteboard, Flash increases the size of the Pasteboard to accommodate them.

Tabbed documents for Mac users.
The Windows operating system has always allowed Flash users to view multiple open documents as tabs in a single window. Flash 8 gives Mac users the same capability. By default, multiple open documents appear as tabs in one window. You can see the documents in separate windows by changing Preferences settings.

Tabbed panels for everyone. In previous versions, Flash grouped panels vertically, which takes up a lot of room on the desktop and leads users to repeatedly collapse and expand panel windows. Flash 8 adds the ability to group multiple panels as tabs in a single window (**Figure i.2**).

Multiple libraries in one panel. In previous versions, each active Flash document had a separate Library panel. In Flash 8, by default, the Library panel contains the libraries of all open documents; as you switch documents, the active document's library appears in the panel. To view another document's library, choose it from a menu in the Library panel (**Figure i.3**). You can pin the library currently on display so it doesn't change when you switch documents; you can also open libraries in separate windows.

Object-level undo. Flash 8's history-tracking feature gives you a choice of techniques for undoing your work. Flash can track each step you take in a document in sequence, and you can undo those steps in reverse order. Alternatively, Flash can track the steps used in creating symbols separately from the other steps you take. That way, you can undo changes to one symbol without undoing changes you made to another symbol or to the document as a whole.

Script Assist mode. In Script Assist mode, Flash 8's Actions panel provides text fields, menus, radio buttons, and check boxes that help you enter ActionScript code in the correct syntax (**Figure i.4**).

Script Assist window

Figure i.4 Assisted scripting returns in Flash 8. The Script Assist mode of the Actions panel helps you to enter scripts. You make choices and enter text in the Script Assist window; Flash writes the ActionScript code using the correct syntax.

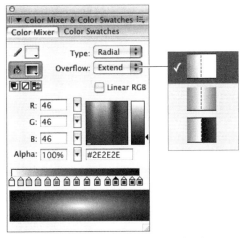

Figure i.5 When you resize a gradient so that it's smaller than the object it's filling, you control the way the gradient fills the gap by choosing an overflow method from the menu in the Color Mixer panel.

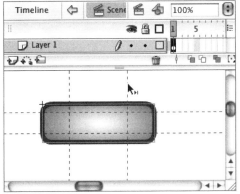

Figure i.6 When you edit a movie-clip symbol that has 9-slice scaling enabled, guidelines appear within the symbol. The draggable guides define the corners of the object. The corner sections don't scale when you resize the object.

Design-Tool Enhancements

Object Drawing mode. Flash's natural-style drawing tools create shapes that interact with one another. For anyone used to using other graphics tools, such as Macromedia FreeHand or Adobe Illustrator, that's a confusing concept. Flash 8's Object Drawing mode enables you to draw shapes that don't interact unless you command them to.

Gradients. Flash 8's gradients can display up to 15 colors. You control how a gradient fills an object when you resize the gradient (**Figure i.5**). You can modify the location of a radial gradient's focal point. You can now use gradients in strokes as well as in fills.

Flash Type. Flash 8 uses a new text-rendering engine that improves the readability of text, especially text at small sizes. Flash Type renders text in both the authoring environment and in Flash Player. Users of Flash Professional 8 can customize the way Flash Type antialiases their text.

9-slice scaling. Flash's default scaling can distort graphic-objects when you resize them; the distortion is particularly noticeable at the corners of the resized objects. Flash 8 offers a technique for improving the looks of scaled movie-clip symbols. By enabling a movie-clip symbol's 9-slice scaling guides, you can define corner regions that don't change when the symbol scales. The result is a consistent look among different-sized copies of the same symbol (**Figure i.6**).

FLASH 8: WHAT'S NEW?

Bitmap caching. When a button or movie-clip symbol contains complex vector graphics, animating the symbol can bog down the playback of your movie. That's true even if the symbol just moves around the Stage without changing its content. Runtime bitmap caching improves playback performance by taking a bitmap "snapshot" of such a symbol and moving the bitmap around the Stage pixel by pixel. Bitmap caching avoids the need to recalculate complex vectors for the symbol in each new position.

Filters and blend modes (Professional only). Flash Professional 8 provides two ways to create special effects for objects. Filters can be applied to text boxes and movie-clip and button symbols to create such effects as glows, drop shadows, or blurs. Blends can be applied only to movie-clip symbols. Flash's blend modes work similarly to those found in Macromedia FireWorks and Adobe Photoshop, allowing you to composite images and control the interaction of colors among overlapping objects.

Custom easing (Professional only). Flash's easing controls have always helped make animations appear more natural by letting you control the rate of change in a tweened animation sequence. Custom easing gives you more precise control, allowing you to set different rates of change for different properties (for example, changing an object's position quickly, but changing its color slowly). You can also vary the rate of change over time: for example, starting the change slowly, speeding up in the middle of the animation sequence, and then slowing down at the end.

Video enhancements (Professional only). Flash Professional 8 offers several new video features:

◆ On2 VP6 is a new codec (compressor/decompressor) for creating Flash Player 8 content. On2 VP6 improves Flash's ability to balance file size and quality for video that you include in your Flash movies.

◆ Flash 8 Vide Encoder is a stand-alone video encoder that can handle batch processing of video files.

◆ Flash 8 Professional supports alpha channels. You can use alpha channels to create transparency effects: for example, compositing video animation and cartoon animation (often called blue- or green-screen work).

◆ Flash 8 Professional supports embedded cue points for synchronizing video and Flash animation.

How to Use This Book

Like all Visual QuickStart Guides, this book seeks to take you out of the passive reading mode and help you get started working in the program. The tasks in the book teach you to use Flash's features. The book is suitable for beginners who are just starting to use Flash and for intermediate-level Flash designers. The initial chapters cover the basics of creating graphic elements by using Flash's unique set of drawing tools. Next, you learn how to turn graphic elements into animations. After that, you learn to create basic user-interface elements, such as rollover buttons. To make your content interactive, you'll work with the Actions panel in Script Assist mode and the Behaviors panel to create basic ActionScript. There's also information about importing and working with various non-Flash content: artwork from other applications and sounds. Finally, you learn to use Flash's Publish feature to create HTML for putting your Flash creations on the Web.

The tasks in the chapters that follow can be carried out in either Flash Basic 8 or Flash Professional 8; in general, the tasks rely on features that are found in both versions, with additional notes where Flash Professional adds other tools.

What You Should Already Know

In order to get you started quickly, this book makes a few assumptions:

◆ Flash Basic 8 or Flash Professional 8 is already installed on your computer.

◆ You're familiar with the workings of your operating system.

◆ You can carry out basic tasks, such as opening, closing, and saving documents; opening, closing, resizing, collapsing, and expanding document windows and dialogs; using hierarchical menus, pop-up menus, radio buttons, and check boxes; and carrying out standard application commands such as copy, cut, paste, delete, and undo.

Cross-Platform Issues

Macromedia designed Flash's authoring environment to have—as much as possible—the same interface on the Macintosh that it has on the Windows platform. Still, differences exist where the user interfaces of the platforms diverge. When these differences are substantial, this book describes the procedures for both platforms. Illustrations of dialog boxes come from both platforms, but generally, there is no special indication as to which platform is shown. If a given feature differs greatly between platforms, the variations are illustrated. If a feature is available only on one platform, that is noted in the text.

Originally, Macintosh computers required Macintosh keyboards, and some key names were unique to that keyboard: for example, Return (instead of Enter) and Delete (instead of Backspace). This book generally uses Enter and Delete for these two key names.

Keyboard Shortcuts

Most of Flash's menu-based commands have a keyboard equivalent. That equivalent appears in the menu next to the command name. When this book first introduces a command, it also describes the keyboard shortcut. In subsequent mentions of the command, however, the keyboard shortcut usually is omitted. You'll find a complete list of these commands on Peachpit Press's companion Web site for this book, http://www.peachpit.com/vqs/flash8/.

Contextual Menus

Both the Macintosh and Windows platforms offer contextual menus. To access one of these contextual menus, Control-click (Mac) or right-click (Windows) an element in the Flash movie. You'll see a menu of commands that are appropriate for working with that element. For the most part, these commands duplicate commands in the main menu; therefore, this book doesn't generally note them as alternatives for the commands described in the book. The book does point out when using the contextual menu is particularly handy or when a contextual menu contains a command that is unavailable from the main menu bar.

The Artwork

The Flash graphics in this book are simple and easy to draw. In most cases, the examples are based on simple geometric shapes, which means you can spend your time seeing the Flash features in action instead of re-creating fancy artwork. To make it even easier for you to follow along, Flash files containing the graphic elements that you need for each task are available on Peachpit Press's companion Web site for this book, http://www.peachpit.com/vqs/ flash8/.

THE FLASH AUTHORING TOOL

Before you get started creating projects in Macromedia Flash 8, it's helpful to take a look around the authoring environment and begin to recognize and manipulate its components. When you open Flash for the first time, you'll see the Flash Start page. This page acts as a gateway to many documents and operations in Flash. When you open a Flash document, you enter the Flash authoring environment. Each Flash document consists of four basic items: the Timeline, a record of every frame, layer, and scene in your movie; the Edit Bar, which displays identifying text and menus for choosing symbols and scenes to work on; the Stage, the actual area in which your movie displays; and the Pasteboard, extra work space that surrounds the Stage. The Stage and Pasteboard are present when you edit a document. You can collapse or close the Timeline and hide the Edit Bar, and you can open any combination of other panels and tools that you need to work with your Flash content.

What does the Flash authoring environment look like? And how do you access tools and different views? This chapter presents a quick tour: subsequent chapters explain in more detail what's what as you get into using each element.

Working with Flash Documents

Most of the basic document operations in Flash—opening, closing, and saving files—are straightforward to experienced computer users. Creating new documents may be a little different than in other programs, because Flash creates a variety of document types. Flash's Start page assists you in opening and creating these various Flash documents.

To set launch preferences:

1. From the Flash application menu (Mac) or Edit menu (Windows), choose Preferences.

   The Preferences dialog appears. The General category is selected by default.

2. From the On Launch menu, *select one of the following* (**Figure 1.1**):

   ▲ No document. Flash's menu bar and panels appear at launch, but no document opens.

   ▲ New Document. Flash opens a new document at launch.

   ▲ Last Documents Open. Flash opens the documents that were open when you ended the previous work session.

   ▲ Show Start Page. (The default setting.) Flash displays the Start page at launch and any time you have closed all the documents during a work session.

3. Click OK.

Figure 1.1 The On Launch options in the General category of the Preferences dialog tell Flash what type of document(s), if any, to open on startup.

WORKING WITH FLASH DOCUMENTS

✔ Tips

■ To change launch preferences to the New Document option quickly, click the Don't Show Again button in the lower-left corner of the Start page. A dialog box appears to remind you that you must change the launch settings in the General tab of the Preferences dialog to see the Start page again.

■ Flash Professional 8 users take note: Flash treats projects as a type of document. If you have a project open in the Project panel, Flash does not display the Start page, even if all other documents are closed.

About Preferences

To see, or not to see, the Start page is just one of many preference settings in Flash. To choose new settings, you open the Preferences dialog. From the Flash application menu (Mac) or Edit menu (Windows), choose Preferences, and select a category from the list in the left-hand pane. Choose settings for that category in the main window. Preferences fall into seven categories: General, ActionScript, Auto Format, Clipboard, Drawing, Text, and Warnings. You'll learn about specific Preferences settings as they relate to specific tasks throughout this book.

Touring the Start Page

Flash's default setting opens the Start page when you launch. The Start page contains active links that enable you to open documents quickly. You can open a new document, a document that you worked on recently, or a template document. You can link to Flash tutorials or to the Macromedia Flash Exchange site, where you can download third-party extensions such as new components, Timeline Effects, and Behaviors as they become available (**Figure 1.2**).

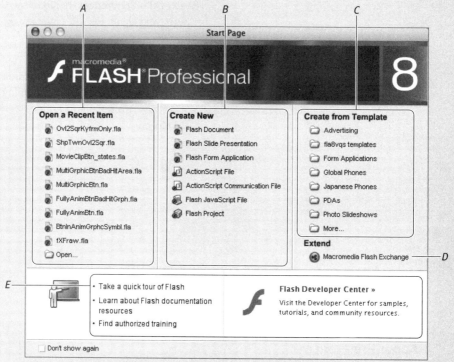

Figure 1.2 The Start page presents common operations you might want to carry out at the beginning of a work session: opening a document you worked on recently (A), creating a new Flash document (B), or creating documents from templates (C). There are also links for browsing the Macromedia Flash Exchange site, to find third-party extensions (D). For new users, there are links to the tutorials that come with Flash as well as other training resources (E).

Figure 1.3 To create a new document in Flash, choose File > New. The New Document dialog opens, with the General View and Flash Document selected by default. Click OK to create a new document.

Open a Recent Item

StopSndBehav.fla

PingPong.fla

TheBeeTree.fla

ManyObjs.fla

MagicWandBeeTest.fla

MakeYourOwnBtn.fla

bigAnimation.fla

testpub.fla

Scale Movie.fla

Open...

Figure 1.4 The Open a Recent Item section of the Start page allows you to view links to the last nine documents you worked on. Clicking a filename opens the document.

To create a new Flash document:

◆ From the Start page, in the Create New section, click the Flash Document link. Flash opens a new blank document.

or

1. Choose File > New, or press ⌘-N (Mac) or Ctrl-N (Windows).

   Flash opens the New Document dialog (**Figure 1.3**). This dialog has two views: General and Templates. General is selected by default.

2. In the General view, select Flash Document.

3. Click OK.

   Flash opens a new blank document.

✔ Tip

■ To switch views in the New Document dialog, click the appropriate tab (Windows) or button (Mac) at the top of the dialog.

To open an existing document:

◆ From the Start page, in the Open a Recent Item section, click the name of a recent file (**Figure 1.4**). Flash opens that file directly.

or

1. From the Start page, in the Open a Recent Item section, click the Open link.

   or

   Choose File > Open.

   The Open dialog appears.

2. Navigate to the file you want to open.

3. Select the file.

4. Click Open.

WORKING WITH FLASH DOCUMENTS

✔ Tips

- In previous versions of Flash running under Windows, multiple open documents automatically appeared as tabs within the application window; documents in the Mac environment were always separate. Flash 8 makes it possible to view multiple open documents as tabs in the Mac environment also (it's the default Preference setting). Inactive documents appear in tabs above the active document. Click a tab to bring that document to the front (**Figure 1.5**). To view documents in separate windows in the Windows environment, you must choose Tile or Cascade from the Window menu. To view documents in separate windows on the Mac, from the Flash application menu, choose Preferences; in the General category, deselect the Open Documents in Tabs check box; and click OK.

- You can change the order of the tabs for open documents by dragging a tab to a new position.

- When you've been working with a document, adding and deleting graphic materials, sounds, video, and so on, the file size builds up because data about the deleted items remains in the file. Choosing File > Save and Compact reduces the file size. However, the Save and Compact command takes longer than a regular Save command and changes the tab order for that document. When you begin editing the file, it again bulks up quickly. You may wish to compact the file only at the end of the authoring process or when file size is crucial—for example, if you need to email the file to a colleague.

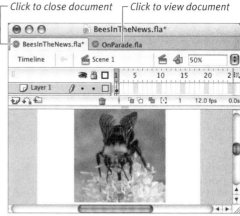

Click to close document   *Click to view document*

Figure 1.5 Viewing multiple open documents as tabs in a single window (always a possibility in the Windows world) is now the default Preference setting in the Mac environment as well. Click an inactive title to bring that document to the front. To close the active document, click the close button in the tab.

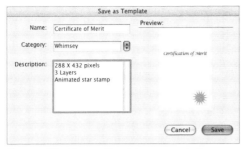

Figure 1.6 The Save as Template command allows you to save Flash documents for reuse. You can create your own template categories and provide a brief description of the template file you're saving in the Save as Template dialog.

Working with Template Documents

If you work repeatedly with one type of Flash document—you create banner ads of a specific size with a consistent background or elements, for example—you can save that basic document as a template.

To create a template document:

1. Open the document that you want to turn into a template.

2. Choose File > Save as Template.

   The Save as Template dialog appears, showing a preview of your document (**Figure 1.6**).

3. In the Name field, type a name for the template.

4. To specify a category, *do either of the following:*

   ▲ To select an existing category, from the Category pop-up menu, choose the desired category.

   ▲ To create a new category, in the Category field, type a name.

5. In the Description field, type a brief summary or reminder of what the template is for.

   Though you can enter as much text as you like in this field, once you click Save, Flash limits the description that accompanies the actual template to the first 255 characters. Still, it's a good idea to give some indication of the intended uses for the template or what its special features are.

6. Click Save.

   Flash saves the file as a master template document in a folder named Templates within the Configuration folder (see, "The Mystery of the Configuration Folder," later in this chapter).

✔ Tip

■ Once you've completed the template, close the document. You may think that after saving the document as a template you're working in a copy made from the template, but you're not. You're still working on the master template document until you close it.

WORKING WITH TEMPLATE DOCUMENTS

To open a new document from a template document:

1. From the Start page, in the Create from Template section, click the name of a specific template folder or click the folder named More (**Figure 1.7**).

   The New from Template dialog appears.

   or

   Choose File > New.

   The New Document/New from Template dialog appears (**Figure 1.8**). The New Document and New from Template dialogs are identical except for their names. Both display two views: General and Templates. The dialog's name changes to reflect the active view. When you click a template folder in the Start page, the Templates view is selected by default in the dialog.

2. From the Category list, choose the appropriate category.

3. From the Templates list, choose the template you want to use.

   The dialog previews the selected template's first frame and provides a brief description of the template, if one is available.

4. Click OK.

   Flash opens a new document with all the contents of the template.

Figure 1.7 Choose a template link in the Start page to access the New from Template dialog.

Figure 1.8 The Templates view of the New from Template (or New Document) dialog displays a preview and a description (when available) for the item selected in the Category and Templates lists.

✔ Tips

- When you choose File > New, Flash displays the document-creation dialog based on the type of file you created previously. The New Document dialog appears if the last file you created was a document. The New from Template dialog appears if the last file was a template.

- On the Mac, when the New from Template dialog opens, the name of the last template you used is highlighted in the Templates list. The preview window, however, shows the first template in the list. If you click OK now, Flash opens the previewed template, not the one that appears to be selected. If you want to use that highlighted template, click its name and wait till it appears in the preview window before clicking OK.

The Mystery of the Configuration Folder

The operating systems that run Flash 8 can be configured for multiple users, storing each user's files and special settings separately. To deal with customized settings, Flash uses Configuration Folders in three folders: The *Application-Level Configuration Folder* governs settings for everyone who uses Flash on the computer; you must have administrative privileges to make changes to this folder. The *All-User-Level Configuration Folder* contains master files for all users; the *User-Level Configuration Folder* contains the files that each user has customized during work with Flash on this computer.

When you create a template document, for example, Flash stores it in a Templates folder inside your User-Level Configuration Folder. The templates that come with Flash are stored in the Application-Level Configuration Folder.

To add, delete, or rename items in a Configuration folder manually, you must have the required access privileges and navigate the hierarchy of nested folders on your hard drive to open the folder.

The folder that will most concern individual Flash users is the User-Level Configuration Folder. The first part of its folder hierarchy is slightly different in each operating system:

Windows XP/2000:
`BootDrive\Documents and Settings\userName\Local Settings\Application Data\`

Mac OS X: `HardDriveName:Users:userName:Library:Application Support:`

From there on, the hierarchy of folders is always the same. For those using the English version of Flash, it's `Macromedia\Flash 8\en\Configuration`. Users of localized versions will see their language code instead of `en` in the folder hierarchy.

Touring the Flash Authoring Environment

A Flash document consists of the Timeline, which holds the frames, layers, and scenes that make up your movie; the Stage, where the graphic content of the movie is displayed; the Edit Bar, which displays information about what you're currently editing and provides access to other scenes and elements; and a Pasteboard, which extends beyond the Stage on all sides (**Figure 1.9**).

✔ Tip

- The Document Properties tab of the Property inspector contains a shortcut to the Document Properties dialog. Just click the Size button. You'll learn more about the Property inspector later in this chapter.

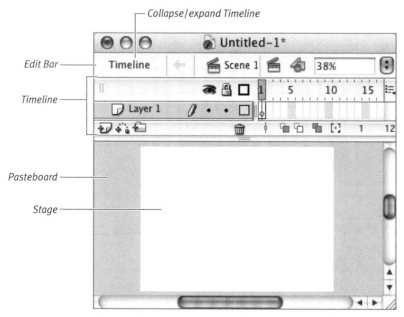

Figure 1.9 A new document opened in Flash consists of the Timeline, the Stage, the Edit Bar, and the Pasteboard.

About the Timeline

The Timeline is a vital, complex organizational tool: it visually represents every element of your movie, and is the framework on which you build your projects. You will use it extensively when you create animations, and I'll go much more deeply into its components later in the book, specifically Chapter 8. For now, you only need to understand the Timeline generally.

Figure 1.10 identifies the major Timeline elements. You can dock the Timeline to any side of a Flash window, float it as a separate window, collapse it, or hide it completely to get more room for working with elements on the Stage.

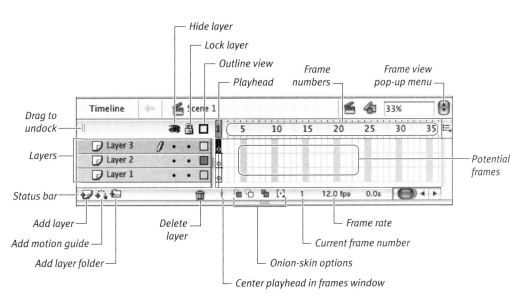

Figure 1.10 The Timeline is the complete record of your movie. It represents all the scenes, frames, and layers that make up the movie. Frames appear in chronological order. Clicking any frame in the Timeline takes you directly to that frame and displays its contents on the Stage.

To undock the Timeline window:

1. Position the pointer over the *gripper* (the textured area) on the left side of the title bar at the top of the Timeline.

The pointer changes to the move icon.

2. Click and drag away from the document window (**Figure 1.11**).

A gray outline represents the Timeline's new position.

3. Release the mouse button.

✔ Tips

■ To redock the Timeline, reverse the procedure. Drag the Timeline preview to the top of the document window or to any other edge. When you drag the Timeline to the right or left edge of the Stage, the Timeline docks vertically.

■ On the Mac, if the Timeline is docked to the bottom or one side of the document window, double-click the gripper to redock the Timeline at the top of the window.

■ To collapse the Timeline window, click the Timeline button in the upper-left corner of the Edit Bar.

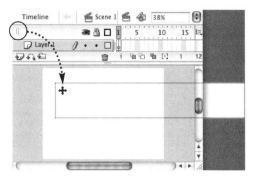

Figure 1.11 Drag the Timeline by the *gripper*—the textured portion of the title bar (top)—and then release the mouse button. The Timeline floats in its own window (bottom).

The Mystery of the Timeline

If you think of your Flash movie as a book, the Timeline is its interactive table of contents: Each scene is like a chapter; each frame is like a page. Imagine that you could point to Chapter 10 in the table of contents, and the book would flip open to the first page of that chapter. In Flash, when you click a frame in the Timeline (or when the playhead enters a frame), that frame appears in your document window.

A Flash movie is much more complex than a book, of course. Each movie "page" may actually be several transparent sheets stacked one on top of another. Flash keeps track of these sheets in what it calls *layers*. And the whole "book" appears to be in motion as you move through the table of contents, with some unseen hand flipping the pages.

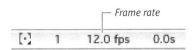

Figure 1.12 Double-clicking the frame-rate display in the Status bar is a quick way to access the Document Properties dialog.

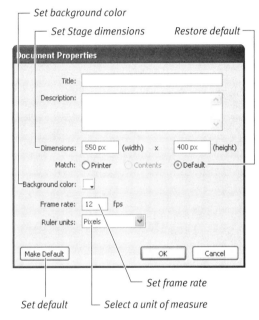

Figure 1.13 The Document Properties dialog is where you set all the parameters for viewing the Stage. Selecting a unit of measure for the rulers resets the unit measurement for all the Stage's parameters. Clicking the color control pops up the current set of colors and lets you choose one for the background. Clicking Make Default sets the parameters for all new documents you create.

About Document Properties

The Document Properties dialog lets you define the Stage (its dimensions, the color of the background on which your artwork appears, and the units of measure for rulers and grids) and set a frame rate for playing your movie. Frames are the lifeblood of your animation, and the *frame rate* is the heart that keeps that blood flowing at a certain speed. Flash's default setting is 12 frames per second (fps)—a reasonable setting for animations viewed over the Web. (By comparison, the standard frame rate for film movies is double that speed.). You'll learn more about how frame rates affect animation in Chapter 8.

In Flash 8, the Document Properties dialog has a feature for creating metadata for .swf files. Metadata allows search engines to find your creations by title and/or keywords when you publish them to the Web. You can also use the Document Properties tab of the Property inspector to set some document properties. You'll learn more about using the Property inspector later in this chapter.

To open the Document Properties dialog:

Do either of the following:

◆ Choose Modify > Document; or press ⌘-J (Mac) or Ctrl-J (Windows).

◆ In the Timeline's Status bar, double-click the frame-rate display (**Figure 1.12**).

The Document Properties dialog appears (**Figure 1.13**).

✔ Tip

■ The Document Properties tab of the Property inspector also contains a short-cut to the Document Properties dialog. Just click the Size button. You'll learn more about the Property inspector later in this chapter.

To create .swf metadata:

1. Open the Document Properties dialog.

2. In the Title field, enter a title for your document.

3. In the Description field, enter descriptive words (*keywords*) (**Figure 1.14**).

   When you publish your movie, the .swf file will contain metadata from the Title and Description fields. To learn about publishing movies, see Chapter 16.

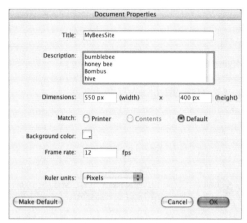

Figure 1.14 By entering a title in the Title field and descriptive keywords in the Description field, you add metadata to your published movie (.swf file), making the metadata available to search engines for searching.

The Mystery of .swf Metadata

In Flash 8, the Document Properties dialog contains two new fields: Title and Description. When you publish your document (see Chapter 16), the text in these fields gets turned into metadata attached to the .swf file. Search engines can use this metadata to help potential users find your creation. Even though earlier versions of Flash did not create .swf metadata, when you publish from Flash 8 to an earlier version, Flash 8 still creates the metadata for that .swf file. Note that the title and keywords in the Description field don't become part of the metadata of the .html file you publish; you must create metadata for the .html file yourself.

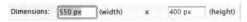

Figure 1.15 To assign new proportions to your Stage, type a width and height in the Dimensions section of the Document Properties dialog.

Figure 1.16 To make your Stage just big enough to enclose the elements in your movie, select the Contents radio button in the Match section of the Document Properties dialog.

To set the size of the Stage:

1. Open the Document Properties dialog, and *do one of the following:*

   ▲ To set the Stage's dimensions, type values for width and height in the appropriate fields of the Dimensions section (**Figure 1.15**). Flash automatically assigns the units of measure currently selected in Ruler Units.

   ▲ To create a Stage big enough to cover all the elements in your movie, in the Match section of the Document Properties dialog, select the Contents radio button (**Figure 1.16**). Flash calculates the minimum Stage size required to cover all the elements in the movie and enters those measurements in the width and height fields of the Dimensions section.

   ▲ To set the Stage size to the maximum print area currently available, in the Match section of the Document Properties dialog, select the Printer radio button. Flash gets the paper size from the Page Setup dialog, subtracts the current margins, and puts the resulting measurements in the width and height fields of the Dimensions section.

2. Click OK.

ABOUT DOCUMENT PROPERTIES

✔ Tips

- If you've entered new dimensions, either manually or by selecting Printer or Contents for matching, you can return to the default Stage dimensions by clicking the Default radio button.

- To set the units of measure for your document, in the Document Properties dialog, from the Ruler Units menu, choose the units of measure you prefer. You can work in inches, decimal inches, points, centimeters, millimeters, and pixels. Flash uses these units to calculate all measured items on the Stage: rulers, grid spacing, and dimensions.

- If you want a banner that's 1 inch tall and 5 inches wide, but you don't know what that size is in pixels (the standard unit of measure used for working on the Web), Document Properties can figure it out for you. First, set Ruler Units to inches. Type 1 in the height field and 5 in the width field. Then, return to Ruler Units and choose pixels. Flash does the math and sets the Stage dimensions. (Note that Flash uses screen pixels in its calculations. This means an inch in your movie may differ from an inch in the real world, depending on the resolution of the monitor on which you view the Flash movie.)

About the Pasteboard

In previous versions of Flash, the Pasteboard (formerly called the *work area*) was a set, limited size. In Flash 8, the Pasteboard grows to accommodate your need for extra space. As you drag items from the Stage to the Pasteboard area, Flash enlarges the Pasteboard to hold them. If you move a large graphic element onto the Pasteboard, and some of it lies outside the area of the open document window, you can see the scroll bar move back toward the center of its range. There is now more Pasteboard area that's hidden from view. Use the scroll bars to view your graphic element and the enlarged Pasteboard. (You'll learn about creating graphic elements in Chapter 2 and repositioning them in Chapter 4.)

Color control

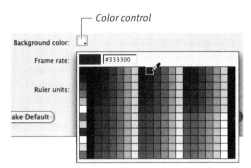

Background color:

Frame rate: #333300

Ruler units:

ake Default

Figure 1.17 To assign your Stage a new color, choose one from the Background Color control in the Document Properties dialog.

Frame rate: 24 fps

Figure 1.18 Typing a frame rate for your movie in the Frame Rate field of the Document Properties dialog sets Flash to display that number of frames in 1 second.

To set the background color:

1. Open the Document Properties dialog.

2. Click the Background Color control.

   The pointer changes to an eyedropper, and a set of swatches appears (**Figure 1.17**).

3. To select a background color, *do either of the following:*

   ▲ Click a swatch with the eyedropper pointer.

   ▲ Click the hexadecimal-color field (to activate it), type a value, and press Enter.

   The selected color appears in the Background Color control.

4. Click OK.

   The Stage now appears in the color you selected.

✔ Tip

■ The Document Properties tab of the Property inspector also contains a Background Color control for selecting the movie's background color. You'll learn more about the Property inspector later in this chapter; you'll learn more about assigning colors with color controls in Chapter 2.

To set the frame rate:

1. Open the Document Properties dialog.

2. In the Frame Rate field, type the number of frames you want Flash to display in 1 second (**Figure 1.18**).

3. Click OK.

   The frame-rate setting appears in the Status bar of the current document.

To save your settings as the default:

◆ In the Document Properties dialog, click the Make Default button.

   The current settings in the Document Properties dialog become the defaults for any new documents.

Touring the Edit Bar

Another feature of the Flash document window is the Edit Bar. Its default position is above the Timeline, docked to the top edge of the Stage. You can also position the Edit Bar below the top-docked Timeline. When the Timeline is floating, or docked to the bottom or side of the Stage, the Edit Bar remains at the top of the Stage. You can even make the Edit Bar disappear entirely.

The Edit Bar lets you know what mode you're working in (editing your document, or editing a drawing-object, group, or symbol within the movie). The Edit Bar's pop-up menus give you the power to switch scenes, to choose a symbol to edit and immediately switch to symbol-editing mode, and to change the magnification for viewing the Stage. When you're editing drawing-objects, groups, or symbols, the Edit Bar identifies the element you're editing (**Figure 1.19**). To learn about editing drawing-objects and groups, see Chapter 5; for symbols, see Chapter 7; for scenes, see Chapter 11.

To reposition the Edit Bar, ⌘-Shift double-click (Mac) or Alt-Shift double-click (Windows) any blank area within the Edit Bar. If the Edit Bar was initially above the Timeline, double-clicking sends it below the Timeline. If the Edit Bar started out in the low position, double-clicking sends it to the top. To hide the Edit Bar, choose Window > Toolbars > Edit Bar. If you hide the Edit Bar, however, you may find it more difficult to know when you're editing drawing-objects, groups, or symbols within your document and when you're working on the Stage in the main document.

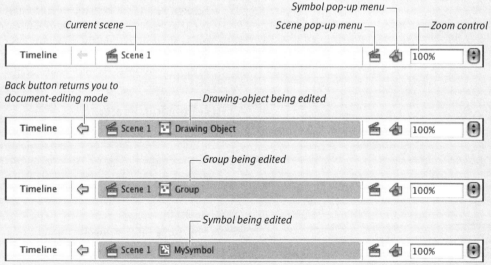

Figure 1.19 The Edit Bar is located above the Stage. You can use it to access symbols and scenes and to change magnification. When you're editing a drawing-object, group, or symbol, the Edit Bar identifies the item you're editing. Clicking the Back button takes you up the hierarchy of items you are editing, eventually returning you to document-editing mode.

Figure 1.20 Flash offers three visual drawing aids: rulers, grids, and guides. To show or hide these features during authoring, use the View menu. Here, for example, is the command for showing grids.

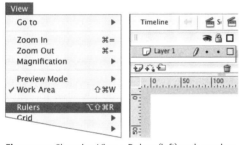

Figure 1.21 Choosing View > Rulers (left) makes rulers visible on the Stage (right).

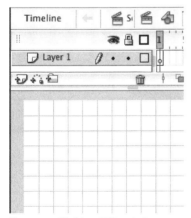

Figure 1.22 Visible grid lines help you position elements on the Stage during authoring.

Using Rulers, Grids, and Guides

Flash offers rulers, grids, and guides as visual aids that help you place graphic elements on the Stage. You turn on these visual aids from the View menu (**Figure 1.20**). Choose the feature you want to use; a checkmark indicates that the feature is currently on. None of the visual aids appear in your final movie.

To show/hide grids, guides, and rulers:

From the View menu, *choose any of the following (or use a keyboard shortcut):*

◆ Choose Rulers, or press Option-Shift-⌘-R (Mac) or Ctrl-Alt-Shift-R (Windows).

Ruler bars appear on the left side and top of the Stage (**Figure 1.21**). You can set ruler units in the Preferences dialog.

◆ Choose Grid > Show Grid, or press ⌘-apostrophe(') (Mac) or Ctrl-apostrophe (') (Windows).

When Show Grid is active, Flash superimposes crisscrossing vertical and horizontal lines on the Stage (**Figure 1.22**). The grid acts as a guide for drawing and positioning elements, the way that graph paper functions in the nondigital world. Flash also uses the grid to align elements when you activate the Snap to Grid feature.

◆ Choose Guides > Show Guides, or press ⌘-semicolon (;) (Mac) or Ctrl-semicolon (;) (Windows).

When Show Guides is active, any guides you've placed become visible. To place guides, see "To work with guides," later in this section.

To set grid parameters:

1. Choose View > Grid > Edit Grid, or press Option-⌘-G (Mac) or Ctrl-Alt-G (Windows).

   The Grid dialog appears (**Figure 1.23**).

2. To set grid spacing, *do the following*,

   ▲ Type a value in the width field.

   ▲ Type a value in the height field (**Figure 1.24**).

3. To select a grid color, *do the following*,

   ▲ Click the Color control.

   The pointer changes to an eyedropper, and a set of swatches appears.

   ▲ Click a color in the swatch set, or click an area of color on the Stage (**Figure 1.25**).

   The new color appears in the Color control in the Grid dialog.

4. To control how close an item must get to the grid before Flash snaps the item to the grid, from the Snap Accuracy menu, choose a tolerance setting.

5. Click OK.

✔ Tips

■ Grids need not consist of perfect squares.

■ You can create new default settings for the grids in all new documents. After entering the desired settings in the Grid dialog, click the Save Default button, and then click OK.

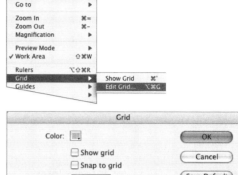

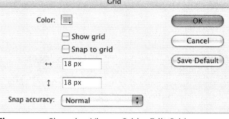

Figure 1.23 Choosing View > Grid > Edit Grid opens the Grid dialog, where you can change grid parameters.

Figure 1.24 Type values in the width and height fields to set grid spacing.

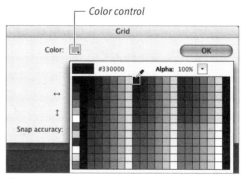

Figure 1.25 To select a new grid color, with the eyedropper pointer, click anywhere in the pop-up set of swatches or on the Stage. The swatch set displays the currently selected color set.

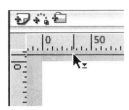

Figure 1.26 As you drag a guideline from the ruler bar, a direction indicator appears next to the selection tool.

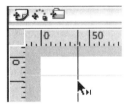

Figure 1.27 You can position individual vertical and horizontal guides anywhere you want on the Stage.

■ To avoid repositioning guides accidentally, choose View > Guides > Lock Guides, or press Option-Shift-semicolon (;) (Mac) or Ctrl-Shift-semicolon (;) (Windows). The directional arrow no longer appears next to the selection tool when you place it over a guideline, and the guides can't be moved. To unlock the guides, choose View > Guides > Lock Guides or press the keyboard shortcut again.

■ If you've placed numerous guides in your document, dragging them from the Stage may get tedious. To remove them all at once, choose View > Guides > Clear All, or access the Guides dialog and click the Clear All button.

To work with guides:

1. With rulers visible, position the pointer over the vertical or horizontal ruler bar.

   If you're using a tool other than the selection tool, the pointer changes to the selection arrow.

2. Click and drag the pointer onto the Stage.

   As you click, a small directional arrow appears next to the pointer, indicating which direction to drag (**Figure 1.26**).

3. Release the mouse button.

   Flash places a vertical or horizontal line on the Stage (**Figure 1.27**).

✔ Tips

■ To set parameters for guides, open the Guide dialog by choosing Guides > Edit Guides or pressing Option-Shift-⌘-G (Mac) or Ctrl-Alt-Shift-G (Windows). To set the guide color, click the Color control, and then use the eyedropper pointer to select a color from the swatch set or from the Stage. Click OK. You can also lock or unlock guides and set their visibility and snapping properties by selecting or deselecting check boxes in the Guides dialog. Click OK to confirm settings and close the dialog.

■ To move a guide, position the selection tool over the guide. A direction arrow appears next to the pointer, indicating that the guide can be dragged. Drag the guide to a new location, and release the mouse button.

■ To remove a guide, drag it completely out of the open document window.

USING RULERS, GRIDS, AND GUIDES

Working with Snapping

Flash's five snapping features help you align elements on the Stage. Snap to Grid helps you position the edge or center of an element to sit directly on top of a user-defined grid. Snap to Guide does the same thing with elements and guidelines. Snap to Objects helps you position one element in relation to another. Snap to Pixels helps you move elements in whole-pixel steps; at magnifications over 400% it displays a 1-pixel-by-1-pixel grid. Snap Align helps you align elements once you've dragged them within a user-definable distance from one another or from the edge of the Stage. By default, Snap Align, Snap to Guides, and Snap to Objects are active each time you launch Flash.

To snap elements to a grid:

◆ Choose View > Snapping > Snap to Grid, or press Shift-⌘-apostrophe (') (Mac) or Ctrl-Shift-apostrophe (') (Windows) (**Figure 1.28**).

or

1. Choose View > Grid > Edit Grid, or press Option-⌘-G (Mac) or Ctrl-Alt-G (Windows).

   The Grid dialog appears.

2. Select the Snap to Grid check box (**Figure 1.29**).

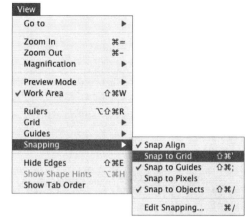

Figure 1.28 Choose View > Snapping > Snap to Grid to get help aligning items to the grid as you move them around the Stage.

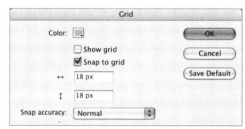

Figure 1.29 In the Grid dialog, selecting the Snap to Grid check box turns on snapping.

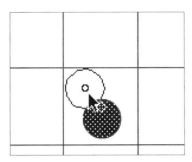

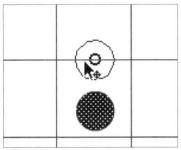

Figure 1.30 As you drag elements, the *snap ring*, a small circle, appears beneath the tip of the pointer (top). The snap ring grows larger when it moves over an item that you've chosen to snap to, such as a grid, a guide, or the edge or center of another element.

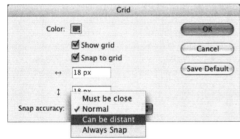

Figure 1.31 Choose a Snap Accuracy setting to determine how close an element must be to the grid before Flash snaps the element to the grid line. Choosing Always Snap forces the edge or center of an element to lie directly on a grid line.

3. Click OK.

A check appears next to the Snap to Grid command in the menu.

As you drag an element, a circle called the *snap ring* appears beneath the tip of the selection tool. As the element nears a grid line, Flash highlights potential snap points by enlarging the snap ring (**Figure 1.30**).

✔ Tips

- The snap ring appears roughly in the place where the selection tool connects with the element you're dragging. Flash can snap an element only by its center point or a point on its perimeter, however. If you have trouble seeing the snap ring, try grabbing the element nearer to its center, an edge, or a corner.

- You can also access the Grid dialog by choosing View > Grid > Edit Grid or pressing Option-⌘-G (Mac) or Ctrl-Alt-G (Windows).

To set parameters for snapping to the grid:

1. Choose View > Grid > Edit Grid.

2. In the Grid dialog, choose a parameter from the Snap Accuracy pop-up menu (**Figure 1.31**).

3. Click OK.

WORKING WITH SNAPPING

To snap elements to guides:

◆ Choose View > Snapping > Snap to
Guides, or press Shift-⌘-semicolon (;)
(Mac) or Ctrl-Shift-semicolon (;)
(Windows).

or

1. Choose View > Guides > Edit Guides,
or press Option-Shift-⌘-G (Mac) or
Ctrl-Alt-Shift-G (Windows).

   The Guides dialog appears (**Figure 1.32**).

2. Select the Snap to Guides check box.

3. Click OK.

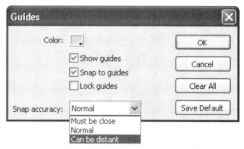

Figure 1.32 In the Guides dialog, you can set the color
and visibility of guides, their status as locked or
unlocked, and how close items must be before they
will snap to the guides.

To set parameters for snapping to guides:

1. Choose View > Guides > Edit Guides.

2. In the Guides dialog, choose a parameter
from the Snap Accuracy pop-up menu.

3. Click OK.

To snap elements to elements:

◆ Choose View > Snapping > Snap to
Objects, or press Shift-⌘-/ (Mac) or
Ctrl-Shift-/ (Windows).

   or

◆ With the selection, line, oval, rectangle,
polystar, free-transform, or fill-transform
tool selected, in the options section of
the Tools panel, click the magnet icon.

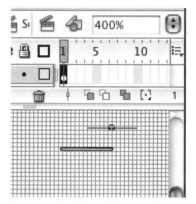

Figure 1.33 With Flash's Snap to Pixels
feature enabled, a 1-pixel grid becomes
visible at magnifications of 400 percent
or greater. You can use this mode for
precise positioning of graphic elements.

To snap elements to pixels:

◆ Choose View > Snapping > Snap to Pixels.

   Flash creates a grid whose squares measure 1 pixel by 1 pixel. To see the grid,
you must set the Stage's magnification
to at least 400 percent (**Figure 1.33**).
You'll learn more about magnified views
in "Viewing at Various Magnifications"
later in this chapter.

✔ Tip

■ Although the Snap to Pixels feature uses
a 1-pixel grid, the graphic elements you
move don't snap to the grid's coordinates
unless you set the element's x and y position to a whole number in the Info panel
or Properties tab of the Property inspector. (You'll learn to set coordinates for
graphic elements in Chapter 4.)

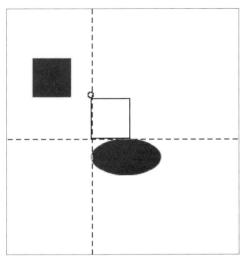

Figure 1.34 Flash's Snap Align feature displays a dotted guideline whenever an element comes within the user-specified distance of another element or the edge of the Stage. You can also set Snap Align to display the dotted guideline for aligning to the centers of elements.

Click to hide Advanced options

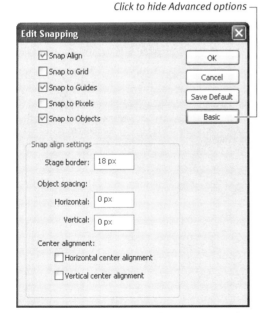

Figure 1.35 You set the tolerance for Snap Align in the Advanced section of the Edit Snapping dialog. Flash's default settings are shown here.

To turn on Snap Align:

◆ Choose View > Snapping > Snap Align. With Snap Align active, as you drag elements on the Stage, Flash displays a dotted-line alignment guide whenever the element gets within a user-specified distance of another element's edge, its center, or the edge of the Stage (**Figure 1.34**).

✔ Tip

■ You can adjust the way Snap Align interacts with elements and the Stage. Choose View > Snapping > Edit Snapping to open the Edit Snapping dialog. Click the Advanced button to view the Snap Align settings. (**Figure 1.35**).

To turn off snapping:

◆ From the View > Snapping menu, choose the snapping option that you want to turn off.

The items with check marks are currently turned on. You can only select one item at a time from the menu.

✔ Tips

■ You can turn off snapping for grids and guides from within the dialogs where you set their parameters. Choose View > Grid > Edit Grid (or View > Guides > Edit Guides); in the dialog that appears, deselect the Snap to Grids (or Snap to Guides) check box.

■ To avoid making multiple trips to the View menu to turn individual snapping modes on and off, choose View > Snapping > Edit Snapping. The Edit Snapping dialog appears, listing all five snapping modes. Select the check boxes for the types you want to activate.

Viewing at Various Magnifications

Flash offers several ways to adjust the magnification of elements on the Stage.

To view elements at actual size:

◆ Choose View > Magnification > 100% (**Figure 1.36**), or press ⌘-1 (Mac) or Ctrl-1 (Windows).

or

◆ In the Zoom Control field at the right side of the Stage's Edit Bar, type 100%. Press Enter.

At 100%, Flash displays elements as close as possible to the size they will be in the final movie. (Some monitors and video cards may display elements at a slightly different size than the system on which you created the element.)

To zoom in or out on the Stage:

1. In the Zoom Control field, type the desired percentage of magnification (**Figure 1.37**).

2. Press Enter.

✔ Tip

■ Click the scroll button next to the Zoom Control field to open a menu that duplicates the View > Magnification submenu. Choose a percentage from this menu to change magnification immediately. This menu also lets you choose Fit in Window (to display the full Stage area in the current window, without scroll bars), Show Frame (to display the full Stage area in the current window, with scroll bars), and Show All (to scale the Stage so that all elements on the Stage and in the Pasteboard appear in the current window).

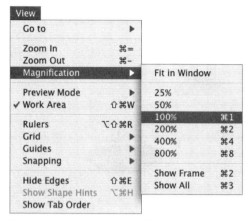

Figure 1.36 Choose 100% magnification to display graphics at the size they will be in the final movie.

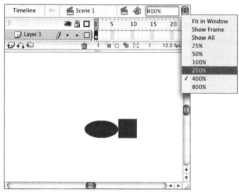

Figure 1.37 Enter a percentage greater than 100 in the Zoom Control field to magnify elements on the Stage. The pop-up menu to the right of the field offers several common magnification levels.

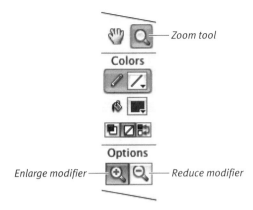

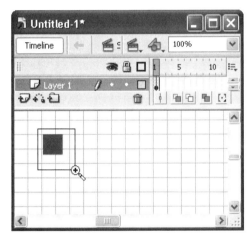

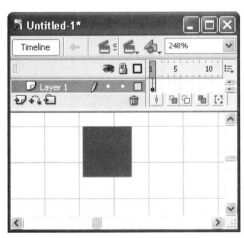

Figure 1.38 Use the zoom tool (top) to draw a selection rectangle around an element (middle). Flash places the element at the center of the enlarged view (bottom).

To reduce or enlarge specific areas:

1. In the Tools panel, select the zoom tool (or press M or Z on the keyboard).

   The pointer changes to a magnifying glass.

2. To enlarge an area or element, click and drag to create a selection rectangle that encompasses the area or element.

   Flash fills the window with your selection (**Figure 1.38**). This technique works whether the zoom tool is set to Enlarge or Reduce mode.

To zoom in or out:

1. With the zoom tool active, in the Tools panel's Options section, *select one of the tool's modifiers:*

   ▲ Enlarge (the magnifying glass icon with the plus sign)

   ▲ Reduce (the magnifying glass icon with the minus sign)

2. On the Stage, click the area or element you want to enlarge or reduce.

   Flash places the spot you clicked at the center of the viewing window and changes the percentage of magnification specified in the Zoom Control field. With the zoom tool set to Enlarge, Flash doubles the percentage; with the zoom tool set to Reduce, Flash halves the percentage.

✔ Tips

■ When you have the zoom tool selected, you can switch temporarily from Enlarge to Reduce, and vice versa, by holding down the Option (Mac) or Alt (Windows) key.

■ To access the zoom tool in Enlarge mode temporarily while using another tool, press ⌘-spacebar (Mac) or Ctrl-spacebar (Windows). To access the tool in Reduce mode, press ⌘-Shift-spacebar (Mac) or Ctrl-Shift-spacebar (Windows).

VIEWING AT VARIOUS MAGNIFICATIONS

About Panels

In addition to the drawing tools, Flash puts a number of authoring tools in *panels*— windows that can stay open on the desktop for quick access as you work. Some panels, such as the Color Mixer, let you set attributes to be used in creating new elements or modifying existing elements. Others, such as the Movie Explorer and Scenes panels, help you organize and navigate your Flash document. One crucial panel, the Property inspector, lets you get information about selected elements and modify them. You'll learn to use individual panels in later chapters of this book. For now, you'll learn general features of panels and how to manage the panel environment.

To open or close a panel window:

◆ From the Window menu, select the desired panel—for example, Color Mixer (**Figure 1.39**).

One of the following actions takes place:

▲ If the selected panel is closed, a window containing that panel opens (**Figure 1.40**).

▲ If the selected panel is collapsed, it expands.

▲ If the selected panel is obscured behind other panels, the selected panel moves to the front of the panel stack.

▲ If the selected panel is already open, expanded, and front-most in the panel stack, using this technique closes the panel.

Figure 1.39
The Window menu contains a list of panels.

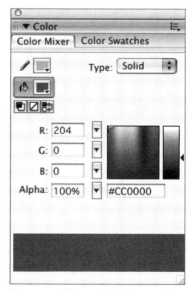

Figure 1.40 This panel window contains the Color Mixer and Color Swatches panels.

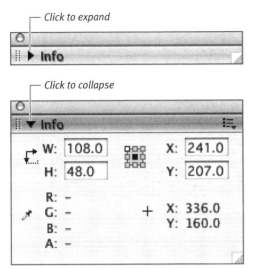

Click to expand

Click to collapse

Figure 1.41 Click the triangle to the left of the panel name to collapse and expand the panel window.

✔ Tips

- There are three other ways to close an open panel: Click the panel window's close button (Mac) or close box (Windows, for undocked panels); from the panel's Options menu, choose Close Panel Group; or Control-click (Mac) or right-click (Windows) the panel's title bar, and choose Close Panel Group from the contextual menu.

- To hide all the open panels (including the Tools panel, the Property inspector, and any open Library panels), press F4. Press F4 again to show the panels.

To collapse or expand a panel window:

◆ Click the triangle to the left of the panel title (**Figure 1.41**).

Tools and Help: Not Like Other Panels

The *Tools panel* (known in some previous incarnations as the *Toolbar* or *Toolbox*) contains Flash's drawing tools and other tools you'll need to create and manipulate graphics for animation. Unlike other panels, the Tools panel can't be collapsed or resized and it can't be grouped with other panels.

The Mac and Windows operating systems handle the Tools panel slightly differently. In Windows, you can dock the Tools panel on either side of the application window. In the Mac OS, the Tools panel always floats as a separate window. Also, in Windows, you can place a subset of the Tools panel tools into a Tools panel (called the *Main Tools panel*) at the top of the application window. You'll learn more about working with the Tools panel and its tools in Chapter 2.

The *Help panel* works just like the majority of the Flash panels, but you won't find it in the Window menu. To access the Help panel, choose Help > Flash Help (or press F1).

To reposition a floating panel window:

◆ Click the gripper on the left side of the panel's title bar, and drag the window to a new location.

On the Macintosh, panels (or panel-groups) are always floating. In Windows, by default, panels are docked in the application window. To change a docked panel to a floating one, position the pointer over the gripper. Click and drag the panel away from the side of the application window.

✔ Tips

■ When you position one floating panel window so that one of its edges lies right next to the edge of another panel window, Flash snaps the two windows. It's not a permanent connection, but it ensures that the two take up as little space together as possible (**Figure 1.42**).

■ In the Windows operating system, you can more permanently dock panels at edges of the application window. Or, if you prefer free-floating panels and want to avoid accidentally docking them, choose Edit > Preferences, select the General category of the Preferences dialog, and select Disable Panel Docking in the Panel Options section.

■ If you just want to move a panel, not dock or undock it, you can click the gray (Mac) or blue (Windows) bar above the panel's title. (The bar for the Property inspector is located on the left side of the panel.)

To resize a floating panel window:

◆ Click and drag the bottom-right corner of the window (Windows) or the resize handle (Mac).

Figure 1.42 These floating panels snap together because of their proximity. They are still independent units. To join them more permanently, you must group them.

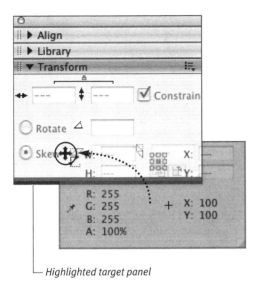

— *Highlighted target panel*

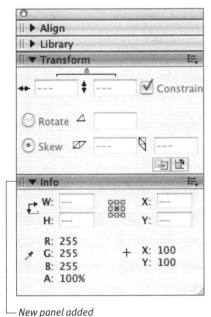

— *New panel added*

Figure 1.43 To group panels, drag one panel over another. When the target panel window is highlighted (top), release the mouse button. The new panel appears in the target window (bottom).

Working with Grouped Panels

Flash 8 offers two ways to group multiple panels in a single window. You can group panels vertically, stacking one above another in a single window; or you can group panels horizontally, as tabbed items in a single window. You can also add a tabbed panel-group to a vertical panel-group window. You can close any panel in a group individually; but the next time you open that panel, it will again appear within the group, unless you specifically remove it from the group. Panels within a vertical panel-group window may also be collapsed and expanded individually.

To group panels vertically:

1. With two or more panel windows open on the desktop, click one panel's gripper. The pointer changes to the move icon.

2. Drag the panel over another open panel window.

   Flash highlights the target panel window. A thick blue (Mac) or black (Windows) line indicates the spot where Flash will insert the added panel. Drag up or down in the target window to move the highlight line to the desired position.

3. Release the mouse button.

   The panel you dragged now appears in the destination window (**Figure 1.43**).

✔ Tips

- To collapse and expand individual panels within the vertical panel-group window, click the triangle to the left of the panel's title or click anywhere in the panel's title bar.

- To expand one panel and collapse all the others in the vertical panel-group window, choose Maximize Panel Group from the panel's Options menu. (To access the Options menu, you must have the panel in expanded mode.)

- To close the whole vertical panel-group window, click the close button (Mac) or close box (Windows, for floating panels).

- To close one panel in the vertical panel-group window, from that panel's Options menu, choose Close Panel Group. The word *group* in this command can seem confusing. Here *group* refers not to the whole vertical panel-group, but to the horizontal panel-group whose Options menu you open. The panel may have multiple tabs, or it may be a single panel (a sort of group of one).

To separate vertically grouped panels:

1. In a vertical panel-group window, click one panel's gripper.

   The pointer changes to the move icon.

2. Drag the panel away from the vertical panel-group window.

   Flash displays a ghosted version of the panel as you drag.

3. Release the mouse button.

   The panel appears in its own window (**Figure 1.44**).

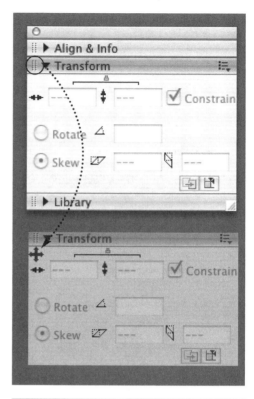

Figure 1.44 To separate one panel from a vertical panel-group, drag the panel's title bar away from the window until you see a ghosted panel (top); then release the mouse button to create a separate panel window (bottom).

WORKING WITH GROUPED PANELS

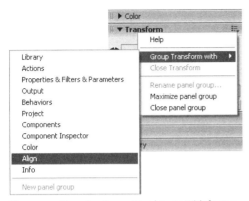

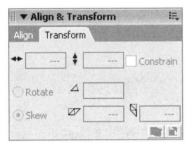

Figure 1.45 Choosing Group *Panel Name* With from a panel's Options menu opens a submenu listing all the open (and groupable) panels. Choose the panel that you want to have as part of a tabbed group with the current panel.

Figure 1.46 The Group *Panel Name* With command creates a panel window containing tabs for the grouped panels.

To create tabbed panels:

1. Open two or more panels (see "About Panels," earlier in this chapter).

2. From the Options menu of an open panel, choose Group *Panel Name* With.

   A submenu appears, listing panels with which this panel can be grouped (**Figure 1.45**). Note that the Tools panel can't be grouped.

3. From the submenu, choose a panel.

   The two panels combine in one window. The title bar identifies the panels in that window, and a tab for each panel appears at the top of the window (**Figure 1.46**). Click a tab to view a different panel.

✔ Tips

■ The Options > Group *Panel Name* With command always lists a set of commonly used panels whether they are open or not. In addition, the menu lists any panels that have been opened during the current work session. If you'd like to group the current panel with a panel that's not on the list open that panel to make it visible in the list.

■ A tabbed panel operates just like a single panel window. You can collapse and expand it, open and close it, even drag it into a vertical group (where it will still display its tabs).

continues on next page

WORKING WITH GROUPED PANELS

- You can close one tab without closing the entire panel-group. From the tabbed panel window's Options menu, choose Close *Panel Name*. The selected panel's tab disappears. Choose that panel from the Window menu, and the tab reappears in the tabbed panel-group window.

- To close a tabbed panel-group that's a member of a vertical panel-group, click the Options menu in the upper-right corner of the tabbed panel-group, and then choose Close Panel Group. Here *group* refers just to the panel-group whose Options menu you open, not to the entire vertical panel-group.

To separate tabbed panels:

1. Open a tabbed panel-group.

2. Select the tab of the panel you wish to separate from the group.

3. From the panel window's Options menu, choose Group *Panel Name* With > New Panel Group.

   The command name isn't intuitive, but making the selected tab a new panel-group puts that panel back into an individual window.

About Workspace Layouts

If you like to work with a certain combination of panels placed in specific locations on your desktop, you can save that combination as a *workspace layout*. The layout remembers which panels are opened, which are grouped, how large each panel or group window should be, and where to place those windows on the desktop.

To save a layout, set up your desktop with the panels the way you like them. Then, choose Window > Workspace Layout > Save Current. Name the layout in the Save Workspace Layout dialog. Click OK. Whenever you want to restore the desktop to that configuration, choose Window > Workspace Layout, and choose your layout from the submenu.

To open the default panel set:

◆ Choose Window > Workspace Layout > Default.

Flash opens the Tools panel, the Property inspector, and one vertical panel-group window containing the Library panel and a tabbed panel-group containing the Color Mixer and Color Swatches panels (**Figure 1.47**).

✔ Tips

■ In the Windows environment, the Actions panel is also part of the default workspace layout.

■ The default workspace layout also combines the Info, Transform, and Align panels into a tabbed group. Opening any member of the trio from the Window menu opens the tabbed group inside the vertical panel-group window.

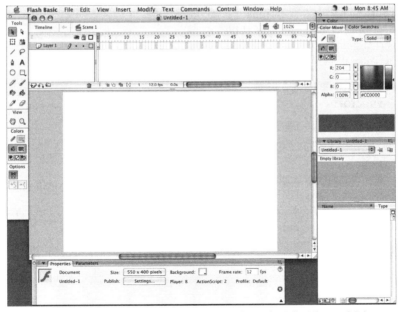

Figure 1.47 The default workspace layout in Flash combines the Color Mixer and Color Swatches panels in a tabbed panel-group, which is grouped vertically with the Library panel and placed on the right side of the desktop.

WORKING WITH GROUPED PANELS

About the Property Inspector

By default, Flash 8 creates a tabbed panel-group known as the *Property inspector*. In Flash Basic the panel-group has two tabs: the Properties tab displays information about the properties and attributes of tools and graphic elements (such as color, style, and font for the text tool); the Parameters tab displays information about components (see Chapter 12). In Flash Professional, the panel has a third tab: Filters, which allows you to add special effects to text and certain symbols (to learn about symbols, see Chapter 7). You can use any of the techniques in the preceding exercises to change the grouping of the Property inspector's panels. For now, leave them in the default panel-group, even though you'll work mostly with just the Properties tab.

The Properties tab of the Property inspector is context-sensitive, changing to reflect the tool or element you have selected. You'll learn about specific versions and tabs of the Property inspector in later chapters. For now, just learn the general rules of operation.

To access the Properties tab of the Property inspector:

◆ Choose Window > Properties > Properties, or press ⌘-F3 (Mac) or Ctrl-F3 (Windows) (**Figure 1.48**).

Flash opens the Property inspector with the Properties tab active. The panel displays information about whatever item you have selected in the Flash document (see "The Power of the Property Inspector").

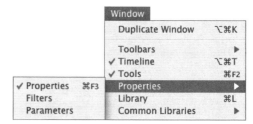

Figure 1.48 To access the Properties tab of the Property inspector, choose Window > Properties; from the submenu, select the tab you want to be active in the panel.

✔ Tips

■ On a Mac, the Property inspector always floats. In Windows, the Property inspector docks to the bottom of the application window by default, but you can make it float as a separate panel by clicking the gripper on the left side of the panel's title bar and dragging the panel away from the bottom of the application window.

■ To open the Property inspector with the Parameters (or Filters in Professional) tab active, from the Window > Properties submenu, choose Parameters (or Filters).

To hide or show the information area:

◆ To hide or show the lower half of the Property inspector, click the triangle in the bottom-right corner of the panel (**Figure 1.49**).

For some elements, the lower half of the Property inspector panel displays extra information. Hiding the information area gives you more room on your desktop.

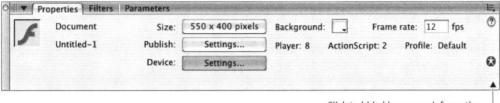

Click to hide/show more information

Figure 1.49 In some situations, the Property inspector displays more information in the lower portion of the panel. Click the triangle in the lower-right corner of the panel to show or hide that information.

Entering Values in the Property Inspector

In many modes, the Property inspector requires you to enter a value in a field to change a parameter. You can always type a new value. When modifying selected items, usually you must press Enter to apply the new value to selected items.

A small triangle to the right of an entry field indicates the presence of a pop-up slider for entering values quickly. Often, a slider previews new values interactively. The following methods work for most sliders:

◆ Click and drag. Click the small triangle, and hold down the mouse button; you can start dragging the slider's lever right away. Release the mouse button. Flash enters the current slider value in the field and—in most cases—applies that value to selected elements automatically.

◆ Click and click. Click the small triangle, and release the mouse button right away; the slider pops up and stays open. You can drag the slider's lever or click various locations on the slider to choose a new value. Flash enters the value in the field. To apply the value to selected items, you must click somewhere off the slider.

The Power of the Property Inspector

Think of the Property inspector as being a context-sensitive superpanel—a panel that changes to reflect whatever item you have selected. The Properties tab of the panel displays information about the active Flash document or a selected tool, graphic element (a shape, grouped shape, or symbol; a text block; a bitmap; or a video clip), or frame. The Parameters tab displays information about a selected component. The Filters tab (Professional only) displays information about special effects applied to text, a movie clip, or a button.

The Properties tab of the Property inspector is also the place for choosing many tools' settings and for changing the attributes of selected elements.

Select the line tool, for example, and the Properties tab of the Property inspector becomes the Line Tool Properties tab (**Figure 1.50**). In this incarnation, the Properties tab presents all the line tool's attributes for you to set: color, thickness, and style. Select a line on the Stage, however, and the Properties tab becomes the Shape Properties tab. Because the selected shape is a line, the Properties tab displays attributes similar to those shown in the Line Tool Properties tab; change the settings in the Properties tab, and Flash changes the selected line to match.

Click a blank area of the Stage, and you'll see the Document Properties tab of the Property inspector, which gives you access to various document settings. Select a symbol instance on the Stage, and the Properties tab reveals the instance's heritage (which master symbol it came from), as well as its height, width, and Stage position. Change those settings in the Properties tab, and Flash makes those changes in the selected symbol instance.

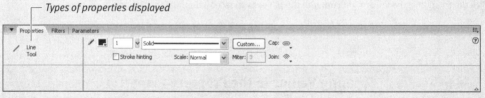

Figure 1.50 The Property inspector displays information about selected items and allows you to modify them. The Line Tool Properties tab of the Property inspector, for example, lets you set the color, thickness, and style for lines that the line tool creates

CREATING
SIMPLE GRAPHICS

About Strokes and Fills

What do *stroke* and *fill* mean? A stroke is an outline, and a fill is a solid area of color. Picture a coloring book, with black lines creating the pictures: Those lines are strokes. When you fill in the areas outlined by strokes—say, with crayon—that colorful area is the fill. In a coloring book, you start with an outline and create the fill inside it. In Flash, you can work the other way around—start with a solid shape and then create the outline as a separate element.

Flash's oval, rectangle, and polystar tools allow you to create an element that's just a stroke or just a fill, or to create the stroke and fill elements simultaneously. The line tool, as you might guess, creates only strokes. The pen tool can create both strokes and fills.

The concept of fills and strokes is a bit trickier to grasp in relation to the brush tool. This tool creates fills. These fills may look like lines or brushstrokes, but they are shapes you can outline with a stroke. Flash has special tools for adding, editing, and removing strokes and fills: the ink bottle, the paint bucket, and the faucet eraser. See Chapter 4 for more details.

This chapter teaches you to use Macromedia Flash 8's drawing tools to create basic shapes from lines and areas of color—in Flash terminology, *strokes* and *fills*. Flash offers natural drawing tools that imitate the feel of drawing or painting on paper with pencil or brush; geometric-shape tools that make it easy to draw predefined shapes; and a pen tool that lets you draw with precision, using Bézier curves.

You can edit all shapes with the Bézier subselection tool—even those drawn with the other tools. You also can modify any shape by tugging on its outline instead of working with Bézier curves points and handles. (To learn about editing shapes, see Chapter 4.)

In previous versions of Flash, all the shapes you created were raw shapes—all strokes and fills interacted with other strokes and fills on the same layer. In Flash 8, you can create raw shapes by using the drawing tools in Merge Drawing mode, or you can use a new feature—Object Drawing mode—to create editable shapes that don't interact with other shapes (you'll learn more about how graphic elements interact in Chapter 5).

Flash also lets you import graphics from other programs. If you create graphics in a program such as Macromedia FreeHand or Adobe Illustrator, you can import them into Flash for animation (see Chapter 14).

Touring the Tools

The Tools panel holds all the tools you need to create and modify graphic elements in Flash 8 (**Figure 2.1**). The Tools section contains tools for creating graphic elements; the View section contains tools for scrolling the Stage and for zooming in and out; the Colors section allows you to set colors for the elements you create; and the Options section provides modifiers appropriate to whatever tool you have currently selected.

You click a tool to select it for use. If the selected tool has options, the appropriate buttons and/or menus for choosing options and settings appear in the Options section at the bottom of the Tools panel.

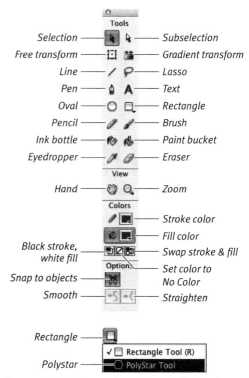

Figure 2.1 The Tools panel contains tools for drawing, editing, and manipulating graphic elements in Flash. The polystar tool appears as a submenu item of the rectangle tool.

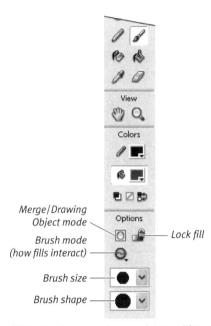

Merge/Drawing Object mode

Brush mode (how fills interact)

Lock fill

Brush size

Brush shape

Figure 2.2 When you select a tool, its modifiers appear in the Options section of the Tools panel. Here the settings for using the brush appear; click a button to toggle settings such as Merge mode; select a setting from a menu, such as Brush mode.

To access tools and options:

1. With the Tools panel open, click a tool—for example, the brush tool.

The Options section of the Tools panel displays the relevant modifiers for the selected tool.

2. Click a button or select an option from a menu in the Options section to modify the way the selected tool works (**Figure 2.2**).

✔ Tips

■ Flash's default setting makes tool tips active (when the pointer hovers over a tool, an identifying label appears). You can change the tool tip setting in the Preferences dialog: Select the General category, select (or deselect) the Show Tool Tips check box, and click OK to close the dialog. (For details on opening the Preferences dialog, see Chapter 1.)

■ In addition to displaying tool names, tool tips show keyboard shortcuts. As you get more familiar with the tools, activating them from the keyboard will speed your operations.

■ If you accidentally close the Tools panel, you can open it as you would any other panel. Choose Window > Tools.

Creating Solid Colors and Gradients

Although you can define fill and stroke colors from most color controls (see the sidebar "The Mystery of Color Controls"), the Color Mixer panel gives you the widest variety of options for defining fill and stroke colors. You can choose colors visually (by clicking a graphic representation of a color space—all the available colors in a given color-definition system) or numerically (by entering specific values for color components). You can also set a color's transparency in the Color Mixer panel. To define new gradients, you must use the Color Mixer panel.

Before you define a color or gradient, you must choose whether the color or gradient applies to fills or strokes by activating the Fill Color control or the Stroke Color control. (The ability to apply gradients to strokes is new in Flash 8.) As you define new colors, Flash updates all the related color controls. If you define a new fill color, for example, that color becomes the current setting for all the tools that use fills.

To assign solid-color attributes in the Color Mixer panel:

1. Access the Color Mixer panel (if it's not open, choose Window > Color Mixer).

2. From the Type menu, choose Solid.

3. To choose a color space, from the panel's Options menu, *do one of the following:*

   ▲ To define colors as mixtures of red, green, and blue, choose RGB.

   ▲ To define colors by percentage of hue, saturation, and brightness, choose HSB (**Figure 2.3**).

Fill Color control
Stroke Color control

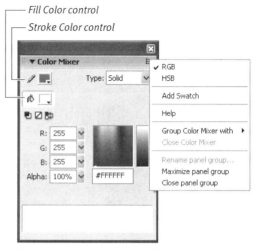

Figure 2.3 The Color Mixer panel lets you choose a color from the color-space window or enter values directly to define a color in the RGB or HSB color space. Choose the desired color space from the Options pop-up menu.

What Are Hex Colors?

The term *hex color* is short for *hexadecimal color*, which is a fancy way of saying "a color defined by a number written in base 16." Hexadecimal coding is the language of bits and bytes that computers speak

Hex coding is the way to specify color in HTML. In Flash, entering a single hex code for your color may be easier than entering three different values for red, green, and blue (RGB).

If you remember studying bases in high-school math, you'll recall that the decimal system is base 10, represented by the numbers 0 through 9. In hex color, to get the extra six digits, you continue coding with letters A through F.

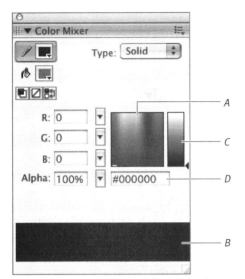

Figure 2.4 The Color Mixer panel displays a color-space window (A), a preview window for the new color (B), a luminosity/ lightness slider (C), and a text field for entering the precise hex value of a color (D). Click in the color-space window to choose a new color visually.

The Mystery of Color Controls

You'll find color controls—a color chip with an open-menu triangle in the lower right corner—throughout Flash. To operate a color control, click the color chip; color swatches pop up, and the pointer changes to an eyedropper. To assign a new color, click a swatch with the eyedropper; with many color controls, you can also click a color on the Stage or the desktop, enter a new value in the Hex Color field, enter a transparency value in the Alpha field, choose No Color, or click the Color Picker button to access the System Color Picker(s).

You can use any Stroke Color or Fill Color control to assign color attributes. The specs for the color you select appear in the Color Mixer panel, and all the other color controls update to match.

4. To determine where Flash applies the new color, *do one of the following:*

   ▲ To set a new stroke color, choose the Stroke Color control by clicking the pencil icon.

   ▲ To set a new fill color, choose the Fill Color control by clicking the paint-bucket icon.

To define a new color visually in the Color Mixer panel:

1. With the Color Mixer panel open, choose a color space.

2. Position the pointer over the desired hue in the color-space window.

3. Click.

   The crosshair cursor appears, and Flash selects the color within the crosshairs (**Figure 2.4**).

✔ Tips

■ If you have trouble clicking exactly the right color, click and drag around within the color-space window. A preview of the new color appears alongside the old color in the preview window. When the color you want appears, release the mouse button. Flash enters the values for that color in the appropriate fields.

■ You can move the color-control eyedropper anywhere over your desktop within Flash to pick up a color. You can use this method to match colors with artwork you've created in Flash.

To define a new color numerically in the Color Mixer panel:

1. With the Color Mixer panel open, choose a color space.

2. To define a new color, *do one of the following:*

   ▲ For RGB colors, enter values from 0 to 255 for red, green, and blue in the R, G, and B fields (**Figure 2.5**).

   ▲ For HSB, enter values for hue, saturation, and brightness in the H, S, and B fields.

To define a color's transparency:

1. With the Color Mixer panel open, define a color.

2. Enter a value in the Alpha field (**Figure 2.6**).

   A value of 100 (100 percent) results in a completely solid color; a value of 0 results in a completely transparent color.

   After you define a new color, you may want to add it to the Color Swatches panel so that you can use it again. (For more information about the Color Swatches panel, see "Creating Color Sets" later in this chapter.)

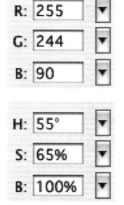

Figure 2.5 Enter RGB values to specify the amount of red, green, and blue that make up the color. Enter HSB values to specify the color by hue, saturation, and brightness. The new color appears in the selected color control.

Figure 2.6 Enter an Alpha value of less than 100 percent to define a transparent color.

CREATING SOLID COLORS AND GRADIENTS

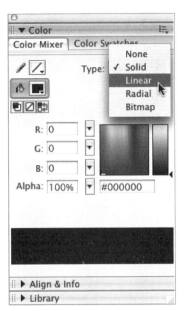

Figure 2.7 Choose Linear from the Type menu to access the tools for defining linear gradients.

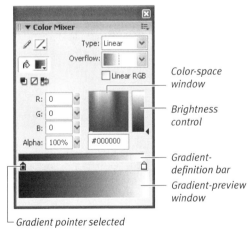

Gradient pointer selected

Figure 2.8 The Color Mixer panel displays the gradient-preview window, gradient-definition bar, and a color-space window.

To create a linear gradient:

1. Open the Color Mixer panel.

2. From the Color Mixer panel's Type menu, choose Linear (**Figure 2.7**).

   The tools and options for defining gradients appear (**Figure 2.8**). The default gradient starts with two pointers, black on the left and white on the right.

3. For Overflow, leave the default setting (Extend).

   Overflow determines how gradient colors fill a shape when you resize the gradient to be narrower than the shape it fills (to learn about resizing gradients, see Chapter 4).

4. To add a new color to the gradient, position the mouse pointer on or below the gradient-definition bar.

   Flash adds a plus sign to the pointer, indicating that you can add a new gradient pointer in this area.

5. Click anywhere along the gradient-definition bar.

   Flash adds a new gradient pointer.

6. To change a gradient pointer's color, click it to select it, and define a new color using any of the methods described in the preceding section.

   or

   Double-click the gradient pointer to open a pop-up swatch set, and *do one of the following*:

   ▲ Click a swatch to copy the swatch color.

   ▲ Click an item on the desktop to copy its color.

   ▲ Enter a new value in the Hex field.

   ▲ Click the Color Picker button in the upper-right corner of the pop-up swatch set to access the System Color Picker for assigning new colors.

   continues on next page

7. Repeat steps 5 and 6 for any additional colors you want in your gradient.

You can add up to 13 pointers (for a total of 15 colors) to a gradient.

8. Drag the pointers to position them on the gradient-definition bar (**Figure 2.9**).

Place pointers closer together to make the transition between colors more abrupt; place them farther apart to spread the transition out over more space.

As you modify the gradient, your changes appear in the Tools panel's Fill Color control. The new gradient also appears in the Properties tab of the Property inspector for any tools that create a fill—say, the oval tool. Those tools are now loaded and ready to create shapes using that gradient.

Gradient starts with white and blends first to gray and then to black

Move pointers in to increase width of outside bands

Click to add pointers

Figure 2.9 Choose a color for each gradient pointer. The colors and positions of the pointers on the bar define a gradient's color transitions.

About Gradients

In addition to solid colors, Flash works with *gradients*—bands of color that blend into each other. Gradients can be linear (parallel bars of color) or radial (concentric rings of color). Gradients can create interesting visual effects and are useful for adding shading—to make a circle look like a sphere, for example. In previous versions of Flash, gradients were used only for fills. In Flash 8, you can also use gradients in strokes.

Flash defines each gradient with a set of markers called *gradient pointers* that indicate which color goes where in the lineup of color bands. You define the color for each pointer. By positioning the pointers on the gradient-definition bar, you control how wide each band of color is. Each gradient can contain as many as 15 colors.

You define new gradients in the Color Mixer panel.

About Using the System Color Pickers

In addition to creating colors in the Color Mixer panel, you can create colors in one of the System Color Pickers. These color pickers let you enter colors in a system that may be more to your liking than the RGB/HSB offered by the Color Mixer panel. The Windows System Color Picker allows you to specify colors according to Hue, Saturation, and Luminosity values. The Macintosh OS offers five different System Color Pickers, including one with CMYK sliders.

To access the System Color Picker(s), Option-double-click (Mac) or Alt-double-click (Windows) the Fill Color or Stroke Color control in the Color Mixer panel, Tools panel, or Properties tab of the Property inspector. You can also access the System Color Picker(s) by clicking the color control once, to open the swatch set, then clicking the Color Picker button in the upper-right corner. Whenever you select or specify a color that will dither, the color picker splits the preview window; half the window shows the dithered color, and the other half shows the nearest Web-safe color.

About Bitmap Fills

In addition to solid fills and gradients, Flash lets you import bitmap images and use them as fills. They work similarly to gradient fills. You might use a bitmap fill to create a tiled repeating image for the background of a Web page. To learn about working with bitmaps and bitmap fills, see Chapter 14.

✔ Tips

■ To reduce the number of colors in a gradient, with the gradient selected in the Color Mixer, drag one or more gradient pointers downward, away from the gradient-definition bar. The pointer disappears as you drag. The gradient changes to blend the colors in the remaining gradient pointers.

■ When a gradient pointer is set to black, the Color Picker's Luminosity setting gets set to 0% (for white, Luminosity gets set to 100%). That setting means the color-proxy window will show a solid black (or solid white) square even if you enter new RGB values or use the crosshair cursor to choose a new color. To change the color of a pointer that's set to black (or white), you must choose a new color from the color-proxy window's pop-up swatch set, reposition the Luminosity slider (on the right side of the Color Picker window), or enter a new Brightness value.

■ To reverse the direction of a gradient's color transition, drag one gradient pointer over another. In a white-to-black gradient (a white pointer on the left and a black pointer on the right), drag the white pointer to the right past the black one. Your gradient goes from black to white.

■ To create an SVG-compliant gradient, select the Linear RGB check box.

To create a radial gradient:

1. Open the Color Mixer panel.

2. From the Type menu, choose Radial.

   The tools for defining circular gradients appear. The gradient-definition bar looks the same as it does for linear gradients, but the preview shows your gradient as a set of concentric circles (**Figure 2.10**). The leftmost pointer defines the inner ring; the rightmost pointer defines the outer ring.

3. Follow steps 3–8 of the previous task, "To create a linear gradient," to define the color transitions in the radial gradient.

✔ Tips

■ To modify an existing gradient, choose it in the Color Swatches panel. Flash switches the Color Mixer panel to gradient mode and displays the selected gradient. Now you can make any changes you need.

■ Gradients can have transparency. You simply use a transparent color in one or more gradient pointers (see "To define a color's transparency" earlier in this chapter). If a gradient has transparency, a grid shows up in the gradient pointer, in the Fill Color or Stroke Color control, and in the transparent part of the gradient in the preview window (**Figure 2.11**).

■ Each pointer in a gradient can have a different alpha setting. To create fade effects, try creating a gradient that blends from a fully opaque color to a transparent one.

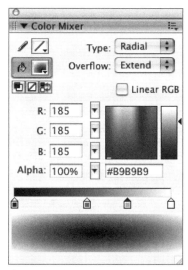

Figure 2.10 Choose Radial from the Type menu to create a circular gradient. The preview window translates the horizontal gradient-definition bar into the appropriate circular color transitions.

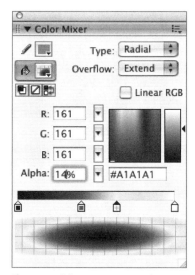

Figure 2.11 When transparent colors make up part of a gradient, grid lines appear in the gradient pointer, the Fill Color or Stroke Color control, and the gradient-preview window.

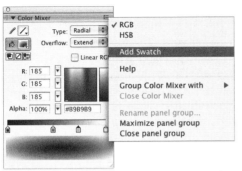

Figure 2.12 The Color Mixer panel's Options menu has a command for adding the current color to the Color Swatches panel.

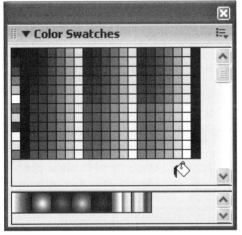

Figure 2.13 Positioning the pointer over a blank spot in the Color Swatches panel changes the pointer to a paint-bucket. Click to add whatever color is currently specified in the Color Mixer panel. Solid color swatches are added to the upper half of the Color Swatches panel; gradient swatches, to the lower half.

Working with Color Swatches

You can save a new color or gradient for the duration of your work session by adding the color currently displayed in the Color Mixer panel to the Color Swatches panel. The Fill Color and Stroke Color controls found in the Tools panel, Properties tab of the Property inspector, and Color Mixer panel also give you quick access to the current set of swatches; you'll learn more about these controls later in this chapter.

To add a color or gradient to the Color Swatches panel:

1. Create a new color or gradient using any of the techniques outlined in the preceding sections.

2. In the Color Mixer panel, *do either of the following:*

   ▲ From the Options menu, choose Add Swatch (**Figure 2.12**).

   ▲ Position the pointer over the blank area of the Color Swatches panel; when the paint-bucket pointer appears, click.

   Flash adds the new solid color or gradient to the appropriate section of the Color Swatches panel (**Figure 2.13**).

Creating Color Sets

Flash stores a default set of colors and gradients in the system color file, but it stores the colors and gradients used in each document with that document. Flash lets you define what colors and gradients make up the default set. In addition, you can create and save other color sets and load them into the Color Swatches panel. This practice makes it easy to maintain a consistent color palette when you're creating several documents for use in a single movie or on a single Web site.

To define a new set of colors:

1. Define the colors and gradients for your color set (see "Creating Solid Colors and Gradients," earlier in this chapter).

   You don't need to define them all at once, but after you have a set you want to save, go to step 2.

2. Access the Color Swatches panel.

3. From the Options menu, choose Save Colors (**Figure 2.14**).

   The Export Color Swatch dialog appears (**Figure 2.15**).

4. Navigate to the folder where you want to store your color set.

5. Enter a name for the color-set in the Save As (Mac), or File Name field (Windows).

6. From the Format (Mac) or Save as Type (Windows) pop-up menu, *choose one of two formats:*

   ▲ To save colors and gradients in Flash's proprietary Flash Color Set (CLR) format, choose Flash Color Set.

   ▲ To save the colors in Color Table (ACT) format, choose Color Table.

   The ACT format saves only colors (not gradients) but lets you share color sets with other programs, such as Macromedia Fireworks.

7. Click Save.

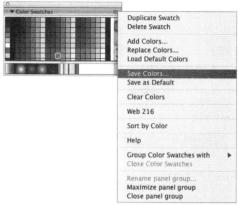

Figure 2.14 The Options menu in the Color Swatches panel offers commands for working with color sets.

Figure 2.15 To save a set of colors for reuse, in the Export Color Swatch dialog, choose Flash Color Set from the Format menu (Mac, top) or Save as Type menu (Windows, bottom).

CREATING COLOR SETS

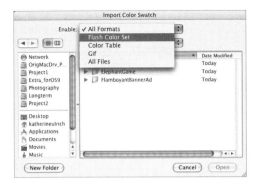

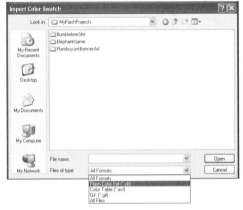

Figure 2.16 To reload a saved set of colors, in the Import Color Swatch dialog, choose Flash Color Set from the Enable menu (Mac, top) or Files of Type menu (Windows, bottom).

To load a set of colors:

1. From the Options menu in the Color Swatches panel, *choose either of the following:*

   ▲ To add to the color set currently displayed in the Color Swatches panel, choose Add Colors.

   ▲ To replace the entire set currently displayed in the Color Swatches panel, choose Replace Colors.

   The Import Color Swatch dialog appears (**Figure 2.16**).

2. To determine what types of files to display, from the Enable pop-up menu (Mac) or Files of Type (Windows) pop-up menu, *choose one of the following:*

   ▲ All Formats, which displays CLR, ACT, and GIF files

   ▲ Flash Color Set, which displays only CLR files

   ▲ Color Table, which displays only ACT files

   ▲ GIF, which displays only GIF files

   ▲ All Files, which displays files of any format

   Note that the Color Table and GIF formats are for color import only; these formats don't handle gradients. Flash Color Set handles both colors and gradients.

3. Navigate to the file you want to import.

4. Click Open.

CREATING COLOR SETS

✔ Tips

- You can add new colors to the Color Swatches panel even if it's closed. But if you want to get feedback when you add a swatch, open the Color Swatches panel in its own window (if the panel is part of a tabbed panel-group, you'll need to ungroup it; see Chapter 1 for details). Resize the panel so that a bit of space appears below the existing swatches. You'll see the new swatch come in.

- You can also delete swatches from the Color Swatches panel. Select the swatch you want to delete. From the Color Swatches panel's Options menu, choose Delete Swatch.

- If the gradients section of the Color Swatches panel is so full that you can't see the latest swatches you added, resize the section by dragging upward on the bar dividing the gradient swatches from the solid color swatches. You may need to resize the whole panel so there is room to drag upward.

- If the swatches in the Color Swatches panel are too small for you, resize the panel. The swatches grow bigger as the window widens.

- To create a new gradient swatch based on an existing one, in the Color Swatches panel, select the swatch you want to tweak. Position the pointer over the blank area below the swatch set. When the paint-bucket tool appears, click to add a copy of the selected swatch. Select the copy in the Color Swatches panel, and it loads into the Color Mixer panel, ready for you to modify.

- The Options menu in the Color Swatches panel also offers some handy shortcuts for dealing with color sets. To reload the default color set, choose Load Default Colors. To remove all color swatches from the current panel window, choose Clear Colors. To load the standard Web-safe colors, choose Web 216. To arrange colors by hue, choose Sort by Color. (Note that you can't undo the color sorting. Be sure to save your current set of colors if there's any chance that you'll want to restore the unsorted order.)

- You can also use the Color Swatches panel to select colors for fills and strokes. The key is first to tell Flash where to apply the new color. You do that by choosing any Stroke Color or Fill Color control and then selecting a color in the Color Swatches panel. Flash puts that color in every Stroke Color or Fill Color control. In the Colors section of the Tools panel, for example, choose the Fill Color control by clicking the paint-bucket icon; then select blue in the Color Swatches panel. Blue now appears in the Fill Color control in the Tools panel, in the Color Mixer panel, and in the Properties tab of the Property inspector.

Setting Fill Attributes

Flash offers five fill types: none, solid, linear gradient, radial gradient, and bitmap. You can create new fill colors and gradients in the Color Mixer panel (see "Creating Solid Colors and Gradients," earlier in this chapter). To assign colors or gradients to selected tools or graphic elements, you can use the Color Mixer panel; the Tools panel; or any fill-related Property inspectors, such as the one that accompanies the rectangle tool. You'll learn about using bitmap fills in Chapter 14.

To assign fill colors from the Tools panel:

1. In the Colors section of the Tools panel, click directly on the color chip in the Fill Color control (the one identified by a paint-bucket icon).

   The Fill Color control highlights, the pointer changes to an eyedropper, and a set of swatches pops up (**Figure 2.17**).

2. To assign a new fill color or gradient, *do one of the following:*

   ▲ To assign a gradient, select one of the linear or radial gradient swatches.

   ▲ To select a solid color, click a solid swatch or an item on the Stage; the color directly below the tip of the eyedropper becomes the assigned fill color.

   ▲ To define a new fill color, enter hex values in the field above the swatches.

   ▲ To define transparency for the current fill color, enter a percentage less than 100 in the Alpha field and press Enter.

   The new color appears in all Fill Color controls (in the Tools panel, Properties tab of the Property inspector, and Color Mixer) and will be used by any of the tools that create fills.

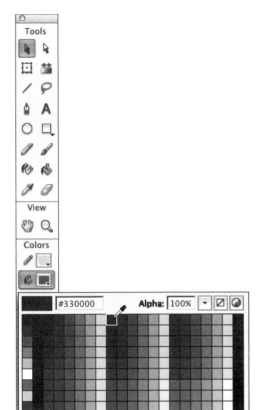

Figure 2.17 To set the fill color from the Tools panel, click the color chip in the Fill Color control. A set of swatches opens and you can choose the new fill color.

✔ Tip

■ To define a color that's not in the swatch set, click the Color Picker button in the top-right corner of the swatch pop-up. Doing so opens a separate color picker window. (For more information about defining colors, see "Creating Solid Colors and Gradients," earlier in this chapter.)

To assign fill colors from the Properties tab of the Property inspector:

1. Access the Properties tab of the Property inspector.

2. In the Tools panel, select one of the tools that creates fills.

   The oval, rectangle, polystar, brush, and bucket tools all create fills. When one of these tools is selected, the Properties tab of the Property inspector displays a Fill Color control (**Figure 2.18**).

3. In the Properties tab of the Property inspector, click directly on the color chip in the Fill Color control (the one identified by a paint-bucket icon).

   The current set of swatches appears.

4. To assign a new fill color, follow the instructions in step 2 of the preceding task.

✔ **Tip**

■ To access a System Color Picker for assigning fill colors, click the color chip in one of the Fill Color controls and then click the Color Picker button from the pop-up swatch window.

SETTING FILL ATTRIBUTES

Figure 2.18 When nothing is selected on the Stage and you select a tool that creates fills, such as the oval tool, the Properties tab of the Property inspector displays a Fill Color control.

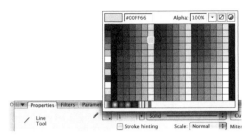

Figure 2.19 Clicking the Stroke Color control in the Properties tab of the Property inspector opens a set of color swatches and provides an eyedropper pointer for selecting a new color.

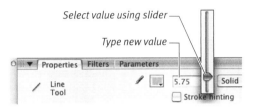

Select value using slider

Type new value

Figure 2.20 Entering a new value in the stroke-height field sets the thickness for strokes created by tools that draw strokes.

Setting Stroke Attributes

A line has three main attributes: color, thickness (also known as *weight* or, in Flash, *stroke height*), and style. You can set all three in the Properties tab of the Property inspector for any tool that creates strokes (the line, pen, oval, rectangle, polystar, pencil, and ink-bottle tools). The Properties tab of the Property inspector also lets you control the way the ends of lines (*caps*) look and the way lines connect (*joins*).

To set stroke properties:

1. With the Properties tab of the Property inspector open, in the Tools panel, choose a tool that creates strokes (line, pen, oval, rectangle, polystar, pencil, or ink bottle).

    The Properties tab of the Property inspector for the selected tool appears, displaying the current settings for strokes.

2. In the Properties tab of the Property inspector, click the Stroke Color control.

    The pointer changes to an eyedropper, and a set of swatches appears (**Figure 2.19**).

3. Select a stroke color.

4. To set the stroke's weight, in the stroke-height field, enter a number between 0.25 and 200, or drag the slider next to the stroke-height field (**Figure 2.20**).

    continues on next page

5. To set the stroke's style, from the stroke-style pop-up menu (**Figure 2.21**), select a style.

There are seven styles to choose from: hairline, solid, dashed, dotted, ragged, stippled, and hatched.

A graphic representation of your selected style appears in the stroke-style menu.

6. To set how the stroke ends, from the Cap pop-up menu, choose a cap style.

▲ None ends the stroke exactly where you stop drawing it.

▲ Round extends the stroke by half the current stroke height, creating a rounded end.

▲ Square extends the stroke by half the current stroke height, creating a square end (**Figure 2.22**).

7. To set the way strokes intersect, click the Join pop-up menu.

▲ Miter creates a sharp point at the intersection of two strokes.

▲ Round creates a slightly curved intersection

▲ Bevel creates a slightly flattened intersection (**Figure 2.23**).

Flash uses all the settings currently active in the Properties tab of the Property inspector any time you choose a tool that creates strokes.

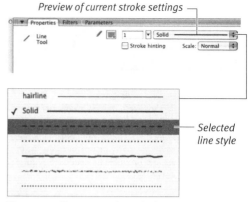

Preview of current stroke settings

Selected line style

Figure 2.21 Choose a stroke style from the pop-up menu in the Line Tool Properties tab of the Property inspector.

Figure 2.22 Set a Cap style in the Properties tab of the Property inspector to control the look of the ends of lines. None keeps the line's original length and makes the end flat, Round extends and rounds the line's end, and Square extends and squares off the end.

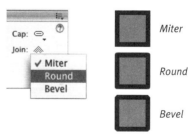

Figure 2.23 Set a join style in the Properties tab of the Property inspector to control the way lines connect. Miter makes a clean pointed corner, Round makes a rounded corner, and Bevel slices a flat piece off the corner.

✔ Tips

■ Use the three buttons at the bottom of the Tools panel's Colors section to set basic stroke (and fill) colors quickly. Clicking the leftmost button of the trio sets the stroke color to black (and the fill color to white). Clicking the rightmost button makes the current stroke and fill colors change places. (Clicking the middle button sets the fill or stroke to No Color when you use the oval, rectangle, and polystar tools.)

■ In Flash, the hairline setting is considered to be a stroke style, not a stroke height. (Use the stroke-style pop-up menu to get the hairline setting.) In symbols, hairlines don't change thickness when you resize the symbol. Other lines in symbols grow thicker or thinner as you scale them up or down. (To learn about symbols, see Chapter 7.)

■ To constrain the way strokes scale in your published movie, with a stroke (or stroke-creating tool) selected, choose a setting from the Scale menu in the Properties tab of the Property inspector. In the default (Normal) mode, a 1-pixel stroke becomes a 2-pixel stroke if your final movie gets enlarged to 200 percent. To prevent a selected stroke from scaling at all, choose None. To allow the stroke to scale in one direction only, choose Horizontal or Vertical.

■ Click the Stroke hinting check box in the Properties tab of the Property inspector to ensure crisp lines on the strokes in your final output. Without it, lines can sometimes appear slightly blurry on some monitors.

■ You can modify Flash's stroke styles. You might, for example, want larger dots in the dotted line or bigger spaces in the dashed line. In the (Line Tool) Properties tab of the Property inspector, select the style you want to modify, and then click the Custom button. The Stroke Style dialog appears, in which you can assign new settings. Click OK to close the dialog and confirm the settings. Those settings continue in force for that style until you change them or end the work session.

■ You can also set stroke color in the Tools panel or Color Mixer panel. In either panel, click the Stroke Color control, and select a color as described in "Setting Fill Attributes," earlier in this chapter.

SETTING STROKE ATTRIBUTES

Merge Drawing vs. Object Drawing

Flash 8 adds a new facet to the way you create graphic elements: there are now two models (or modes) for creating strokes and fills.

In **Merge Drawing** mode, the strokes and fills you create are raw shapes (just as they were in previous versions of Flash). Raw shapes are ready for editing directly on the Stage; raw shapes on a single layer interact with one another, dividing and replacing strokes and fills that overlap or intersect (you'll learn more about how shapes interact in Chapter 5).

In **Object Drawing** mode, the strokes and fills you create are still directly editable on the Stage, but they don't interact with other shapes on the same layer. To anyone who's used a previous version of Flash, these shapes may seem a little unpredictable. In some ways, shapes created in Object Drawing mode act as if they were isolated on a separate layer or protected using the Group command (you'll learn more about working with grouped shapes in Chapter 5 and about shapes on separate layers in Chapter 6). But shapes created in Object Drawing mode can be modified directly on the Stage (see Chapter 4), whereas grouped objects can't. In fact Object Drawing mode creates a whole new type of creature.

Flash's default mode for drawing tools is Merge Drawing. To turn on Object Drawing mode, select a tool that creates strokes and/or fills, and then click the Object Drawing button in the Options section of the Tools panel (**Figure 2.24**). Once you activate Object Drawing mode for any tool, all tools that create strokes and fills are set to Object Drawing mode. To return to Merge Drawing mode, you must click the Object Drawing button again to deselect Object Drawing mode (or press J on the keyboard to toggle between Merge Drawing and Object Drawing). Whatever Merge/Object Drawing setting is active when you end a work session will be active the next time you open Flash.

For many tasks, you'll see no difference between working with shapes created in Merge Drawing mode and shapes created in Object Drawing mode; in some tasks, however, the difference is crucial. For the exercises in this book, unless otherwise noted, you can use either drawing mode when creating shapes.

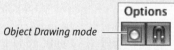

Object Drawing mode

Figure 2.24 You can set the drawing tools to create shapes that don't interact with other shapes on the same layer. Select Object Drawing mode in the Options section of the Tools panel.

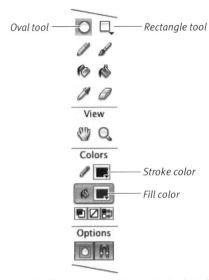

Figure 2.25 The Tools panel with the oval tool selected.

Figure 2.26 When the Fill Color control is selected in the Colors section of the Tools panel, clicking the No Color button allows whatever tool you select to create a shape with no fill.

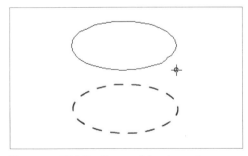

Figure 2.27 Click the Stage and drag to create an oval. You see a preview outline of your shape (top). Release the mouse button, and Flash creates an oval outline using the current color, thickness, and style settings. In this case, the oval tool is set to black stroke color, no fill, dashed stroke style, and a stroke height of 1 point (bottom).

Making Geometric Shapes

Flash provides separate tools for drawing ovals, rectangles, and polygons or stars. The tools work similarly; all can draw a shape as an outline (just a stroke) or as a solid object (a fill). You can also create a geometric shape with a fill and a stroke simultaneously.

To create geometric outlines:

1. In the Tools panel, select a geometric-shape tool—for example, the oval tool (**Figure 2.25**).

2. In the Colors section of the Tools panel, click the paint-bucket icon to select the Fill Color control.

3. In the Colors section of the Tools panel, select No Color (**Figure 2.26**).

   This setting enables the tool to draw outlines without a fill.

4. Use the current stroke color and line weight, or select new ones (see "Setting Stroke Attributes," earlier in this chapter).

5. Move the pointer over the Stage.

   The pointer turns into a crosshair.

6. Click and drag to create the geometric shape (**Figure 2.27**).

   Flash previews the shape as you drag.

7. Release the mouse button.

   Flash draws the geometric shape as an outline.

✔ Tips

- Flash provides a line tool for drawing simple straight lines (strokes). To use the line tool, select it in the Tools panel and set its stroke attributes; with the line-tool pointer (a cross hair) active, click and drag on the Stage. You see a preview line as you drag. Flash creates the finished line, with the correct attributes, when you release the mouse button.

- To draw a perfect circle (or square), hold down the Shift key while you draw with the oval or rectangle tool.

- To make ovals (or rectangles) grow outward from the center point as you draw, position the pointer where you want the center of the shape to be; hold down the Alt key (Windows) or Option key (Mac) as you drag. Shapes drawn with the polystar tool always grow from the center.

- There are other ways to set geometric tools to draw just outlines. Click the Tools panel's Fill Color control directly on the color chip. A pop-up set of fill swatches opens. Now, click the No Color button near the top-right corner of the swatch pop-up. You can also use the Mixer panel: Select the Fill Color control, and then choose None from the Type menu.

Shapely Terminology

The question of what to call the graphic elements created with Flash's drawing tools has always been a bit of a stumper, and the addition of Object Drawing mode makes it more perplexing. The general term *shape* might apply to the form of the element (round versus rectangular), or it might be used to distinguish something created in Merge Drawing mode from something created in Object Drawing mode. The term *object* has a specific meaning in ActionScript (see Chapter 7). To avoid confusion, here's how this book will talk about these elements.

A **shape** is any stroke and/or fill created with Flash's drawing tools. A **drawing-object** is a shape created in Object Drawing mode or by using the Modify > Combine Objects command (see Chapter 5). A **merge-shape** (or **raw shape**) is a shape created in Merge Drawing mode. A **grouped shape** (or **group**) is a set of shapes that have been combined to act as a unit via Flash's Group command (see Chapter 5).

The term **graphic-object** refers to drawing-objects, groups, and symbols. A graphic-object is a container that holds shapes; each type of graphic-object has specific rules that govern its behavior, for example, controlling how its contents interact with other graphic elements. (The word *graphic* here distinguishes these items from ActionScript objects.)

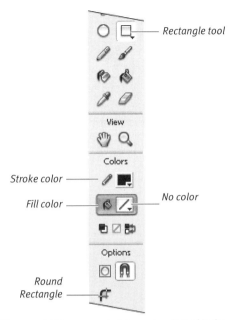

Stroke color

Fill color — No color

Round
Rectangle

Figure 2.28 When you select the rectangle tool in the Tools panel, the Round Rectangle modifier appears in the Options section. This setting gives you more control in creating rectangles with blunt corners.

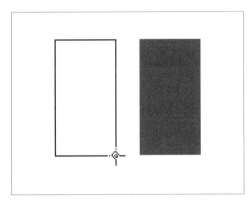

Figure 2.29 As you drag the rectangle tool, Flash creates an outline preview of a rectangle (left). To complete the fill shape, release the mouse button (right).

To create geometric fills:

1. In the Tools panel, select a geometric-shape tool—for example, the rectangle (**Figure 2.28**).

2. To set the tool to create just a fill, in the Colors section of the Tools panel, *do the following,*

   ▲ Click the pencil icon to activate the Stroke Color control.

   ▲ Click the No Color button.

   Flash enables the selected tool to draw fills without outlines.

3. Select a fill color (see "Setting Fill Attributes," earlier in this chapter).

4. Move the pointer over the Stage.
   The pointer changes to a crosshair.

5. Click and drag to create the geometric fill.
   Flash previews the shape as you drag (**Figure 2.29**).

6. Release the mouse button.
   Flash draws a geometric fill, using the currently selected fill color.

✔ Tips

■ In "Setting Stroke Attributes," earlier in this chapter, you learned to use the Join setting in the Properties tab of the Property inspector to make line segments connect with mitered, beveled, or rounded corners. The rectangle tool can override that Join setting. Select the rectangle tool; in the Options section of the Tools panel, click the Round Rectangle button; and enter a value in the Corner Radius field of the Rectangle Settings dialog (**Figure 2.30**). With a 0 setting, the rectangle tool uses the Join setting; at higher settings, the tool creates rounded corners (the higher the setting, the more rounded the corners).

MAKING GEOMETRIC SHAPES

- To reset the rectangle tool's corner radius to 0 quickly, Shift-double-click the rectangle tool or Shift-click the Round Rectangle button.

- You can change a rectangle's corner radius as you draw. Drag on the Stage with the rectangle tool to create your shape. Before releasing the mouse button, press the up-arrow key to reduce the corner-radius value; press the down-arrow key to increase it. The preview rectangle changes interactively as you press the arrow keys. Release the mouse button to complete your shape.

- You can create polygons and star shapes with the polystar tool (choose it from the rectangle tool's submenu in the Tools panel). To set the number of sides in the polygon and to switch from polygons to stars, you must enter tool settings via the PolyStar Tool Properties tab of the Property inspector. With the polystar tool selected, click the Options button in the Properties tab of the Property inspector. The Tool Settings dialog appears. Enter values for the number of sides and how sharp the star points are, and then click OK to close the dialog.

- You can draw precision ovals and rectangles by using the Oval Settings and Rectangle Settings dialogs. To access this feature, select the oval or rectangle tool. Option-click (Mac) or Alt-click (Windows) the Stage. The appropriate settings dialog appears. Enter values for your shape's height and width. These values describe the height and width of the rectangle or the bounding box that contains the oval. Select the Draw from Center check box to place your shape's center at the spot you clicked; deselect the check box to place the top-left corner of the shape, or bounding box, at the spot you clicked.

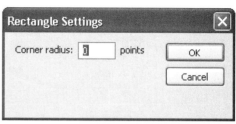

Figure 2.30 Enter a value of 0 in the Corner radius field of the Rectangle Settings dialog to create a rectangle that uses the Join property you've set in the Properties tab of the Property inspector. Enter a larger value to round the corners of your rectangle precisely.

Creating Freeform Shapes

Flash offers three tools for creating freeform shapes: the pencil, pen, and brush. The pencil and pen tools create stroke outlines, and the brush tool creates fills without strokes. The pencil tool creates only outlines, even if you draw a closed shape. The pen tool automatically fills a closed shape with the current fill color. Once you've created a shape, you can always modify it—say, to fill an empty outline or add an outline to a plain fill shape.

The pencil tool lets you draw lines (strokes) naturally (as you would with a real-world pencil, but using the mouse or a graphics tablet and pen). Flash hides information about the anchor points and curves of a stroke drawn with the pencil. With the pen tool, you place anchor points and adjust Bézier curves to create strokes.

For the tasks below, make sure the grid is visible (see Chapter 1) and set drawing preferences as follows: choose Edit > Preferences (Windows) or Flash > Preferences (Mac) to open the Preferences dialog; select Drawing from the Category list, and select the Show Pen Preview and Show Solid Points check boxes; leave the other items at their default settings.

About Drawing Assistance

Flash's pencil tool offers two assisted line-drawing modes: Straighten and Smooth. For total freedom in drawing, the pencil's Ink mode leaves shapes exactly as you create them.

Straighten mode refines any blips and tremors in a rough hand-drawn line into straight-line segments and regular arcs. This mode also carries out what Flash calls *shape recognition*. Flash evaluates each rough shape you draw, and if the shape comes close enough to Flash's definition of an oval or rectangle, Flash turns your rough approximation into a shape neat enough to please your high-school geometry teacher.

Smooth mode transforms your rough drawing into one composed of smooth, curved line segments. Note that Smooth mode doesn't recognize shapes; it simply smoothes out the curves you draw. Smoothing reduces the number of points in a shape, resulting in smaller files which in turn improves the performance of your final, published work.

Tolerance settings are all-important, especially for Straighten mode. You can set Flash to change almost anything ovoid into a circle and anything slightly more oblong into a rectangle. You set the degree of drawing assistance in the Preferences dialog. Choose Flash > Preferences (Mac) or Edit > Preferences (Windows); in the Preferences dialog that opens, choose Drawing from the Category list, and then choose tolerance levels from the Connect Lines, Smooth Curves, Recognize Lines, and Recognize Shapes menus. Click OK to close the dialog.

To draw freeform strokes with the pencil tool:

1. In the Tools panel, select the pencil tool, or press Y.

2. In the Options section, from the Pencil Mode menu (**Figure 2.31**), *choose one of the following assistance modes:*

   Straighten resolves minor variations into straight-line segments.

   Smooth resolves minor variations into smooth curves.

   Ink provides very little assistance, leaving minor variations.

3. Move the pointer over the Stage.
   The pointer turns into the pencil tool.

4. Click, and draw a squiggle (**Figure 2.32**).
   Flash previews your rough line.

5. Release the mouse button.
   Flash recasts the line you've drawn according to the assistance mode you chose in step 2, creating a set of straight-line segments and regular curves.

✔ Tip

■ You can apply smoothing and straightening (even shape recognition) after you've drawn an outline or shape by selecting it on the Stage and then clicking the Straighten or Smooth modifier of the Selection tool (you'll learn more about making and modifying selections in Chapter 4).

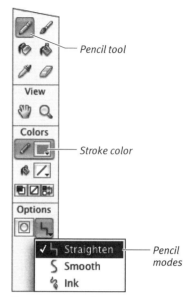

Pencil tool

Stroke color

Pencil modes

Figure 2.31 When the pencil tool is selected, the Tools panel displays a pop-up menu of pencil modes.

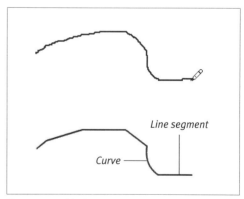

Line segment

Curve

Figure 2.32 With the pencil in Straighten mode, when you draw a squiggle, Flash previews it for you. When you release the mouse button, Flash applies straightening, turning your rough squiggle (top) into a set of straight-line segments and smooth curves (bottom).

Figure 2.33 Select the pen tool to create paths.

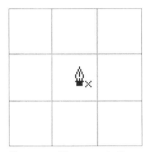

Figure 2.34 The x next to the pen tool indicates that you're about to start a new path. Click to place the first anchor point.

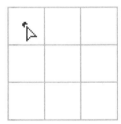

First point previewed

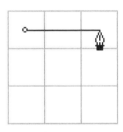

Preview line segment

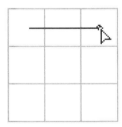

Click to place second point

Completed line segment

Figure 2.35 Flash previews points as you place them (top), and it adds a stroke to the path as soon as you complete a segment (bottom).

To draw freeform strokes with the pen tool:

1. In the Tools panel, select the pen tool, or press P (**Figure 2.33**).

2. Set the stroke attributes for your path.

3. Move the pointer over the Stage.

   The pen tool appears with a small *x* next to it (**Figure 2.34**). The *x* indicates that you're ready to place the first point of a path.

4. Click where you want your line segment to begin.

   The pointer changes to a hollow arrowhead; a small circle indicates the location of the anchor point on the Stage.

5. Reposition the pen tool where you want your line segment to end.

   Flash extends a preview of the line segment from the first point to the tip of the pen as you move around the Stage.

6. Click.

   Flash completes the line segment using the selected stroke attributes. The anchor points appear as solid squares (**Figure 2.35**).

continues on next page

CREATING FREEFORM SHAPES

7. To add a straight segment to your line, click the Stage where you want the segment to end, and release the mouse button (**Figure 2.36**).

8. To add a curve segment, click the Stage where you want the curve segment to end, and then drag the pointer.

   Flash places a preview point on the Stage, the pointer changes to a hollow arrowhead, and Bézier handles appear (**Figure 2.37**).

9. Drag the pointer in the opposite direction from which you want your curve to bulge.

   The Bézier handles extend from the anchor point, growing in opposite directions as you drag. Flash previews the curve you're drawing (**Figure 2.38**).

Figure 2.36 Continue clicking to add segments to your freeform shape. A quick click (top) adds a straight line segment (bottom).

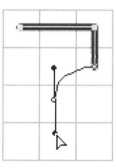

Figure 2.37 Click and drag to create a curve point; as you drag, the point's Bézier handles activate. The bulge of the curve grows away from the direction of your drag. To make the curve bulge upward, drag downward.

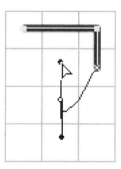

Figure 2.38 To make the curve bulge downward, drag upward. Dragging the handles out further deepens the curve.

CREATING FREEFORM SHAPES

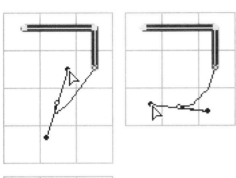

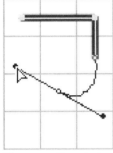

Figure 2.39 Move the handles clockwise or counterclockwise around the point to modify the curve shape. Drag the handles in or out to make the curve deeper or shallower.

Figure 2.40 When you finish positioning handles for a segment and release the mouse button, Flash adds a stroke to the segment.

Figure 2.41 To create a closed shape, position the pointer over the first anchor point you placed. When you see the hollow circle icon, click that first point. Flash adds the finishing segment and fills the shape with the current fill color.

10. Still keeping the mouse button down, drag the pointer to reposition the Bézier handle.

    Dragging the handle clockwise or counterclockwise around its anchor point controls the direction of the bulge; dragging the handle further from the anchor point deepens the curve (**Figure 2.39**).

11. When the curve preview looks the way you want, release the mouse button.

    Flash completes your curve segment with a stroke (**Figure 2.40**).

12. To create an open path, ⌘-click (Mac) or Ctrl-click (Windows) the Stage.

    or

    To create a closed shape, *do the following:*

    ▲ Position the pointer over your first anchor point.

       Flash previews the closing segment of your shape. A small hollow circle appears next to the pen tool (**Figure 2.41**).

    ▲ Click the first anchor point.

       Flash closes the shape, adding a stroke to the path and filling the shape with the currently selected fill color.

    Once the path is complete, the pen tool pointer displays a small *x*, indicating that the tool is ready to place the first anchor point of a new path.

✔ Tips

- There are other ways to end open paths. Choose Edit > Deselect All, or press ⌘-Shift-A (Mac) or Ctrl-Shift-A (Windows). In the Tools panel, click the pen tool (or any other tool). You can also double-click the last point you placed. This technique works best when the path ends with a straight-line segment that doesn't involve Bézier handles.

- You don't have to close a path at the beginning point. The hollow circle appears next to the pen pointer when you position the pointer anywhere over a stroke. Clicking any anchor point in the path you're currently drawing closes off a shape at that point; the shape fills automatically with the current fill color. Clicking between anchor points creates an outline shape (to force that shape to fill, double-click just inside of the stroke).

- If you click a path that's separate from the one you're creating, Flash joins the two paths.

About Path Math in Flash

A *path*—a series of points and connecting lines—is the skeleton of your graphic-object. With most Flash tools, the math that goes into creating a path takes place behind the scenes. You draw a complete line or a shape; Flash places points (without showing them), connects them, and adds a stroke. With the pen tool, you place the defining points (called *anchor points*) and adjust the curve segments that connect them (using controllers called *Bézier handles*). When you've finished placing points with the pen tool, Flash fleshes out the path by applying a stroke to it.

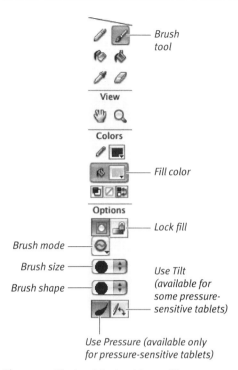

Figure 2.42 The brush tool and its modifiers.

To create freeform solid fills with the brush tool:

1. In the Tools panel, select the brush tool or press B (**Figure 2.42**).

2. To optimize the brush for particular painting tasks, in the Options section of the Tools panel, *do any of the following,*

   ▲ From the Brush Size pop-up menu, choose a size for the brush tip.

   ▲ From the Brush Shape pop-up menu, choose a shape for the brush tip.

   continues on next page

About the Brush Tool

Flash's brush tool offers a way to create free-flowing swashes of color. These shapes are actually freeform fills drawn without a stroke. The brush tool lets you simulate art-work you'd create in the real world with a paintbrush or marking pen. A variety of brush sizes and tip shapes helps you create a painterly look in your drawings.

If you have a pressure-sensitive drawing tablet, the brush can interact with it to create lines of varying thickness, imitating the thick and thin lines of real-world brushwork. The more pressure you apply, the thicker the brushstroke (**Figure 2.43**).

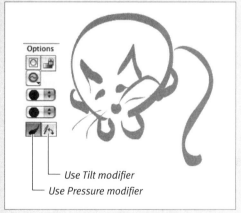

Figure 2.43 Selecting the brush tool's Use Pressure modifier activates the pressure-sensitive capabilities of a connected pressure-sensitive pen and graphics tablet. To produce lively lines of varying thickness, apply more or less pressure as you draw. Flash created all the lines in this cat with a single brush size and shape.

CREATING FREEFORM SHAPES

▲ From the Brush Mode pop-up menu, choose a painting mode; for this exercise, choose Paint Normal (**Figure 2.44**). The brush tool always creates merge-shape fills. The painting modes allow you to control how brush stroke fills act when you use the brush tool to paint over other shapes.

Overlapping shapes interact in different ways depending on whether they are merge-shapes or drawing-objects. (You'll learn about how overlapping shapes interact in Chapter 5.)

▲ To paint brushstroke fills that can vary in thickness, choose Use Pressure (this option appears only when a graphics tablet is connected to your computer).

3. Select or define a solid fill color using any of the techniques outlined earlier in this chapter.

4. Move the pointer over the Stage.

The pointer changes to reflect the current brush size and shape.

5. Click and draw on the Stage.

Flash previews your brushwork (**Figure 2.45**).

6. When you complete your shape, release the mouse button.

Flash creates the final shape in the currently selected fill.

✔ Tip

■ You can change the size of your brushstroke by changing the magnification at which you view the Stage. To create a fat stroke without changing your brush-tip settings, set the Stage view to a small percentage. To switch to a thin stroke, zoom out to a higher percentage (**Figure 2.46**). Be sure to check your work in 100% view.

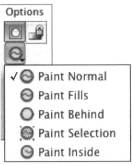

Figure 2.44 The Brush Mode options give you control over how fills created with the brush tool interact with other shapes on the same layer. Choosing Paint Normal lets you paint merge-shape fills that act like any other fills when they overlap other shapes.

Figure 2.45 Drawing with the brush creates a preview of your shape (top); Flash recasts the shape as a vector graphic with the currently selected fill color.

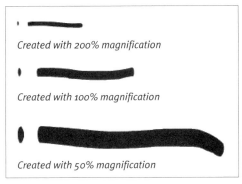

Created with 200% magnification

Created with 100% magnification

Created with 50% magnification

Figure 2.46 Flash created these three brushstrokes with exactly the same brush size—only the magnification level of the Stage changed for each stroke.

CREATING FREEFORM SHAPES

Figure 2.47 Deselect the Lock Fill modifier to paint with an unlocked gradient.

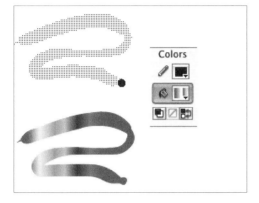

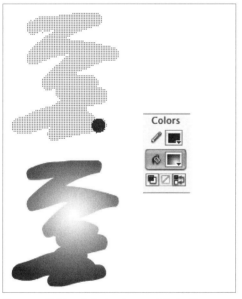

Figure 2.48 A brushstroke shape painted with an unlocked linear-gradient fill (top) and one painted with radial-gradient fill (bottom).

To paint with gradients:

1. Follow steps 1 and 2 in the preceding task.

2. Using one of the methods described earlier in this chapter, select (or define) a linear or radial gradient fill.

3. To lock or unlock the gradient, in the Options section of the Tools panel, *do either of the following,*

   ▲ To paint shapes that contain the full gradient spectrum, deselect Lock Fill (**Figure 2.47**).

   ▲ To paint shapes that reveal just a portion of the gradient, select Lock Fill.

4. Paint with the brush as described in steps 4–6 in the preceding task.

   Flash can't preview the shape you paint with a gradient fill. The preview shape has a black-and-white pattern.

   Flash redraws the painted shape, using the current lock-fill and fill-color setting (see the sidebar "The Mystery of Gradients and Flash's Drawing Models").

   For unlocked fills, the full gradient is visible in the shape (**Figure 2.48**).

   continues on next page

For locked fills, just a portion of the gradient is visible in the shape (**Figure 2.49**).

✔ Tips

- Try painting a variety of brushstrokes in both drawing modes; use locked and unlocked gradients; use different areas of the Stage; and make the shapes different lengths. Notice the way each shape displays the gradient.

- To predetermine the location of the center of a locked gradient, first paint a brushstroke shape with an unlocked gradient. When you switch to painting with Lock Fill active, the virtual underlying gradient aligns with the last unlocked gradient you painted. You can then delete the unneeded unlocked gradient or use the paint-bucket tool to change it to a locked gradient (see Chapter 4).

- After you've created a shape with a gradient fill, you can adjust the location of the center of the gradient by using the gradient transform tool (see Chapter 4).

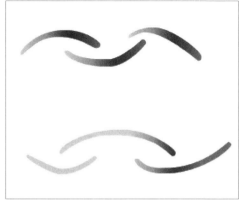

Figure 2.49 With the brush tool's Lock Fill modifier deselected, each brushstroke fill you paint contains the full range of the current gradient (top); with Lock Fill selected, each brushstroke fill appears to reveal a section of a gradient that runs the width of the Stage and Pasteboard (bottom).

The Mystery of Gradients and Flash's Drawing Models

When you use the brush tool to paint a shape with a gradient fill and the Lock Fill modifier is deselected, it makes no difference if you're painting in Merge Drawing mode or Object Drawing mode. Flash centers the gradient in the shape's bounding box (an invisible rectangle that's just the right size to enclose the shape); the full gradient is visible in the shape.

When you paint the same kind of shape and Lock Fill is selected, however, shapes created in the two drawing modes behave differently.

For locked fills, Flash creates a virtual gradient that underlies the Stage and Pasteboard. Each shape you create with a locked fill reveals just the portion of the gradient that corresponds to that area of the Stage. If you paint multiple merge-shapes with a locked gradient, the same virtual gradient underlies each shape; you can use the gradient-transform tool to shift the gradient within all the shapes. Multiple drawing-objects each have their own personal virtual gradient. These virtual gradients are all centered in the same way, so initially it looks like it works the same way as for merge-shapes. But the gradient transform tool shifts the gradient in each drawing-object separately. You'll learn more about working with multiple shapes and using the gradient-transform tool in Chapter 4.

The Mystery of Brush Smoothness Settings

Flash 8 gives you control over how your brushstrokes translate into vector shapes. To access this control, in the Properties tab of the Property inspector for the brush tool, enter a value in the Smoothing field. The stroke-smoothness setting determines how closely Flash re-creates each movement of the brush as a separate vector segment; the setting ranges from 0 to 100, and the default is 50. The lower the setting, the more faithfully Flash reproduces the shapes you draw. (It does this by using more vectors, which has an impact on the size and animation performance of your final file.) With a higher setting, Flash re-creates your flourishes more roughly, using fewer vectors.

To see the difference most clearly, select the brush tool, assign a smoothing value of 1, and use the mouse (not a graphics pen) to draw a curvy line on the Stage. Now change the smoothing setting to 10. Draw a second curvy line. Using the subselection tool (you'll learn about using this tool in Chapter 4), select each shape. The line drawn with smoothing set to 1 displays many more points—that is, it contains many more vector segments.

Adding Strokes and Fills

As you've learned earlier in this chapter, you can use the line, pencil, pen, and geometric-shape tools to create outline shapes (strokes without fills). Using the brush, pen, and geometric shape tools, you can create fill shapes that have no stroke outline. At any point, you can add the missing element to such shapes. The ink-bottle tool adds strokes that outline plain fill shapes; the paint bucket tool adds fills inside of plain outline shapes. (You can also use these tools to modify strokes and fills; see Chapter 4.)

To add strokes to fills:

1. On the Stage, draw a fill that has no stroke, or work with an existing unstroked shape.

For merge-shapes, make sure the fill is deselected; for drawing-objects, the fill can be selected or deselected.

2. In the Tools panel, select the ink-bottle tool or press S (**Figure 2.50**).

3. In the Ink Bottle Tool Properties tab of the Property inspector, set the desired stroke attributes (see "Setting Stroke Attributes," earlier in this chapter).

4. Position the pointer over a fill shape that has no stroke.

The pointer appears as a little ink bottle, spilling ink.

Ink bottle —

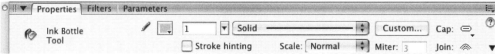

Figure 2.50 The ink-bottle tool applies all the stroke attributes currently set in the (Ink Bottle Tool) Properties tab of the Property inspector.

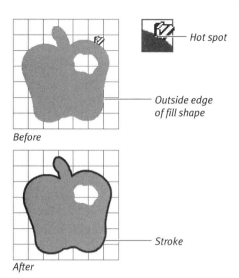

Hot spot

Outside edge of fill shape

Before

Stroke

After

Figure 2.51 As you move the ink bottle over a filled shape, the hot spot appears as a white dot at the end of the ink drip that's spilling out of the bottle. To add a stroke around the outside edge of your fill shape, position the hot spot along that edge (top) and then click. Flash adds a stroke with the current attributes set in the (Ink Bottle Tool) Properties tab of the Property inspector (bottom).

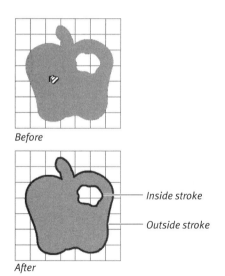

Before

Inside stroke

Outside stroke

After

Figure 2.52 Position the ink bottle's hot spot in the middle of your fill shape (top), and then click. Flash uses the current stroke attributes to add a stroke around the outside and inside of your shape (bottom).

5. With the ink bottle's hot spot, click a fill shape in one of the following ways:

▲ To add a stroke around the outside of your shape, click near the outside edge of the shape (**Figure 2.51**).

▲ To add a stroke around the inside of a shape that has a hole cut out of it, click near the inside edge of the shape.

▲ To outline both the outside of a shape and the hole inside the shape, click in the middle of the shape (**Figure 2.52**).

Flash adds strokes to the outside edge, inside edge, or both, using the Properties tab of the Property inspector's current settings for color, thickness, and style.

✔ Tip

■ In previous versions of Flash, strokes could only be solid colors. In Flash 8, you can use gradients for strokes. In step 3 of the preceding task, in the Properties tab of the Property inspector, choose a linear or radial gradient from the Stroke Color control's pop-up swatch set. Why might you want a gradient stroke? For an oval shape, adding a thick stroke with a radial gradient can help to create the illusion of 3D depth or make the shape appear to glow.

ADDING STROKES AND FILLS

To fill an outline shape with solid color:

1. On the Stage, draw an outline stroke that has no fill, or work with an existing outline shape.

   The outline can be selected or deselected.

2. In the Tools panel, select the paint-bucket tool, or press K (**Figure 2.53**).

3. From the Gap Size menu in the Options section of the Tools panel, choose the amount of assistance you want (**Figure 2.54**).

   If you draw your shapes precisely, medium or small gap closure serves you best; you don't want Flash to fill areas that aren't meant to be shapes. If your drawings are rougher, choose Close Large Gaps. This setting enables Flash to recognize less-complete shapes.

4. From any Fill Color control, select a solid fill color.

5. Place the paint bucket's hot spot (the tip of the drip of paint) inside the outline shape (**Figure 2.55**).

6. Click.

   The shape fills with the currently selected fill color (**Figure 2.56**).

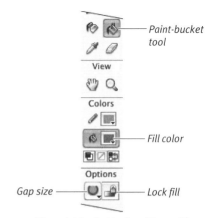

Figure 2.53 The paint-bucket tool and its modifiers.

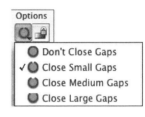

Figure 2.54 The Gap Size menu controls Flash's capability to fill shapes that aren't fully closed.

Figure 2.55 The hot spot on the paint-bucket tool is the little drip at the end of the spilling paint. The hot spot changes to white when you move the paint bucket over a darker color.

Figure 2.56 Clicking inside an outline shape with the paint bucket (top) fills the shape with the currently selected fill color (bottom).

Figure 2.57 The paint bucket can't fill this apple shape with the setting of Close Large Gaps and a magnification of 100 percent (left). But in a 50 percent view, the paint bucket with the same large-gap closure setting recognizes this shape as complete and fills it.

View

Colors

Options

— Deselect
Lock Fill

Figure 2.58 Deselect the Lock Fill button to fill a shape with an unlocked gradient.

✔ Tips

■ You may be unaware that your shape has any gaps. If nothing happens when you click inside a shape with the paint bucket, try changing the Gap Size setting in step 3.

■ Gap-closure settings are relative to the amount of magnification you're using to view the Stage. If the paint bucket's largest gap-closure setting fails at your current magnification, try again after reducing magnification (**Figure 2.57**).

To fill outline shapes with unlocked gradients:

1. In the Tools panel, select the paint-bucket tool.

2. In the Color Mixer panel, define a new gradient (see "Creating Solid Colors and Gradients," earlier in this chapter),

   or

   From any Fill Color control, select an existing linear or radial gradient (see "Setting Fill Attributes," earlier in this chapter).

3. In the Options section of the Tools panel, make sure that Lock Fill is deselected (**Figure 2.58**).

continues on next page

ADDING STROKES AND FILLS

4. Follow steps 5 and 6 in the preceding task.

Each outline shape you click fills with the gradient currently displayed in the Fill Color control. If you chose a linear gradient in step 2, Flash centers the gradient within the outline shape (**Figure 2.59**). If you chose a radial gradient, the location you click with the paint bucket's hot spot determines where the center of the gradient appears (**Figure 2.60**).

To fill outline shapes with locked gradients:

1. Follow steps 1 and 2 in the preceding task.

2. In the Options section of the Tools panel, select Lock Fill.

3. Follow steps 5 and 6 in "To fill an outline shape with solid color," earlier in this section.

Each outline shape you click fills with a portion of the gradient currently set in the Fill Color control (see the sidebar "The Mystery of Gradients and Flash's Drawing Models").

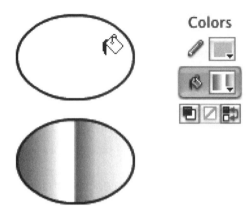

Figure 2.59 You can use the paint-bucket tool to apply a linear-gradient fill. The gradient is centered within the outline shape's bounding box.

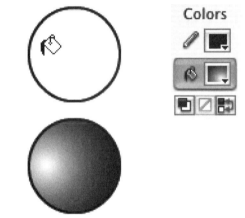

Figure 2.60 The paint-bucket tool can also apply a radial-gradient fill. Click where you want to locate the center of the gradient.

Gradients Add Overhead

Gradients are lovely, but they increase file sizes and thereby slow the loading of published movies. Each area of gradient fill requires an extra 50 bytes of data that a solid fill doesn't need.

In addition, gradients take processor power. If you use too many, you may see slower frame rates, or slower animations, in your finished movie

ADDING STROKES AND FILLS

Working with Text

Flash's text tool doesn't just create graphic-objects in the shape of letters, it creates text boxes filled with live type; in the authoring environment, the contents of a text box are fully editable. As you create text elements, you must decide how they will be used in the published movie and assign them a text-type property. If you want the end user to interact with a text field (for example, to enter personal information), set the text box's text-type property to *input*. If you want to update the text at runtime (for example, using ActionScript to download and display new basketball scores to a sports site), set the text-type property to *dynamic*. If the text will just sit there looking pretty, set the text-type property to *static*.

Flash 8 uses a new text-rendering engine called Flash Type, which makes fonts more legible (especially at small sizes). This legibility shows up in the authoring environment, as you create your movies, but it also comes into play for your end users if you publish your files for Flash Player 8 (see Chapter 16).

In this chapter, you learn about using static text. The manipulation of input and dynamic text fields requires a more advanced level of ActionScripting than this book can cover; if you need to know more, check out *Macromedia Flash 8 Professional Advanced; Visual QuickPro Guide,* from Peachpit Press.

Using the Text Tool

The text tool creates blocks of editable text. You can set the text to read horizontally or vertically. You can also apply a variety of text attributes to text—including text and paragraph styles.

To create a single line of text for use as a graphic element:

1. In the Tools panel, select the text tool or press T (**Figure 3.1**).

   For this task, use the current settings for type and paragraph styles. You learn to change these settings in upcoming tasks.

2. Move the pointer over the Stage.

   The pointer turns into a crosshair with a letter *A* in the bottom-right corner (**Figure 3.2**).

3. Click the Stage at the spot where you want your text to start.

   Flash creates a resizable text box with a blinking insertion point, ready for you to enter text (**Figure 3.3**).

   Each corner of the text box has a draggable resize handle; the round handle in the upper-right corner indicates that word wrap hasn't been set on this text box.

4. Start typing your text.

   The text box grows to accommodate whatever you type (**Figure 3.4**).

5. When you finish typing, click elsewhere on the Stage or change tools.

   Flash hides the text box, leaving just the text visible. When you click this text with the selection tool, Flash selects the text box so that you can reposition it or change the text's attributes directly.

Figure 3.1 Select the text tool in the Tools panel to start creating text boxes on the Stage.

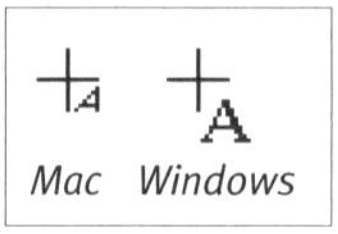

Figure 3.2 The text-tool pointer.

Figure 3.3 Click the Stage with the text tool to create a text box. The round resize handle indicates that the text box does not have word wrap turned on.

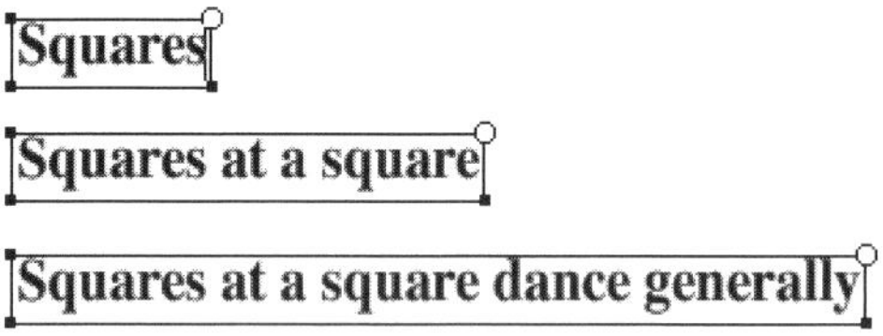

Squares

Squares at a square

Squares at a square dance generally

Figure 3.4 As you type, the box grows horizontally to accommodate your text. The text won't wrap.

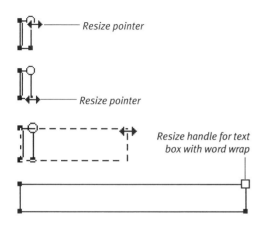

Resize pointer

Resize pointer

Resize handle for text box with word wrap

Squares at a square dance

Squares at a square dance generally dance with squares|

Figure 3.5 Click and drag any resize handle to create a text box with a specific width. The top-right handle changes to a square, indicating that the text you enter will wrap to fit the column width of the text box. The text box continues to grow in length—but not width—as you enter more text.

To create a text box with set width and word wrap:

1. With the text tool selected in the Tools panel, click the Stage at the spot where you want your text to start.

2. Move the pointer over any of the resize handles.

   The pointer changes to a double-headed arrow.

3. Click and drag one of the handles until your text box is as wide as you want it (**Figure 3.5**).

   The resize handle in the upper-right corner changes to a square, indicating that word wrap is set for this text box.

4. Release the mouse button.

   The blinking insertion point appears in the text box.

5. Enter your text.

   Flash wraps the text horizontally to fit inside the column that the text box defines. The box automatically grows longer (not wider) to accommodate your text.

✔ Tips

■ To reposition a text box with the text tool active, position the pointer along the edge of the text box. The pointer changes to the selection arrow. Now you can drag the text box to a new location.

■ To restore a text box to its original state (where text doesn't wrap), double-click the square in the upper-right corner. It changes to the circle that indicates the box will grow horizontally.

Setting Text Attributes

The Properties tab of the Property inspector has two slightly different modes for setting text attributes. When you choose the text tool in the Tools panel, the Properties tab is labeled Text Tool; this tab provides options for setting typeface, font size, style, spacing between letters, line spacing, and color; for controlling *tracking* (the amount of space between letters and words in a chunk of selected text); for defining text as superscript or subscript; and for creating live links between text and URLs. When you select an existing text box, the label for the Properties tab disappears, but the panel displays all the text-attribute options just listed and adds options for setting attributes of the text box itself, such as size and location on the Stage. When you need to distinguish one tab from the other, this book will refer to them as as the Text Tool Properties tab and the Text Properties tab; when referring to either or both tabs, this book will use the Text (Tool) Properties tab.

You can set attributes in advance so that as you type, the text tool applies them automatically, or you can apply attributes to existing text. The text tool always uses whatever settings currently appear in the Text (Tool) Properties tab (**Figure 3.6**).

For the following tasks, keep the Properties tab of the Property inspector open (choose Window > Properties > Properties if it's not already open).

✔ Tip

■ In addition to setting text attributes in the Text (Tool) Properties tab, you can set the font, size, style, paragraph alignment, and tracking from the Text menu. You can use the Text menu to change the properties of selected text or to load text properties into the text tool.

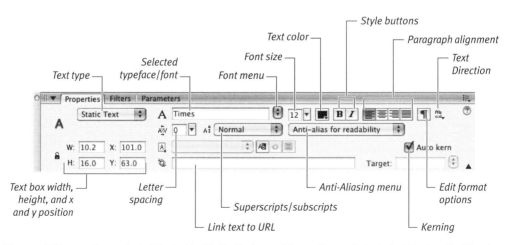

Figure 3.6 When you have selected the text tool in the Tools panel (or you have selected a text block on the Stage), the Properties tab of the Property inspector displays the type attributes to be created by the text tool (or applied to the current text selection).

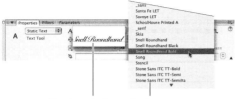

Preview window   Font menu

Figure 3.7 As you move the pointer through the font list in the Text (Tool) Properties tab of the Property inspector, you see a preview of each installed font.

Vertical Text

Using Flash's static text boxes, you can create a single vertical text column, or create text that flows from column to column. You can set the columns to read left to right (as in English) or vice versa (as in Japanese text). With the text tool active, you can set the text-flow direction in the Properties tab of the Property inspector by choosing one of the vertical modes from the Change Orientation of Text menu (**Figure 3.8**). You work with vertical text boxes just as you do with horizontal ones, resizing to set word wrap—in vertical text, the "wrap" forces words to the next column not the next line. As you enter text, Flash places one character below another until the text reaches the bottom edge of the box. Then text jumps to the next column. You can force text to flow to the next column by adding a paragraph return.

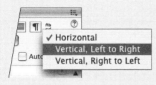

Figure 3.8 When you have selected the text tool or a text box, the Properties tab of the Property inspector displays a text-direction menu, with options for setting the direction in which your text flows.

To select text to apply character attributes:

Do either of the following:

◆ With the text tool selected, drag over existing text to highlight just a portion of text.

◆ With the selection tool active, click a text box to select all the text within it.

✔ Tips

■ You can select multiple text boxes with the selection tool and modify them at the same time. (You'll learn more about selections in Chapter 4.)

■ The contact-sensitivity settings in the General category of the Preferences dialog also apply to selecting text boxes with a selection outline. (You'll learn more about making such selections in Chapter 4.)

To choose an installed typeface:

1. Select the text you want to modify.

2. In the Text Properties tab of the Property inspector, click the scroll arrow to the right of the Font field.

   A scrolling list of your installed fonts appears, together with a font-preview window (**Figure 3.7**).

3. Move the pointer over a font name.

   Flash highlights the font name and displays its preview.

4. Click to select the currently highlighted font and close the scrolling list.

   The selected font name appears in the Font field. Flash changes the selected text to the new font.

SETTING TEXT ATTRIBUTES

✔ Tips

- You can also enter a font by typing its name in the Font field in the Text (Tool) Properties tab. The field isn't case-sensitive, but you must type accurately. If you make a mistake in typing the name of an installed font, Flash assumes that it's dealing with a missing font and substitutes the system default font.

- Another way to select a font is to choose it from the Text > Font menu.

- You can allow end users to copy text from static text boxes. During authoring, select the text that you want users to be able to copy. In the Text Properties tab of the Property inspector, click the Selectable Text button (the button labeled with the letters *Ab*, just below the pop-up menu for creating superscripts and subscripts).

The Mystery of Device Fonts

When you assign an installed font to a static text box, usually you want the text to look exactly the same during playback as it does during authoring. Yet you have no way of knowing if your end users will have the font that you assigned installed on their system. In order to re-create your static text box font accurately during playback, Flash saves information about the outlines of the letter forms with the published (SWF) file (you'll learn more about publishing files in Chapter 16). During playback, Flash Player uses those outlines to draw the letters correctly. Saving outline information increases the size of your SWF file. Device fonts allow you to eliminate that information. You can apply device fonts two ways: Select one from a font menu, or choose Use Device Fonts from the Anti-Aliasing menu in the Text (Tool) Properties tab of the Property inspector.

By choosing a device font from one of the font menus, you retain control over the style of type Flash displays but give up the use of a specific typeface. Three device fonts appear in the font menu in the Text (Tool) Properties tab and the Text > Font menu: _sans, _serif, and _typewriter. During movie playback of static text for which you chose a specific device font, the end user's system supplies a font that has the same type style. For static text set as _serif, the end users' system supplies a font with *serifs*, those little hooks and tails you see at the ends of some letters' strokes in typefaces such as Times Roman. For _sans (short for *sans serif*, or without serifs), the end user's system supplies a plainer font, one without hooks and tails; Helvetica and Arial are good examples. For _typewriter, the end user's system supplies a monospaced font (one in which each letter form takes up the same amount of space, like the letters on a typewriter); Courier is one example.

Choosing a specific font for your static text and then choosing Use Device Fonts from the Anti-Aliasing menu in the Text (Tool) Properties tab of the Property inspector gives the end user's system the greatest liberty in choosing a substitute font; the system looks for the closest match from its installed fonts, but there's no guarantee that it will substitute a font with the same style as the font you originally specified.

Although the use of Device Fonts helps to keep your SWF files slim, the results are often unattractive. If you want to try this option, be sure to test your published movie on a variety of systems to get a feel for what your users might actually wind up seeing. The savings in file size may not be worth the loss of quality.

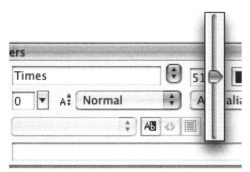

Figure 3.9 Drag the font-size slider to change the point size of selected text interactively on the Stage.

The Mystery of Anti-aliasing

Anti-aliasing is a method of *rendering* (drawing lines and curves) that softens edges. For text, this means making the letter forms appear slightly blurry. Anti-aliasing text at large point sizes makes it easier to read, but at smaller sizes, text may appear fuzzy and indistinct. In previous versions of Flash, applying anti-aliasing to text in small sizes made that text difficult to read. Flash Type (the new font-rendering engine found in Flash 8) allows you to apply anti-aliasing to small type sizes and still have readable text, provided that the text isn't animated.

To set the font size:

1. Select the text you want to modify.

2. In the Text Properties tab of the Property inspector, double-click (or click and drag) in the Font Size field to highlight the current value.

3. Enter the desired point size.

4. Press Enter.

or

1. Click the triangle to the right of the Font Size field.

   A slider pops open (**Figure 3.9**).

2. Drag the slider's lever to choose a value between 8 and 96 points.

   Flash previews the changes on the Stage as you drag the slider lever.

3. Click outside the slider to confirm the new font size.

✔ Tips

■ For even quicker changes, click and drag the slider triangle. When you release the slider's lever, Flash confirms the new font size automatically.

■ To enter font sizes outside the slider's range, you must type the value in the Font Size field.

To set the font rendering method:

1. Select the text you want to modify.

2. In the Text tab of the Property inspector, from the Anti-Aliasing menu (**Figure 3.10**), *choose one of the following:*

   Use device fonts. Choose this setting when smaller file sizes are more important than being able to re-create the precise font outlines on the end user's system (see "The Mystery of Device Fonts").

   Bitmap text (no anti-alias). Choose this setting when you want your text to have hard edges instead of softened (*anti-aliased*) edges. Fonts are embedded in your published movie, without anti-aliasing. (Bitmap text can greatly increase your SWF file size.)

   Anti-alias for animation Choose this setting for animated text boxes or when you plan to publish your movie to Flash Player 7 or below. Flash embeds font outlines for these text boxes but ignores some information about aligning and kerning to help speed playback. Flash Type doesn't do the rendering.

   Anti-alias for readability (the default setting for publishing to Flash Player 8; see Chapter 16). Choose this setting for text boxes that you don't plan to animate. The Flash Type font-rendering engine draws text with this setting on the Stage as you create your FLA file. When you publish, Flash embeds the fonts in the SWF file. The Flash Type engine renders this text for playback.

   Custom anti-alias (found only in Flash Professional). Choosing this setting gives you access to the Custom Anti-Aliasing dialog, where you can determine how soft and blurry the anti-aliased letter forms are. The dialog's Sharpness and Thickness settings control the transitional blurred area between each letter and the background against which it appears.

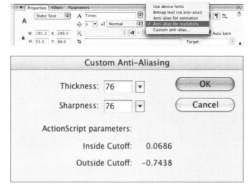

Figure 3.10 To control the degree of anti-aliasing, in the Text (Tool) Properties tab of the Property inspector, select an option from the Anti-Aliasing menu (top). If you are working with Flash Professional, the Custom Anti-Aliasing option gives you access to a dialog for setting more precise anti-aliasing controls (bottom).

✔ Tips

■ Even when you choose an option that evokes Flash Type anti-aliasing, certain situations cause Flash to turn off anti-aliasing. When you skew, flip, or distort a text box, Flash Type doesn't anti-alias that text. Flash Type doesn't work on fonts larger than 255 points. (Note that when you zoom in on a text box during authoring, you may effectively be asking to see fonts at a size larger than 255 points, even though the text box is set to a smaller point size.) In the published Flash Player 8 movie (the SWF), anti-aliasing is applied; but when you view the magnified text on the Stage, you won't see anti-aliasing.

■ You can also select a font size from the Text > Size menu.

Figure 3.11 You can choose a color for text created with the text tool from the color control in the Text (Tool) Properties tab of the Property inspector.

B *I*

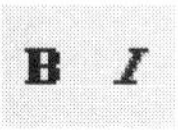

Figure 3.12 Access bold and italic styles by clicking the Bold (left) and Italic (right) buttons in the Text (Tool) Properties tab of the Property inspector.

To choose a text color:

1. Select the text you want to modify.

2. In the Text Properties tab, click the Text (Fill) Color control (note that text in Flash is a type of fill).

   The standard color-control swatch set appears (**Figure 3.11**).

3. Select a color.

   Because Flash considers text to be a fill, you can change the text color by using any of the methods described for setting fill attributes in Chapter 2.

✔ Tip

■ Flash changes all the settings in the Text (Tool) Properties tab to match the attributes of selected text, which means that by selecting text, you load the text tool with that text's attributes. Keep blocks of text with formatting you use often on the Pasteboard, and click to re-create their settings for the text tool.

To choose a type style:

1. Select the text you want to modify.

2. In the Text Properties tab of the Property inspector, *do one of the following:*
   - ▲ To create boldface type, click the Bold button (**Figure 3.12**).
   - ▲ To create italic type, click the Italic button.
   - ▲ To create type that is both boldface and italic, click the Bold and Italic buttons.

✔ Tip

■ You can also toggle boldface type by pressing Shift-⌘-B (Mac) or Ctrl-Shift-B (Windows). (Take special note of that Shift key if you're used to using another application for creating text: muscle memory is likely to make your fingers skip the Shift because it's not part of the usual command.) To toggle italic, press Shift-⌘-I (Mac) or Ctrl-Shift-I (Windows).

To apply tracking (letter spacing):

1. Within a text box in a Flash document, select the text to track.

2. In the Text Properties tab's Letter Spacing field, enter the desired point size.

   A negative value reduces the space between the letters; a positive value increases it (**Figure 3.13**).

3. Press Enter.

   or

1. In the Text Properties tab's Letter Spacing field, click the triangle to the right of the field.

   A slider pops open.

2. Drag the slider's lever to a value between −60 and 60.

   Flash previews the changes interactively on the Stage as you drag.

3. Release the slider to confirm the new spacing.

✔ Tips

■ To increase tracking of selected text in 0.5-point increments, choose Text > Letter Spacing > Increase or press Option-⌘-right arrow (Mac) or Ctrl-Alt-right arrow (Windows). To decrease tracking, choose Text > Letter Spacing > Decrease, or use the keyboard commands with the left arrow. Add the Shift key to the keyboard shortcuts for narrower and wider tracking; this method increases or decreases space in two-pixel increments.

■ You can also track interactively by using the keyboard shortcuts. The space between letters continues to expand or contract as long as you hold down the key combination.

■ To reset the font's original letter spacing, choose Text > Letter Spacing > Reset or press Option-⌘-up arrow (Mac) or Ctrl-Alt-up arrow (Windows).

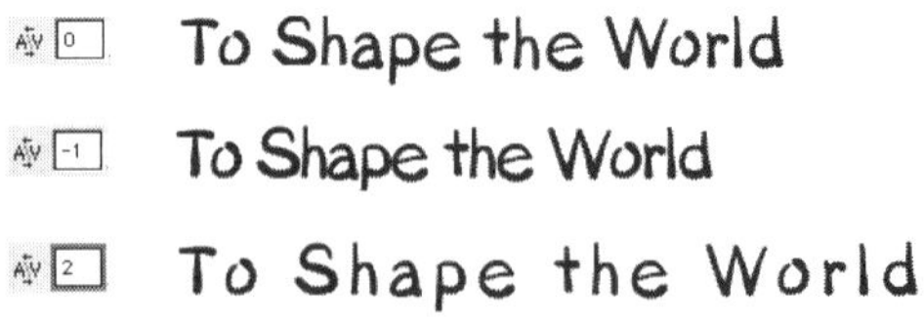

Figure 3.13 Enter a negative letter-spacing value to bring characters closer together. Enter a positive value to space characters out. Enter 0 to use a font's built-in tracking value.

What Is Kerning?

Whereas *tracking* affects the space between characters and words in an entire line or paragraph of text, *kerning* affects the space between a pair of letters. Because of the way fonts are constructed, with each letter being a separate element, some pairs of letters look oddly spaced when you type them. The space between a capital *T* and a lowercase *o*, for example, may seem too large because of the white space below the crossbar of the *T*. To make the characters look better, you can reduce the space between them, or *kern in* the pair. Some letters may seem to be too close together—say, a *t* and an *i*. You can *kern out* the pair so that it looks better.

Font designers often build into their fonts special information about how to space troublesome pairs of letters. Flash takes advantage of that embedded kerning information when you select the Auto Kern check box in the Text (Tool) Properties tab of the Property inspector. It's a good idea to turn on kerning to make your type look its best.

You can kern manually in Flash instead of using the embedded kerning or in addition to it. Select the character pair that you want to kern; then use Flash's Letter Spacing feature to bring the letters closer together or move them farther apart.

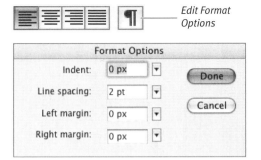

Edit Format Options

Figure 3.14 In the Text (Tool) Properties tab of the Property inspector, click the Edit Format Options button (top) to access a dialog for setting text attributes such as alignment, indents, margins, and space between lines of text (bottom).

Setting Paragraph Attributes

Flash allows you to work with paragraph formatting much as you would in a word processor. The Text (Tool) Properties tab of the Property inspector lets you set right and left margins, a first-line indent, line spacing, and alignment (flush left, flush right, centered, or justified) (**Figure 3.14**). You can set paragraph attributes in advance so that as you type, the text tool applies them automatically. And you can apply paragraph attributes to existing text. The text tool uses whatever settings currently appear in the Text (Tool) Properties tab of the Property inspector.

In the following tasks, you learn to modify existing text; keep the Properties tab of the Property inspector open. (Choose Window > Properties > Properties if it's not already open.)

To select paragraphs to modify:

Do one of the following:

◆ With the text tool, click within the paragraph you want to modify.

◆ With the text tool, click and drag to select multiple paragraphs within one text box.

◆ With the selection tool, click a text box to select all the paragraphs within the box.

To set paragraph alignment:

1. Select the paragraphs you want to modify.

2. In the Text Properties tab of the Property inspector, *do one of the following* (**Figure 3.15**):

   ▲ To align horizontal text on the left (vertical text on the top), click the first alignment button.

   ▲ To center horizontal or vertical text, click the second alignment button.

   ▲ To align horizontal text on the right (vertical text on the bottom), click the third alignment button.

   ▲ To justify text (force all lines except the last line of a paragraph to fill the full column width), click the fourth alignment button.

✔ Tip

■ To select all the paragraphs within a text block, click with the text tool anywhere inside the text block; and then choose Edit > Select All. Flash highlights the entire text block.

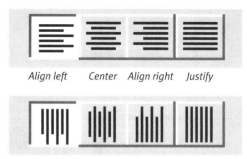

Align left   *Center*   *Align right*   *Justify*

Align top   *Center*   *Align bottom*   *Justify*

Figure 3.15 The paragraph-alignment buttons allow you to format the text of a paragraph in four ways. A graphic representation of the selected paragraph-alignment style appears on each button in the Text (Tool) Properties tab of the Property inspector. The images on the buttons reflect whether the text box is set for horizontal (top) or vertical (bottom) text flow.

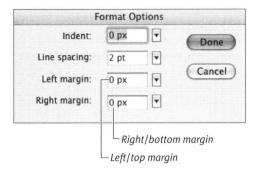

Right/bottom margin
Left/top margin

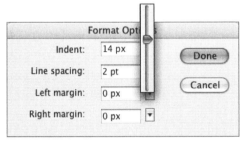

Figure 3.16 You can enter a value for right and left margins (horizontal text) or top and bottom margins (vertical text) directly in the appropriate box of the Format Options dialog (top) or use the slider to select a value (bottom).

To set margins:

1. In the Text (Tool) Properties tab of the Property inspector, click the Edit Format Options button (the one with the paragraph symbol).

   The Format Options dialog appears.

2. In the Left Margin or Right Margin field, enter the desired margin size.

   The units of measure used for the margin are the ones set in the Document Properties dialog (see Chapter 1).

3. Click Done (**Figure 3.16**).

   Flash uses the values that you enter to create margins from the left and right sides of the text box. Your audience won't see the margins unless you're creating text that they can edit, in which case you can make the border of the text box visible.

✔ Tips

- For easy entry of new values, click the triangle to the right of the Margin field. A slider pops open. Drag the slider's lever to choose a value between 0 and 720 pixels.

- Flash incorporates the current margin settings into text boxes as you create them. With margins set to the default (0 pixels), clicking the text tool on the Stage creates a small text box, just large enough for the blinking insertion point. If you get a longer text box than you expect when you click the Stage with the text tool, check your margin settings in the Text (Tool) Properties tab of the Property inspector and adjust them as needed.

SETTING PARAGRAPH ATTRIBUTES

To set a first-line indent:

◆ In the Format Options dialog, in the Indent field, use the value-entry techniques described in the preceding task to enter a value for indenting the first line of text in the paragraph.

Flash calculates the indent from the left margin; when the left margin is set to 0, Flash measures the indent from the left edge of the text box.

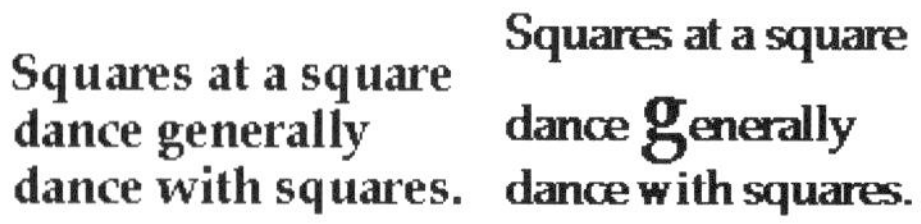

To set line spacing:

◆ In the Format Options dialog, in the Line Spacing field, use the value-entry techniques described earlier in this chapter to enter a value for the amount of space you want between lines of text.

If your text contains various point sizes, Flash bases the spacing between two lines on the larger font (**Figure 3.17**).

✔ Tip

■ *Points* are the most common unit of measure for working with type. Regardless of the units you've set in the Document Properties dialog, Flash always enters the line-spacing value with the abbreviation *pt* (for points).

■ If you're using a font that creates larger line spacing than you like, enter a negative number for line spacing. Acceptable values for the line spacing field are -36 points to 72 points.

Squares at a square
dance generally
dance with squares.

Squares at a square
dance 𝐠enerally
dance with squares.

Figure 3.17 The line spacing for the text block on the left is set to o points. The space you see between lines is the space specified as part of the font. Because the text is all one size, the spacing above and below the middle line of text is the same. In the text block on the right—with the same o-point line spacing—one letter is a larger point size. Flash increases the space between lines to make room for the larger text

MODIFYING SIMPLE GRAPHICS

One way to modify Macromedia Flash 8 graphics is to select one or more shapes and edit them by changing their attributes (such as color, size, and location) in the Properties tab of the Property inspector or in other appropriate panels.

You can also modify the shape of an element. Some operations—such as straightening lines, adjusting Bézier curves, and assigning new attributes—require that the element be selected. Others, such as reshaping a line segment or curve with the selection tool, require the element to be deselected. A few operations allow you to edit the element whether it's selected or not—using the paint-bucket tool to change a fill color, for example.

This chapter covers using the selection, lasso, and subselection tools to select and modify the elements you learned to make in Chapter 2. You also learn about using the Properties tab of the Property inspector and other panels to modify elements' attributes.

Setting Selection Preferences

There are two basic ways to make selections: one is to click an element directly, and the other is to enclose all or part of an element with a selection outline. You can set preferences to gain more control over these two methods. For the click method, you choose whether you must Shift-click to select multiple items or whether you can merely click additional items to add to a selection. For the selection-outline method, you decide if the outline must fully enclose a drawing-object to select it or if enclosing any part of a drawing-object selects the whole thing.

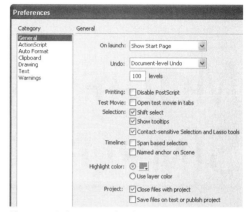

Figure 4.1 Select General in the Category list of the Preferences dialog to choose a selection method.

To set selection methods for the selection tools:

1. From the Edit menu (Windows) or the Flash application menu (Mac), choose Preferences. The Preferences dialog appears.

2. From the Category list, choose General (**Figure 4.1**).

3. In the Selection section, *choose either of the following check boxes:*

   Shift Select. In Shift Select mode (Flash's default setting), you must Shift-click to add items to the current selection. With Shift Select turned off, each new item you click with the selection tool is added to the current selection.

   Contact-sensitive selection and lasso tools. With contact-sensitive selection turned on (the default mode), whenever a selection outline touches a drawing-object, a text field (see Chapter 3), a grouped shape (see Chapter 5), or a symbol instance (see Chapter 7), Flash selects the whole thing. This setting has no effect on merge-shapes; a selection outline always defines the precise area of the merge-shape that is selected (see the next section, "Making Selections").

4. Click OK.

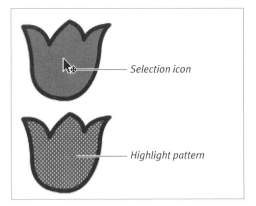

Figure 4.2 When the pointer sits above a filled area, it changes into the selection arrow (the cross icon appears next to the pointer, indicating that the tool is ready to move or select an item). Click a fill to select it. A dot pattern in a contrasting color highlights the selected fill.

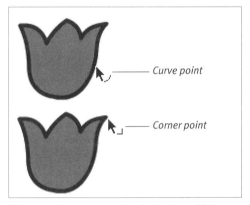

Figure 4.3 As you prepare to select a line, additions to the pointer icon indicate what kind of point lies beneath the pointer.

Making Selections

Merge-shapes and drawing-objects behave differently when being selected. What you think of as a single shape may contain several segments. When you use the rectangle tool to create a square outline, that "square" consists of four line segments. If you create the square as a merge-shape, Flash treats each segment as a separate shape. Clicking one side of a merge-shape square just selects one segment. To fully select the square, you must select each segment (you could use Shift-click to add the remaining sides to the initial selection). If you create the square as a drawing-object, Flash treats the four segments as a unit. Clicking any side of a drawing-object square selects the whole square.

Flash highlights selected areas of merge-shapes with a pattern of tiny dots. Make sure all the parts of the merge-shape stroke or fill you intend to select display this pattern.

To select merge-shapes by clicking:

1. To prepare for this task, in Merge Drawing mode, create one or more shapes; use at least one fill and a stroke made of multiple line segments (see Chapter 2).

2. In the Tools panel, select the selection tool, or press V on the keyboard.

3. To select a fill, position the pointer over the fill.
   The selection icon appears next to the selection pointer.

4. Click the fill.
   Flash highlights the selected fill with a dot pattern (**Figure 4.2**).

5. To select a stroke, position the pointer over a line segment (**Figure 4.3**).

continues on next page

Flash appends a little arc or a little right-angle icon to the selection tool. These icons indicate that the tool is over a point in a line segment and show what type of point it is: a curve or a corner point. (For more information about points, see the sidebar "About Curve and Corner Points" later in this chapter).

6. Click the segment.

Flash highlights just the segment you clicked (**Figure 4.4**).

7. To include additional segments or fills in your selection, *do either of the following:*

▲ If you're using Flash's default selection style (Shift Select), Shift-click each item you want to include. Flash adds each item to the highlighted selection (**Figure 4.5**).

▲ If you turned off the Shift Select option in the Preferences dialog, click each item you want to include. Flash adds each new item to the highlighted selection.

✔ Tips

■ Double-clicking any segment in a series of connected merge-shape line segments selects all the segments.

■ Double-clicking the fill of a merge-shape that has a fill and a stroke selects the fill and the stroke together.

■ To switch to the selection tool temporarily while using another tool, press ⌘ (Mac) or Ctrl (Windows). The selection tool remains in effect as long as you hold down the modifier key.

■ To select everything that's currently on the Stage, choose Edit > Select All, or press ⌘-A (Mac) or Ctrl-A (Windows).

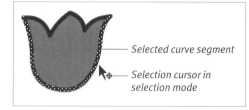

Figure 4.4 When you click a merge-shape line, Flash selects and highlights just one segment.

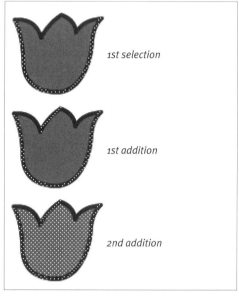

Figure 4.5 With Flash's default Preferences setting for selections, Shift-click unhighlighted line segments or fill areas to add them to a selection.

Figure 4.6 When you position the selection tool over an unselected drawing-object (left), the pointer displays the same icons as for merge-shapes (move/select cross for fills, curve-point arc or corner-point angle for strokes). Click anywhere on the drawing-object, and Flash selects the entire drawing-object, highlighting its bounding box (right).

To select drawing-objects by clicking:

1. To prepare for this task, in Object Drawing mode, use the rectangle or polystar tool to create a shape that has a fill and a stroke made of multiple line segments (see Chapter 2).

2. Deselect the shape.

 When you create a shape with a tool in Object Drawing mode, the finished shape is automatically selected. To practice selecting it, you must first deselect it. (The quickest way to deselect it is to click an empty area of the Stage or press ESC.)

3. In the Tools panel, select the selection tool, or press V on the keyboard.

4. Position the pointer over any portion of the shape.

 The appropriate icon appears next to the selection pointer as described in the preceding task.

5. Click the shape.

 Flash selects the entire shape and highlights its bounding box—a rectangle that encloses the shape (**Figure 4.6**).

✔ Tip

- The bounding box for a round or irregular drawing-object is easy to see because it sits outside the shape like a frame; but for a rectangular shape, the bounding box frame sites on top of the rectangle's edges. Depending on the color of your drawing-object rectangle, the highlighted bounding box can be difficult to see. If you have trouble seeing the highlight on selected drawing-object rectangles, choose a contrasting highlight color in the General category of the Preferences dialog.

MAKING SELECTIONS

To use a contact-sensitive selection rectangle:

1. Make sure the selection preferences are set for contact sensitivity (see "Setting Selection Preferences," earlier in this chapter).

2. In the Tools panel, select the selection tool.

3. Click and drag to pull out a selection rectangle (**Figure 4.7**).

   This rectangle isn't a graphic element; it just defines the boundaries of your selection.

4. Continue dragging until the rectangle encloses all the merge-shapes you want to select and at least some part of each drawing-object.

   Be sure to start dragging at a point that allows you to create a rectangle big enough to enclose the elements you want.

5. Release the mouse button.

   Merge-shapes. Flash highlights any portions of fill or stroke that fall inside the selection rectangle; portions of merge-shape fills or strokes that lie outside the rectangle remain unselected (**Figure 4.8**).

   Drawing-objects. If the selection rectangle touches any part of a drawing-object, Flash selects the entire thing, highlighting its bounding box.

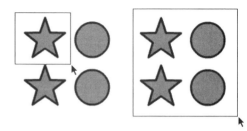

Figure 4.7 Clicking and dragging with the selection tool creates a selection rectangle (left). Be sure to start from a point that allows you to enclose all the elements you want to select within the rectangle (right). Release the mouse button, and Flash selects those elements.

Drag selection rectangle

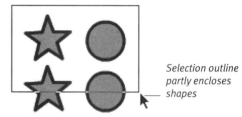

Selection outline partly encloses shapes

Selected shapes

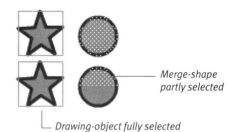

Merge-shape partly selected

Drawing-object fully selected

Figure 4.8 When Flash's default contact-sensitive selection mode is active, a selection includes any drawing-objects that are touched or partially enclosed by the selection rectangle. Only the parts of merge-shapes that fall within the selection rectangle are selected. (Here the star shapes are drawing-objects, and the circles are merge-shapes.)

Drag selection rectangle

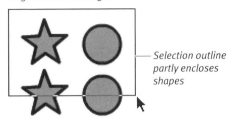

Selection outline
partly encloses
shapes

Selected shapes

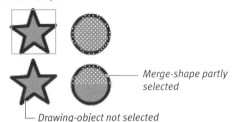

Merge-shape partly
selected

Drawing-object not selected

Figure 4.9 When contact-sensitivity is inactive, a selection includes just those parts of merge-shapes that fall within the selection rectangle. For drawing-objects to be selected, they must be fully enclosed by the selection rectangle. (Here the star shapes are drawing-objects, and the circles are merge-shapes.)

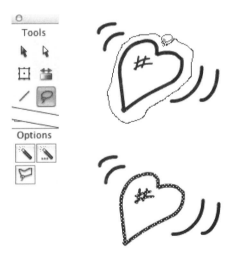

Figure 4.10 The lasso tool lets you select elements that are oddly shaped or too near other elements to allow use of the selection rectangle. Any merge-shapes inside the selection outline become highlighted and selected when you release the mouse button. Whether or not drawing-objects must be fully enclosed in your selection outline to be selected depends on the contact sensitivity setting in the Preferences dialog.

To use a non-contact-sensitive selection rectangle:

1. Make sure contact sensitivity is turned off (see "Setting Selection Preferences," earlier in this chapter).

2. Follow steps 2 through 4 in the preceding exercise, but this time, fully enclose the drawing-objects you want to select.

   Merge-shapes. Flash highlights any portions of fill or stroke that fall inside the selection rectangle; portions of merge-shape fills or strokes that lie outside the rectangle remain unselected (**Figure 4.9**).

   Drawing-objects. Flash selects only those drawing-objects that are completely enclosed within the selection rectangle. If the selection rectangle touches or includes just a part of a drawing-object, Flash leaves the entire object deselected.

✔ Tips

- If the lines or shapes you want to select are located close to other lines, you may have difficulty selecting just what you want with a rectangle. The lasso tool can create an irregular selection outline. In the Tools panel, select the lasso tool, or press L. Click and draw a freeform line around the elements you want to select (**Figure 4.10**). Close the selection outline by bringing the lasso pointer back over the spot where you began the selection outline. Release the mouse button. Flash highlights whatever falls inside the shape you drew with the lasso.

continues on next page

- The lasso tool is also capable of contact sensitivity with respect to drawing-objects. When preferences are set to Contact Sensitive Selection and Lasso tools, if you include any portion of a drawing-object in your freeform selection outline, the drawing-object is selected. If contact sensitivity is turned off, to select a drawing-object, you must fully enclose it in the selection outline.

- The lasso's Polygon mode lets you define a selection area with a series of connected straight-line segments. With the lasso tool selected, click the Polygon mode button in the Options section of the Tools panel. Now you can click your way around the elements you want to select (**Figure 4.11**). Double-click to end the selection outline.

- You can combine the regular lasso tool with the polygon lasso in creating a single selection outline. To access Polygon mode temporarily, hold down Option (Mac) or Alt (Windows) as you click.

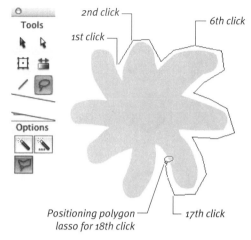

Figure 4.11 In Polygon mode, the lasso tool creates a series of connected line segments to outline whatever element you want to select. Double-clicking finishes the shape by drawing a line from the point where you double-clicked to the starting point.

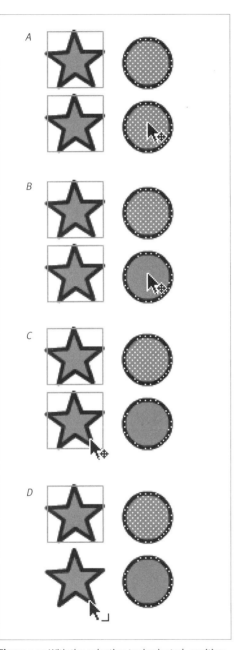

Figure 4.12 With the selection tool selected, position the pointer over the element you want to remove from the selection (A). Shift-click the item to deselect it (B). Repeat the process to deselect another item (C and D). (In this image, the stars are drawing-objects, and the circles are merge-shapes.)

To deselect individual items:

1. In the Tools panel, select the selection tool.

2. Hold down the Shift key.

3. Click any highlighted drawing-objects or merge-shape strokes or fills you want to remove from the current selection.

   Flash deselects the items you clicked (**Figure 4.12**). No matter which method you used to select items, you must Shift-click with the selection tool to remove items from a selection.

✔ Tips

- To deselect everything, choose Edit > Deselect All, or press Shift-⌘-A (Mac) or Ctrl-Shift-A (Windows).

- To deselect all elements quickly, click the selection tool in an empty area of the Stage or Pasteboard.

Using the Clipboard

Flash supports the standard cut, copy, and paste operations familiar to most computer users. Flash also provides special pasting operations for graphic elements; you can paste items in the center of the Stage or in the exact same location they were in when you copied or cut them. (Copying and pasting frames of animation require working with other commands; you'll learn about those in Chapter 8.)

To perform basic editing operations on a selection:

1. Select the elements you want to delete, cut, or copy.

2. From the Edit menu (**Figure 4.13**), *choose one of the following:*

   ▲ To delete the selection, choose Clear, or press the Delete key. Flash removes the selected items.

   ▲ To cut the selection, choose Cut, or press ⌘-X (Mac) or Ctrl-X (Windows). Flash copies the selected items to the Clipboard and removes them from the Stage.

   ▲ To copy the selection, choose Copy, or press ⌘-C (Mac) or Ctrl-C (Windows). Flash copies the selected items to the Clipboard.

   After you cut or copy an item, it resides on the Clipboard until your next cut or copy operation. You can retrieve the Clipboard's contents with one of the Paste commands.

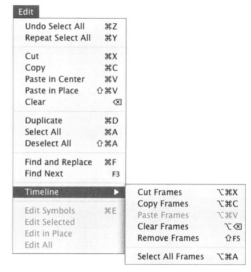

Figure 4.13 The Edit menu offers all the basic cut, copy, and paste commands, as well as some special commands for working with graphics and animations.

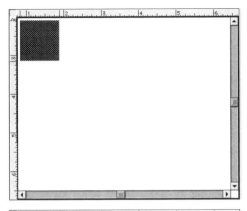

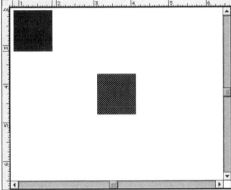

Figure 4.14 When you copy a selected graphic element (top) and choose Edit > Paste in Center, Flash pastes a copy of the element from the Clipboard to the center of the current view (bottom).

To paste the Clipboard's contents in the center of the window:

◆ Choose Edit > Paste in Center, or press ⌘-V (Mac) or Ctrl-V (Windows).

Flash pastes the Clipboard's contents in the center of the current view (**Figure 4.14**).

To paste the Clipboard contents in their original location:

◆ Choose Edit > Paste in Place, or press Shift-⌘-V (Mac) or Ctrl-Shift-V (Windows).

Flash pastes the Clipboard contents back into their original location on the Stage. The value of this command will become more apparent when you get into working with layers and animation; it can be crucial to have elements appear in precisely the same spot but on a different layer or frame.

✔ Tips

■ The Duplicate command is another way to make copies. Select the elements you want to copy. Choose Edit > Duplicate, or press ⌘-D (Mac) or Ctrl-D (Windows). Flash creates a copy of the selected items. The duplicate appears on the Stage, offset from the original item. The duplicate is selected, to prevent a merge-shape duplicate from interacting with the original. (For more information on interaction between elements, see Chapter 5.) The Duplicate command doesn't change the contents of the Clipboard.

■ Alternately, with the selection or lasso tool active, you can Option-click (Mac) or Alt- or Ctrl-click (Windows) and drag any selected element to create a copy.

USING THE CLIPBOARD

Resizing Graphic Elements

Flash gives you several ways to resize, or *scale*, graphic elements. You can scale selected elements interactively on the Stage. You can also set specific scale percentages or dimensions for your element in the Transform panel, the Properties tab of the Property inspector, and the Info panel.

To resize a graphic element interactively:

1. In the Tools panel, select the free-transform tool (**Figure 4.15**).

2. On the Stage, click the element you want to resize.

   Flash selects and highlights the element and places transformation handles on all four sides and at the corners of the element's bounding box.

3. In the Tools panel, choose the Scale modifier.

4. Position the pointer over a handle.

   The pointer changes to a double-headed arrow, indicating the direction in which the element will grow or shrink as you pull or push on the handles.

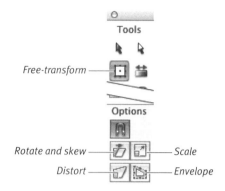

Figure 4.15 The free-transform tool enables you to select and scale elements interactively.

RESIZING GRAPHIC ELEMENTS

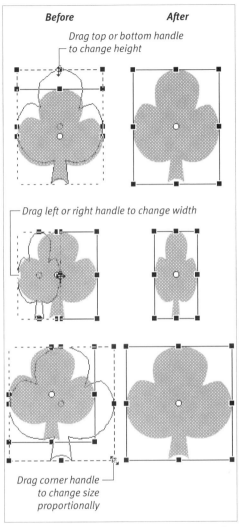

Before   **After**

Drag top or bottom handle
to change height

Drag left or right handle to change width

Drag corner handle
to change size
proportionally

Figure 4.16 Activating the free-transform tool's Scale modifier places a set of handles around a selected element. Click and drag the handles to change the size of the element.

5. To resize the graphic element, *do one of the following:*

- ▲ To change the graphic element's width, click and drag one of the side handles.

- ▲ To change the element's height, click and drag the top or bottom handle.

- ▲ To change the size of the element proportionally, click and drag one of the corner handles.

Dragging toward the center of the element reduces it; dragging away enlarges it (**Figure 4.16**).

✔ Tips

- ■ If you have made a selection with the selection tool, you can activate transformational handles for the selection by choosing Modify > Transform > Scale. Flash chooses the free-transform tool and its Scale modifier in the Tools panel.

- ■ In the default scaling mode, the selection scales graphic elements from the control point opposite the one you're dragging. To scale relative to the center of a selection, hold down the Option key (Mac) or Alt key (Windows) as you drag. Both handles move away from the center of the selection as you drag. For symbols (see Chapter 7), it's the reverse: the default mode scales the symbol from its transformation point (which is the center by default) and pressing the Option key (Mac) or Alt key (Windows) lets you scale from the opposite control point.

- ■ Don't use the subselection tool to select an element by its path when you want to scale it. Choosing the free-transform tool automatically deselects the selected path.

RESIZING GRAPHIC ELEMENTS

To resize an element by using the Transform panel:

1. With the Transform panel open, on the Stage, select the element you want to resize.

   A value of 100% appears in the Width and Height fields of the Transform panel.

2. To resize the element, *do either of the following:*

   ▲ To resize proportionally, select the Constrain check box next to the Width and Height fields, and enter a new value in either field (**Figure 4.17**). As you enter the value in one field, Flash automatically updates the other field.

   or

   ▲ To allow the aspect ratio to change, in the Transform panel, deselect the Constrain check box; enter new percentages in the Width field and Height field.

   A value less than 100% shrinks the element; a value greater than 100% enlarges the element.

3. Press Enter.

   Flash resizes the element.

✔ Tips

■ As long as a shape remains selected on the Stage, the Transform panel resizes the shape on an absolute scale (always applying the percentage you enter into the panel to the element's original size). To make changes on a relative scale—for example, to shrink the shape to 50 percent and then shrink the shrunken shape to 20 percent—you must deselect the element after the first transformation and then select it again and enter the percentage for the second transformation.

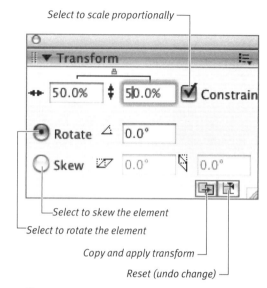

Figure 4.17 Enter new values in the Transform panel's Width and Height fields to resize an element. (The transform panel also lets you enter values for scaling, rotating, and skewing selected elements).

■ To scale several elements at the same time, select all the elements and then use any of the scaling methods described earlier in this section. The bounding box that contains the elements scales relative to its center point, and the entire selection grows or shrinks to fit the new box.

■ To undo a Transform panel's transformation quickly, click the Reset button in the bottom-right corner of the Transform panel or press Ctrl-Shift-Z (Windows) or Shift-⌘-Z (Mac). For merge-shapes, you must not have deselected the element; for drawing-objects, text boxes (see Chapter 3), groups (see Chapter 5), and symbols (see Chapter 7), you can select the object and click Reset in the Transform panel at any time to restore the item to 100% size.

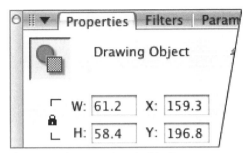

Figure 4.18 The Properties tab of the Property inspector displays the width and height of the bounding box of a selected element. Enter new values to resize the element.

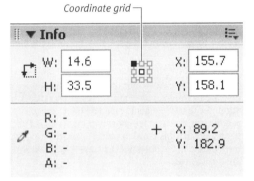

Figure 4.19 You can enter precise dimensions for an element's width and height in the Info panel. The coordinate grid shows whether changes will be relative to the transformation point or to the top-left corner of the element's bounding box. To apply the values you entered in the panel to the selected graphic element, click the Stage or press Enter.

■ To transform a copy of the element, click the Copy and Apply Transform button in the Transform panel. This feature can be tricky if you use it with merge-shapes, because Flash doesn't offset the copy it makes. You must be sure to move the copy yourself before deselecting it.

■ The Transform panel always resizes drawing-objects, text boxes, groups (see Chapter 5), and symbols (see Chapter 7) on an absolute scale. If you deselect the resized item, then select it again, you still see the new values for width and height.

■ You can also enter specific width and height values for a selected element in the (Shape) Properties tab of the Property inspector (**Figure 4.18**) and the Info panel (**Figure 4.19**). To constrain proportions in the Properties tab of the Property inspector, click the lock button to the left of the Width and Height fields. (The lock button settings on the Property inspector and the Transform panel work in synch; changing one panel's lock button also changes the other's.)

■ The Info panel lets you change the element's size relative to the top-left corner of its bounding box or relative to the element's *transformation point*. (For graphic-objects, the transformation point is always the center of the object, you can set the point's location for symbols, see Chapter 7.) Click the upper-left corner on the coordinate grid in the Info panel to transform in relation to that corner of the element; click the center of the grid to transform in relation to the element's transformation point.

■ The Info panel's coordinate grid setting persists and applies to each element you select on the Stage, whether the panel is open or not. If you use the Property inspector to enter new height and/or width values for an element, and it resizes from the corner when you wanted the center, open the Info panel and change the coordinate grid setting.

Positioning Graphic Elements

If you aren't happy with the position of an element, you can always move it. You can position elements visually by dragging them around on the Stage with the selection tool. You can also position a selection numerically by specifying a precise Stage location in x- and y-coordinates. You can enter the x- and y-coordinates in either the (Shape) Property inspector or the Info panel.

To reposition an element via the Properties tab of the Property inspector:

1. With the Properties tab of the Property inspector open, on the Stage, select an element.

   The coordinates for the element's current position appear in the x and y fields in the Properties tab, and a label—for example, *Drawing Object*—appears, identifying the type of element selected (**Figure 4.20**).

2. To position the element, *do one or both of the following:*

   ▲ Enter a new x-coordinate for the element's position along the horizontal axis.

   ▲ Enter a new y-coordinate for the element's position along the vertical axis.

3. Press Enter to confirm the last coordinate value you entered.

   Whenever you tab to or click another field, or press Enter, Flash confirms your change, and the element moves to its new position (**Figure 4.21**).

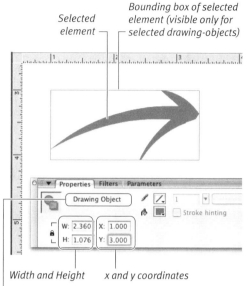

Selected element — *Bounding box of selected element (visible only for selected drawing-objects)*

Width and Height   *x and y coordinates*

Type of element selected

Figure 4.20 With an element selected on the Stage, the Properties tab of the Property inspector reveals attributes of that element, including the x- and y-coordinates of the upper-left corner (or center) of its bounding box. This drawing-object is located 1 inch to the right along the horizontal axis and 3 inches down the vertical axis.

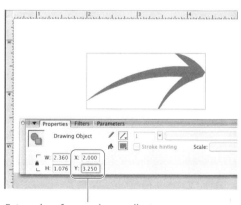

Enter values for x- and y-coordinates

Figure 4.21 Changing the x- and y-coordinates in the Properties tab of the Property inspector changes the location of a selected element. This arrow is now located 2 inches to the right along the horizontal axis and 3.25 inches down the vertical axis.

Tips for Positioning Elements Visually

◆ Select a shape before trying to move it. You can move unselected shapes by dragging them with the selection tool, but it's easy to mistakenly edit the shape instead (see "Modifying Shapes: Selection Tool," later in this chapter). Selecting a shape ensures that the selection tool will activate its move icon (not the curve or corner point icon) when you click and drag. An outline preview of the shape helps you position the element as you drag it.

◆ Turn on rulers (View > Rulers) to help position elements. As you drag an element around the Stage, markers indicating the height and width of the element's bounding box appear in the ruler area (**Figure 4.22**). (To learn more about bounding boxes, see the sidebar "How Flash Tracks Elements.")

◆ When Snap Align is active, as it is by default, Flash displays guidelines for aligning your selection with other objects on the Stage as you drag (**Figure 4.23**). (To learn more about Snap settings, see Chapter 1.)

◆ Use the four arrow keys on the keyboard to move selected elements precisely; the amount depends on the magnification at which you view the Stage. At 100% magnification, the arrows move items in 1-pixel increments; at 200% magnification, it's 0.5-pixel increments. With Snap to Pixels active, the arrows move items in 1-pixel increments regardless of the Stage magnification.

◆ To beef up the arrow keys' ability to move selected elements, hold down the Shift key. When viewing the Stage at 100% magnification, each press of Shift-arrow moves a selected element 10 pixels.

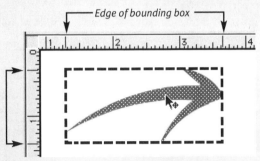

Figure 4.22 The longer lines in the ruler area indicate the edges of the element you're dragging.

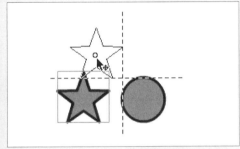

Figure 4.23 With Snap Align turned on, Flash displays guidelines as you drag a selection when you have more than one element on the Stage.

How Flash Tracks Elements

To keep track of an element's size and position on the Stage, Flash encloses each element in a *bounding box*—an invisible rectangle just big enough to hold the element. Flash then treats the Stage as a giant graph, with the top-left corner of the Stage as the center of the x- and y-axis (**Figure 4.24**). Flash locates elements by means of x- and y-coordinates on that graph. The units of measure for the graph are those currently selected in the Document Properties dialog (to learn more about document properties, see Chapter 1). The Property inspector and the Info panel show you the x- and y-coordinates for an element's current position and also display the height and width of the element's bounding box.

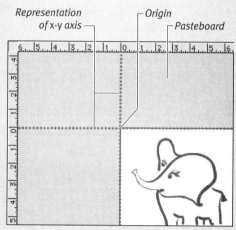

Figure 4.24 The dotted line here represents the x-y axis of the Stage. The origin—the o point both horizontally and vertically—is the top-left corner of the Stage.

By entering new x- and y-coordinates and values for Height and Width in the Properties tab of the Property inspector or the Info panel, you can change an element's position and size. (For more information about resizing elements, see "Resizing Graphic Elements," earlier in this chapter.)

For authoring purposes, Flash calculates an element's position on the Stage either from the top-left corner of the element's bounding box or from the element's transformation point. For shapes, text boxes, and groups, the transformation point is at the exact center of the bounding box; you can set the point's location for symbols and create different settings for individual symbol instances (see Chapter 7). Whether Flash uses the top-left corner or the transformation point, depends on the current setting of the Info panel's *coordinate grid* (the little nine-squares diagram). To determine which part of a graphic element the x- and y-coordinates refer to, choose the desired point in the Info panel's coordinate grid. Click the grid's top-left square to position elements by the top-left corner of the bounding box. Click the central square to position elements by the transformation point. The coordinate-grid setting applies to the coordinate you enter in both the Info panel and the Properties tab of the Property inspector. The setting remains in effect for all graphic elements until you change it in the Info panel.

When you use ActionScript to dynamically move symbols at runtime, the rules for calculating an item's position are different, but that's beyond the scope of the tasks you'll be working on in the book.

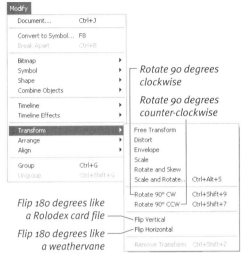

Rotate 90 degrees clockwise

Rotate 90 degrees counter-clockwise

Flip 180 degrees like a Rolodex card file

Flip 180 degrees like a weathervane

Figure 4.25 The Modify > Transform submenu offers commands for flipping graphic elements vertically and horizontally. It also offers commands for rotating an element in 90-degree increments, both clockwise and counterclockwise.

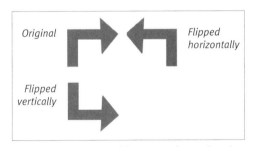

Original

Flipped horizontally

Flipped vertically

Figure 4.26 The results of flipping an element by using the Flip commands in the Modify > Transform submenu.

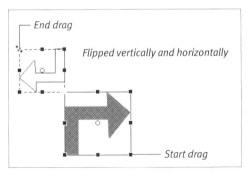

End drag

Flipped vertically and horizontally

Start drag

Figure 4.27 The free-transform tool's Scale modifier can flip and scale an element simultaneously. Here, the Scale modifier is flipping the element both vertically and horizontally.

Flipping, Rotating, and Skewing

Flash lets you flip, rotate, and skew selected elements. You can either manipulate elements freely with the free-transform tool's Rotate and Skew modifier or use a variety of commands to do the job with more precision.

To flip a graphic element:

1. Select the element you want to flip.

2. Choose Modify > Transform.

3. From the submenu (**Figure 4.25**), *choose either of the following:*

   ▲ To reorient the element so that it spins 180 degrees around its vertical central axis like a weathervane, choose Flip Horizontal.

   ▲ To reorient the element so that it spins 180 degrees around its horizontal central axis like a Rolodex file, choose Flip Vertical.

   Figure 4.26 shows the results of the two types of flipping.

✔ Tip

■ You can flip and scale elements simultaneously by using the free-transform tool's Scale modifier. With the selected element in Scale mode, drag one handle all the way across the bounding box and past the handle on the other side. To flip a selected element vertically and horizontally, for example, drag the handle in the bottom-right corner diagonally upward, past the handle in the top-left corner (**Figure 4.27**). The flipped element starts small and grows as you continue to drag away from the element's top-left corner. Flash previews the flipped element; release the mouse button when the element is the size you want.

To rotate an element in 90-degree increments:

1. Select the element you want to rotate.

2. Choose Modify > Transform.

3. From the submenu, *choose either of the following:*

   ▲ To rotate the element counterclockwise 90 degrees, choose Rotate 90° CCW.

   ▲ To rotate the element clockwise 90 degrees, choose Rotate 90° CW.

   Flash rotates the element 90 degrees. You can repeat the command to rotate the element 180 and 270 degrees or back to its starting point.

To rotate an element by a user-specified amount:

1. Access the Transform panel (**Figure 4.28**). If the panel isn't open, choose Window > Transform.

2. Click the Rotate radio button.

3. To specify the direction and amount of rotation, *do either of the following:*

   ▲ To rotate the element counterclockwise, enter a negative value (–1 to –360) in the Rotation field.

   ▲ To rotate the element clockwise, enter a positive value (1 to 360).

4. Press Enter.

   Flash rotates the selected element by the amount you specified.

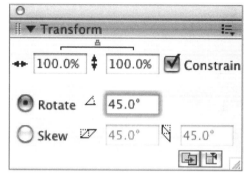

Figure 4.28 The Transform panel lets you rotate graphic elements in precise increments. Positive values rotate the element clockwise; negative values rotate it counterclockwise.

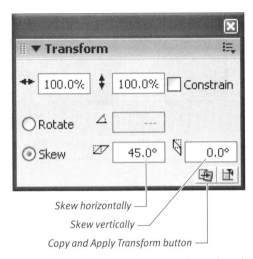

Figure 4.29 Use the Transform panel to skew selected elements. You can set separate values for horizontal and vertical skewing.

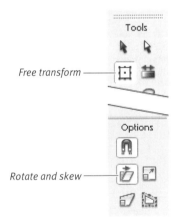

Figure 4.30 Select the free-transform tool's Rotate and Skew modifier to access handles for rotating or skewing a selected element interactively.

To skew an element by a user-specified amount:

1. With the Transform panel open, select the element you want to skew.

2. In the Transform panel, click the Skew radio button.

3. Enter the desired skew values in the horizontal and vertical fields (**Figure 4.29**).

4. To complete the transformation, press Enter.

✔ Tip

- To skew a copy of the selected element, in the Transform panel, click the Copy and Apply Transform button.

To rotate or skew an element interactively:

1. Select the element you want to rotate or skew.

2. In the Tools panel, select the free-transform tool; then click the Rotate and Skew modifier (**Figure 4.30**).

   Solid square handles appear on all four sides and at the corners of the element's bounding box.

   continues on next page

FLIPPING, ROTATING, AND SKEWING

3. To modify the selected element, *do either of the following:*

▲ To rotate the element, position the pointer over one of the corner handles.

The pointer changes to a circular arrow. Click and drag in the direction you want to rotate the element. Flash spins the element around its transformation point, previewing the rotation as you drag (**Figure 4.31**).

▲ To skew the element, position the pointer over one of the side handles of the element's bounding box.

The pointer changes to a two-way arrowhead. Click and drag the side handle in the direction you want to skew the element. Flash previews the skewing as you drag (Figure 4.31).

4. Release the mouse button.

Flash redraws the modified element.

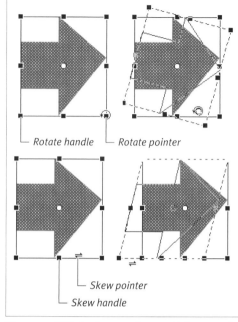

Rotate handle   *Rotate pointer*

Skew pointer

Skew handle

Figure 4.31 With the free-transform tool's Rotate and Skew modifier selected, you can drag one of the corner handles of a selected element's bounding box to rotate that element (top). Drag one of the side handles to skew the element (bottom).

✔ Tips

■ By default, the transformation point corresponds to a point at the center of a shape's bounding box. You can change that. With the free-transform tool, drag the hollow circle that represents the transformation point to a new location

■ To rotate an element around one of its corners instead of its transformation point, press Option (Mac) or Alt (Windows) while dragging. The handle diagonally across from the one you're manipulating becomes the point of rotation.

■ When you select an object with the free-transform tool, watch carefully as you move the pointer near the handles. If you pause directly on top of a corner handle, the icon changes to the double-headed arrow that allows you to scale the object. Move the pointer slightly away from the corner handle, and the icon changes to the rotation arrow. Click and drag to rotate the object. Position the pointer along the edge of the bounding box between handles, and the icon changes to the two-way arrows. Click and drag in the direction you wish to skew the object.

■ To constrain rotation by 45-degree increments, hold down the Shift key while rotating.

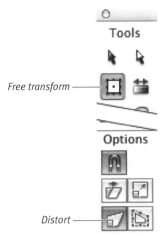

Figure 4.32 Choose the free-transform tool's Distort modifier to reposition the corner points of the bounding box containing your selection independently.

Distorting Graphic Elements

The free-transform tool's Distort modifier allows you to distort a graphic element by changing the shape of its bounding box. You can reposition one or more corners of the box individually; you can manipulate paired corner handles simultaneously to turn the rectangular box into a trapezoid; and you can stretch, shrink, and/or skew the box by moving the side handles of the bounding box. The selected element(s) stretch or shrink to fit the new bounding box. The Distort modifier works only on merge-shapes and single, selected drawing-objects; Distort doesn't work on multiple drawing-objects, text boxes (see Chapter 3), groups (see Chapter 5), or symbols (see Chapter 7).

To distort an element freely:

1. Using the free-transform tool, select the element you want to distort.

   A bounding box with transformational handles appears.

2. In the Tools panel, select the Distort modifier (**Figure 4.32**).

   Note that the center point of your selection disappears, indicating that you are in Distort mode.

3. Position the pointer over one of the transformational handles.

   The pointer changes to a hollow arrowhead.

DISTORTING GRAPHIC ELEMENTS

4. To change the shape of the bounding box, *do one of the following:*

▲ To relocate one corner of the element's bounding box, position the pointer over one of the corner handles; then click and drag the handle to the desired location. You can position each corner handle independently (**Figure 4.33**).

▲ To skew the element, position the pointer over one of the side handles; then drag the handle to the desired position. The element skews toward the direction you drag.

▲ To stretch the element as you skew it, move the selected side handle away from the element's center (**Figure 4.34**).

▲ To shrink the element as you skew it, move the selected side handle toward the element's center.

5. Release the mouse button.

Flash redraws the selection to fill the new bounding-box shape.

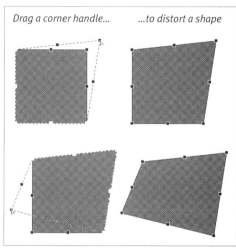

Figure 4.33 Use the free-transform tool's Distort modifier to redefine the shape of an element's bounding box. You can drag each corner handle separately.

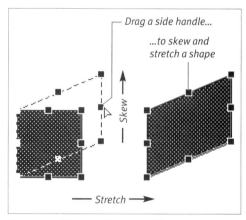

Figure 4.34 When the Distort modifier is selected, dragging the side handles of a selected element's bounding box skews the element. To enlarge (or shrink) the element at the same time, move the side handle away from (or in toward) the center of the original shape.

Distorted Perspective

As beginning art students discover, it's not difficult to add depth to objects made up of rectangular shapes. You adjust the appropriate edges to align with imaginary parallel lines that converge at a distant point on the horizon—the *vanishing point*. Doing so creates the illusion that the objects recede into the distance. Adding perspective to nonrectangular shapes takes a bit more experience and the ability to imagine the way that those shapes should look. The Distort modifier of Flash's free-transform tool helps you because it encloses your selected shape—circle, oval, or squiggle—within a rectangular bounding box. All you need to do is adjust that box as you would a rectangular shape.

Beginning art students learn about 1-point, 2-point, and 3-point perspective. The *points* here refer to the vanishing point. By selecting elements in your artwork carefully, and by using the distort tools to make the edges of the bounding box seem to line up with those converging lines, you can add perspective to graphic elements even if they don't contain the parallel lines that would make it easy for you to fake the depth perception you want.

✔ Tips

- You can use the free-transform tool to distort multiple merge-shapes simultaneously. Select the merge-shapes you want to modify. Then, using the Distort modifier of the free-transform tool, redefine the shape of the bounding box that surrounds the shapes. The shapes change as a unit.

- When you select multiple drawing-objects, the free-transform tool's Distort modifier is inactive. To distort multiple drawing-objects simultaneously, you must combine them into a single drawing-object (see "Converting Shape Types," later in this chapter).

- If your selection mixes one or more merge-shapes with a single drawing-object, the Distort modifier of the free-transform tool is available, and you can distort the merge-shapes and that one drawing-object.

- Although you can use the free-transform tool on text boxes, groups, and symbols, the Distort modifier doesn't work on these items. If your selection includes merge-shapes and one or more text boxes, groups, or symbols, the free-transform tool's Distort modifier is available, but the distortion affects only the merge-shapes.

To distort graphic elements symmetrically:

1. Follow steps 1 and 2 of the preceding task to prepare an element for distorting.

2. To taper the element, *do either of the following:*

   ▲ To make the top of the bounding box narrower than the bottom, Shift-click and drag the top-right corner handle toward the top-left corner handle, or vice versa (**Figure 4.35**).

   ▲ To make the top of the bounding box wider than the bottom, Shift-click and drag the top-right corner handle away from the top-left corner handle, or vice versa.

   As you drag, the two corner handles move in tandem, coming together if you drag in or moving apart if you drag out.

3. Release the mouse button.

   Flash redraws the bounding box and its contents. If you dragged in, the box appears to taper toward the top. If you dragged out, the box appears to taper toward the bottom. You can follow these procedures for the sides or bottom of the bounding box to taper the box in any direction.

✔ Tips

■ To access the free-transform tool's hollow-arrowhead pointer temporarily without selecting the Distort modifier, press ⌘ (Mac) or Ctrl (Windows). Then you can drag or Shift-drag to distort selected elements.

■ If you make a mistake while distorting a graphic, and you choose Edit > Undo so you can fix it, your graphic will be select-ed with the free-transform tool but the Distort modifier won't be active. You must reselect the Distort modifier in the Tools panel to continue your distortion.

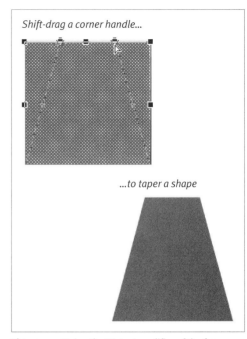

Shift-drag a corner handle...

...to taper a shape

Figure 4.35 Using the Distort modifier of the free-transform tool, Shift-click and drag a corner handle to taper selected elements.

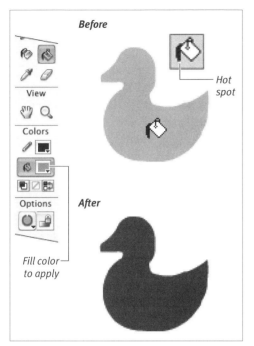

Figure 4.37 Clicking a fill with the paint bucket applies whatever color is selected in the Fill Color control. Use this technique to change existing fills.

Modifying Fills and Strokes

Flash provides two methods for modifying existing fills and strokes: you can apply new attributes with a tool (the paint bucket tool for fills, the ink bottle tool for strokes), or you can select the fill or stroke on the Stage and choose new attributes in an appropriate panel. For fills or strokes that contain a gradient, you can also modify the way the gradient fits in the shape by using the gradient-transform tool.

To change fill color with the paint-bucket tool:

1. In the Tools panel, select the paint-bucket tool, or press K.

2. Select new fill attributes (see Chapter 2).

3. Click the paint bucket's hot spot (the tip of the drip of paint) somewhere inside the fill you want to change.

   The fill can be selected or deselected. The fill changes to the new color (**Figure 4.37**).

MODIFYING FILLS AND STROKES

Use Panels to Change Selected Fills and Strokes

You can modify the fill and stroke attributes of a selected graphic element by changing the settings in any appropriate panel. For example, draw an oval with a red fill and a 1-point, solid blue stroke; then select the whole shape (note that if you create the oval as a drawing-object, Flash automatically selects it). Now access the Properties tab of the Property inspector; it displays the attributes of the selected shape (or drawing-object). Select green from the Fill Color control; the oval fill changes to green. Increase the stroke height or choose a new stroke style; the oval stroke changes to match.

You can choose new colors for selected fills and strokes from any appropriate panel—Color Mixer, Color Swatches, Tools, or Property inspector.

When a selected merge-shape has a stroke or fill set to No Color, however, the only way to change that setting is to add a fill or stroke by using the paint-bucket or ink-bottle tool (see Chapter 2).

When your selected shape is a drawing-object, changing the fill or stroke attributes in a panel adds the missing element (**Figure 4.36**).

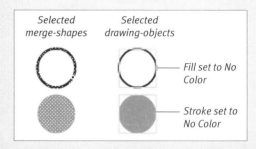

Selected merge-shapes   Selected drawing-objects

Fill set to No Color

Stroke set to No Color

Select new attributes

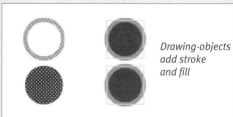

Properties | Filters | Parameters

Drawing Object

W: 94.5   X: 67.0

H: 97.5   Y: 133.0

5

Stroke h

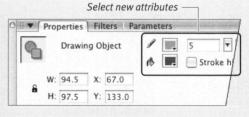

Drawing-objects add stroke and fill

Figure 4.36 Changing the attributes of a drawing-object whose fill or stroke was originally set to No Color causes Flash to add the missing element, whereas doing the same thing for a selected merge-shape has no effect.

With nothing selected, click stroke or fill

With fill and stroke selected, click stroke or fill

With just fill selected, click stroke

With part of stroke selected, click selection

Warning: Clicking a selected fill with unselected stroke does nothing

Figure 4.38 You don't have to select a stroke to change its attributes; just click the stroke or the unselected fill with the ink bottle. Warning: If the fill is selected, you must click the stroke itself; you can't click the selected fill to change an unselected stroke.

- To pick up the color of a stroke or fill and use it for both strokes and fills, Shift-click with the eyedropper tool. Flash loads the selected color into the Fill Color and Stroke-Color controls in the Tools panel, the Color Mixer panel, and the Properties tab of the Property inspectors relevant to the selected color.

To change stroke color with the ink-bottle tool:

1. In the Tools panel, select the ink-bottle tool, or press S.

2. Select new stroke attributes (see Chapter 2).

3. Click the ink bottle's hot spot (the tip of the drip of paint) *in one of the following ways:*

   ▲ Click directly on the stroke.

   ▲ If a shape has both stroke and fill, and both are deselected, click the fill.

   ▲ If a shape has both stroke and fill, and both are selected, click the fill.

   ▲ If a shape has both stroke and fill, and only the fill is selected, click the stroke.

   The stroke takes on its new attributes (**Figure 4.38**).

✔ Tips

- To save time, you can copy the fill and stroke attributes of one element and apply them to another. In the Tools panel, select the eyedropper tool, or press I. The pointer changes to an eyedropper. To copy a fill color or gradient, position the eyedropper over a fill and click. To copy all of a stroke's attributes, position the eyedropper over the stroke and click. Flash switches tools; the paint bucket appears for fills, the ink bottle for strokes. The attributes of the clicked item appear in all related panels; when you click a fill, for example, the fill type and fill color appear in the Tools panel, the Color Mixer panel, and the Properties tab of the Property inspector. You can then use the loaded paint-bucket or ink-bottle tool to apply the attributes to a different graphic element.

MODIFYING FILLS AND STROKES

To change a gradient fill's center point:

1. In the Tools panel, select the gradient-transform tool (**Figure 4.39**).

2. Position the pointer over the graphic element whose gradient you want to modify; the gradient can be located in a fill or in a stroke.

The pointer changes to the gradient-transform pointer.

3. Click.

Handles for manipulating the gradient appear (**Figure 4.40**). You can rotate the gradient or change its size and/or center point.

4. Position the pointer over the gradient's center-point handle, the circle icon.

The move icon appears.

5. Drag the center-point handle to reposition the center point of the gradient (**Figure 4.41**).

Figure 4.39 The fill-transform tool (left) and the pointer with which you manipulate gradients (right).

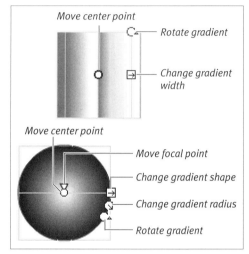

Figure 4.40 Handles for transforming gradients appear when you click a gradient with the gradient-transform pointer.

Before *After*

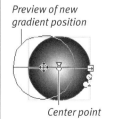 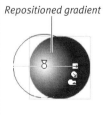

Figure 4.41 Drag the center-point handle to reposition the center of the gradient within your shape.

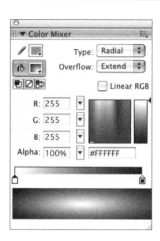

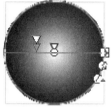

Currently defined gradient

To change a radial gradient's focal point:

1. Follow steps 1–3 in the preceding task.

2. Position the gradient-transform pointer over the focal-point handle, the triangle. The pointer changes to a triangle.

3. Drag the focal-point handle to a new location (**Figure 4.42**).

    The focal point, the most concentrated amount of the gradient's central color, shifts to the new location.

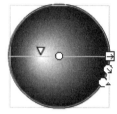

Preview of new focal point position

Repositioned focal point

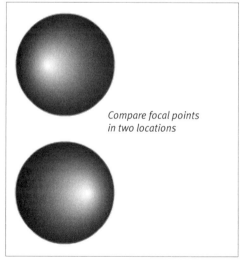

Compare focal points in two locations

Figure 4.42 This gradient blends from white (in the left-most gradient pointer) to black (in the right-most). This arrangement puts white at the center of a radial gradient, giving the illusion of highlighting on a three-dimensional object. By moving the focal point, you can mimic changes in the way light hits the object.

To resize a gradient in a fill or stroke:

1. With the gradient-transform tool selected in the Tools panel, click the graphic element that contains the gradient you want to modify.

2. To change the way the gradient fits inside the fill or stroke, *do one of the following*:

   ▲ To change the width of a linear gradient, drag the square handle (**Figure 4.43**).

   The pointer changes to a double-headed arrow. Dragging toward the center of your shape squeezes the transition into a narrower space; dragging away from the center of your shape spreads the transition over a wider space.

   ▲ To change the shape of a radial gradient, drag the square handle (**Figure 4.44**).

   The pointer changes to a double-headed arrow. Dragging toward the center of your shape creates a narrower oval space for the transition; dragging away from the center of your shape creates a wider oval space.

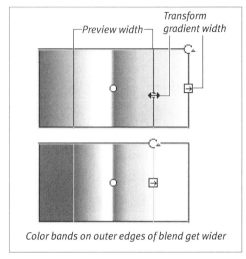

Figure 4.43 With a linear gradient selected, use the gradient-transform tool to drag the square handle inward and create a narrower rectangle for a gradient.

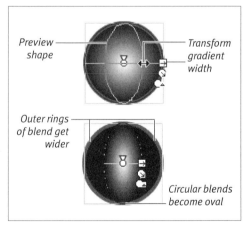

Figure 4.44 With a radial gradient selected, use the gradient-transform tool to drag the square handle inward to create a narrower oval for a gradient.

MODIFYING FILLS AND STROKES

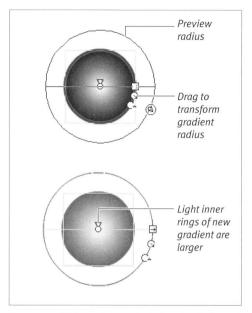

Figure 4.45 With a radial gradient, drag the first round handle outward to create a larger radius.

Preview radius

Drag to transform gradient radius

Light inner rings of new gradient are larger

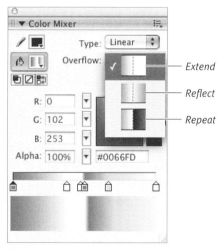

Figure 4.46 When you're set to publish your movie to Flash Player 8 (see Chapter 16), the Color Mixer panel's Overflow menu is active. You can choose how Flash fills out a gradient that you have made narrower than the shape it sits in.

Extend

Reflect

Repeat

▲ To change the radius of a radial gradient, drag the circular handle next to the square handle (**Figure 4.45**).

The pointer changes to an arrow within a circle. Dragging toward the center of your shape squeezes the transition into a smaller circular space; dragging away from the center of your shape spreads the transition over a larger circular space.

To control overflow (for Flash Player 8):

1. Follow the steps in the preceding task to create a gradient that is narrower than the shape it sits in.

2. In the Color Mixer panel, from the Overflow menu (**Figure 4.46**), *choose one of the following:*

   ▲ To extend the colors in the leftmost and rightmost gradient pointers, choose Extend (the first menu item).

   ▲ To repeat the gradient, but with the colors in reverse order, choose Reflect (the second menu item).

   ▲ To repeat the gradient with colors in the original order, choose Repeat.

   Note that to view the Overflow menu, your Publish Settings must be set to publish for Flash Player 8 (see Chapter 16). If you're set to publish to earlier versions of Flash Player, the Overflow menu is inactive.

MODIFYING FILLS AND STROKES

125

The Mystery of Gradient Overflow

When you resize a gradient to be narrower than the shape it sits in, you create a gap. In previous versions, Flash always filled that gap by extending the colors on the outside edges of the gradient. In Flash 8, when you're publishing for Flash Player 8 (see Chapter 16), you control the filling of that gap by choosing an Overflow setting in the Color Mixer panel. There are three overflow styles to choose from: Extend, Reflect, and Repeat (**Figure 4.47**).

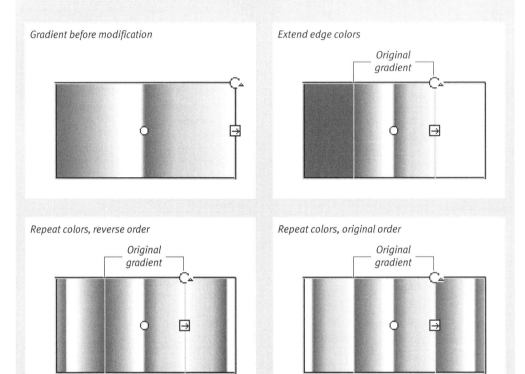

Gradient before modification

Extend edge colors

Repeat colors, reverse order

Repeat colors, original order

Figure 4.47 When you resize a gradient to make it narrower, Flash 8's default overflow style, Extend, fills the gap by extending the colors on the outside of the gradient (top-right). Reflect fills the gap by reversing the order of the colors and displaying however many bands fit the space (bottom-left). Repeat starts the gradient over again, showing the bands in the original order (bottom-right).

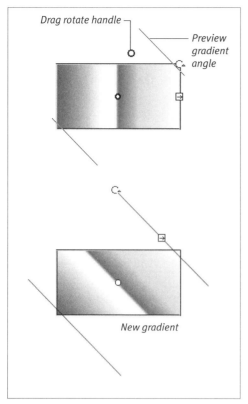

Drag rotate handle

Preview gradient angle

New gradient

Figure 4.48 As you drag the gradient's rotate handle with the gradient-transform tool, you spin the gradient around its center point.

To rotate a gradient fill:

1. With the gradient-transform tool selected in the Tools panel, click the fill or stroke containing the gradient you want to modify.

2. To rotate the gradient, *do either of the following:*
   - ▲ To rotate a linear gradient, drag the round handle (**Figure 4.48**).
   - ▲ To rotate a radial gradient, drag the round handle farthest from the square handle.

   The pointer changes to a circular arrow. You can rotate the gradient clockwise or counterclockwise.

✔ Tips

■ Click and drag with the paint-bucket tool to rotate the gradient as you apply it. To constrain the gradient angle to vertical, horizontal, or 45-degree angles, hold down the Shift key as you drag.

■ When you rotate a gradient interactively with the paint-bucket tool, the Fill Color control continues to display the gradient in its vertical position, but the rotation persists for some tools. If you switch to the brush or paint bucket tool, it uses the rotated gradient. (The oval and rectangle tools use the original unrotated gradient.) To remove the angle modification, use the paint-bucket tool to modify the gradient again, or choose another fill and then choose the gradient again.

MODIFYING FILLS AND STROKES

Modifying Shapes: Selection Tool

All the strokes and fills you create in Flash can be edited after you've drawn them. You can edit them in their more naturalistic form, using the selection tool, or you can work directly with the path's anchor points and Bézier curves by using the subselection and pen tools (see "Modifying Shapes: Subselection Tool," later in this chapter). You can also apply the pencil tool's editing assistance after the fact.

When you use the selection tool, the shape you want to modify must be deselected. If the segment is selected, the selection tool moves the segment as a unit. Always note what kind of icon the selection pointer is displaying as it hovers over the line you want to modify.

For the following tasks, make sure the item you want to modify is deselected. These tasks all deal with modifying strokes, but the same techniques work for modifying fills by reshaping their outlines (see the sidebar "The Mystery of Fill Outlines").

About Curve and Corner Points

Flash's selection and pen/subselection tools let you modify an element's curves and lines. The subselection tool lets you do so by moving the curve and corner points that define the element's path and by rearranging the curves' Bézier handles. When you drag a selection rectangle to enclose a path with the subselection tool, Flash reveals any curve points' Bézier handles. (Corner points have no handles.)

When you use the selection tool, Flash hides all that technical stuff. You simply pull on a line to reshape it. Still, the selection tool has its own hidden version of curve and corner points, which are evident only in the changing icons that accompany the tool as it interacts with a line or curve (**Figure 4.49**).

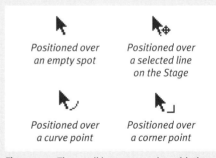

Positioned over an empty spot

Positioned over a selected line on the Stage

Positioned over a curve point

Positioned over a corner point

Figure 4.49 The small icons appearing with the selection pointer indicate what type of graphic element lies beneath the pointer.

For the selection tool, corner points appear at the end of a segment or at the point where two segments join to form a sharp angle. All those other in-between points—even if they fall in the middle of a line segment that happens to be completely flat—are curve points. When you tug on a curve point with the selection tool, you pull out a range of points in a tiny arc. When you tug on a corner point with the selection tool, you pull out a single point.

Clean Up Rough Pencil-Tool Sketches

In Chapter 2, you learned about using the pencil tool with assistance to draw shapes freehand and have Flash clean them up. Rather than have Flash assist you with everything while you draw, you may prefer to sketch with the pencil tool's free-form Ink mode. Flash can recognize pencil-drawn lines and apply smoothing and straightening after you draw them.

To smooth or straighten existing pencil-drawn lines, select them. With the selection tool active, in the Tools panel, click the Smooth or Straighten button. Flash smoothes the curves or straightens the line segments in the selected lines according to the tolerances currently set in the Drawing category of the Preferences dialog (see Chapter 2). You can also smooth or straighten selected lines by choosing Modify> Shape > Smooth or Modify> Shape > Straighten.

If a line still looks too rough after your first attempt, apply the Smooth or Straighten command again. Repeated smoothing eventually flattens your curves; repeated straightening eventually turns curve segments into straight-line segments (**Figure 4.50**).

You can also make Flash recognize shapes you've sketched with the pencil tool. Select your rough version of an oval or rectangle. With the selection tool active, in the Tools panel, click the Straighten button; or, from the Modify menu, choose Shape > Straighten. If the shape is recognizable under the tolerances currently set in the Preferences dialog, Flash recasts the shape as a perfect oval or rectangle. If at first Flash fails to recognize your rough shape, try again. Often, the newly straightened shape falls within the parameters Flash needs to recognize it.

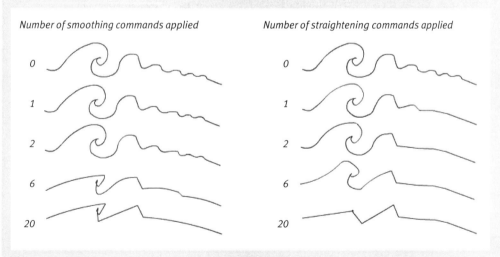

Figure 4.50 Invoking the Smooth and Straighten commands several times can change the appearance of a line dramatically.

To activate the end of a segment with the selection tool:

1. Position the pointer over the end point of a deselected line segment.

The corner-point modifier appears.

2. Click the end point.

The end of the segment becomes active.

3. Reposition the end point *in any of the following ways:*

▲ Drag away from the existing line or curve to lengthen the segment (**Figure 4.51**).

▲ Drag toward the existing line or curve to shorten the segment (**Figure 4.52**).

▲ Drag at an angle to the original line to pivot a straight-line segment to a new position or reshape the end of a curve segment (**Figure 4.53**).

As you drag, the end of the line changes to a small circle, showing that the line is active for modifications; Flash previews the modified segment as you drag

4. Release the mouse button.

Flash redraws the line segment.

Figure 4.51 Drag away from the existing curve or line segment (top) to lengthen it (bottom).

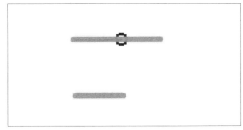

Figure 4.52 Drag toward the existing line or curve segment (top) to shorten it (bottom).

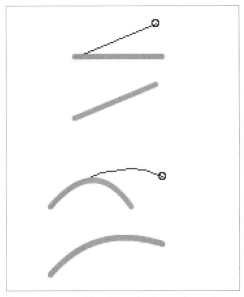

Figure 4.53 Reposition the end point to change the direction of the line or curve segment.

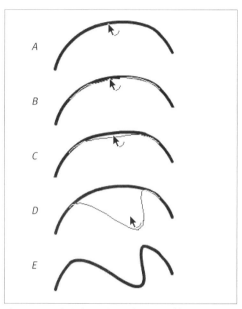

Figure 4.54 Click the middle of a curve (A). Flash activates the curve segment (B). Drag the curve to a new position (C, D). When you release the mouse button, Flash redraws the curve (E).

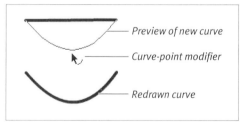

Preview of new curve

Curve-point modifier

Redrawn curve

Figure 4.55 Although this line doesn't look curved (top), Flash considers all its middle points to be curve points. Drag one of those points to create a line that looks like a curve (bottom).

To reshape curves with the selection tool:

1. Position the selection tool's pointer over the middle of a curve segment.

   The curve-point modifier appears.

2. Click and drag the curve to reshape it (**Figure 4.54**).

   Flash previews the curve you're drawing.

3. Release the mouse button.

   Flash redraws the curve.

To turn straight-line segments into curve segments with the selection tool:

1. Position the selection tool's pointer over the middle of a line segment.

   The curve-point modifier appears.

2. Click and drag the line to reshape it (**Figure 4.55**).

   Flash previews the curve that you're drawing.

3. Release the mouse button.

   Flash redraws the line, giving it the curve you defined.

To create new corner points with the selection tool:

1. Position the selection tool's pointer over the middle of a line or curve segment.

   The curve-point modifier appears.

2. Option-click (Mac) or Ctrl-click (Windows).

   After a brief pause, the selection tool's modifier changes to the corner-point modifier, and a circle appears where the pointer intersects the line. You're now activating a corner point.

3. Drag to modify the line or curve segment and add a new corner point (**Figure 4.56**).

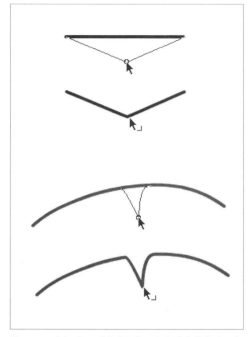

Figure 4.56 Option-click (Mac) or Ctrl-click (Windows) to create a new corner point for editing your line. Dragging a corner point from a straight-line segment creates a sharp V (top). Dragging a corner point from a curve creates a V with curving sides that comes to a sharp point (bottom).

The Mystery of Fill Outlines

You can't see the outline of a filled shape unless you give the shape a stroke, but fills do have outlines that act just like strokes for modification purposes. The selection, pen, and subselection tools all work to reshape fills just as they do to reshape strokes, as outlined in the tasks in this chapter (**Figure 4.57**).

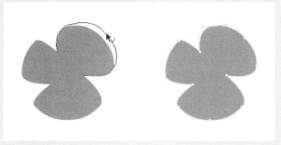

Figure 4.57 When you position the pointer over the edge of a fill shape, the selection tool displays either the curve-point or corner-point modifier. Clicking the edge of the fill activates part of the outline for reshaping (left). Selecting the edge of a fill shape with the subselection tool highlights the path and anchor points that outline the shape. You can reposition anchor points and Bézier handles to modify the fill shapes (right).

Figure 4.58 Use the subselection tool to modify the path of a line segment.

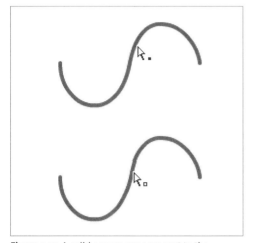

Figure 4.59 A solid square appears next to the subselection tool when it's ready to select the entire path (top). When a hollow square appears (bottom), the tool is ready to select and manipulate a single anchor point.

Figure 4.60 Using the subselection tool, drag a corner point to reposition it.

Modifying Shapes: Subselection Tool

The subselection tool allows you to reveal and manipulate the anchor points that define a line segment or curve. You can reposition these points to modify lines and curves, and you can manipulate a point's Bézier handles to modify the slope and depth of the curve. You can add and delete points and convert existing curve points to corner points, or vice versa, with the pen tool.

To view a path and anchor points:

1. In the Tools panel, choose the subselection tool, or press A (**Figure 4.58**).

   The pointer changes to a hollow arrow.

2. On the Stage, click the line or curve you want to modify.

   Flash selects and highlights the entire path and shows the anchor points. In Flash's default editing mode, anchor points appear as hollow squares in a contrasting highlight color. To manipulate a particular point, you must select it directly.

To select an anchor point:

1. Follow the steps in the preceding task, and then position the pointer over the middle of the highlighted path.

   The anchor-point modifier (a small square) appears next to the hollow-arrow icon (**Figure 4.59**).

2. Click an anchor point.

   Flash highlights the selected point. With Drawing Preferences set to Show Solid Points, selected corner points appear as solid squares; selected curve points appear as solid circles with Bézier handles.

MODIFYING SHAPES: SUBSELECTION TOOL

✔ Tips

■ If you know where a point is in your element, you can skip the step of clicking the path to highlight all the anchor points. To select the point directly, double-click it.

■ You can select multiple points on a path directly with the subselection tool. Draw a selection rectangle that includes the points you want to select. Flash highlights the entire path and selects any points that fall within the rectangle.

■ To view anchor points as hollow squares and selected points as solid, you need to change Flash's editing preferences. From the Edit menu (Windows) or the Flash menu (Mac), choose Preferences to open the Preferences dialog. Choose the Drawing category, and deselect the Show Solid Points check box.

To move corner points:

1. Use the subselection tool to highlight the path and anchor points of the element you want to modify.

2. Position the pointer over a corner point.

3. Click and drag the desired corner point to a new location.
   Flash redraws the path (**Figure 4.60**).

✔ Tip

■ Corner points are often easy to identify withouth highlighting the path. You can click and drag such points directly without first highlighting the path. If you don't click right on the point, however, you'll move the whole path, not just the intended point.

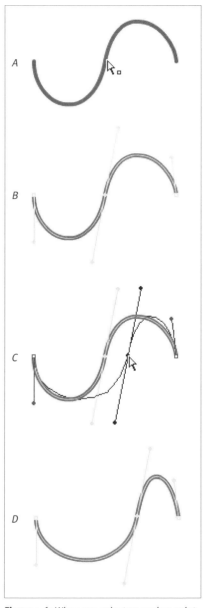

Figure 4.61 When you select an anchor point (A), Flash highlights the entire path (B). You can drag the anchor point to modify the path (C). The path and anchor points remain highlighted when you're done (D).

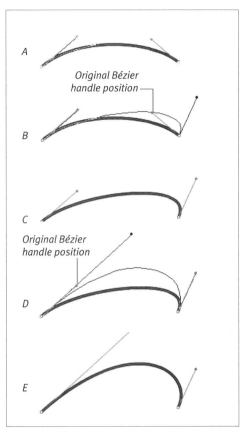

Figure 4.62 When you select anchor points, their Bézier handles appear (A). Leaning a Bézier handle away from a curve (B) makes that curve segment more pronounced (C). Leaning the handle toward the curve flattens that part of the curve. Dragging the Bézier handle away from its anchor point (D) makes the curve deeper (E); dragging the handle toward the anchor point makes the curve shallower.

To move a curve point:

1. Use the subselection tool to highlight the path and anchor points of the element.

2. Position the pointer over a curve point. The anchor-point modifier appears.

3. Click and drag the point to a new location (**Figure 4.61**).

   Flash previews the new curve as you drag.

   After you move a curve point, the path remains selected, and the Bézier control handles become active so that you can further manipulate the curve.

To reshape a curve with the Bézier handles:

1. With the subselection tool, click the curve you want to modify.

2. Click one of the anchor points that define the curve you want to modify. Bézier handles appear.

3. Click and drag one of the Bézier handles. The pointer changes to an arrowhead.

4. To modify the curve, *do one or more of the following:*

   ▲ To make the curve more pronounced, position the Bézier handle farther from the curve in the direction in which the curve bulges.

   ▲ To make the curve flatter, position the Bézier handle closer to the curve.

   ▲ To make the curve bulge in the opposite direction, move the Bézier handle past the existing curve, in the opposite direction from the current bulge.

   ▲ To make the curve deeper, position the Bézier handle farther from the anchor point.

   ▲ To make the curve shallower, position the Bézier handle closer to the anchor point.

   Flash previews the new curve as you manipulate the Bézier handle (**Figure 4.62**).

✔ Tips

■ To select an anchor point and activate its Bézier handles quickly, use the subselection tool to draw a selection rectangle around the curve you want to modify. Even if the path wasn't highlighted, Flash selects any anchor points that fall within the selection and activates their handles.

■ You can move selected anchor points with the arrow keys. To move in larger increments, press the Shift-arrow key.

To convert corner points to curve points:

1. Using the subselection tool, click the path you want to modify.

   Flash highlights the path and its anchor points.

2. Position the hollow-arrow pointer over a corner point.

   The anchor-point modifier appears.

3. Click the anchor point to select it.

4. To pull Bézier handles out of the point, Option-drag (Mac) or Alt-drag (Windows) away from the selected corner point.

   Flash converts the corner point to a curve point (**Figure 4.63**).

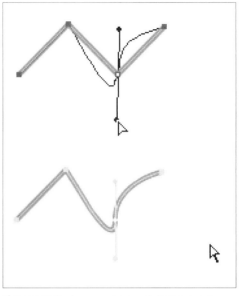

Figure 4.63 To change a corner point into a curve point (one with Bézier handles) using the subselection tool, Option-drag (Mac) or Alt-drag (Windows) a selected corner point (top). You pull a Bézier handle out of the point instead of relocating the point. When you release the mouse button, Flash redraws the curve (bottom).

Figure 4.64 When you position the pen tool over a curve point, a small caret appears next to the pointer (top). With the caret modifier active, click the curve point to reduce it to a corner point (bottom). Flash redraws the path accordingly.

Figure 4.65 When you position the pen tool over a corner point, a small minus sign appears next to the pointer (top). With the minus-sign modifier active, click the corner point to reduce it to no point at all (bottom). Flash redraws the path accordingly.

To convert curve points to corner points:

1. With the path you want to modify selected, in the Tools panel, choose the pen tool.

2. Position the pen pointer over a curve point. The convert-to-corner-point modifier (a small caret) appears next to the pen icon.

3. Click the curve point.

   Flash converts the curve point to a corner point and flattens the curved path (**Figure 4.64**).

✔ Tip

■ You can also select a path using the pen tool. Position the pen tool over a deselected stroke or fill outline, and click. Now you're ready to start converting anchor points.

To delete anchor points:

1. With the path you want to modify selected, in the Tools panel, choose the pen tool.

2. Position the pen pointer over a corner point. The remove-point modifier (a minus sign) appears next to the pen icon.

   Note that if the point you want to delete is currently a curve point, you must first follow the steps in the preceding exercise to convert it to a corner point.

3. Click the corner point.

   Flash removes the anchor point and reshapes the path to connect the remaining points (**Figure 4.65**).

✔ Tip

■ You can also delete one or more anchor points (both corner and curve points) by selecting them with the subselection tool and pressing Delete.

To add new anchor points to a curve segment:

1. With the path you want to modify selected, choose the pen tool from the Tools panel.

2. Position the pen pointer over the path between two curve points.

   The add-point modifier (a plus sign) appears next to the pen icon.

3. Click the path.

   Flash adds a new curve point (**Figure 4.66**).

✔ Tips

■ If you need to add points to a straight-line segment (one that's made up solely of corner points), first convert one of the corner points that define the segment to a curve point. Then you'll be able to add another curve point between them.

■ To add points to the end of an open path, position the pen pointer over the end of the path. When the x to the right of the pen pointer disappears, click the last anchor point, and then continue clicking to add more points.

■ To switch between the pen and subselection tools quickly, use the keyboard shortcuts: A accesses the subselection tool, P accesses the pen tool.

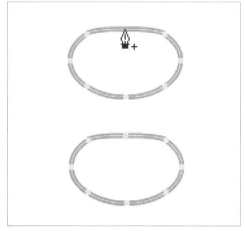

Figure 4.66 When you position the pen tool between existing curve points, a small plus sign appears next to the pointer (top). With the plus-sign modifier active, click the path to add a new curve point (bottom). Note that the pen tool can't add points between corner points.

Modifying Shapes with the Eraser Tool

Flash's eraser tool allows you to modify shapes by deleting parts of fills and strokes. To use the eraser tool, click and scrub on the Stage, as you'd rub an eraser over a piece of paper.

The eraser tool has five modes; you select a mode from the Eraser Mode menu in the Options section of the Tools panel. The eraser modes govern how the tool interacts with fills and strokes. For simple shapes on a single layer, Erase Normal is a good setting; it enables the eraser tool to remove any line or fill you drag over. The other eraser modes limit what the tool affects: in Erase Fills, the tool affects only fills; in Erase Lines, the tool affects only strokes; in Erase Selected Fills, the tool only erases from fills that have been selected; and in Erase Inside, the tool affects only the fill in which you begin an erasure. These modes become important when you work with complex graphics with multiple elements (see Chapter 5).

Another eraser option is the Faucet modifier. The faucet speeds removal of lines and fills. Clicking a deselected line with the eraser in Faucet mode deletes all the segments that make up that line. If multiple merge-shape strokes and/or fills are selected, clicking any of the selected items with the faucet deletes the entire selection. (If multiple drawing-objects are selected, however, the faucet deletes the individual fills you click, one at a time; the faucet can't delete selected drawing-object strokes.)

In addition, the Faucet mode overrides the complex eraser mode settings. For example, with the eraser set to Erase Lines, you can't scrub to erase a fill; but without changing the Erase Lines setting, you can choose the Faucet mode and then click a fill to erase it.

The eraser tool's quickest trick is to clear the decks completely. Double-click the eraser tool in the Tools panel to delete the entire contents of the Stage.

Converting Shape Types

Flash 8 offers a variety of shape types: fills, strokes, merge-shapes, drawing-objects, and text. It's possible to convert some types of shapes into others. For example, you can convert strokes to fills; you can convert merge-shapes to drawing-objects and vice versa; and you can convert text, a special type of fill, to a regular merge-shape fill.

To convert strokes to fills:

1. Select a stroke on the Stage.

2. Choose Modify > Shape > Convert Lines to Fills (**Figure 4.67**).

   Flash converts the line to a fill shape that looks exactly like the line. You can now edit the "line's" outline as though you were working with a fill created with the brush tool (**Figure 4.68**).

Figure 4.67 Choose Modify > Shape > Convert Lines to Fills to transform strokes into fills.

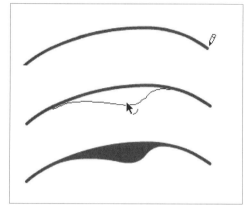

Figure 4.68 You can convert a stroke, such as this line drawn with the pencil tool (top), to a fill. The fill then has its own editable outlines (middle and bottom).

The Mystery of Text Fills

Flash considers text to be a type of fill, but the letter forms don't act like fill shapes you sketch with the drawing tools. The letter shapes are unified as text within a container that acts as a single graphic-object. Flash allows you to *break apart* text—that is, divide one text block containing multiple editable characters into multiple text blocks, each containing one editable character. This feature lets you scale, reposition, or distort individual letters. The ability to place letters in separate text boxes also comes in handy for animating text. (You learn more about animation techniques in Chapters 8–11.) These single-letter text boxes are still graphic-objects, however. To convert text fills to true merge-shape fills, you must break them apart twice: once to get them into separate text boxes, then a second time to convert each letter to a merge-shape. This technique is useful when you have a small amount of text, you can't (or don't want to) supply to every end user, but you need to ensure the text looks exactly the same in the finished product.

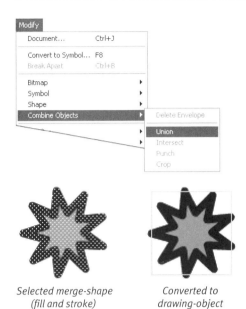

Selected merge-shape (fill and stroke)   *Converted to drawing-object*

Figure 4.69 Choose Modify > Combine Objects > Union to convert all the shapes selected on the Stage into a single drawing-object.

Figure 4.70 Choose Modify > Break Apart to convert drawing-objects to merge-shapes.

To convert merge-shapes to drawing-objects:

1. Select a merge-shape on the Stage.

2. Choose Modify > Combine Objects > Union.

   Flash converts the selected shape to a drawing-object; it remains selected (**Figure 4.69**).

To convert drawing-objects to merge-shapes:

1. Select a drawing-object on the Stage.

2. Choose Modify > Break Apart, or press ⌘-B (Mac) or Ctrl-B (Windows) (**Figure 4.70**).

   Flash converts the selected drawing-object to a merge-shape; it remains selected.

✔ Tip

■ The Modify > Combine Shapes commands (Union, Intersect, Punch, and Chop) work on multiple, selected drawing-objects; the last three work on overlapping drawing-objects. In effect, these commands convert the drawing-objects to merge-shapes (so that they interact) and then convert the resulting shape(s) back into a drawing-object. You'll learn more about combining drawing-object shapes in Chapter 5.

CONVERTING SHAPE TYPES

To divide text blocks into single-letter text boxes:

1. Select a text block on the Stage.

2. Choose Modify > Break Apart (**Figure 4.71**).

   Flash places each letter in its own text box and selects all the text boxes. Each text box is just wide enough to hold one letter. Each letter is fully editable on its own, although the group is no longer linked.

To transform letters into merge-shapes:

1. Follow the steps in the preceding task to place letters in individual text boxes.

2. Choose Modify > Break Apart.

   This second Break Apart command transforms the editable letters into raw shapes on the Stage (**Figure 4.72**). You can edit them as you would any other fill, but you can no longer change their text attributes with the text tool.

Figure 4.71 Choose Modify > Break Apart to place each letter of a text block in its own text box.

Figure 4.72 Applying the Break Apart command once transforms selected text (top) into single-letter text boxes (middle); applying the command again creates merge-shapes out of the individual letters (bottom).

COMPLEX GRAPHICS ON A SINGLE LAYER

In Chapters 2 and 4, you learned to make and modify simple individual shapes from lines (strokes) and fills by using Macromedia Flash 8's drawing tools. In your movies, you'll want to use many shapes together, and you'll need to combine strokes and fills in complex ways. You might combine several shapes, such as ovals and rectangles, to create a robot character, for example. To work effectively with complex graphics, you must understand how multiple graphic elements—both merge-shapes and drawing objects—interact when they're on the same layer or on different layers. In this chapter, you learn how to work with multiple graphic elements on one layer in a Flash document. To learn more about the concept of layers, see Chapter 6.

Two of Flash's drawing tools—the brush tool and the eraser—offer special modes for use with multiple fills and strokes on a single layer. In this chapter, unless you're specifically requested to do otherwise, leave both tools at their default settings of Paint Normal (for the brush tool) and Erase Normal (for the eraser).

When Merge-Shapes Interact

You can think of each frame in a Flash movie as being a stack of transparent acetate sheets. In Flash terms, each sheet is a layer. Graphics on different layers have a depth relationship: Items on higher layers block your view of items on lower layers, just as a drawing on the top sheet of acetate would obscure drawings on lower sheets.

Imagine that you have two layers in your movie. If you draw a little yellow square on the bottom layer and then switch to the top layer and draw a big red square directly over the yellow one, the little square remains intact, but you can't see it. The square on the top layer is in the way.

On a single layer in Flash, however, merge-shapes interact with one another, almost as though you were painting with wet finger paint. Here's a quick run down of how lines (strokes) and shapes (fills) created in Merge Drawing mode interact within a single layer.

When Merge-Shape Lines Intersect

Intersecting merge-shape lines drawn on the same layer affect one another. Draw one line in Merge Drawing mode, and then draw a second line that intersects the first. The second line cuts—or, in Flash terminology, *segments*—the first. Segmentation happens whether the lines are the same color or different colors, but it's easiest to see with contrasting colors (**Figure 5.1**).

You might expect that the second line you drew would wind up on top of the first, but sometimes, that's not the case. Start with a red line, and then draw a blue line across it; the blue line jumps *behind* the red one when you release the mouse button. Flash creates a stacking order for merge-shape lines based on the hex-color value of the line's stroke-color setting. The higher the hex value of the stroke color, the higher the line sits in a stack of merge-shape lines drawn on the Stage. A merge-shape line whose stroke color is set to a hex value of 663399 always winds up on top of one whose stroke color is set to 333399.

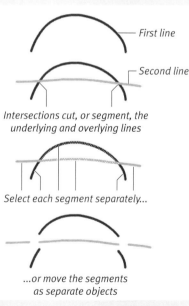

First line

Second line

Intersections cut, or segment, the underlying and overlying lines

Select each segment separately...

...or move the segments as separate objects

Figure 5.1 When you draw one line across another in Merge Drawing mode, every intersection creates a separate segment.

When Merge-Shape Lines and Fills Intersect

Even the invisible outlines that describe painted brush-stroke fills can cut other lines when they're created in Merge Drawing mode. When you draw merge-shape lines over merge-shape fills, you can wind up with lots of little segments. Try drawing lines with the pencil tool and shapes with the brush tool set to Merge Drawing mode. If you paint a brush stroke that intersects a line, the brush stroke remains one solid object, but the line gets segmented (**Figure 5.2**). If you draw a line that intersects a brush stroke, the line cuts the brush stroke, and the invisible outline of the brush stroke cuts the line (**Figure 5.3**).

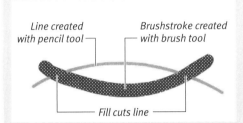

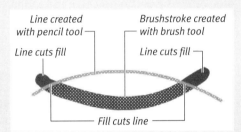

Figure 5.2 When a merge-shape fill overlays a merge-shape line, the fill segments the line. As the selection highlighting shows, the fill remains one solid object.

Figure 5.3 When a merge-shape line overlays a merge-shape fill, the line cuts the fill, and the fill's invisible outline cuts the line.

When Merge-Shape Fills Intersect

When intersecting fills created in Merge Drawing mode are the same color, the newer fill adds to the merge-shape (**Figure 5.4**).

When fills of different colors interact, the newer fill replaces the older one (**Figure 5.5**). If the new fill only intersects the old, it still replaces the part where the two overlap.

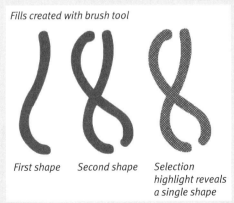

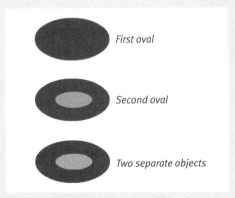

Figure 5.4 When you draw overlapping fills in the same color in Merge Drawing mode, Flash puts the two shapes together to create a single merge-shape.

Figure 5.5 When one merge-shape fill overlaps another of a different color, the fills don't meld but remain separate. The second oval here replaces the first where they overlap.

Working with Groups

Groups serve several functions. They allow you to prevent selected merge-shapes from interacting. They also let you lock down the attributes of shapes and preserve spatial relationships among graphic elements.

To create a group:

1. Select one or more items on the Stage using any of the methods discussed in Chapter 4 (**Figure 5.6**).

2. Choose Modify > Group, or press ⌘-G (Mac) or Ctrl-G (Windows) (**Figure 5.7**). Flash groups the items, placing them within a bounding box (**Figure 5.8**). The visible bounding box lets you know that the group is selected. When the group isn't selected, the bounding box is hidden.

✔ Tip

- If you choose Modify > Group when nothing is selected, you immediately enter group-editing mode. Anything you draw on the Stage now is part of a new group.

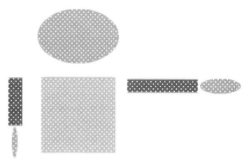

Figure 5.6 The first step in grouping is selecting the shapes you want to use in the group.

Figure 5.7 Choose Modify > Group to unite several selected shapes as a group.

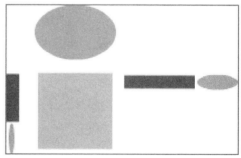

Figure 5.8 When you select the group, a highlighted bounding box appears, surrounding the grouped shapes.

Preventing Interactions

Shapes created in Merge Drawing mode act as if their paint is still wet. Here are some ways to dry the paint and prevent interactions.

Drawing-objects. In Drawing Object mode, the drawing tools create merge-shapes, but Flash isolates them inside a container. The container acts as a semi-permeable membrane. Fills and strokes inside the drawing-object container don't interact with fills and strokes outside the container. You can modify the outlines and the fill and stroke attributes of a drawing-object directly on the Stage (see Chapter 4). You can also open a drawing-object container to work with its merge-shape contents directly.

Groups. When you group selected fills and strokes, they stop interacting with other fills and strokes. Grouped items also stop being directly editable. To modify any attributes of the shapes in a group, you must enter a special editing mode.

Symbols. When you create a symbol, its fills and strokes don't interact with the fills and strokes of other graphic elements. Symbols also require editing in a special mode. Symbols do more than just prevent graphic elements from interacting; symbols let you save your work for reuse and keep file sizes down (see Chapter 7).

Layers. Placing merge-shapes on separate layers prevents them from interacting (see Chapter 6).

Sublayers. When you put several drawing-objects, groups, and/or symbols on the same layer in a Flash document, they stack up, one on top of another. It's as if the objects reside on sublayers within the one layer (see the sidebar "Understanding Stacking Order").

To return objects to ungrouped status:

1. Select the group that you want to return to ungrouped status.

2. Choose Modify > Ungroup, or press Shift-⌘-G (Mac) or Ctrl-Shift-G (Windows).

   Flash removes the bounding box and selects all the items.

✔ Tips

■ If you prefer using a two-key shortcut rather than a three-key shortcut, the command for breaking apart symbols also works to ungroup groups. That command is ⌘-B (Mac) or Ctrl-B (Windows).

■ Interactions between strokes and fills occur not only when you draw a shape but also when you place a copy of a shape or move a shape. Be careful when placing copies of merge-shape fills and strokes on a single layer; you can inadvertently add to or delete part of an underlying merge-shape. If you ungroup a grouped shape that overlaps merge-shapes on a single layer, the shapes will segment one another.

WORKING WITH GROUPS

Working with Grouped Elements

Grouping is a useful way to prevent shapes from interacting and to preserve spatial relationships among shapes as you work with elements on the Stage. Although you can also group drawing-objects, for the tasks in this section, you want to see the interaction with merge-shapes; make sure the Object Drawing button in the Options section of the Tools panel is deselected.

To prevent interaction between merge-shapes on one layer:

1. In the Tools panel, choose the oval tool in Merge Drawing mode.

2. Set the stroke color to No Color and the fill color to red.

3. On the Stage, draw a fairly large oval (**Figure 5.9**).

4. In the Tools panel, switch to the selection tool, and select the oval you just drew.

5. To make the oval a grouped element, Choose Modify > Group (**Figure 5.10**).

6. Back in the Tools panel, choose the oval tool and a different fill color.

7. On the Stage, draw a smaller oval in the middle of your first oval (**Figure 5.11**).

   When you finish drawing the new oval, it immediately disappears behind the grouped oval (**Figure 5.12**). That's because grouped objects always stack on top of ungrouped objects (see the sidebar "Understanding Stacking Order," later in this chapter).

8. Switch to the selection tool, and reposition the large oval so that you can see the small one (**Figure 5.13**).

9. Deselect the large oval, and select the small oval (**Figure 5.14**).

Figure 5.9 The oval before grouping.

Figure 5.10 The oval after grouping.

Figure 5.11 Draw a second oval on top of the grouped oval.

Figure 5.12 The ungrouped oval stacks beneath the grouped oval.

Figure 5.13 Drag the grouped oval to make the ungrouped oval visible.

Figure 5.14 Select the small oval.

Figure 5.15 After grouping, the small oval—the most recently created group—pops to the top of the stack.

10. To make the small oval a grouped element, Choose Modify > Group.

Flash puts the small oval in a bounding box and brings it to the top of the stack (**Figure 5.15**). Flash always places the most recently created group on the top of the stack. Now you can reposition the two ovals however you like, and they won't interact.

✔ Tips

■ In terms of stacking order, drawing-objects work much like groups. Try the task above with the following changes: in step 1 set the oval tool to Object Drawing mode; skip step 5; and in step 6, set the oval tool to Merge Drawing mode. The small oval disappears behind the larger one. You don't need to group a drawing-object to keep it separate from a merge-shape.

■ You can group several shapes so that you can manipulate them as a unit but keep them in the same relationship to one another. You might, for example, make the eyes and eyebrows in a face a single group. That would let you create new facial expressions by repositioning the eye elements or changing their size.

■ You can group grouped objects. To position several merge-shapes on top of one another, group them as individuals first. Position them as you like. Then group all the items to preserve their relationship.

■ You can lock groups so that you don't accidentally move or modify them. Select the group that you want to lock. Then, choose Modify > Arrange > Lock, or press Opt-⌘-L (Mac) or Ctrl-Alt-L (Windows). You can no longer select the item. To make it available again, choose Modify > Arrange > Unlock All, or press Opt-Shift-⌘-L (Mac) or Ctrl-Alt-Shift-L (Windows). You can't unlock locked items selectively.

WORKING WITH GROUPED ELEMENTS

Editing Groups

Although you can transform a group as a whole (scale, rotate, and skew it), you can't directly edit the individual shapes within the group the way you can edit an ungrouped shape. To edit the shapes within a group, you must use the Edit Selected command.

To edit the contents of a group:

1. In the Tools panel, select the selection tool.

2. On the Stage, select the group you want to edit.

3. Choose Edit > Edit Selected.

   Flash enters group-editing mode (**Figure 5.16**). The Edit Bar just above the Stage Timeline changes to indicate that you're in group-editing mode. The bounding box for the selected group disappears, and Flash dims all the items on the Stage that aren't part of the selected group. These dimmed items aren't editable; they merely provide context for editing the selected group.

Document-editing mode

Click the Back button to return to document-editing mode

Group-editing mode

Double-click away from the group to return to document-editing mode

Grayed shapes don't belong to the group that's being edited

Figure 5.16 These eyes and eyebrows are a selected group (top). In group-editing mode (bottom), the other items on the Stage are grayed out to indicate that you can't edit them.

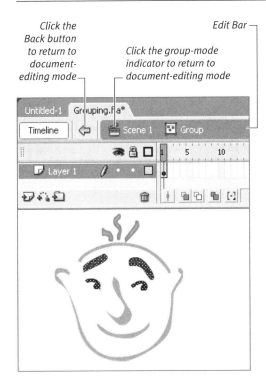

Click the Back button to return to document-editing mode

Edit Bar

Click the group-mode indicator to return to document-editing mode

Figure 5.17 You have several ways to return to document-editing mode when you're editing a group. Choose Edit > Edit All or Edit Document. Or, click items in the Edit Bar: The Back button, the scene name, and the Scene pop-up menu (not shown) all let you resume editing the movie.

4. Make changes to the contents of the group.

5. To return to document-editing mode, *do one of the following:*

▲ Choose Edit > Edit All (**Figure 5.17**).

▲ Double-click the Stage or the work area away from the shapes in the group you're editing.

▲ Click the current scene name in the Edit Bar.

▲ Click the Back button in the Edit Bar.

✔ Tips

- To enter group-editing mode quickly, double-click a grouped item on the Stage with the selection tool.

- When the Properties tab of the Property inspector is open, you can see—and change—the height, width, and x- and y-coordinates of the bounding box of a selected group (**Figure 5.18**).

- When you're editing a group nested within another group, clicking the Back button moves you up one level in the nesting hierarchy.

- You can also enter group-editing mode for a selected item by choosing Edit > Edit in Place. When you edit groups, there is no difference between this command and Edit > Edit Selected. There is a difference when you use these commands to edit symbols. You'll learn about symbols in Chapter 7.

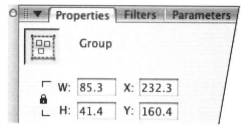

Figure 5.18 The Property inspector displays the height, width, and x- and y-coordinates for the bounding box of a group you've selected on the Stage. Enter new values to change any of those parameters.

Editing the Contents of Drawing-Objects

As you learned in Chapter 4, you can modify drawing-objects as they sit on the Stage. But you can also work directly with the merge-shapes inside the drawing-object container. To do so, you must enter drawing-object–editing mode. There is no menu command for entering this edit mode, but double-clicking a drawing-object on the Stage opens that object for editing.

In drawing-object–editing mode—as in group-editing mode—selected shapes appear in full color, and other shapes appear dimmed. In drawing-object–editing mode, you can modify or delete the original merge-shapes or add new merge-shapes. Note that a drawing-object can contain only merge-shapes. If you create a new drawing object while in drawing-object–editing mode, Flash converts your original drawing-object to its constituent merge shapes, adds the new drawing-object(s), selects all these items, and groups them.

To return to document-editing mode, use the same techniques discussed in "Editing Groups," earlier in this section.

Controlling Stacking Order

Within a single layer, text boxes, grouped objects and drawing-objects stack as if they were sitting on sublayers above any ungrouped merge-shapes. Stacking order exists even if objects don't literally lie on top of one another. If you have a group on one side of the Stage and a drawing-object on the other, you can't see which one stacks higher than the other; but if you drag the objects so they overlap, the order becomes apparent. (Symbols, which you'll learn about in Chapter 7, are another type of graphic-object that stacks on top of ungrouped merge-shapes.)

Understanding Stacking Order

Merge-shapes on a single layer always stay on the same layer, segmenting one another whenever they inhabit the same space on the Stage. All graphic-objects (drawing-objects, groups, and symbols) stack on top of one another. By default, Flash stacks each new graphic-object that you create on top of the preceding one; the last graphic-object created winds up on top of all the others (**Figure 5.19**). A higher-level graphic-object obscures any graphic-object that lies directly beneath it.

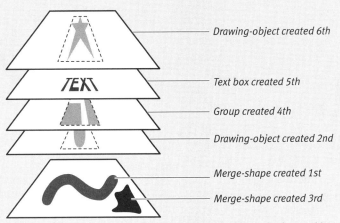

Drawing-object created 6th

Text box created 5th

Group created 4th

Drawing-object created 2nd

Merge-shape created 1st

Merge-shape created 3rd

Figure 5.19 This schematic shows Flash's default stacking order for graphic-objects. The most recently created graphic-object is on top. Merge-shapes are always on the bottom.

You can change the stacking order of graphic-objects via the Modify > Arrange menu. You can move objects up or down in the stacking order one level at a time, or you can send an object to the front or bottom of the stack of sublayers.

To change position in the stack by one level:

1. On the Stage, create at least three graphic-objects.

   Use any combination of grouped shapes or drawing-objects.

2. Select one of the graphic-objects.

3. From the Modify > Arrange menu, *choose either of the following:*

   ▲ To move the selected item up one level, choose Bring Forward, or press ⌘-up arrow (Mac) or Ctrl-up arrow (Windows).

   ▲ To move the selected item down one level, choose Send Backward, or press ⌘-down arrow (Mac) or Ctrl-down arrow (Windows).

   Flash moves the selected item up (or down) one sublayer in the stacking order (**Figure 5.20**).

To move an element to the top or bottom of the stack:

1. On the Stage, select one of the graphic-objects you created in the previous task.

2. From the Modify > Arrange menu, *choose either of the following:*

   ▲ To bring the item to the top of the stack, choose Bring to Front, or press Option-Shift-up arrow (Mac) or Ctrl-Shift-up arrow (Windows).

   ▲ To move the item to the bottom of the stack, choose Send to Back, or press Option-Shift-down arrow (Mac) or Ctrl-Shift-down arrow (Windows).

   Flash places the selected item at the top (or bottom) of the heap.

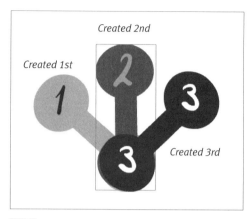

Figure 5.20 Each dumbbell here is a separate group (top). Choose Modify > Arrange > Bring Forward (middle) to move a selected group up one level in the stacking order (bottom).

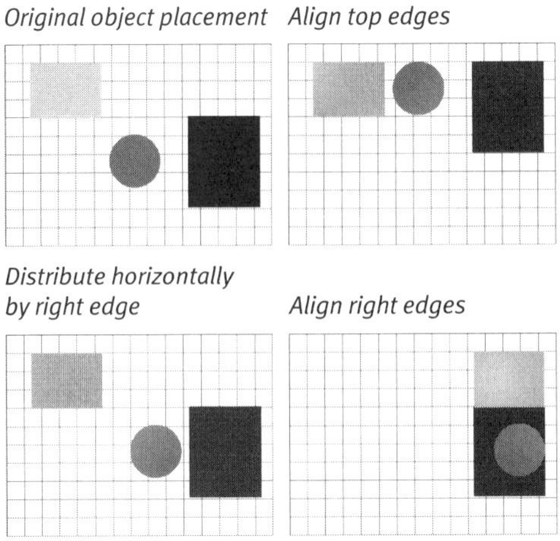

Original object placement *Align top edges*

Distribute horizontally by right edge *Align right edges*

Figure 5.21 Flash's Align panel can line up selected objects in various ways. Here are a few alignment choices used on the same set of objects.

Aligning Elements

As you get into the process of animation, you'll discover how important alignment can be. Flash's grids, guides, and Snap features (see Chapter 1) help you align items on the Stage manually. Flash also offers automated alignment through the Align panel. You can line up selected items by their top, bottom, left, or right edges or by their centers (**Figure 5.21**). You can align the items to each other or align them to the Stage—for example, you can place the top edge of all selected items at the top edge of the Stage. Flash can also resize one item to match the dimensions of another —making them the same width, for example.

To access alignment options:

◆ Choose Window > Align, or press ⌘-K (Mac) or Ctrl-K (Windows) (**Figure 5.22**). The Align panel appears (**Figure 5.23**). You can apply any of the alignment options to selected items on the Stage.

ALIGNING ELEMENTS

Figure 5.22 Choose Window > Align to open the Align panel.

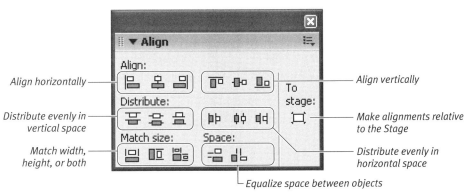

Align horizontally

Distribute evenly in vertical space

Match width, height, or both

Align vertically

Make alignments relative to the Stage

Distribute evenly in horizontal space

Equalize space between objects

Figure 5.23 The Align panel offers options for aligning selected items horizontally and vertically, distributing items evenly in horizontal or vertical space, forcing items to match each other (or the Stage) in width and height, and creating even spacing between items.

To align items:

1. On the Stage, select the items that you want to align.

2. In the Align section of the Align panel (**Figure 5.24**), *choose one of the following options:*

   ▲ Align left edge

   ▲ Align horizontal center

   ▲ Align right edge

   ▲ Align top edge

   ▲ Align vertical center

   ▲ Align bottom edge

   Flash rearranges the selected objects.

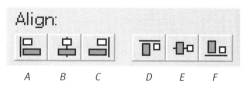

Figure 5.24 You can align items horizontally by their left edges (A), centers (B), or right edges (C). You can align items vertically by their top edges (D), centers (E), or bottom edges (F).

✔ Tips

- The Match Size section of the Align panel contains three buttons for forcing selected items to have the same width or height. To expand all items to be the same width as the widest item, choose Match Width (the far-left button); to expand all items to be the same height as the tallest item, choose Match Height (the middle button); to do both, choose Match Width and Height (the far-right button).

- You can make your alignment adjustments relative to the edges of the Stage by clicking the To Stage button. For example, with To Stage selected, choosing Align Bottom Edge puts the bottom edges of all the selected items at the bottom of the Stage. Choosing Match Size makes selected items as tall as the Stage.

- In addition to aligning items horizontally and vertically, you can create equal horizontal or vertical space among three or more items. The buttons in the Distribute section of the Align panel let you equalize the horizontal space between selected elements' left edges, centers, or right edges or equalize the vertical space between selected items' top edges, centers, or bottom edges.

- Use the Align panel's Space options to create equal horizontal or vertical space between items' inside edges.

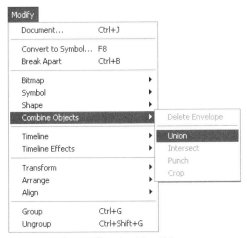

Figure 5.25 The Modify > Combine Objects menu offers commands for uniting overlapping drawing-objects in four ways.

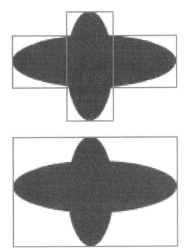

Figure 5.26 Applying the Modify > Combine Objects > Union command to drawing-object fills of the same color (top) melds the fills and creates a single drawing-object (bottom).

Combining Drawing-Objects

The shapes you create in Object Drawing mode don't interact with one another or with shapes you create in Merge Drawing mode, even when they overlap. But you can force them to do so by using the Modify > Combine objects commands.

To unite multiple drawing-objects:

1. Use the drawing tools, in Object Drawing mode, to create overlapping shapes:

   ▲ Make two or more overlapping fills with the same colors.

   ▲ Make two or more overlapping shapes with fills and strokes; use different colors for the fills and strokes in each shape.

2. Select the overlapping fills that are the same color.

3. Choose Modify > Combine Objects > Union (**Figure 5.25**).

   The two fills become a single shape (**Figure 5.26**).

continues on next page

4. Select the overlapping shapes of different colors.

5. Repeat step 3.

The fills and strokes of the shapes segment one another, but you wind up with a single drawing-object containing all those segmented shapes (**Figure 5.27**). To access those shapes, double-click the drawing-object to edit it (**Figure 5.28**).

✔ Tip

■ You can also use the Modify > Combine Objects > Union command to combine a mix of merge-shapes and drawing-objects into a single drawing-object.

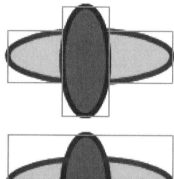

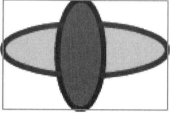

Figure 5.27 Applying the Modify > Combine Objects > Union command to shapes of different colors (top) causes the selected fills and strokes to replace and segment one another as merge-shapes would. The resulting shapes unite in a single drawing-object (bottom).

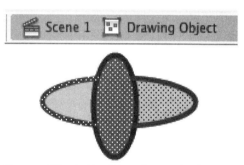

Figure 5.28 Try double-clicking the new drawing-object after you've applied Union to drawing-objects of different colors. In drawing-object–editing mode, you can see how the shapes segment one another. Each chunk of stroke and fill is a separate shape.

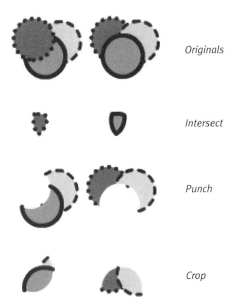

Originals

Intersect

Punch

Crop

Figure 5.29 The last three commands in the Modify > Combine Objects menu have different results depending on which object lies on top of the stack. Intersect creates a new shape from the intersection of all selected shapes, using the top shape's attributes. With Punch, the top shape takes a bite out of the others and removes it; the remaining shapes keep their original attributes. With Crop, the top shape takes the same bite but this time removes everything else; the resulting shapes keep their original attributes.

To use one drawing-object to remove part of another:

1. Use the drawing tools in Object Drawing mode to create two or more overlapping shapes with a variety of fills and strokes.

2. From the Modify > Combine Objects menu, *choose one of the following:*

    Intersect retains fills and strokes only where all the selected shapes overlap and deletes all other fills and strokes. The resulting shape(s) take stroke and fill attributes from the topmost shape.

    Punch uses the topmost drawing-object like a cookie cutter to *remove* any shapes directly below it. (Imagine the shape left in the cookie dough after you've cut out a cookie; that's what Punch creates.) The resulting shape(s) retain their original attributes.

    Crop uses the topmost object like a cookie cutter to *select* a new shape from any shapes that lie below it. (Imagine the cookie cutter again, but this time you wind up with the cookie itself.) The resulting shape(s) retain their original attributes (**Figure 5.29**).

✔ Tips

-   When you select merge-shapes, the Modify > Combine Objects menu only offers the Union command. You can use this command instead of grouping merge-shapes. The Union command preserves the spatial relationships between shapes but gives you the ability to change fills and strokes directly on the Stage as you did in Chapter 4.

-   If you choose Modify > Combine Objects > Intersect and all your shapes disappear, it means there was no place where they all intersected. That result may seem self evident, but if you've selected many shapes or your shapes are complex, it may be difficult to see.

COMBINING DRAWING-OBJECTS

Using Gradients in Multipart Shapes

When you're applying gradients to multipart graphics, you can choose whether to give each part its own separate gradient (as you learned to do in Chapter 4) or to spread one gradient across all the parts. To truly spread a single gradient across multiple shapes, you must use merge-shapes. You can create a similar effect by using drawing-objects and locked gradients, but applying gradients to drawing-objects sometimes yields unpredictable results.

To repeat one gradient in multiple fills:

1. On the Stage, create a graphic made of several fills.

    They can be merge-shapes or drawing-objects.

2. Deselect all the shapes.

3. In the Tools panel, select the paint bucket.

4. Deselect the Lock Fill modifier.

5. Define a new gradient fill, or use any Fill Color control to select an existing one (see Chapter 2).

6. Click each fill to which you want to apply the gradient.

    Flash applies the same gradient to each shape separately (**Figure 5.30**). The full range of the gradient appears within each shape.

✔ Tip

■ You can also apply separate gradients to multiple fills simultaneously. Select the fill shapes on the Stage, and then define a new gradient fill or use any Fill Color control to select an existing one. Flash applies the gradient separately to each selected shape.

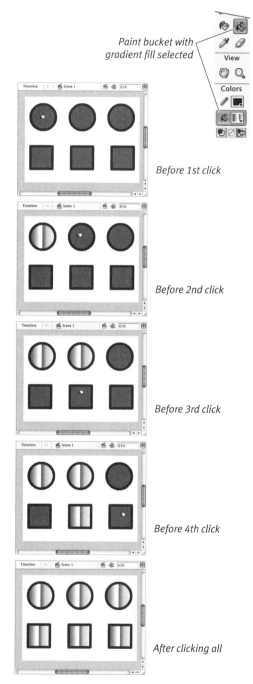

Paint bucket with gradient fill selected

Before 1st click

Before 2nd click

Before 3rd click

Before 4th click

After clicking all

Figure 5.30 Applying unlocked gradient fills to multiple shapes results in multiple versions of the full gradient. This applies both to merge-shapes (the circles) and to drawing-objects (the squares).

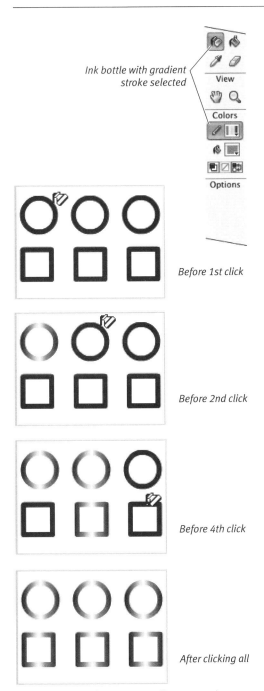

Ink bottle with gradient stroke selected

Before 1st click

Before 2nd click

Before 4th click

After clicking all

Figure 5.31 To apply separate gradients to strokes, use the ink-bottle tool to click unselected strokes.

To repeat one gradient in multiple strokes:

1. On the Stage, create a graphic made of several strokes.

   They can be merge-shapes or drawing-objects.

2. Deselect all the strokes.

3. In the Tools panel, select the ink bottle.

4. Define a new gradient stroke or use any Stroke Color control to select an existing one (see Chapter 2).

5. Click each stroke to which you want to apply the gradient.

   Flash applies the same gradient to each stroke separately (**Figure 5.31**). The full range of the gradient appears within each stroke.

✔ Tip

■ The ink bottle doesn't give you the choice to apply locked or unlocked gradients. To apply separate gradients to strokes (the equivalent of unlocked gradients), you must use the steps given in this task.

USING GRADIENTS IN MULTIPART SHAPES

To spread one gradient across multiple merge-shape fills:

1. On the Stage, create a graphic made of several merge-shape fills.

2. On the Stage, select the fills to which you want to apply the gradient.

3. In the Tools panel, select the paint bucket.

4. Deselect the Lock Fill modifier.

5. Define a new gradient fill, or use any Fill Color control to select an existing one (see Chapter 2).

   Separate gradients appear in each fill.

6. Use the paint bucket to click any of the selected merge-shape fills.

   Flash spreads a single gradient across all the selected fills (**Figure 5.32**). It's as if Flash creates an underlying gradient that fills a bounding box containing all the selected shapes; each shape reveals its portion of that underlying gradient.

✔ Tips

- Moving one of the shapes in the task above disconnects the shape's fill from the underlying gradient. The shape still shows the same slice of the gradient, but in fact the moved shape contains a separate copy of the gradient fill.

- If you select Lock Fill in step 4, Flash again spreads one gradient across all your merge-shapes, but this time Flash centers the underlying gradient at the left edge of the Stage. You can verify the location by clicking one of the shapes with the gradient-transform tool (see "To modify gradients underlying multiple merge-shapes," later in this chapter).

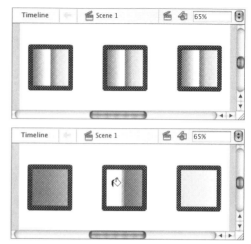

Figure 5.32 When you choose a gradient fill with several merge-shapes selected, Flash first applies separate gradients to each shape (top). When you then click one of the selected fills directly with the paint-bucket tool (and Lock Fills deselcted), Flash spreads the gradient across all the fills. For linear gradients, the center of the gradient is at the center of the selected shapes; for radial gradients, where you click becomes the center of the gradient.

- Because drawing-objects are separate containers, you can't create a single underlying gradient for multiple drawing-object fills. You can fake the appearance of doing so, however, by using the technique in the previous tip but using drawing-object fills.

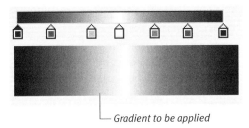

Gradient to be applied

Figure 5.33 When strokes are selected on the Stage and you choose a gradient for the stroke attribute, Flash applies separate gradients to each drawing-object stroke (the circles) and a single underlying gradient to all the selected merge-shape strokes (the squares).

Figure 5.34 When you use the ink bottle to click any stroke in a selection that includes multiple merge-shape strokes, Flash applies an underlying gradient again. This time it's centered in the merge-shape you click and overflows to the other merge-shapes.

To spread one gradient across multiple merge-shape strokes:

1. On the Stage, create an object made of several merge-shape strokes.

2. On the Stage, select the strokes to which you want to apply the gradient.

3. In the Tools panel, select the ink bottle.

4. Define a new gradient stroke, or use any Stroke Color control to select an existing one (see Chapter 2).

   Flash spreads a single gradient across all the selected merge-shape strokes; the gradient is centered within the selection (**Figure 5.33**).

✔ Tips

■ If you follow the steps of the previous task, but use drawing-object strokes, Flash centers a separate gradient within each drawing-object stroke.

■ If you use the ink bottle to directly click any of the selected merge-shape strokes, Flash applies a single underlying gradient, centering it within the shape you clicked and using the current overflow setting (see Chapter 4) to extend the gradient to the other selected shapes (**Figure 5.34**).

To modify gradients underlying multiple merge-shapes:

1. Follow the steps in the preceding tasks to create a gradient that underlies several merge-shape strokes or fills.

2. In the Tools panel, choose the gradient-transform tool.

3. Click any of the shapes that contain the underlying single gradient.

   The gradient-transform handles appear (**Figure 5.35**). You can use them to modify the gradient to make it narrower or wider, to rotate it or change its center point (see Chapter 4).

Gradient underlying merge-shape strokes

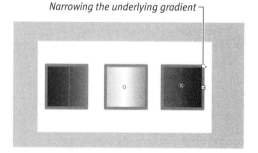

Gradient underlying merge-shape fills, centered across shapes

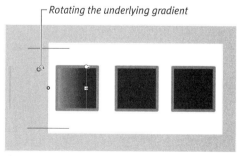

Gradient underlying merge-shape fills, centered at left edge of Stage

Figure 5.35 When a single gradient underlies multiple merge-shape fills or strokes, you can click any of the shapes with the gradient-transform tool and modify the gradient beneath all those shapes.

✔ Tip

■ When you apply locked gradient fills to drawing-objects, each object contains a separate virtual gradient; their centers line up at the left side of the Stage. If you try to modify the gradient inside one of these drawing-objects by using the gradient-transform tool, you'll see that they're in fact separate gradients (**Figure 5.36**).

Locked gradients in drawing-object fills

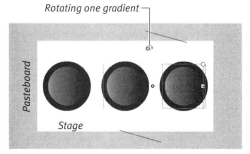

Figure 5.36 When you apply a locked gradient fill to multiple drawing-objects, it may look as if one virtual gradient underlies them all. But click one of the drawing-objects with the gradient-transform tool and modify the selected gradient, and your changes affect the color spectrum in only the object you clicked.

How Can You Tell What You're Painting or Erasing?

Flash provides accurate previews only when you use the Paint/Erase Normal modes. In the complex painting modes, the brush tool paints a temporary fill over every object it touches on the Stage, obscuring all fills and lines below. When you release the mouse button, Flash calculates and redraws the new fill according to the paint mode you've selected in the Tools panel. Similarly, with the eraser tool, Flash temporarily obliterates everything the eraser touches, creating the proper erasure only after you release the mouse button.

About the Complex Paint and Erase Modes

In addition to Paint Normal mode, where you have a choice of creating merge-shape fills (which interact with other merge-shapes) or drawing-object fills (which don't), and Erase Normal mode (where the eraser eats up everything you drag it over), Flash offers four special modes that govern the way that brushstroke fills (**Figure 5.37**) or erasures (**Figure 5.38**) interact with existing strokes and fills.

Note that the Object Drawing button is disabled when you choose one of the special brush modes, and it isn't even an option when you choose the eraser tool.

When the brush or eraser is set to Paint/Erase Selected Fills or Paint/Erase Inside, it isn't supposed to affect strokes. However, these tools do occasionally create a gap when they intersect strokes that have a stroke-height setting greater than 1 pixel. If this happens to you, undo your brushstroke or erasure and try it again. Try not to touch the exact same spot in the stroke that left a gap before.

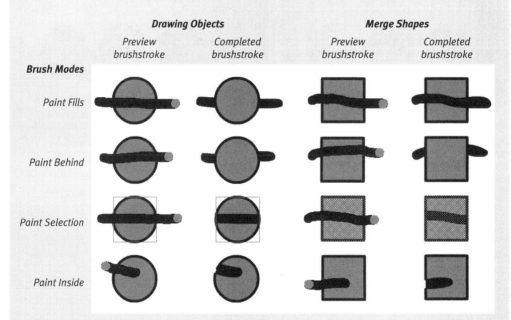

Figure 5.37 The special paint modes give you extra control over how the tools work with existing strokes and fills on the Stage. They behave somewhat differently with merge-shapes and drawing-objects.

USING GRADIENTS IN MULTIPART SHAPES

The eraser tool in Erase Inside mode does not work on copies of drawing-objects. If you're trying to erase inside a drawing-object and nothing's happening, select the drawing-object and break it apart (choose Modify > Break Apart), then choose Modify > Combine Objects > Union to restore it to drawing-object status. Erase Inside works on the restored drawing-object.

In the special paint modes, the paint brush tool always creates merge-shapes. This means that some of the names of the special modes can be a bit misleading. Paint Behind can truly paint a full brush stroke behind a drawing-object; but a merge-shape segments the brush stroke (**Figure 5.39**).

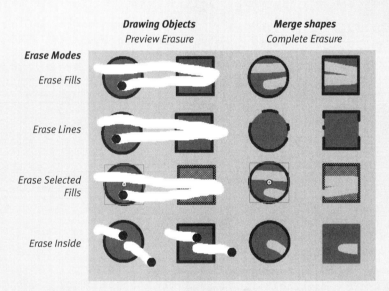

Figure 5.38 The special erase modes control how the eraser deals with strokes and fills.

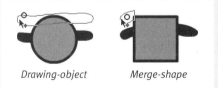

Drawing-object   *Merge-shape*

Figure 5.39 Using the paint brush tool in one of the special painting modes always creates merge-shape fills. These brush strokes were created in Paint Behind mode. The merge-shape segements the brushstroke, chopping out the middle of the brushstroke shape, the drawing-object doesn't.

GRAPHICS ON MULTIPLE LAYERS

6

In Flash 8, you create an illusion of three-dimensional depth by overlapping graphic elements. As you learned in Chapter 5, you can create this overlapping effect on one layer by stacking drawing-objects, groups, and symbols. The more elements the layer contains, however, the more difficult it becomes to manipulate and keep track of their stacking order. Layers help you to bring that task under control.

You can think of a Flash document as being like a stack of filmstrips: a sheaf of long, clear acetate strips divided into frames. Each filmstrip is analogous to a Flash layer. Shapes painted on the top filmstrip obscure shapes on lower strips; where the top filmstrip is blank, elements from lower strips show through.

When you place items on separate layers, it's easy to control and rearrange the way the items stack up. You can make shapes appear to be closer to the viewer by putting them in a higher layer. Additionally, raw shapes on different layers don't interact, so you don't need to worry about grouping merge-shapes or having one merge-shape inadvertently delete another. You can hide and show layers and label them to make it easier to work with multiple layers and elements in a Flash document.

Touring the Timeline's Layer Features

Flash graphically represents each layer as one horizontal section of the Timeline and provides controls for viewing and manipulating these graphic representations. Several features make it easier to work with graphics on layers, such as viewing the items on layers as outlines and assigning different colors to those outlines so you can easily see which items are on which layers. You can lock layers so you don't edit their contents accidentally, and you can hide layers to make it easier to work with individual graphics in a welter of other graphics. You can create special guide layers for help in positioning elements, masks for hiding and revealing layer contents selectively, and guides for animating motion along a path. (You learn more about motion paths in Chapter 9.)

Complex movies contain dozens of layers. Viewing and navigating such hefty Timelines can get tedious and confusing. Flash lets you create layer folders to organize the layers in a movie. You can keep all the layers related to one character or element together in one folder, for example. Flash considers a folder to be another type of layer, and the methods for adding and deleting layer folders are similar to those for adding and deleting layers. Layer folders don't by themselves hold graphic content, however, and folders have neither frames nor keyframes in the Timeline. (Keyframes are special frames in which you place your graphic elements; you'll learn about them in Chapter 7.)

Figure 6.1 offers a road map to the important layer features in the Timeline.

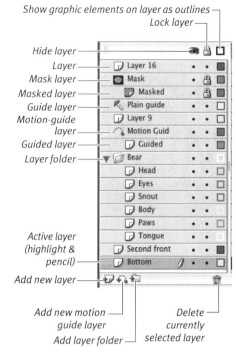

Figure labels (clockwise): Show graphic elements on layer as outlines · Lock layer · Hide layer · Layer · Mask layer · Masked layer · Guide layer · Motion-guide layer · Guided layer · Layer folder · Active layer (highlight & pencil) · Add new layer · Add new motion guide layer · Add layer folder · Delete currently selected layer

Figure 6.1 The Timeline represents all the layers in a Flash movie graphically. Layer folders let you organize layers in a complex movie. You can do much of the work of creating and manipulating layers and folders by clicking buttons in the Timeline.

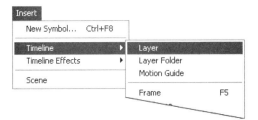

Figure 6.2 Choose Insert > Timeline > Layer to add a new layer to the Timeline.

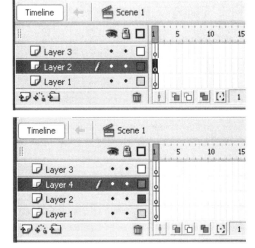

Figure 6.3 Select the layer that you want to wind up beneath the new layer (top); Flash inserts a new layer directly above the selected layer and gives the new layer a default name (bottom).

Creating and Deleting Layers and Folders

You can add new layers and layer folders as you need them while creating the ingredients of a particular scene in your movie.

To add layers and folders:

1. In the Timeline, select a layer or folder layer.

   Flash always adds the new layer or folder directly above the one you selected, so be sure to select the layer or folder that should wind up directly beneath the new one. To add a layer or folder beneath the current bottom layer, create the layer first, and then click and drag it to reposition it at the bottom of the stack.

2. To add a layer, *do either of the following*:
   ▲ Choose Insert > Timeline > Layer (**Figure 6.2**).
   ▲ In the Timeline, click the Insert Layer button.

   Flash adds a new layer and gives it a default name—for example, *Layer 4* (**Figure 6.3**).

continues on next page

3. To add a folder, *do either of the following:*

▲ Choose Insert > Timeline > Layer Folder.

▲ In the Timeline, click the Insert Layer Folder button.

Flash adds a new layer folder and gives it a default name—for example, *Folder 1* or *Folder 2* (**Figure 6.4**).

Flash bases the number in the default names on the number of layers or folders already created in the active scene of the movie, not on the number of layers and folders that currently exist. Flash tracks layer and folder numbers separately; the first folder you insert among numerous layers gets the name *Folder 1.*

To delete layers or folders:

1. In the Timeline, select the layer or folder you want to delete.

2. Click the Trash icon (**Figure 6.5**).

Flash removes that layer (and all its frames) or that folder (and all the layers it contains) from the Timeline.

✔ Tip

■ The contextual menu for layers offers some choices that otherwise are available only via buttons in the Timeline—for example, the Delete Layer and Delete Folder commands (**Figure 6.6**). To access this menu, Control-click a layer on the Mac or right-click it in Windows.

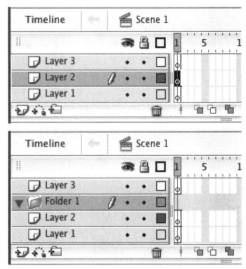

Figure 6.4 Select the layer that should be below the new folder (top). Flash creates a new folder above the layer you selected (bottom). Flash names new folders based on the number of folders that have been created in the current scene of the movie.

Delete layer or folder

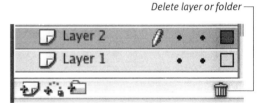

Figure 6.5 Click the Trash icon to delete a selected layer or folder.

Figure 6.6 The contextual menu for layers gives you easy access to layer commands, including some that you can otherwise access only via buttons—for example, Delete Layer. To access the contextual menu for layers, Control-click (Mac) or right-click (Windows) the icon of the layer you want to work with.

Layer selected for deletion

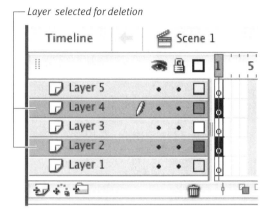

After deletion

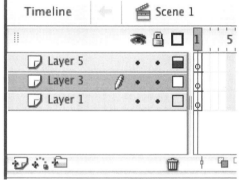

Figure 6.7 To delete noncontiguous layers, ⌘-click (Mac) or Ctrl-click (Windows) the layers you want to add to your selection; then click the Trash icon.

To delete multiple layers and/or folders:

1. In the Timeline, select the first layer or folder you want to remove.

2. ⌘-click (Mac) or Ctrl-click (Windows) every layer or folder you want to remove.

   This method of selection allows you to choose multiple layers that aren't contiguous (**Figure 6.7**).

3. Click the Trash icon.

   Flash removes the selected layers (and their frames) from the Timeline.

   If your selection includes folders containing layers, a dialog appears, warning that deleting the layer folder will also delete all the layers it contains.

4. To delete the folder and its layers, click Yes.

   or

   To cancel the delete operation, click No.

✔ Tips

- You can also Control-click (Mac) or right-click (Windows) selected layers or folders to bring up the context menu, which contains commands for deleting layers and folders.

- To select a range of layers, click the lowest layer you want to delete; then Shift-click the highest layer you want to delete. Flash selects the clicked layers and all the layers in between.

- You can drag selected layers to the Trash icon to delete them instead of selecting and clicking the Trash icon in two steps.

- You can't delete all the layers in the Timeline. If you select all the layers and folders and click the Trash icon, Flash keeps the bottom layer and deletes the rest. Even if the bottom layer is nested in a folder, Flash keeps it and promotes it to regular layer status.

Controlling Layers and Folders

Layer properties are the settings that define the look and function of a layer. Remember that layer folders are also a type of layer in Flash. You can name layers and folders. You can hide or show layers and folders, lock them to prevent editing their contents, and view them in outline form. Flash generally gives you two ways to control the properties of a selected layer or folder: set the property in the Layer Properties dialog, or set the property via button controls located in the Timeline.

To work with the Layer Properties dialog:

1. In the Timeline, select the layer whose properties you want to define or change.

2. Choose Modify > Timeline > Layer Properties.

   The Layer Properties dialog appears (**Figure 6.8**).

3. To name the layer, enter text in the Name field.

4. To define the layer type, *select one of the following radio buttons.*
   - ▲ Normal
   - ▲ Guide (can be set only via the Layer Properties dialog or the contextual menu)
   - ▲ Guided
   - ▲ Mask
   - ▲ Masked
   - ▲ Folder

   For a description of layer types, see the sidebar "Layer Types Defined."

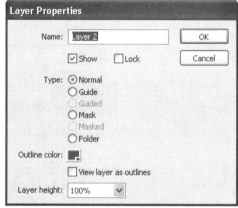

Figure 6.8 You can define a layer's type and other features in the Layer Properties dialog. Most of these properties can also be set directly in the Timeline. The only properties that can't be set in the Timeline are Layer Height, Outline Color, and Type: Guide (which makes the layer act as a set of guide lines for positioning elements).

Layer Properties Dialog vs. Timeline-Based Layer Controls

If you just want to set layer visibility, lock layer contents, or view layer elements as outlines, it makes no difference whether you call up the Layer Properties dialog to do so or click the various layer-property controls in the Timeline. Selecting a property in the dialog offers no more permanence than setting that property in the Timeline.

The Layer Properties dialog does offer functions that lack button equivalents: creating plain guide layers, changing the height of a layer in Timeline view, choosing an outline color, and changing an existing layer from one type to another.

The Timeline offers the capability to create motion guides, whereas the Layer Properties dialog doesn't.

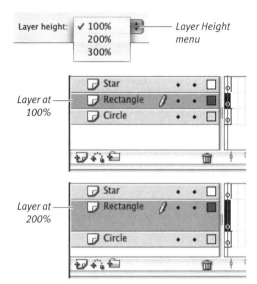

Figure 6.9 Choose a larger percentage from the Layer Height menu in the Layer Properties dialog to increase the height of a selected layer.

5. To make the contents of a layer (or folder layer) invisible, deselect the Show check box.

To make the contents visible, select the box.

6. To prevent changes in contents of a layer or folder, select the Lock check box.

To permit changes, deselect the box.

7. To view the contents of a layer as outlines, select the "View layer as outlines" check box.

To view the contents as solid graphic elements, deselect the box.

8. To choose a color for the outlines on this layer, use the Outline Color control to choose a color (see Chapter 2, "Creating Solid Colors and Gradients").

You can change this property only via the Layer Properties dialog.

9. To change the height at which layers or folders display in the Timeline, choose a percentage from the Layer Height pop-up menu (**Figure 6.9**).

Flash offers two enlarged layer views. The larger layers in the Timeline are especially useful for working with sounds. The waveform of each sound appears in the layer preview in the Timeline, and some sounds are difficult to see at the 100% setting. (You learn more about sounds in Chapter 15.)

You can change this property only via the Layer Properties dialog.

10. Click OK.

Flash applies all the selected settings to the current layer.

CONTROLLING LAYERS AND FOLDERS

175

✔ Tips

■ To change the size of the graphic representation of all the layers in the Timeline, choose a size from the Frame View pop-up menu located in the top-right corner of the Timeline. The Preview and Preview in Context options display thumbnails of the contents of each frame in the layers.

■ To change a folder into a regular layer, change its layer type to Normal. Because layer folders have no frames in the Timeline, the first frame of the resulting layer winds up without a keyframe. If you try to draw on the layer right away, you'll get an error message. To make the layer usable, add a keyframe to frame 1. (For more information about working with keyframes, see Chapter 8.)

■ Double-clicking the folded-page icon or folder icon in the Timeline opens the Layer Properties dialog for that layer or folder.

■ When you select the "View layer as outlines" check box for a layer folder, Flash displays the contents of all the layers contained in the folder as outlines. Although you can specify an outline color for a layer folder, the color has no effect on what you see on the Stage. When you turn on outline view for the folder, each layer within the folder displays its contents in the outline color set for that layer.

■ You can tell Flash to use the layer-outline color for the bounding box that highlights selected graphic elements. Doing so helps you keep track of the fact that selections are on different layers. Open the Preferences dialog—from the Flash menu (Mac) or Edit menu (Windows), choose Preferences—choose the General category and click the Use Layer Color button in the Color Highlight section.

Layer Types Defined

Flash creates six types of layers:

Normal. The default layer type is normal; all the items in a normal layer appear in your final movie.

Guide. Flash creates two types of guide layers: *guides* and *motion guides*. Lines or shapes on plain guide layers serve as reference points for placing and aligning elements on the Stage. You can define plain guide layers via the Layer Properties dialog or the contextual menu. A merge-shape line on a motion-guide layer becomes a path that an animated graphic element can follow (see Chapter 9). You can't define motion-guide layers directly from the Layer Properties dialog; you must set them from the Timeline or from the contextual menu for layers. Graphic elements on both types of guide layers do not get exported to the final movie. (You can use guide layers to make notes to yourself; they'll be deleted when you publish your document.)

Guided. Guided layers contain the graphic elements that will animate by following the path on a motion guide layer. You must link the guided layer to the motion-guide layer.

Mask. A mask layer hides and reveals portions of linked layers that lie directly beneath the mask layer.

Masked. Masked layers contain elements that can be hidden or revealed by a mask layer.

Folder. Folder layers allow you to organize layers hierarchically. Setting the layer properties of a folder automatically sets the properties for all the layers within that folder. Collapsing (or expanding) folders hides (or reveals) the frames for all the layers within that folder in the Timeline.

Setting Layer Properties via the Timeline

The Timeline represents each layer or layer folder as a horizontal field containing a name and three buttons for controlling the way the layer or folder's contents look on the Stage. You can hide a layer or folder (making all the elements on that layer or within that folder temporarily invisible), lock a layer or folder (making the contents visible but uneditable), and view the items on the layer or within the folder as outlines. These controls are helpful when you're editing numerous items on several layers.

To rename a layer or folder:

1. In the Timeline, double-click the layer or folder name.

Flash activates the name's text-entry field.

2. Type a new name.

3. Press Enter, or click anywhere outside the name field.

To hide the contents of a layer or folder:

◆ In the Timeline for the layer or folder that you want to hide, click the bullet in the column below the eye icon (**Figure 6.10**).

Flash replaces the bullet with a red X, indicating that the contents of the layer or folder no longer appear on the Stage. The invisible setting doesn't affect the final movie. When you publish a movie (see Chapter 16), Flash includes all the contents of hidden layers and folders.

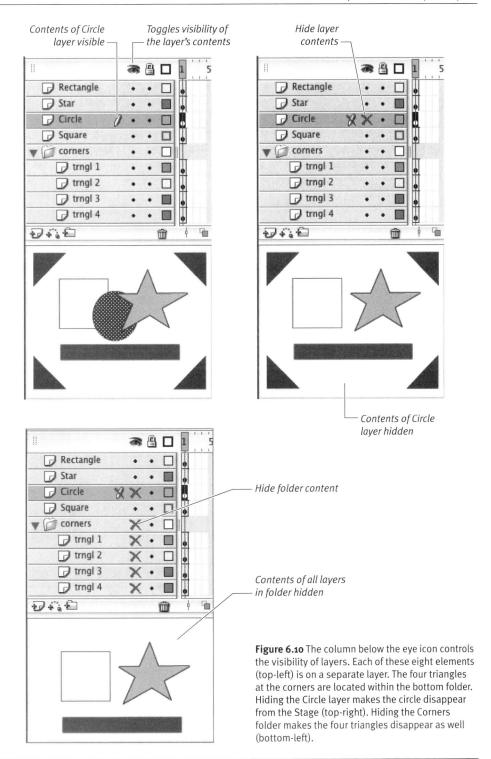

Contents of Circle layer visible

Toggles visibility of the layer's contents

Hide layer contents

Contents of Circle layer hidden

Hide folder content

Contents of all layers in folder hidden

Figure 6.10 The column below the eye icon controls the visibility of layers. Each of these eight elements (top-left) is on a separate layer. The four triangles at the corners are located within the bottom folder. Hiding the Circle layer makes the circle disappear from the Stage (top-right). Hiding the Corners folder makes the four triangles disappear as well (bottom-left).

SETTING LAYER PROPERTIES VIA THE TIMELINE

To show the hidden contents of a layer or folder:

◆ In the Timeline for the layer or folder that you want to show, click the red *X* in the column below the eye icon.

Flash replaces the *X* with a bullet and displays the contents of the layer or folder.

To lock a layer or folder:

◆ In the Timeline for the layer or folder that you want to lock, click the bullet in the column below the padlock icon (**Figure 6.11**).

Flash replaces the bullet with a padlock icon. The contents of the layer or folder appear on the Stage, but you can't edit them. Locking a layer or folder doesn't affect the final movie.

To unlock a layer or folder:

◆ In the Timeline for the layer or folder that you want to unlock, click the padlock icon.

Flash replaces the padlock with a bullet and makes the contents of the layer or folder editable.

To view the contents of a layer or folder as outlines:

◆ In the Timeline for the layer or folder that you want to view as outlines, click the solid square in the column below the square icon (**Figure 6.12**).

Flash replaces the solid square with a hollow square, indicating that the layer or folder is in outline mode. The contents of a layer appear on the Stage as outlines in the color that the square indicates. The elements on each layer within a folder appear in the outline color associated with their own layer, not in the outline color of the folder. Placing a layer or folder in outline mode doesn't affect the final movie.

SETTING LAYER PROPERTIES VIA THE TIMELINE

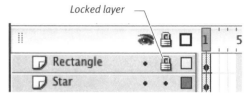

Locked layer

Figure 6.11 The padlock icon indicates that a layer is locked. The contents of a locked layer appear on the Stage, but you can't edit them.

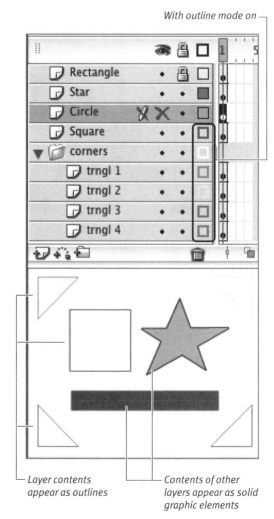

With outline mode on

Layer contents appear as outlines

Contents of other layers appear as solid graphic elements

Figure 6.12 A hollow square in the outline-mode column indicates that graphic elements on that layer appear as outlines. Setting a folder to outline mode automatically changes all the layers within it to outline mode.

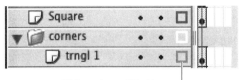

Click to view solid objects

Figure 6.13 Clicking the hollow square in the outline-mode column returns you to viewing the contents of that layer or folder as solid graphic elements.

To view the contents of a layer or folder as solid graphic elements:

◆ In the Timeline for the layer or folder whose contents you want to view as solid, click the hollow square (**Figure 6.13**).

Flash replaces the hollow square with a solid square, indicating that the layer or folder is no longer in outline mode. The contents of the layer or folder appear on the Stage as solid graphic elements.

Working with Layer-View Columns

Flash provides several shortcuts for working with the three layer-view columns in the Timeline. The following tips describe hiding and showing layer or folder content; the controls in the Timeline for locking and unlocking layer contents and for viewing layer contents as outlines work the same way.

◆ To hide the contents of several layers or folders quickly, click the bullet in the column below the eye icon and drag through all the layers or folders you want to hide. As the pointer passes over each bullet, Flash changes it to a red *X*.

◆ To show numerous layers or folders quickly, click a red *X* in the eye column and drag through all the layers or folders whose contents you want to show.

◆ To hide the contents of all layers or folders but one, Option-click (Mac) or Alt-click (Windows) the bullet in the eye column of the layer or folder you want to see. Flash puts an *X* in that column for all the other layers or folders.

◆ To hide the contents of all the layers and folders, ⌘-click (Mac) or Ctrl-click (Windows) the eye column of any layer or folder, or click the eye icon in the column header. Flash puts an *X* in that column for all the layers. To show the contents of all the layers and folders, ⌘-click or Ctrl-click an *X* or click the eye icon again.

Controlling Layer Visibility in the Timeline

In addition to controlling the visibility and editability of the contents of a layer or folder, when you organize layers in folders, you gain control of which layers appear in the Timeline. When you close a folder, layers within it disappear from the Timeline; making it much easier to view and navigate. Closing the layer folder has no effect on the contents of each layer within it, however. All the elements on those layers continue to display on the Stage in whatever mode you chose for them before closing the folder.

When you create new layer folders, they are open by default.

To close layer folders in the Timeline:

◆ In the Timeline, click the triangle to the left of the open folder icon (**Figure 6.14**).

The triangle rotates to the closed position, and the icon changes to a closed folder. The Timeline hides all the layers contained within the layer folder.

To open layer folders in the Timeline:

◆ In the Timeline, click the triangle to the left of the closed folder icon.

The triangle rotates to the open position, and the icon changes to an open folder. The Timeline displays all the layers contained within the layer folder.

✔ Tip

■ You can open or close all the folders in a movie at the same time via the contextual menu. Access the menu by Control-clicking (Mac) or right-clicking (Windows) any Timeline layer. Then, choose Expand All Folders or Collapse All Folders (**Figure 6.15**).

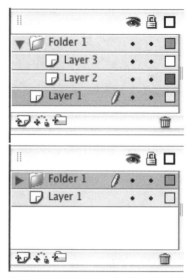

Figure 6.14 Clicking the triangle to the left of the folder icon toggles between open (top) and closed (bottom) folder views.

Figure 6.15 To open all folders at the same time, Control-click (Mac) or right-click (Windows) any layer to access the contextual menu for layers. Then choose Expand All Folders.

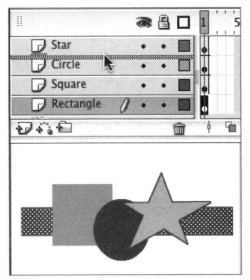

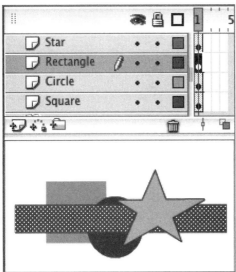

Figure 6.16 The gray line (top) represents the new location for the Rectangle layer you're dragging. Release the mouse button to drop the layer into its new position. Flash selects the layer and its contents (bottom). The rectangle shape moves from the bottom of the heap, below the square and circle, to just under the star.

Controlling the Stacking Order of Layers

As you add more layers to your document, you may need to rearrange them so that the graphic elements that should appear in the foreground cover graphic elements that appear in the background.

Layers make it easy to change the stacking order of numerous elements at the same time. You can, for example, bring all the elements on one layer to the top of the stack by dragging that layer to the top of the list in the Timeline. Doing so brings those elements to the front of the Stage (overlapping any items on other layers) in every frame of the movie.

To reorder layers:

1. In a document with several layers, in the Timeline, position the mouse pointer over the layer you want to move.

2. Click and drag the layer.

 Flash previews the layer's new location with a thick gray line.

3. Position the preview line in the layer order you want (**Figure 6.16**).

4. Release the mouse button.

 Flash moves the layer to the new location and selects it in the Timeline.

Organizing Layers in Folders

After you have created folders, you can drag existing layers into the folders to organize the Timeline. Repositioning a folder in the Timeline changes the stacking order of all the layers within that folder.

To move existing layers into folders:

1. In a document with several layers and folders, in the Timeline, position the mouse pointer over the layer you want to place in a folder.

2. Click and drag the layer over the folder where you want to place it.

   As you drag, Flash previews the layer's new location with a thick gray line; when you position the mouse directly over a folder, the preview line disappears. On Windows, the folder icon also highlights, turning gray (**Figure 6.17**).

3. Release the mouse button.

   Flash moves the layer into the folder, indents the layer name in the Timeline, selects the layer in the Timeline, and selects the layer's contents on the Stage.

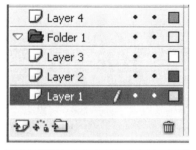

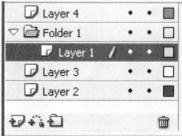

Figure 6.17 When you drag a layer over a folder layer, the preview bar disappears (in Windows, the folder icon also turns gray) (top). Release the mouse button to drop the layer into that folder. Flash selects the layer and its contents (bottom).

Drag right to position inside folder

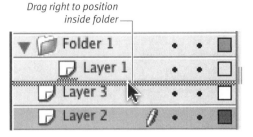

Drag left to position outside folder

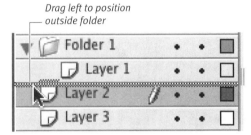

Figure 6.18 When you position layers at the bottom of a folder, you need to let Flash know whether you want the layers to wind up inside or outside the folder. The bump on top of the preview bar for the layer indicates where the layer will go.

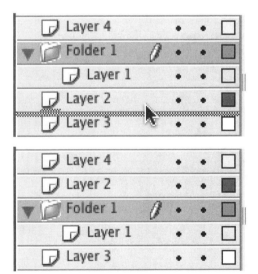

Figure 6.19 You reposition folder layers the same way you reposition other layers. Drag the folder, preview the location (top), and release the mouse button to place the folder (bottom).

✔ Tips

■ Positioning layers beneath an open folder containing layers is a bit tricky. When you position a layer's preview line after the last layer in the folder, Flash defaults to adding the layer to the folder. You can close the folder to prevent putting the layer inside the folder. Or, with the folder open, watch the layer's preview line carefully as you drag. With the layer in position beneath the last layer in the folder, drag slightly to the left. The gray bump on the top of the preview bar moves over to the left (**Figure 6.18**). Release the mouse button, and the layer winds up outside the folder.

■ To change the order of folder layers in the stack of Timeline layers click and drag the folder. Flash previews the folder's new location with a thick grayline (**Figure 6.19**). Release the mouse button; Flash moves the folder layer and selects it in the Timeline. The contents of the layers in the folder aren't selected on the Stage.

■ To nest folders within folders, drag one existing folder into another. Or, select a layer within a folder, and choose Insert > Timeline > Layer Folder (or click the Insert Layer Folder button).

Working with Graphics on Different Layers

Unless you lock shapes, or lock or hide layers, the graphics on all layers are available for editing, but you can add shapes only to the active layer (the one that's currently selected). You can use any of the techniques you learned in Chapter 4 to modify merge-shapes and drawing-objects.

To activate a layer:

◆ To select the layer where you want to add a graphic-object, *do either of the following:*

▲ In the Timeline, click the layer name.

The area containing the layer name highlights and a pencil icon appears to the right of the layer name. Flash selects all the graphic-objects on that layer.

▲ On the Stage, click a graphic-object.

Flash selects that graphic-object and highlights the layer name as described above.

To edit shape outlines on inactive layers:

1. In a document with shapes on two or more layers, using the selection tool, position the pointer over a shape on an inactive layer (one without the pencil icon).

The curve or corner-point icon appears.

2. Drag the outline of the shape on the inactive layer.

3. Release the mouse button.

Flash redraws the shape (**Figure 6.20**). The layer that was active originally remains active.

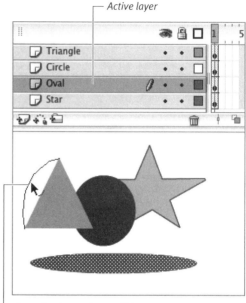

Active layer

Use selection tool to modify shape on inactive layer

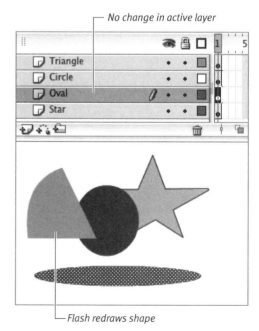

No change in active layer

Flash redraws shape

Figure 6.20 Oval is the active layer, but you can still edit shapes on inactive layers. Modifying a shape's outline with the selection tool doesn't activate the shape's layer.

Active layer

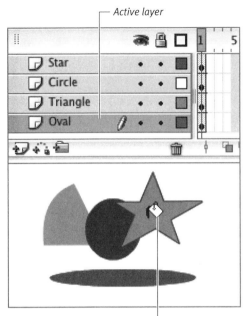

Use paint bucket to modify
fill on inactive layer

No change in active layer

Flash fills shape with new color

Figure 6.21 Using the paint-bucket tool to change a
fill color on an inactive layer doesn't activate that layer.

To edit fills across layers:

1. In a document with shapes on two or
   more layers, select the paint-bucket tool
   from the Tools panel.

2. From the Color Mixer panel, choose a
   new color.

3. Position the paint-bucker over a shape
   on an inactive layer and click.

   Flash fills the shape with the new color,
   but the layer remains inactive
   (**Figure 6.21**).

✔ Tip

- When you're working with merge-shapes,
  get into the habit of creating each one on
  a separate layer. That way, if you need to
  tweak the stacking order, you can. It won't
  hurt to have drawing-objects on separate
  layers too; more layers don't increase the
  file size of your final movie.

WORKING WITH GRAPHICS ON DIFFERENT LAYERS

Cutting and Pasting Between Layers

Flash allows you to create and place graphics only on the active layer of a document. But you can copy, cut, or delete elements from any visible, unlocked layer. You can select items on several layers, cut them, and then paste them all into a single layer. Or, cut items individually from one layer, and redistribute them to separate layers.

To paste across layers:

1. Create or open a document that contains several layers.

2. Place at least one element on all but one layer.

   To make the elements easier to work with, create them as drawing-objects, or group each merge-shape. Leave one layer empty.

3. On the Stage, select a shape.

   Flash highlights the layer in the Timeline.

5. Choose Edit > Copy.

6. In the Timeline, select the empty layer.

7. Choose Edit > Paste in Center.

   Flash pastes the copy of the shape in the empty layer, in the middle of the window (**Figure 6.22**). Now you can move the shape to a new position, if you wish.

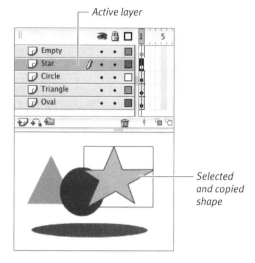

Active layer

Selected and copied shape

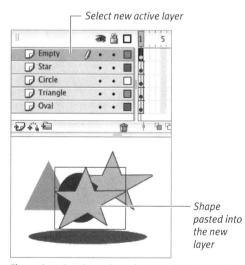

Select new active layer

Shape pasted into the new layer

Figure 6.22 Copying a shape from one layer to another involves selecting the shape (top), copying it, selecting the target layer, and then pasting the copy there. The Paste in Center command (middle) positions the pasted shape in the center of the window (bottom).

Active layer is the layer of the item last selected

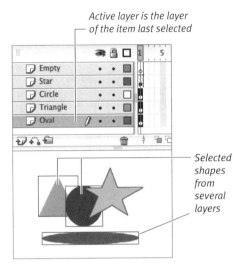

Selected shapes from several layers

After cutting the shapes

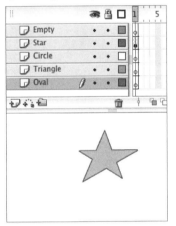

Figure 6.23 The first step in consolidating items from several layers on a single new layer involves selecting all the items and cutting them. Later, you'll paste them into the new active layer.

To use the Paste in Place command across layers:

1. In a document that has several layers containing shapes and one layer that has no shapes, select one shape.

   In the Timeline, the layer containing the selected shape becomes the active layer.

2. Using the techniques you learned in Chapter 4, add other shapes to your selection.

   In the Timeline, the layer containing the most recent addition to the selection becomes the active layer.

3. Choose Edit > Cut.

   Flash removes the selected shapes (**Figure 6.23**).

4. In the Timeline, select the empty layer.

continues on next page

Where Do Pasted Graphic Elements Go?

A Flash document can have only one layer active at a time. Any new shapes you create wind up on the currently selected, or active, layer. The same is true of placing copies of shapes or instances of symbols; if you copy and paste an element, Flash pastes the copy on the active layer. When you drag a symbol instance from the Library window, it winds up on the active layer.

5. Choose Edit > Paste in Place (**Figure 6.24**).

Flash pastes all the shapes back into their original locations on the Stage but on a different layer (**Figure 6.25**). Try hiding the empty layer temporarily; you should no longer see those shapes.

✔ Tips

■ You've already learned that selecting an element on the Stage causes Flash to select that element's layer in the Timeline. As you move elements between layers, it helps to know that selections work the other way around, too. When you select a layer in the Timeline, Flash selects all the elements for that layer on the Stage.

■ The process of cutting elements and using the Paste in Place command is, obviously, time-consuming, because you have to keep selecting new layers as you place the elements. To automate the process, use the Distribute to Layers command (see "Distributing Graphic Elements to Layers," later in this chapter).

Figure 6.24 Choose Edit > Paste in Place to paste items back into their original positions.

Shapes after pasting in place

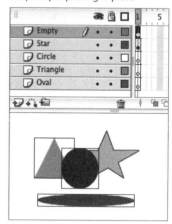

Click to hide the layer

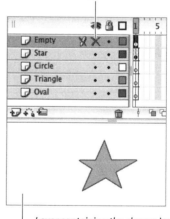

Layer containing the shapes is now hidden

Figure 6.25 The Paste in Place command positions the pasted items in the new layer. Each shape occupies the same coordinates it had on its former layer, but now all the shapes are together in the new layer. Hide the new layer to make sure you moved the elements from their old layers.

Two Ways to Paste

Flash offers two pasting modes: Paste in Center and Paste in Place. Paste in Center puts elements in the center of the open Flash window. (Note that the center of the window may not necessarily be the center of the Stage; if you want to paste to the center of the Stage, you must center the Stage in the open window.) Paste in Place puts an element at the same x- and y-coordinates it had when you cut or copied it. Paste in Place is useful for preserving the precise relationships of all elements in a scene as you move items from one layer to another.

Layers set to preview in context

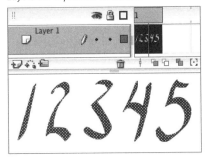

After Distribute to Layers

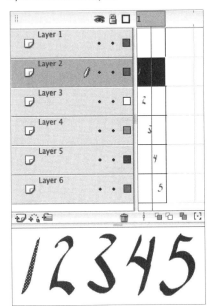

Figure 6.26 Selecting elements on the Stage and choosing Modify > Timeline > Distribute to Layers automatically cuts each element and pastes it in place in a new layer. The new layers follow the order in which you placed the elements on the Stage originally. In this series of numbers, the numeral 1 was drawn first, so it winds up at the top of the section of new layers.

Distributing Graphic Elements to Layers

As you draw elements for your movie, you may not always remember to create a new layer for each one. Using the Cut and Paste in Place commands can be tedious. Flash's Distribute to Layers feature automates the process, putting each element of a selection on a separate layer. This feature comes in handy when you start creating a type of animation called *motion tweening*, in which each element being animated must be on its own layer. (You'll learn more about motion tweening in Chapter 9.)

To place selected elements on individual layers:

1. Open a new document, and, on the Stage, create several separate shapes on a single layer.

2. Choose Edit > Select All.
   Flash highlights all the shapes.

3. Choose Modify > Timeline > Distribute to Layers, or press Shift-⌘-D (Mac) or Ctrl-Shift-D (Windows) (**Figure 6.26**).
   Flash creates a layer for each shape and adds the new layers to the bottom of the Timeline. Each shape winds up in the same location on the Stage, but on a separate layer.

✔ Tips

■ Distribute to Layers works with selected graphic-objects (text boxes, drawing-objects, groups, and symbols) as well as with selected raw shapes. (You learn about symbols in Chapter 7.) Flash distributes each selected graphic-object to its own layer; the various elements of the drawing-object, group, or symbol remain joined.

■ When you use Distribute to Layers, any unselected elements remain on their original layer. Only the selected shapes move to new layers.

Working with Guide Layers

Flash offers two types of guide layers: guides and motion guides. Plain old guides can contain any kind of content: lines, shapes, or symbols. The contents of a regular guide layer merely serve as a point of reference to help you position items on the Stage. Flash doesn't include the graphic content of guide layers in the final exported movie.

Motion-guide layers contain a single line that directs the movement of an animated element along a path. (To learn more about creating and animating with motion guides, see Chapter 9.) Another distinction to remember is that Flash creates motion guides by adding a new layer directly to the Timeline. To create plain guides, you must redefine an existing layer as a guide layer.

To create a plain guide layer:

1. *Do either of the following:*

   ▲ Create a new layer in the Timeline (for example, by clicking the Insert Layer button). Flash selects the new layer.

   ▲ Select a layer that already exists.

2. Control-click (Mac) or right-click (Windows) the layer you want to define as a guide, and choose Guide from the contextual menu (**Figure 6.27**).

   Flash turns the selected layer into a guide layer and places a little T-square icon before the layer name (**Figure 6.28**).

   You can rename the layer to identify it as a guide, if you wish.

Figure 6.27 Select Guide as the layer type in the contextual menu for layers to change a normal layer to a guide layer.

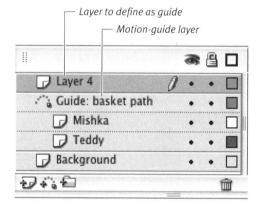

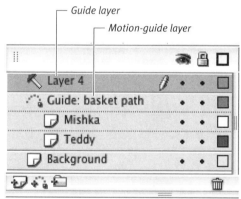

Figure 6.28 Select a layer (top) and define it as a guide layer. In the Timeline, Flash identifies the guide layer with a T-square icon; compare that with the icon for the motion-guide layer (bottom).

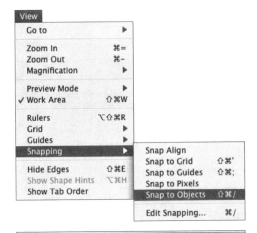

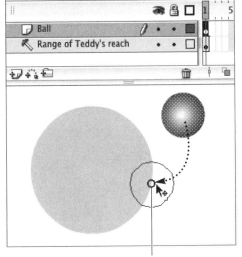

Center point snaps to other elements as you drag

Figure 6.29 Choose View > Snapping > Snap to Objects (top) to force items that you drag to snap to other lines or shapes, such as those on a guide layer (bottom).

3. To make guide elements easier to use, *do either of the following:*

▲ Choose View > Snapping > Snap to Objects (**Figure 6.29**).

Flash forces items that you draw or drag to snap to lines or shapes.

▲ Choose View > Snapping > Snap Align.

Flash displays alignment guides as you drag shapes or graphic-objects near to other shapes or graphic-objects. Now you can more easily align items to the elements on your guide layers.

✔ Tips

■ When you've placed guide elements where you need them for a certain scene, lock the guide layer so you don't move the guides accidentally as you draw on other layers.

■ The Snap to Guide feature sounds like it might help you snap to items on a guide layer, but it doesn't. The guides in this mode are the guide lines you drag out from rulers (see Chapter 1).

■ Because the graphic content of guide layers doesn't become part of your published movie, you can use guide layers as a space for making notes to yourself, or instructions to other people who may be working on the file.

Working with Mask Layers

Mask layers are special layers that allow you to hide and show elements on underlying layers. In the final movie, shapes on the Mask layer become holes that let items on linked layers show through.

Figure 6.30 Select Mask from the contextual menu for layers to define a layer as a mask.

To create a mask layer:

1. *Do either of the following:*

   ▲ Create a new layer in the Timeline (for example, by clicking the Insert Layer button). Flash selects the new layer.

   ▲ Select a layer that already exists.

   In general, you should create (or select) a layer directly above the layer containing content you want to mask, although you can always create the mask separately and link the masked layers to it later.

2. Right-click (Windows) or Control-click (Mac) the layer to access the contextual menu for layers, and choose Mask (**Figure 6.30**).

   Flash automatically defines the layer as a mask, links the layer beneath the selected layer to the mask, and locks both layers so that masking is in effect (**Figure 6.31**). You can also rename the layer to identify it as a mask, if you wish.

✔ Tips

■ To link existing layers to a mask layer quickly, drag them in the Timeline so they sit directly below the mask or one of its linked layers.

■ Once you have linked a layer to the mask, you can create additional new linked layers for that mask quickly. Select the linked (masked) layer; and then follow the steps for creating a new layer. Flash adds the new layers as masked layers directly above the selected layer.

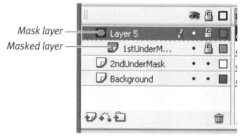

Mask layer —
Masked layer —

Figure 6.31 The mask-layer icon imitates the masking effect with a dark mask shape over a checkerboard pattern. Masked layers are indented and have a checkerboard pattern on the layer icon in the Timeline, indicating that the layer is masked.

■ Positioning a layer beneath a list of masked layers can be tricky. When you position a layer's preview line after the last layer in the masked set, you have the choice of adding the layer to the masked set or placing it at the main level of the Timeline. Use the preview line's subtle clues to place the layer where you want it. Position the layer directly beneath the last masked layer. To add the layer to the masked set, drag slightly to the right; the bump on the top of the preview bar moves over to the right. To add the layer to the main level of the Timeline, drag slightly to the left; the bump follows suit.

To create the mask:

1. Create one or more layers containing graphic elements you want to reveal only through a mask.

2. Create a mask layer above your masked-content layers, and make sure that it's selected, visible, and unlocked.

The layer should be highlighted in the Timeline, and the eye and padlock columns should contain bullets (not X or padlock icons).

3. Use the drawing tools to create a merge-shape fill on the mask layer (**Figure 6.32**).

Flash uses only fills to create the mask and ignores any strokes on the mask layer.

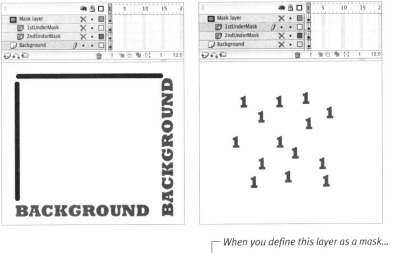

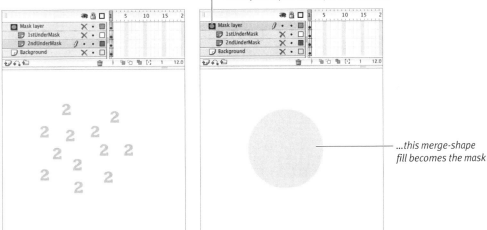

— When you define this layer as a mask...

...this merge-shape fill becomes the mask

Figure 6.32 The content for the layers that the mask will reveal is just like any other content. You create a hole in the mask from a fill shape. All the mask elements must be on the same sublevel of the layer. In other words, you must either use only merge-shapes or combine all your shapes into a single drawing-object, group, or symbol.

✔ Tips

■ It's best to limit your mask to a single merge-shape or a single graphic-object (a drawing-object, a group, a symbol, or a static text box). If the mask layer contains multiple merge-shapes, the mask may work initially. Move one of the parts, however, and Flash stops treating that shape as part of the mask. If the mask layer contains a merge-shape and a graphic-object, Flash uses just the merge-shape to create the mask. If the mask layer contains multiple graphic-objects, Flash uses just the bottom-most one. (For more details on stacking order for graphic-objects, see Chapter 5.)

■ If you want to use multiple shapes in a mask, select them and turn them into a single unit: choose Modify > Combine Objects > Union to turn them into a single drawing-object; choose Modify > Group to turn them into a single group.

■ You can also set up mask and masked layers in the Layer Properties dialog (see "Controlling Layers and Folders," earlier in this chapter).

Figure 6.33 The Show Masking command in the contextual menu for layers locks all layers linked to the selected mask.

To see the mask's effect:

◆ Lock the mask layer and all linked layers.

or

1. Control-click (Mac) or right-click (Windows) a mask (or masked) layer.

2. From the contextual menu, choose Show Masking (**Figure 6.33**).

   Flash automatically locks the mask layer and all the layers linked to it.

   In document-editing mode, you must lock the mask layer and any masked layers beneath it to see the mask effect (**Figure 6.34**). You can see the effect without locking the layers in one of Flash's test modes (see Chapter 8).

Transparent fill helps you see what the mask will reveal

Masking not on

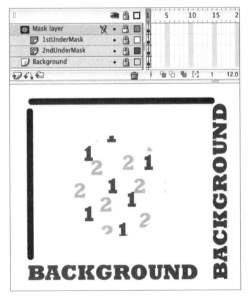

Masking turned on

Figure 6.34 After defining the mask and masked layers, you must lock them to see the mask in effect in document-editing mode.

To edit a mask:

1. In the Timeline, select the mask layer.

2. Make sure that the layer is visible and unlocked.

3. Use any of the techniques you learned in preceding chapters to create and edit fills.

✔ Tips

■ To break the connection between a mask and its linked layers, redefine the layer type for the masked layer in the Layer Properties dialog.

■ If you delete a mask layer, Flash redefines all the layers linked to it as normal layers.

■ Keep in mind that masks use processor power. Using too many masks can slow the frame rate in your final movie. In addition, masked-off areas are published in your final movie and add to file size.

The Mystery of Masks

A mask layer is like a window envelope (the ones you get bills in). The envelope may contain whole sheaves of papers covered with numbers, but the outside presents a blank white front with only a little window that lets you see the portion of the bill showing your name and address. The mask layer is the window envelope, and the linked, or masked, layers are the papers inside.

In Flash, you create the window in the envelope by drawing and painting on a mask layer. (As you'll learn in Chapter 11, you can animate that window to create special effects.) A merge-shape fill on the mask layer becomes a window in the final movie. That window reveals whatever lies on the linked (or masked) layers inside the envelope. Within that envelope, you can have several layers that act just like any other Flash layers.

Here's where it gets a bit tricky. Any areas of the envelope (the mask layer) that you leave blank hide the corresponding areas of all the layers inside the envelope (the masked layers). But the same blank areas of the envelope allow all *unlinked* layers outside and below the envelope to show through.

WORKING WITH SYMBOLS

In previous chapters, you learned to create and edit static graphics. Ultimately, you'll want to animate those graphics, and you're likely to want to use the same graphic over and over again. You may want an element to appear several times in one movie, or you may want to use the same element in several movies. You can save graphic elements for reuse by storing them in a library; to do that, you first turn the graphics into *symbols*.

Every Flash document has its own library; the library contains the symbols you create and other *assets,* reusable elements that you import for use in your movie (see the sidebar "Library Terminology").

In this chapter, you learn to work with libraries and to create symbols that are static graphics. In later chapters, you learn about creating animated symbols and buttons (see Chapters 11 and 12), working with bitmapped graphics (see Chapter 14), and adding sounds (see Chapter 15).

Library Terminology

The general term for an item stored in a Flash library is an *asset.* More specifically, graphics created with Flash's drawing tools and stored in a library are called *symbols;* fonts stored in a library are called *font symbols;* and imported sounds, video clips, and bitmaps (which are always stored in a library) are just called *sounds, video clips,* and *bitmaps.* Flash refers to each copy of a library asset that you use in a movie as an *instance* of that asset.

Understanding the Library Panel

The Library panel offers several ways to view a library's contents and allows you to organize your symbols, sounds, video clips, and bitmaps in folders. The Library panel provides information about when an item was last modified, what type of item it is, and how many times the movie uses it. The Library panel also contains shortcut buttons and menus for working with symbols. Flash has shortcuts for creating new folders, for renaming elements, and for deleting items quickly.

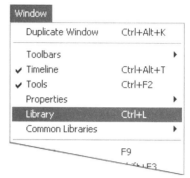

Figure 7.1 Choose Window > Library to open the Library panel of the currently active Flash document.

To open the library of the current movie:

◆ Choose Window > Library, or press ⌘-L (Mac) or Ctrl-L (Windows) (**Figure 7.1**).

The Library panel appears on the desktop (**Figure 7.2**). The Library panel contains the libraries of all the Flash documents currently open on your desktop.

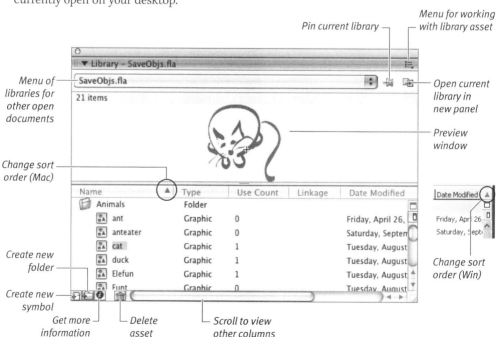

Figure 7.2 The Library panel lists the assets assigned to the current document. Items are sorted by the selected column; click the Sort Order button to reverse the current sort order.

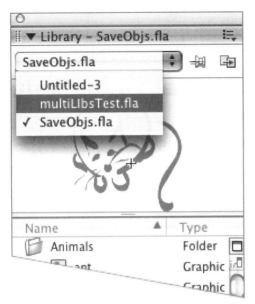

Figure 7.3 The Library panel contains the libraries of all the currently open documents. To view a different library without switching documents, choose one from the menu of open documents.

To view the library of another open document:

1. Open two or more Flash documents.

2. With the library panel, open, *do either of the following:*

   ▲ In the Library panel, from the menu of open documents, choose the desired inactive document (**Figure 7.3**)

   or

   ▲ Select the open document whose library you want to view.

   If your Preferences setting is to view open documents in a tabbed window, click that document's tab; if you're viewing documents in separate windows, click the desired window to make it active.

   The contents of the Library panel change to display the assets of the selected document.

✔ Tip

■ You can also open a separate Library panel for inactive documents. Follow the steps in the preceding task. Then, click the New Library Panel button (the one with the double-document-arrow icon) just below the Options menu. Flash opens the library in a new panel window.

To open the library of a closed Flash document:

1. Choose File > Import > Open External Library, or press Shift-⌘-O (Mac) or Ctrl-Shift-O (Windows) (**Figure 7.4**).
   The Open As Library dialog appears.

2. Navigate to the file whose library you want to open, select it, and click Open.

   The Library panel appears on the desktop, making those symbols available for use in other movies (see "Copying Symbols Between Movies" later in this chapter).

   When you open another file as a library following these steps, you can't add to or modify the contents of that library. In Windows, Flash grays out the library background. On a Mac, the change is subtler; the names of library assets are gray, but the background remains white. In addition, in the library of an external file, the shortcut icons and most of the Options-menu choices are disabled.

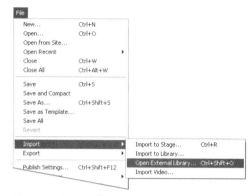

Figure 7.4 Choose File > Import > Open External Library to access symbols from the library of a closed Flash document.

✔ Tips

■ A word of warning: With multiple documents and multiple libraries open, it's easy to get confused about which library you're working with. When you open the library of an external file, Flash prevents you from making changes to the library assets. But if you have several documents and their libraries open simultaneously, it's possible to make changes to the library of an inactive document. For example, you can delete an asset from the library of a document that is open but not currently active. If you try to add a new symbol, Flash brings the inactive document forward and makes it the active document.

■ The variety of menus from which you can open a library of some sort can be daunting at first. Here's a short rundown. To open the Library panel for an open, active document, use Window > Library; to view the library of an open, inactive document, choose it from the menu of open documents in the Library panel; to open the library of a closed document, choose File > Import > Open External Library; to open one of the common libraries, choose Window > Common Libraries (see the sidebar "What Are Common Libraries?").

What Are Common Libraries?

Flash makes a set of *common libraries* available from the menu bar—a sort of library of libraries. Flash 8 ships with three common libraries, but you can add your own. The libraries in the Common Libraries menu are Flash files that live in the Libraries folder of the application-level Configuration folder (see the sidebar "The Mystery of the Configuration Folder" in Chapter 1). If you have administrative privileges, you can add FLA files to that folder. If you don't have privileges, you must add a folder named Libraries to the User-Level Configuration folder. Any files you add to that Libraries folder also appear in the Common Libraries menu when you restart the application (**Figure 7.5**). Choosing an item from the Common Libraries menu opens only the library, not the file itself.

You might create a common library to keep all the symbols, sounds, video clips, and bitmaps for a work project accessible from the menu bar. As you create or import assets, add a copy of each item to a special file and call it something like MyCurrentWork. Make the file one of your common libraries. When you choose MyCurrentWork from the Window > Common Libraries menu, Flash opens the library containing all your project's items.

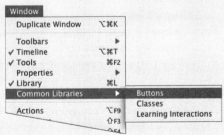

Figure 7.5 The Common Libraries menu gives you quick access to the libraries of Flash Documents located inside a Libraries folder that's available to all users.

To view the wide Library panel:

◆ In the open Library panel, click the Wide Library View button (**Figure 7.6**).

Flash widens the window to accommodate all columns.

To view the narrow Library panel:

◆ In the open Library panel, click the Narrow Library View button.

Flash narrows the window to the minimum allowable panel width.

To resize library columns:

1. In the Library panel, position the pointer over a column-head divider.

The pointer changes to a double-arrow divider-moving icon.

2. Click and drag the divider (**Figure 7.7**).

✔ Tip

■ Flash tracks how many times you use a symbol instance, but the Use Count column doesn't display the latest number automatically. To change that setting, from the Library panel's Options menu, choose Keep Use Counts Updated. (This setting can slow Flash.) To update use counts periodically, choose Update Use Counts Now as needed.

■ When in doubt about whether to make a graphic element a symbol or not, opt for making it a symbol. You can always break it apart into its original shapes, and unused symbols add nothing to the size of the published movie. For a symbol whose use count is 0, Flash exports 0 bytes of data to the published SWF file. Check it out for yourself by generating a size report when you publish (see Chapter 16).

UNDERSTANDING THE LIBRARY PANEL

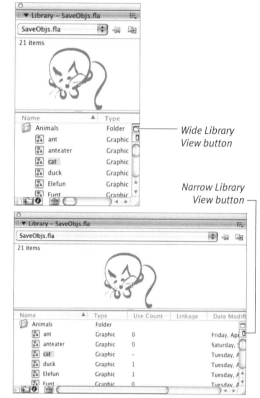

Wide Library View button

Narrow Library View button

Figure 7.6 Click the Wide Library View button to open a wide Library panel. Click the Narrow Library View button to open a narrow one.

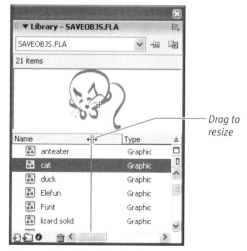

Drag to resize

Figure 7.7 Drag the divider between column headers to resize a column.

Figure 7.8 From the Options menu in the Library panel, choose New Folder to create a library folder.

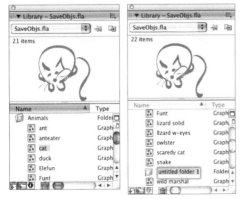

Select root-level item　　*To add root-level folder*

New Folder button　　Enter folder name

Select item within a folder　　*To add subfolder*

Figure 7.9 To create new folders and subfolders, click the New Folder button.

Understanding Library Hierarchy

Flash lets you create folders and subfolders to organize assets hierarchically within the library.

To create a library folder:

1. Open the Library panel.

2. To select a location, *do either of the following:*
   - ▲ To add a root-level folder, select an item at the root level.
   - ▲ To add a subfolder, select an item within the folder where you want to add the new subfolder. (Do not select the folder itself.)

3. To create the new folder, *do either of the following:*
   - ▲ From the pop-up Options menu in the top-right corner of the window, choose New Folder (**Figure 7.8**).
   - ▲ At the bottom of the window, click the New Folder button (**Figure 7.9**).

   Flash creates a new folder, selects it, and activates the text entry field.

4. Type a name for your folder.

5. Press Enter.

To work with library folders:

1. In the Library panel, select a closed folder.

2. To open a closed folder, *do either of the following:*
   - ▲ Double-click the folder icon.
   - ▲ From the Library panel's Options menu, choose Expand Folder.

   The folder's contents appear in the Library panel (**Figure 7.10**).

3. To close an open folder, *do either of the following:*
   - ▲ Double-click the folder icon.
   - ▲ From the Library panel's Options menu, choose Collapse Folder.

✔ Tip

- ■ To open all library folders at the same time, from the Library panel's Options menu, choose Expand All Folders. To close all folders, choose Collapse All Folders.

Figure 7.10 Open folders in the Library panel to display their contents.

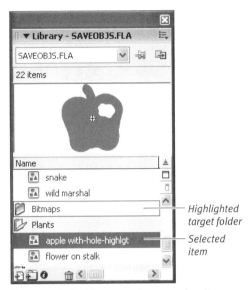

Figure 7.11 In the Library panel, you can drag items between folders. The target folder highlights when it's ready to receive the dragged item.

Highlighted target folder

Selected item

To move items between library folders:

1. In the open Library panel, select the item you want to move.

2. Drag the selected item over the icon of the destination folder.

   Flash highlights the target folder (**Figure 7.11**).

3. Release the mouse button.

   Flash moves the item into the new folder.

✔ Tips

■ To move an item to a new folder quickly, from the Library panel's Options menu, choose Move to New Folder. A dialog for naming the new folder appears. Type a name and press Enter. Flash creates a folder on the same level as the selected item and places that item inside.

■ To sort library items, in the Library panel, click the heading of the column you want to sort by. To sort items by name, for example, click the Name column header. Flash highlights the chosen column header and sorts the Library panel by the items in that column.

■ To change the sort order, click the Sort button, which toggles between alphanumeric and reverse alphanumeric order. In Windows, the button always appears on the far-right side of the column headings; on a Mac, the Sort button appears as a small triangle next to the heading of the currently selected column (see Figure 7.2).

UNDERSTANDING LIBRARY HIERARCHY

Converting Graphics to Symbols

Not all graphics in a Flash movie are symbols; you need to take special steps to define the items you create as symbols. You can convert elements you've already created into symbols or create symbols from scratch in the symbol editor. Symbols reside in the library of the document in which you create them. You can copy a symbol from one document to another or from one library to another document; the symbol then resides separately in each document's library.

The standard library of a Flash document contains all the symbols used in that document; it can also contain unused symbols.

The following task covers creating static graphic symbols. But you can also turn graphics into symbols that are animations (see Chapter 11) or buttons (see Chapter 12).

Why Use Symbols?

Flash uses vectors to hold down file size: Each vector shape is just a set of instructions—a recipe for creating the shape. This fact makes vector shapes efficient to begin with. Symbols allow you to reuse elements in a way that's more efficient than duplicating vector shapes.

A symbol is a master recipe. Imagine a busy restaurant that serves three kinds of soup—chicken noodle, cream of chicken rice, and chicken with garden vegetables—and each pot of soup has its own cook. The head chef could go over with each cook all the steps required to make chicken broth, but that would involve a lot of repetition and take a lot of time. If the restaurant has a master recipe for chicken broth, the chef can instruct all the cooks to make a pot of chicken broth and then tell each cook just those additional steps that distinguish each dish—add noodles for chicken noodle; add rice and cream for cream of chicken rice; and add potatoes, carrots, and peas for garden vegetable.

Symbols act the same way in Flash. The full recipe is in the library. Each instance on the Stage contains just the instructions that say which recipe to start with and how to modify it—for example, use the recipe for the red rectangle, but make it twice as large, change the color to blue, and rotate it 45 degrees clockwise. Because symbols can themselves contain other symbols, it really pays to break your graphic elements into their lowest-common-denominator parts, make each individual part a symbol, and then combine the parts into larger symbols or graphics.

Each *instance* of a symbol (each place you use the same symbol in your Flash document) is linked to one master symbol. Instead of adding a full set of instructions for each instance, Flash adds a note to repeat the instructions, possibly with certain modifications. This method of reusing elements helps keep the published file size small. In addition, if you decide you want the symbol to look different (you want a perfect circle instead of an oval in your logo, for example), you can update one master graphic element instead of making the same change over and over in your document.

Figure 7.12 Choose Modify > Convert to Symbol to turn a selected existing graphic into a symbol.

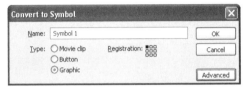

Figure 7.13 The Convert to Symbol dialog lets you name your symbol, define its type, and set its registration point. (Click the Advanced button to expand the box to set linkages for sharing and import/export.)

Selected merge-shape

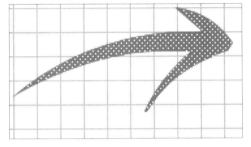

Converted to a symbol

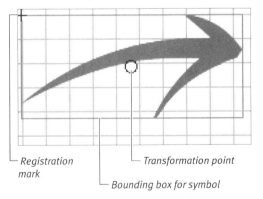

Registration mark

Transformation point

Bounding box for symbol

Figure 7.14 A selected merge-shape on the Stage is highlighted with dots. When you convert that shape to a symbol, the bounding box is the only item that gets highlighted. A crosshair indicates where the symbol's registration mark is. A circle indicates the symbol's transformation point.

To turn an existing graphic into a symbol:

1. On the Stage, select the graphic element(s) you want to convert to a symbol.

   Flash highlights the selected element(s).

2. Choose Modify > Convert to Symbol (**Figure 7.12**), or press F8 on the keyboard.

   The Convert to Symbol dialog appears (**Figure 7.13**). Flash gives the symbol a default name—for example, Symbol 16—based on the number of symbols previously created for the library.

3. If you don't want to use the default name, type a new name for your symbol.

4. Choose Graphic as the symbol type.

5. To set the symbol's registration mark (see the sidebar "Registration Mark vs. Transformation Point vs. Info Panel Coordinates"), click one of the squares in the registration model.

   By default, Flash registers a symbol by the upper-left corner of its bounding box. Click a different square on the registration model—another corner, the center, or the middle of a side—to make Flash register the symbol by the corresponding point on the symbol's bounding box.

6. Click OK.

   Flash adds the symbol to the library. The selected graphic element(s) on the Stage become an instance of the symbol. A crosshair appears, indicating the location of the registration mark; a circle, known as the *transformation point*, appears at the center of the symbol (**Figure 7.14**). You can no longer edit the item directly on the Stage; you must open it in one of Flash's symbol-editing modes.

CONVERTING GRAPHICS TO SYMBOLS

✔ **Tips**

■ A graphic symbol can consist of one or more merge-shapes, drawing-objects, grouped shapes—you name it. You can even include symbols within symbols. Whatever is selected on the Stage when you choose Convert to Symbol becomes part of the symbol.

■ To convert graphic elements to a symbol quickly, select the elements on the Stage and drag the selection to the lower half of the document's Library panel. The Convert to Symbol dialog appears. Name and define your symbol as described in the preceding task.

■ The registration model is elusive. It appears only in the Convert to Symbol dialog. That means you get one chance to select a point on the symbol's bounding box or at its center and make that the registration point. However, you can always go into symbol-editing mode and reposition the graphic elements in relation to the registration mark (see "Editing Master Symbols," later in this chapter).

About Symbol Types

In Flash, you must specify a symbol type for each symbol. (In previous versions of Flash, this was called the symbol's behavior.) You have three choices: graphic, button, and movie clip.

Graphics are, as you might expect, graphic elements, but they can also be animated graphic elements. The feature that distinguishes one symbol type from another is the way the symbol interacts with the Timeline of the movie in which it appears. Graphic symbols operate in lock step with the Timeline of the movie in which they appear. A static graphic symbol takes up one frame of the movie in which you place it (just as any graphic element would). A three-frame animated graphic symbol takes up three frames of the movie (see Chapter 11).

Buttons have their own four-frame Timeline; a button sits in a single frame of the main movie Timeline but displays different frames as a user's mouse interacts with the button (see Chapter 12).

Movie clips have their own multiframe Timeline that plays independently of the main movie Timeline (see Chapter 11).

CONVERTING GRAPHICS TO SYMBOLS

Registration Mark vs. Transformation Point vs. Info Panel Coordinates

The symbol's *registration mark* (the small crosshair) is the point that Flash considers to be the 0, 0 point for the symbol at runtime. Flash uses that point to *register* the symbol—that is, to locate it via coordinates on the Stage, during playback (for example, when you use ActionScript to move a symbol in response to user input). The registration mark stays the same for all instances of the symbol.

The *transformation point* (the small circle) is the point you can use for snapping operations. It's the reference point Flash uses for transforming the symbol. When you rotate a symbol by using the free-transform tool in Rotate and Skew mode, for example, the transformation point is the pivot around which the symbol spins. Flash places the transformation point in the center of the master symbol, but you can change the location of the transformation point of individual symbol instances by using the free-transform tool.

The Info panel locates symbols in space during authoring; the Info panel doesn't use the registration mark to position elements, however. The Info panel positions elements by the top-left corner of their bounding box or by the transformation point, whichever one is selected in the panel's coordinate grid (see Chapter 4).

The fact that Flash positions symbols differently during authoring and at runtime can be very confusing. One way to insure that you see runtime coordinates in the Info panel (and Property inspector) is to position a symbol's registration mark at the top-left corner of a bounding box containing all the graphic-objects in the symbol; then position the transformation point at the center of that bounding box. This is what happens by default when you select elements on the Stage and convert them to a symbol (choose Modify > Convert). A registration mark in this position may not be ideal for positioning a symbol via scripting though. (Imagine scripting the movement of a flying bird, you might prefer to calculate its position using a reference point at the tip of the beak, not a point in the top-left corner of an imaginary rectangle surrounding the bird.) Alternatively, you could position the registration mark and transformation point in the same location, then always select the central square in the Info panel's coordinate grid. For symbol instances, use the free-transform tool to double-click the transformation point; it centers itself on the registration mark.

CONVERTING GRAPHICS TO SYMBOLS

Creating New Symbols from Scratch

You can avoid the conversion process described in the preceding section by creating graphics directly in symbol-editing mode. This practice makes all the tools, frames, and layers of the Flash editor available, but Flash defines the element you're creating as a symbol from the start.

To create a new symbol:

1. To enter symbol-editing mode, *do one of the following:*

   ▲ Choose Insert > New Symbol, or press ⌘-F8 (Mac) or Ctrl-F8 (Windows).

   ▲ From the Library panel's Options menu, choose New Symbol (**Figure 7.15**).

   ▲ In the bottom-left corner of the Library panel, click the New Symbol button (**Figure 7.16**).

   The Create New Symbol dialog appears.

2. Type a name for your symbol.

3. Choose Graphic as the symbol type.

Figure 7.15 From the Library panel's Options menu, choose New Symbol to create a symbol from scratch.

— New Symbol button

Figure 7.16 Click the Library panel's New Symbol button to create a symbol from scratch.

4. Click OK.

Flash enters symbol-editing mode. Flash displays the name of the symbol you're creating in the Edit Bar, places a crosshair in the center of the Stage, and hides the Pasteboard (**Figure 7.17**). The crosshair indicates the symbol's registration mark.

5. Create your graphic on the Stage of the symbol editor as you would in the regular editing environment.

continues on next page

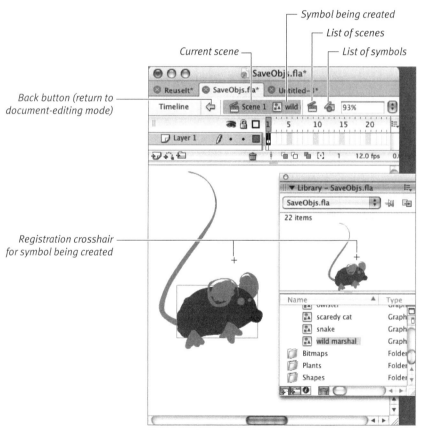

Figure 7.17 In symbol-editing mode, the name of the symbol being worked on appears in the Edit Bar just above the Stage.

6. To return to document-editing mode, *do one of the following:*

▲ Choose Edit > Edit Document. Flash returns you to the current scene.

▲ In the Edit Bar, click the Back button or the Current Scene link (**Figure 7.18**). Flash returns you to the current scene.

▲ From the Edit Scene pop-up menu in the Edit Bar, choose a scene (**Figure 7.19**). Flash takes you to that scene.

✔ Tips

■ When you're creating new symbols, be sure to consider how the registration mark should work with your finished symbol so you can place your graphic elements appropriately in relation to the registration crosshair. Will you want to align this symbol by its center? Then position your elements evenly around the crosshair. Will you want to align this symbol along an outer edge or corner? Then position your elements accordingly.

■ When you enter symbol-editing mode for an existing symbol, the registration crosshair may be outside the current viewing area. To bring the registration mark to the center of your window, choose View > Magnification > Show Frame.

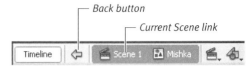

Back button

Current Scene link

Figure 7.18 Click the Back button or the Current Scene link to return to document-editing mode.

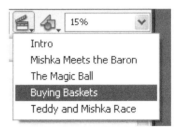

Figure 7.19 Choose a scene from the Edit Scene pop-up menu to return to document-editing mode.

Where Am I?

When you edit symbols in a Flash document, the current window switches to symbol-editing mode. It's easy to get confused about whether you're editing the main document or a symbol. Learn to recognize the following subtle visual cues; they're the only indication that you're in symbol-editing mode.

In symbol-editing mode, a Flash document displays the name of the scene and symbol you're editing in the Edit Bar and activates the Back button. The Pasteboard disappears. Also, a small crosshair, which acts as a registration point for the symbol, appears on the Stage. If you entered symbol-editing mode via the Edit in Place command, any elements on the Stage that aren't being edited appear in a ghostly form. Apart from these changes, the Timeline, the Stage, and the tools all appear and work just as they do in document-editing mode.

Preview location of symbol on the Stage

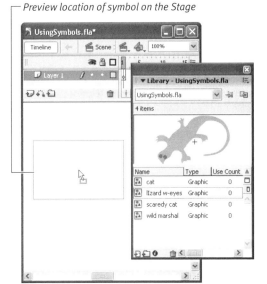

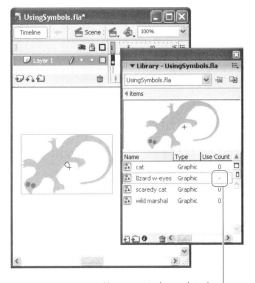

Use count to be updated

Figure 7.20 When you drag a symbol from the Library panel to the Stage (top), Flash places the symbol on the Stage, selects it, and updates that symbol's use count internally (bottom). When you aren't keeping use counts updated constantly, the dash in the Use Count column indicates a change. To see the actual figure, choose Update Use Counts Now from the Library panel's Options menu.

Using Symbol Instances

A *symbol instance* is a pointer to the full description of the symbol. Symbols help keep file sizes small. If you converted a graphic on the Stage to a symbol, you have one symbol instance on the Stage. To use the symbol again, or if you created your symbol in symbol-editing mode, you'll need to get a copy out of the library and onto the Stage.

To place a symbol instance in your movie:

1. In the Timeline, select the layer and keyframe where you want the graphic symbol to appear.

   Flash can place symbols only in keyframes. If you select an in-between frame, Flash places the symbol in the preceding keyframe. (To learn more about keyframes, see Chapter 8.)

2. Open the library containing the symbol.

3. In the Library panel, navigate to the symbol you want; click it to select it.

   Flash highlights the chosen symbol and displays it in the preview window.

4. Position your pointer over the preview window.

5. Click and drag a copy of the symbol onto the Stage.

   Flash previews the symbol's location on the Stage with a rectangular outline as you drag (**Figure 7.20**).

6. Release the mouse button.

   Flash places the symbol on the Stage and selects it.

✔ Tip

- To place a symbol instance quickly, drag the symbol name directly from the Library panel to the Stage without using the pre-viewed image.

215

Modifying Symbol Instances

You can change the appearance of individual symbol instances without changing the master symbol itself. As with any other element, you can resize and reposition an instance (for example, scale and rotate it) by using the tools in the Tools panel, panels, and the Properties tab of the Property inspector (see Chapter 4).

You can also change a symbol instance's color and transparency, but the method differs from the methods you've learned for assigning colors to merge-shapes and drawing-objects. You modify the color, intensity, and transparency of a symbol instance via the Color menu in the Properties tab of the Property inspector.

To change an instance's brightness:

1. On the Stage, select the symbol instance you want to modify.

2. Access the Properties tab of the Properties inspector.
   Settings for the symbol instance appear.

3. From the Color menu, choose Brightness.
   A field for entering a new brightness percentage appears (**Figure 7.21**).

4. Enter a value in the Brightness field.
   A value of –100 makes the symbol black; a value of 0 leaves the symbol at its original brightness; a value of 100 makes the symbol white (**Figure 7.22**).

5. Press Enter.
   Flash applies the brightness setting to the selected symbol on the Stage.

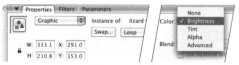

Figure 7.21 Use the Brightness settings in the Color section of the Properties tab to change the intensity of a symbol instance. Enter a high value to make the symbol instance lighter or a low value to make it darker.

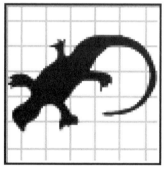

–100 percent brightness setting

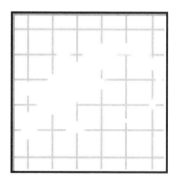

100 percent brightness setting

Figure 7.22 At its extremes, the Brightness setting lets you turn a symbol instance completely black or completely white.

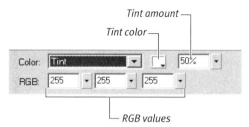

Tint amount
Tint color
RGB values

Figure 7.23 Use the Tint settings in the Color section of the Properties tab to change the color of a symbol instance.

Figure 7.24 Use the Alpha settings in the Color section of the Properties tab to change the transparency of a symbol instance.

To change the instance's color:

1. On the Stage, select the symbol instance you want to modify.

2. In the Properties tab of the Property inspector, from the Color menu, choose Tint.

   Tint settings appear (**Figure 7.23**).

3. To choose a new color, *do either of the following:*

   ▲ In the Red, Green, and Blue fields, enter new RGB values.

   ▲ Click the Tint Color control, and choose a color from the pop-up swatch set.

4. Type a percentage in the Tint Amount field.

   The tint percentage indicates how much of the new color to blend with the existing colors. Applying a tint of 100 percent changes all the lines and fills in the symbol to the new color. Applying a lesser percentage mixes some of the new color with the existing colors in the symbol. It's almost like placing a transparent film of the new color over the symbol.

5. Press Enter.

   Flash applies the tint settings to the selected symbol on the Stage.

To change the instance's transparency:

1. On the Stage, select the symbol instance you want to modify.

2. In the Properties tab of the Property inspector, from the Color menu, choose Alpha (**Figure 7.24**).

3. Enter a new value in the Alpha field.

   A value of 0 makes the symbol completely transparent; a value of 100 makes the symbol completely opaque.

4. Press Enter.

   Flash applies the alpha setting to the selected symbol on the Stage.

217

To change the instance's tint and alpha simultaneously:

1. On the Stage, select the symbol instance you want to modify.

2. In the Properties tab of the Property inspector, from the Color menu, choose Advanced.

   A Settings button appears to the right of the menu.

3. Click the Settings button.

   The Advanced Effect dialog appears (**Figure 7.25**). This dialog contains sliders and text boxes for changing red, green, blue, and alpha values.

4. Adjust the values to fine-tune the color and transparency of the symbol instance.

5. To apply the color effect, click OK.

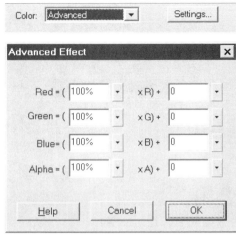

Figure 7.25 Click the Advanced Settings button in the Properties tab (top) to access the Advanced Effect dialog (bottom). Enter new values to change the color and transparency of a symbol instance.

The Mystery of Advanced Effect Settings

The Advanced Effect settings allow you to change the RGB values and alpha values for a symbol instance simultaneously. The sliders in the left-hand column control what percentage of the RGB and alpha values that make up the colors in the original symbol appear in the symbol instance. The sliders on the right add to or subtract from the red, green, blue, and alpha values of the original colors.

Imagine a symbol with three ovals. One is pure red, one is pure green, and one is pure blue. The alpha setting is 50 percent. Changing the red slider in the left-hand column (the percentage of the current red value) affects only the red oval. The green and blue ovals contain 0 percent red; doubling the value makes no visible change. Moving the right-hand slider upwards adds red to everything, including the green and blue ovals. These ovals start to change color when you increase the red value. (If you move the right-hand slider downward, decreasing the red value, you'll see no difference in the green and blue ovals where there was no red to begin with.)

✔ Tips

- Instead of pressing Enter to confirm a value you enter in one of the fields on the Properties tab of the Property inspector, you can click elsewhere in the Properties tab or click the Stage.

- To preview new color values interactively, click and drag the triangle to the right of an entry field. Flash updates the symbol on the Stage as you drag the slider lever. When you release the slider, Flash confirms the change; you don't need to press Enter.

- You can change the transformation point of individual symbol instances. Using the free-transform tool, click the small white circle in the middle of the symbol instance. Drag the circle to a new location. Flash uses the transformation point for rotating and scaling the symbol.

- When you use the free-transform tool to scale a symbol instance, it scales in relation to the instance's transformation point (by default, the center of the symbol instance). Hold down the Option key (Mac) or Alt key (Windows) to scale relative to the corner diagonally opposite the one you're dragging.

Timeline Effects: A Dubious Source of Symbols

Flash's Timeline Effects commands (found in the Insert menu) are Macromedia's attempt to help less-experienced Flash users create a few common special effects and simple animations. If you use Timeline Effects, Flash creates symbols for you (some are static symbols, such as the ones described in this chapter; others are animated symbols, which are described in Chapter 11). You should not reuse or modify timeline-effects symbols according to the methods described in this chapter; doing so risks interfering with the effect. If you attempt to edit such symbols, you'll see a warning dialog; if you attempt to reuse such symbols, however, you won't be warned. In general, Timeline Effects are not a good option for creating animation and effects in Flash. For a brief description of how Timeline Effects work, see the sidebar "A Note About Timeline Effects," in Chapter 11.

Swapping One Symbol Instance for Another

Flash allows you to replace one symbol instance with another while retaining all the modifications you've made in the symbol instance. If, for example, you want to change the look of a logo in certain places in your site but not everywhere, you can create the new logo as a separate symbol and swap it in as needed. (To change the look for every instance, edit the master logo symbol directly, as you learn to do in "Editing Master Symbols," later in the chapter.) You perform symbol swapping in the Properties tab of the Property inspector (**Figure 7.26**).

To switch symbols:

1. On the Stage, select the symbol instance you want to change.

2. In the Properties tab of the Property inspector, click the Swap button.

   The Swap Symbol dialog appears, listing all the symbols in the current document's library (**Figure 7.27**). In the Windows operating systems, Flash highlights the name of the symbol you're modifying and places a bullet next to its name in the Symbol list.

3. From the Symbol list, select the replacement symbol.

   The original symbol remains bulleted; Flash highlights the new symbol and places it in the preview window.

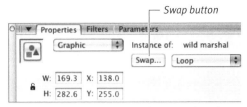

Swap button

Figure 7.26 The Swap button in the Properties tab lets you replace a selected symbol instance with an instance of a different symbol from the same document.

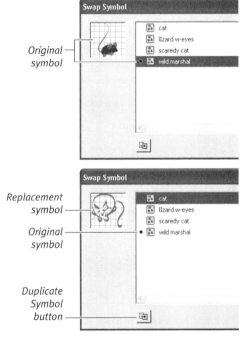

Original symbol

Replacement symbol

Original symbol

Duplicate Symbol button

Figure 7.27 Select a replacement symbol from the list in the Swap Symbol dialog, and click OK to exchange one symbol for another.

Unmodified instance of mouse

Unmodified instance of cat

Instance of mouse scaled and rotated before swapping

After swapping: scaling and rotation applied to cat

Figure 7.28 When you swap symbols, any modifications you have made for the selected instance you're swapping apply to the replacement instance.

4. Click OK.

Flash places the new symbol on the Stage, locating the new symbol where the old one was located and applying any modifications you previously made for that instance (**Figure 7.28**).

✔ Tips

■ To swap symbols quickly, double-click the new symbol in the Swap Symbol dialog. Flash replaces it and closes the dialog.

■ The Duplicate Symbol button in the Swap Symbol dialog lets you make a copy of whatever symbol is selected in the list. If you know you need to tweak the master version of the replacement symbol for this instance, but you also want to keep the current version, click the Duplicate symbol button, name it in the dialog that appears, and click OK. Make sure you select the duplicate as the replacement in the Swap Symbol dialog, and click OK. You can edit the duplicate's master symbol later.

SWAPPING ONE SYMBOL INSTANCE FOR ANOTHER

Editing Master Symbols

After you create a symbol, you can refine and modify it in symbol-editing mode. Unlike modifications of a symbol instance, which affect just that instance on the Stage, leaving the master symbol in the library unchanged, modifications made in symbol-editing mode affect the master symbol and all instances of that symbol in your movie.

You can enter symbol-editing mode in several ways.

To enter symbol-editing mode from the Stage:

1. On the Stage, select the symbol you want to edit.

2. To open the symbol editor, *do one of the following*:

   ▲ Choose Edit > Edit Symbols, or press ⌘-E (Mac) or Ctrl-E (Windows) (**Figure 7.29**).

   ▲ Choose Edit > Edit Selected.

   ▲ From the pop-up list of symbols in the Edit Bar, choose the symbol you want to edit (**Figure 7.30**).

   Flash opens the symbol editor in the current window.

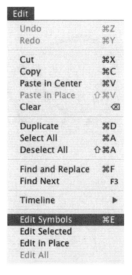

Figure 7.29 Choosing Edit > Edit Symbols takes you from document-editing mode to symbol-editing mode. If you have selected a symbol on the Stage, choosing Edit > Edit Selected also takes you to symbol-editing mode.

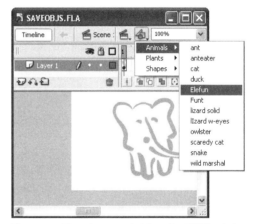

Figure 7.30 Choosing a symbol from the Edit Symbol pop-up menu in the Edit Bar takes you into symbol-editing mode.

Symbol being edited

Figure 7.31 The Edit in Place command allows you to see your symbol instance in context with other items on the stage. The symbol instance appears in full color; the other elements on the Stage are grayed out. In this mode, changes made to the instance affect the master symbol and all the instances in the movie.

✔ Tips

■ There are three ways to enter symbol-editing mode directly from the Library panel: double-click the icon next to a symbol's name; double-click a symbol in the preview window; or select the symbol you want to edit, and from the Options menu, choose Edit. The symbol opens in symbol-editing mode in the active Flash document on your desktop.

■ After you've placed an instance of a symbol on the Stage, you may want to change the master symbol to make it fit with the items around it. The Edit in Place command lets you edit your master symbol in context on the Stage with all other items grayed out (**Figure 7.31**). To evoke the Edit in Place command, choose Edit > Edit in Place; or, Control-click (Mac) or right-click (Windows) the symbol instance you want to edit, and, from the contextual menu that appears, choose Edit in Place. Any changes you make affect all instances of that symbol.

■ You can also enter Edit in Place mode quickly by double-clicking a symbol instance on the Stage.

■ You can edit a symbol in a completely separate window. Select an instance of the symbol on the Stage, Control-click (Mac) or right-click (Windows) to access the contextual menu, and choose Edit in New Window. The symbol opens in a separate window. The edit bar shows the name of the symbol being edited, but there is no Back button; to return to document-editing mode, close the window.

Duplicating Master Symbols

Although you can always modify the instances of a symbol on the Stage, if you need to use one variation of a symbol over and over, you can duplicate the original master symbol and then modify the duplicate to create a new master symbol with those variations.

To create a duplicate symbol:

1. In the Library panel, select the symbol you want to duplicate.

2. From the Options menu, choose Duplicate (**Figure 7.32**).

   Flash opens the Duplicate Symbol dialog, giving the duplicate symbol a default name (**Figure 7.33**).

3. If you want, type a new name for your symbol.

4. Choose Graphic as the symbol type.

5. Click OK.

   Flash adds the new symbol to the library at the same level in the hierarchy as the original (**Figure 7.34**). The duplicate doesn't link to the original symbol in any way. You can change the duplicate without changing the original, and vice versa.

Figure 7.32 From the Library panel's Options pop-up menu, choose Duplicate to make a copy of the selected symbol.

Figure 7.33 In the Duplicate Symbol dialog, you can name the new symbol (the default name is the original name plus the word *copy*) and assign its type.

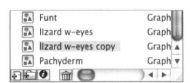

Figure 7.34 Flash puts duplicated symbols at the same library level as the original symbol.

— *Delete selected item*

Figure 7.35 Click the trash can icon to delete a selected library item.

Figure 7.36 You can also choose Delete from the Library panel's Options menu to remove selected symbols from the active document.

Deleting Master Symbols

Deleting symbols can be a little trickier than deleting shapes or groups on the Stage. Deleting one instance of a symbol from its place on the Stage is easy; use the methods for cutting or deleting graphics discussed in Chapter 4. Deleting symbols from the library isn't difficult but does require some thought, because instances of the symbol may still be in use in your movie.

To delete one symbol from the library:

1. In the Library panel, select the symbol you want to remove.

2. To delete the symbol, *do either of the following*:
   ▲ At the bottom of the window, click the Delete button (the trash-can icon) (**Figure 7.35**).
   ▲ From the pop-up Options menu in the top-right corner of the window, choose Delete (**Figure 7.36**).

✔ Tip

■ In earlier versions of Flash, deleting symbols from the library was a permanent operation. Flash even warned you of that fact when you chose to delete master symbols from the library. With Flash 8, you can undo deletions from a library.

To delete a folder of symbols from the library:

1. Select the folder you want to remove.

2. Follow step 2 of the preceding task.

   Flash removes the folder and all the symbols it contains from the library.

✔ Tip

- Always check the usage numbers before you delete library items (**Figure 7.37**). You don't want to delete a symbol that you're currently using in a movie, which is especially easy to do if you've nested symbols within symbols. Some earlier versions of Flash warned you when you tried to delete an item that was in use in a movie. Flash 8 doesn't.

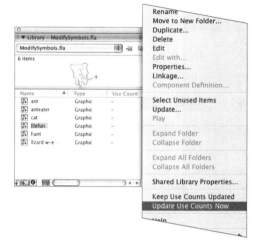

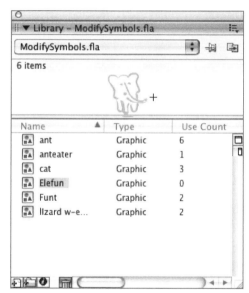

Figure 7.37 Be sure to update use counts before deleting a symbol (in the Library panel, choose Options > Update Use Counts Now). Then check to be sure the item you want to delete isn't being used in the movie.

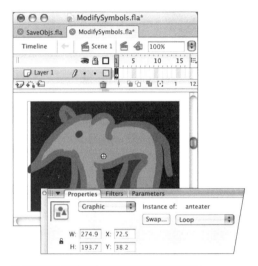

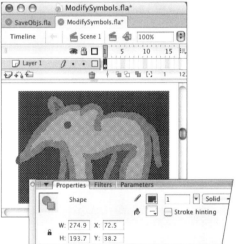

Figure 7.38 The Properties tab of the Property inspector reveals that the selected graphic is a symbol instance (top). To break the link with its master symbol, choose Modify > Break Apart. The Properties tab of the Property inspector reveals that the selection now consists of shapes; it's no longer a symbol instance (bottom).

Converting Symbol Instances to Graphics

At times, you'll want to break the link between a placed instance of a symbol and the master symbol. You may want to redraw the shape in a specific instance but not in every instance, for example. To convert a symbol back to an independent shape or set of shapes, break it apart, just as you break apart grouped shapes (see Chapter 5).

To break the symbol link:

1. On the Stage, select the symbol instance whose link you want to break.

2. Choose Modify > Break Apart, or press ⌘-B (Mac) or Ctrl-B (Windows) (**Figure 7.38**).

   Flash breaks the link to the symbol in the library and selects the symbol's elements. The Properties tab of the Property inspector no longer displays information about the instance of the symbol; it displays information about the selected shapes.

   If you grouped any of the original elements, they remain grouped after you break the link; ungrouped elements stay ungrouped. Any symbols that existed within the original symbol remain as instances of their respective master symbols. Now you can edit these elements as you learned to do in previous chapters.

Copying Symbols Between Movies

It's easy to reuse symbols. You can transfer symbols via the Clipboard, copying or cutting symbols from one Flash document and using one of the paste commands to place them in another. You can also view the libraries of other Flash documents (whether open or closed) and drag their symbols to the Stage of the currently active Flash document.

To transfer symbols between open documents:

1. Open the source document (the one containing symbols that you want to reuse).

2. Open or create the destination document (the one in which you would like to reuse existing symbols).

3. Open the Library panel.

   The panel contains the libraries of both open documents. By default, it displays the library of the document that you're currently viewing—in this case, the destination document that you just opened.

4. To see the assets of the source document, choose its name from the menu of open documents in the Library panel (**Figure 7.39**).

Inactive document

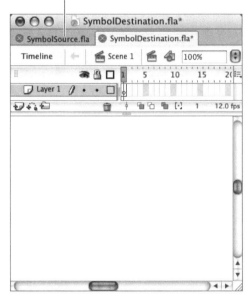

Choose an inactive document

Figure 7.39 The Library panel displays the assets of the currently active open document. To view the library of an inactive but open document, choose the document from the menu of open documents.

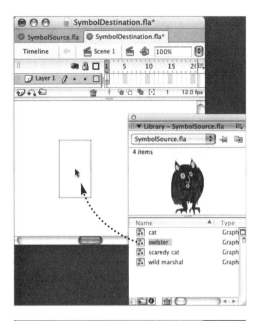

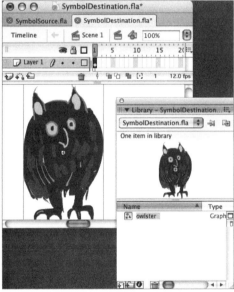

Figure 7.40 You can drag a symbol from a source library by its preview image or by its name. Placing a symbol on the Stage of your destination document adds the symbol to that document's library.

5. In the Library panel, select a symbol and drag it to the Stage of the destination document (**Figure 7.40**).

Flash places the symbol at the root level of the destination document's library.

✔ Tips

- You may want to copy items from one library to several documents, but each time you change documents, the Library panel changes too. To make the desired source library hold still, make it active in the Library panel and click the pin icon to the right of the menu of open documents (**Figure 7.41**). Now you can view any open document, and the Library panel doesn't change.

- Another option is to open the source library in a separate panel. With the source library active in the Library panel window, click the New Library Panel button (the double-document-arrow icon to the right of the pin icon). Flash opens the library in a new panel. You can drag assets from the source-document's Library panel to the Stage of a destination document or to the Library panel of the destination document.

- If you're viewing documents in separate windows, instead of tabbed in a single window, you can drag symbols directly from one document to another. Flash adds the new symbols at the root level of the destination document's library.

Figure 7.41 To keep the Library panel from updating to display the assets of the currently active document, click the horizontal pin icon (top). The pinned library remains visible in the panel no matter what other documents you bring forward to look at. To allow the library to change again, click the upright-pin icon (bottom).

Figure 7.42 Flash allows you to resolve symbol conflicts when you attempt to import or drag in a symbol with the same name as an existing symbol.

- If you drag a symbol to the Stage, and a symbol with that name already exists in the root level of the destination file's library (or if you try to place that duplicate symbol in a folder containing a symbol with that name), Flash displays a warning dialog (**Figure 7.42**). You can cancel the transfer, replace the existing symbol with the one you're transferring, or choose not to replace the existing symbol. When you choose the last option, be forewarned that Flash places a new instance of the existing symbol on the Stage where you placed the one you were dragging; the new symbol isn't added to the destination library. If you cancel the operation, you can rename one of the conflicting symbols and repeat the operation of dragging in the source symbol.

- You don't have to open a source document to drag symbols from its library. Choose File > Import > Open External Library to open just the Library panel for that document. Select a symbol, and drag it to the destination Stage or to the destination Library panel.

- You can use the File > Import > Import to Library command to bring other individual asset files—such as video clips, sounds, and bitmaps—into your movie as well. (You'll learn more about importing non-Flash graphics in Chapter 14; Chapter 15 covers importing sounds.)

COPYING SYMBOLS BETWEEN MOVIES

The Mystery of Object-Level Undo

Every computer user gets familiar with the Undo command. Ctrl-z (Windows) or ⌘-z (Mac) becomes an automatic "oops" response to fix mistakes. Flash 8 provides two types of undo: Document-level Undo and Object-level Undo.

In Document-level Undo, Flash tracks every undoable step you take. Open the History panel (choose Window > Other Panels > History); you'll see them listed in order. In Object-level Undo, Flash also tracks every undoable step but makes a distinction between steps that pertain to working in the main document and steps that pertain to working on master symbols.

Object-level Undo tracks the steps for each master symbol separately; each time you create a master symbol, Object-level Undo starts a separate History-panel list for that symbol. Within one work session (provided you haven't made changes in the History panel yourself), whenever you edit that master symbol, the History panel loads the steps for that symbol; any edits you make are added to the list. If you edit a different symbol, the panel loads the steps for that symbol. When you leave symbol-editing mode and return to document-editing mode, the History panel displays only the steps you've used in the main document.

Note that modifications you make to an instance of a symbol on the Stage are part of the history of the document, not of the master symbol.

To change from one type of undo to the other, from the Edit menu (Windows) or the Flash application menu (Mac), choose Preferences. In the General category, from the Undo menu, choose the style you want. To track the history of master symbols separately, choose Object-level Undo; to track all your steps in one integrated list, choose Document-level Undo. It's best to choose your undo style at the beginning of a work session. If you switch in the middle, Flash wipes the current History panel clean.

FRAME-BY-FRAME ANIMATIONS

Frame-by-frame animation was the traditional form of animation used before the days of computers. Live-action movies and video are really a form of frame-by-frame animation. The camera captures motion by snapping a picture every so often. Animation simulates motion by showing drawings of elements at various stages of a movement.

Traditional animators, such as those who worked for the early Walt Disney or Warner Bros. studios from the 1930s through the 1960s, had to create hundreds of images, each one slightly different from the next, to achieve every movement of each character or element in the cartoon. To turn those drawings into animations, they captured the images on film, putting a different image in each frame of the movie.

Traditional animators painted individual characters (or parts of characters) and graphics on transparent sheets called *cels*. They stacked the cels to create the entire image for the frame. The cel technique allowed animators to save time by reusing parts of an image that stayed the same in more than one frame.

In Macromedia Flash 8, you, too, can make frame-by-frame animations by placing different content in different frames. Flash calls the frames that hold new content *keyframes*.

Using the Timeline

In the Timeline, you have five size options for viewing frames and two options for previewing thumbnails of frame contents. A Flash movie may contain hundreds of frames; the Timeline's scroll bars enable you to access frames not currently visible in the Timeline window. You can also undock the Timeline so that it floats as a separate window and resize it to show more or fewer frames.

Figure 8.1 shows the Timeline for a movie with one layer and 15 defined frames.

To resize the Timeline's area:

1. Open a new Flash document.

   The default Timeline appears.

2. Position the pointer over the gripper (the textured area on the left side of the title bar at the top of the Timeline).

3. Click and drag away from the document window.

   A gray outline represents the Timeline window's new position.

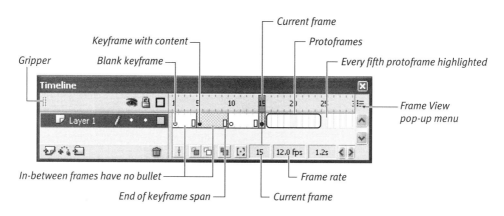

Figure 8.1 Similar to an interactive outline, the Timeline represents each frame of your movie. Click any frame, and Flash displays its contents on the Stage.

4. With the Timeline in its new location, release the mouse button.

The Timeline turns into a separate resizable window.

✔ Tips

■ To redock the Timeline, reverse the procedure. Click the Timeline's gripper, and drag toward the top of the document window. Position the pointer over the Edit Bar above the Stage, and release the mouse button. The Timeline redocks.

■ For those who like a floating Timeline window, it can be a challenge not to redock the Timeline accidentally as you move windows around on your desktop. Windows users can prevent the Timeline from docking by holding down the Ctrl key as you drag.

The Mystery of Timeline Display

When you create a new Flash document, the Timeline displays a single layer with hundreds of little boxes. The first box has a solid black outline and contains a hollow bullet; the rest of the boxes are gray outlines. Every fifth box is solid gray. The box with the black outline and hollow bullet is a *keyframe*; the gray boxes are placeholder frames, or *protoframes*.

When you define a range of live frames by adding keyframes (see "Creating Keyframes," later in this chapter), the outline for the range of frames changes to black in the Timeline.

For a blank keyframe (one that has no content on the Stage), the Timeline displays a hollow bullet. For a keyframe that has content, the Timeline displays a solid bullet.

Any in-between frames that follow a keyframe that has content display that content on the Stage. In the Timeline, the last in-between frame of a span contains a hollow rectangle. If you've set Frame View to Tinted Frames (the default), the in-between frames with content also have a tinted highlight in the Timeline.

USING THE TIMELINE

To view frames in the Timeline at various sizes:

◆ In the Timeline, from the Frame View menu, choose a display option (**Figure 8.2**).

Flash resizes the frame representations in the Timeline to reflect your choice. **Figure 8.3** shows some of the frame views available.

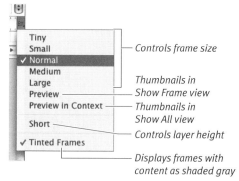

Figure 8.2 The Timeline's Frame View pop-up menu lets you control the display of frames in the Timeline.

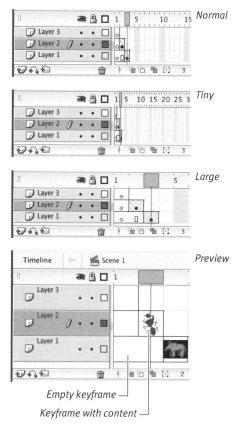

Figure 8.3 Flash can display the frames in the Timeline in a variety of sizes, from Tiny to Large. You can also preview the contents of each frame in the Timeline.

Selected frame

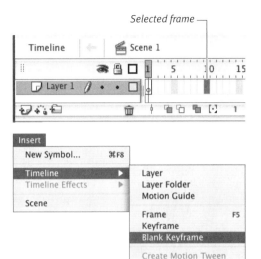

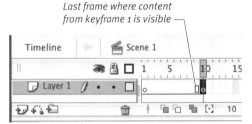

Last frame where content from keyframe 1 is visible

Figure 8.4 Select a frame in the Timeline (top) and then choose Insert > Timeline > Blank Keyframe (middle) to add a new blank keyframe (bottom).

✔ Tip

- These tasks access frame-related commands from the main menu bar, but all the relevant commands for working with frames are available from the contextual frame menu as well. Control-click (Mac) or right-click (Windows) a frame in the Timeline to bring up the contextual frame menu.

Creating Keyframes

Flash offers two commands for creating keyframes. Insert > Timeline > Blank Keyframe defines a keyframe that's empty, and Insert > Timeline > Keyframe defines a keyframe that duplicates the content of the preceding keyframe in that layer. Use the Insert > Timeline > Blank Keyframe command when you want to change the contents of the Stage completely. Use Insert > Timeline > Keyframe when you want to duplicate the content of the preceding keyframe.

To add a blank keyframe to the end of your movie:

1. Create a new Flash document.

   The new document by default has one layer and one blank keyframe at frame 1.

2. In the Timeline, click the protoframe for frame 10 to select it.

3. Choose Insert > Timeline > Blank Keyframe (**Figure 8.4**).

   Flash revises the Timeline to give you information about the frames you've defined. A hollow rectangle appears in frame 9, and a black line separates frame 9 from frame 10. This line indicates where the content for one keyframe span ends and the content for the next keyframe begins. Flash replaces the gray bars separating protoframes 2–9 with gray tick marks and removes the gray highlight that appeared in every fifth frame of the undefined frames.

To create a blank keyframe in the middle of your movie:

1. Follow the steps in the preceding task to create a single-layer, 10-frame movie.

2. In the Timeline, click frame 1 to select it.

3. Draw a shape on the Stage.

   Flash updates the Timeline, adding a solid bullet to frame 1 (**Figure 8.5**).

   With Tinted Frames selected in the Frame View menu (Flash's default setting), Flash shades frames 1–9 with gray. The shading indicates that keyframe 1 has content that remains visible until frame 10 in this layer. A hollow rectangle appears in frame 9, indicating the end of the span of in-between frames that displays the content of keyframe 1.

   Frame 10 still contains a hollow bullet, meaning that it has no content. (Try clicking frame 10 to see that the Stage is blank.)

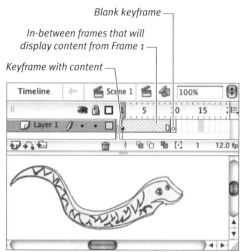

Blank keyframe

In-between frames that will display content from Frame 1

Keyframe with content

Figure 8.5 When you place content in a keyframe, Flash displays that frame in the Timeline with a solid bullet. The gray tint on the frames between keyframes indicates that content from the preceding keyframe appears during these frames. The hollow square indicates the end of the span of in-between frames displaying the same content. The hollow circle indicates a blank keyframe.

Current frame

Display content from
preceding keyframe

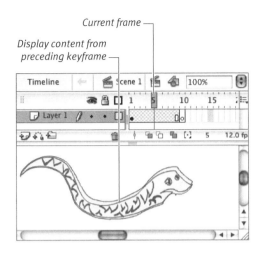

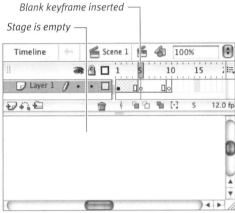

Blank keyframe inserted

Stage is empty

Figure 8.6 When you convert an in-between frame that displays content to a blank keyframe, Flash removes content from the Stage for that frame. Frames 6–9 are tinted when they display the content of frame 1 (top). When you insert a blank keyframe at frame 5 (bottom), the tint disappears, because these frames now display the content of the most recent keyframe, frame 5, which is empty.

4. In the Timeline, in the area above the layers, click the number 5 or drag the playhead to position it in frame 5.

Flash displays frame 5 on the Stage. Notice that this in-between frame continues to display the content of the preceding keyframe, frame 1.

5. Choose Insert > Timeline > Blank Keyframe.

Flash converts the selected in-between frame to a keyframe and removes all content from the Stage in that frame (**Figure 8.6**).

To duplicate the contents of the preceding keyframe:

1. Follow steps 1–3 in the preceding task. You should have a document with content in keyframe 1.

2. In the Timeline, select frame 3.

   The playhead doesn't move into the protoframe area, but frame 3 is highlighted as the current selected frame.

3. Choose Insert > Timeline > Keyframe.

   Flash creates a new keyframe, duplicates the contents of frame 1 in frame 3, and places a solid bullet in the Timeline at frame 3 and a hollow rectangle in frame 2 (**Figure 8.7**). The content of frames 1 and 3 is totally separate. Try selecting frame 1 and making changes—move the graphic or delete it. Now select frame 3 again; it remains unchanged.

✔ Tips

- The word *insert* used in connection with keyframes is a bit misleading. Choosing Insert > Timeline > Keyframe *adds* frames only if you've selected a protoframe. If you select an existing in-between frame, Insert > Timeline > Keyframe converts that frame to a keyframe and leaves the length of the movie as it was. The Insert > Timeline > Frame command always adds frames to your movie.

- You can't add a keyframe between back-to-back keyframes. With keyframes in frames 5 and 6, select frame 5 and choose Insert > Timeline > Blank Keyframe. The playhead moves to frame 6, but Flash doesn't add a new blank keyframe. With frame 5 selected, you must choose Insert > Timeline > Frame. Flash creates an in-between frame at frame 6. Now select frame 5 or frame 6 and choose Insert > Timeline > Blank Keyframe; Flash converts frame 6 to a keyframe.

Current frame

Content of the first keyframe

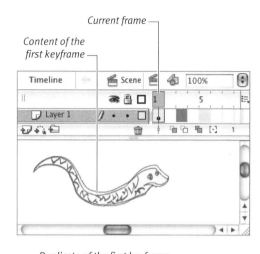

Duplicate of the first keyframe

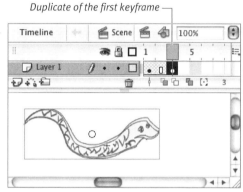

Figure 8.7 The Insert > Timeline > Keyframe command creates a keyframe that duplicates the contents of the preceding keyframe in that layer.

Keyframe Mysteries: Insert vs. Convert

In addition to the Insert > Timeline > Keyframe and Insert > Timeline > Blank Keyframe commands, Flash offers commands for converting frames to keyframes. Choose Modify > Timeline > Convert to Keyframes (or press F6) or choose Modify > Timeline> Convert to Blank Keyframes (or press F7). These conversion commands are also found in the contextual menu for frames—Control-click (Mac) or right-click (Windows) a frame in the Timeline to access the menu.

Whether you should insert or convert keyframes depends on how many frames you have selected when you issue the command and how many frames you want to create. The Insert commands create a single keyframe regardless of how many frames you have selected; the Modify commands create multiple keyframes, one for each selected frame.

With a single frame selected, the Insert > Timeline > Keyframe command and the Modify > Timeline> Convert to Keyframe command work identically. If you select one protoframe or in-between frame, both commands transform that frame to a keyframe and duplicate the content of the preceding keyframe (if any). If you select a keyframe that is followed by an in-between frame or protoframe, both commands transform that following frame to a keyframe with the same content as the selected frame. Neither command has any effect on a selected keyframe that is followed by another keyframe.

With multiple protoframes or in-between frames selected, the Insert > Timeline > Keyframe command creates a single keyframe, usually in the same frame as the playhead (if you select frames at the end of your movie, Flash places the new keyframe in the last selected frame). The remaining selected frames become in-between frames.

With multiple protoframes or in-between frames selected, the Modify > Timeline> Convert to Keyframes command creates a keyframe in every selected frame.

The commands for blank keyframes work similarly. Insert > Timeline > Blank Keyframe creates one keyframe in the same frame as the playhead; the remaining frames become in-between frames. Modify > Timeline> Convert to Blank Keyframe creates a blank keyframe in all the selected frames.

Creating In-Between Frames

The frames that appear between keyframes are in a sense tied to the keyframe that precedes them. They display its content and allow you a space in which to create tweened animation (see Chapters 9 and 10). Flash makes the connections between these frames clear by highlighting them and placing a hollow rectangle at the end of the keyframe span.

To add in-between frames:

1. Open or create a Flash document with keyframes and content in frame 1 and frame 2.

2. In the Timeline, position the playhead in keyframe 1.

3. Choose Insert > Timeline > Frame, or press F5 on the keyboard (**Figure 8.8**). Flash adds an in-between frame (**Figure 8.9**). Your movie now contains a keyframe at frame 1, an in-between frame at frame 2, and another keyframe at frame 3.

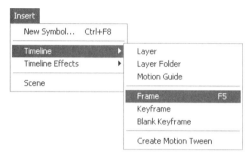

Figure 8.8 Choose Insert > Timeline > Frame to add in-between frames to the Timeline.

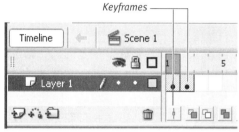

Timeline before evoking Insert > Timeline > Frame

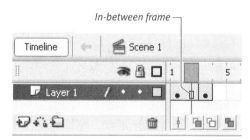

Timeline after evoking Insert > Timeline > Frame

Figure 8.9 The Insert > Timeline > Frame command adds an in-between frame after the selected frame. Unlike Insert > Timeline > Keyframe and Insert > Timeline > Blank Keyframe, which convert a selected in-between frame or protoframe to a keyframe, the Insert > Timeline > Frame command adds a new frame to your movie.

What Are Keyframes and In-Between Frames?

In the early days of animation, it took veritable armies of artists to create the enormous number of drawings that frame-by-frame animation requires. To keep costs down, the studios broke the work into categories based on the artistic skill required and the pay provided. The work might start with creating spec sheets for each character. Then came storyboards that outlined the action over the course of the animation. Eventually, individual artists drew and painted hundreds of cels, each slightly different, to bring the animation to life.

To make the process manageable, animators broke each movement into a series of the most crucial frames that define a movement, called *keyframes,* and frames that incorporate the incremental changes necessary to simulate the movement, called *in-between frames*.

Keyframes define a significant change to a character or graphic. Imagine a 25-frame sequence in which Bugs Bunny starts out facing the audience and then turns to his right to look at Daffy Duck. This scene requires two keyframes—Bugs in a face-on view and Bugs in profile—and 23 in-between frames.

In the early days, some artists specialized in creating keyframes. Other artists—usually lower-paid—had the job of creating the frames that fell in between the keyframes. These in-betweeners (or tweeners, for short) copied the drawings in the keyframes, making just the slight adjustments necessary to create the intended movement in the desired number of frames while retaining the continuity of the character. In Chapters 9 and 10, you learn how to turn Flash into your own personal wage slave. The program takes on the drudgery of in-betweening for certain types of animation.

In Flash, you must use keyframes to define any change in the content or image, no matter how large or small the change. Flash doesn't use the term *in-between frames;* it uses the term *frame* for any frames that aren't defined as keyframes. For clarity, the tasks in this book use the term *in-between frames* to refer to any defined frames that aren't keyframes.

CREATING IN-BETWEEN FRAMES

Selecting Frames

Flash offers two styles for selecting frames in the Timeline. The default selection style, frame-based selection, treats every frame as an individual. The span-based style treats frames as members of a *keyframe span*—the keyframe plus any in-between frames that follow it and display its content. In the span-based selection style, clicking one frame in the middle of a span selects the entire span.

Except where noted, the examples in this book use Flash's default selection style, frame-based selection.

To choose a selection style:

1. From the Edit menu (Windows) or from the Flash application menu (Mac), choose Preferences.

   The Preferences dialog appears.

2. From the Category list, select General.

   The General settings appear in the right-hand pane of the dialog (**Figure 8.10**).

3. In the Timeline section, *choose either of the following frame-selection styles:*

   ▲ To manipulate keyframe spans in the Timeline, select the Span Based Selection check box.

   ▲ To manipulate individual frames in the Timeline, deselect the Span Based Selection check box.

To make frame-based selections:

In the Timeline, *do one of the following:*

◆ To select one protoframe, click it.

◆ To select two protoframes and all the frames between them, Shift-click the two protoframes.

◆ To select a keyframe, click it.

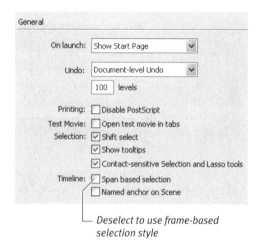

Deselect to use frame-based selection style

Figure 8.10 Choose the way frame selection works in the Timeline from the General category of the Preferences dialog.

Figure 8.11 With Flash's span-based frame-selection style, you can Shift-click to select keyframe spans that aren't contiguous.

◆ To select the last frame in a keyframe span, click it.

◆ To select just a middle frame in a keyframe span, click that frame.

◆ To select an entire keyframe span, double-click a middle frame in the keyframe span.

◆ To add frames to your selection, Shift-click the frames. Flash selects all the frames between the playhead and the frame you Shift-click.

◆ To select a range of frames, click and drag through the frames.

To make span-based selections:

In the Timeline, *do one of the following:*

◆ To select one protoframe, click it.

◆ To select two protoframes and all the frames between them, Shift-click the two protoframes.

◆ To select a keyframe, click it.

◆ To select the last frame in keyframe span, click it.

◆ To select one in-between frame, ⌘-click (Mac) or Ctrl-click (Windows) that frame.

◆ To select an entire keyframe span, click a middle frame in the keyframe span.

◆ To select an entire keyframe span, Shift-click the first or last frame in the span.

◆ To add other spans to your selection, Shift-click the spans. The selection can include noncontiguous spans (**Figure 8.11**).

◆ To select a range of frames in the Windows operating system, Ctrl-drag through the frames.

SELECTING FRAMES

✔ Tips

- In both selection styles, you can select all the frames in a layer by clicking the layer name. In the span-base selection style, you can also select all the frames in a layer by double-clicking any frame.

- In both selection styles, you can select noncontiguous frames by ⌘-clicking (Mac) or Ctrl-clicking (Windows) each frame that you want to include.

- Can't remember what selection style is set in the Preferences dialog? Here's an easy way to check. In span-based selection style, when hovering over a keyframe or the last frame of a span, the pointer is a double-headed arrow. Over an in-between frame, the pointer is an arrow with a small square. In frame-based selection style, when hovering over a selected keyframe or an end-of-span frame, the pointer is an arrow with a square; over an in-between frame, the pointer is an arrow (**Figure 8.12**).

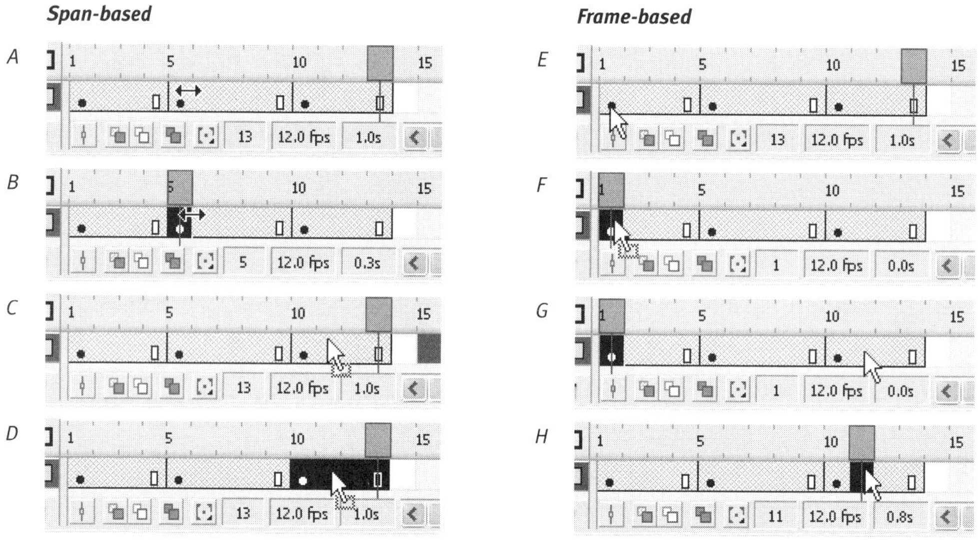

Figure 8.12 In the span-based selection style, the pointer becomes a double-headed arrow when it's over a keyframe (A) or an end-of-span frame. Clicking selects that frame individually (B). Over an in-between frame, the pointer changes to an arrow with a square (C); clicking selects the whole keyframe span (D). In the frame-based selection style, the pointer is a plain arrow when it's over a keyframe (E) or an end-of-span frame; clicking selects that frame (F). Over an in-between frame, the pointer is a plain arrow (G); clicking selects just that frame (H).

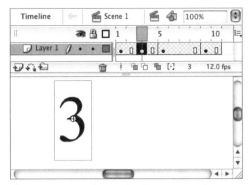

Figure 8.13 To practice moving frames around, create a document with keyframes at frames 1, 3, 5, and 9. Each keyframe contains a text box with the number of the frame.

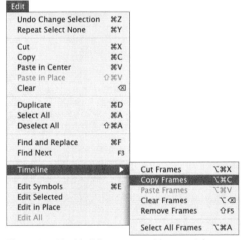

Figure 8.14 Flash's Edit menu provides special commands for copying and pasting frames in the Timeline.

Manipulating Frames in One Layer

You can't copy or paste frames by using the standard Copy and Paste commands that you use for graphic elements. Flash's Edit menu provides special commands for copying and pasting frames. Flash also lets you drag selected frames to new locations in the Timeline.

For the following tasks, open a new Flash document. Create a 10-frame movie with keyframes at frames 1, 3, 5, and 9. Using the text tool, place a text box in each keyframe, and enter the number of the frame in the text box; this technique makes it easy to tell what frame winds up where as you practice. Your document should look like **Figure 8.13**.

To copy and paste a single frame:

1. In the Timeline, select keyframe 3.

2. Choose Edit > Timeline > Copy Frames, or press Option-⌘-C (Mac) or Ctrl-Alt-C (Windows) (**Figure 8.14**).

    Flash copies the selected frame to the Clipboard.

    continues on next page

3. In the Timeline, click frame 4 to select it as the location for pasting the copied frame.

4. Choose Edit > Timeline > Paste Frames, or press Option-⌘-V (Mac) or Ctrl-Alt-V (Windows).

Flash pastes the copied frame into frame 4 (**Figure 8.15**).

5. Paste another copy into frame 5 (**Figure 8.16**).

Flash replaces the contents of keyframe 5 with the content of keyframe 3.

6. Paste another copy into protoframe 12.

Flash extends the movie to accommodate the pasted frame. Note that the playhead won't move to protoframe 12 until after you've pasted the copy to create a defined frame.

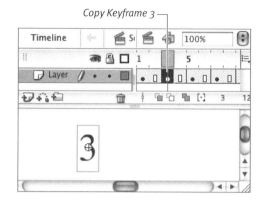

Copy Keyframe 3

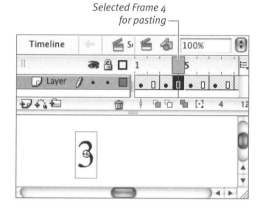

Selected Frame 4 for pasting

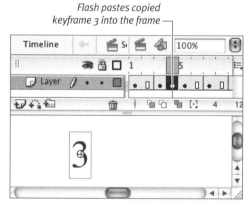

Flash pastes copied keyframe 3 into the frame

Figure 8.15 When you paste a frame with new content into an in-between frame, Flash converts the frame to a keyframe.

Flash replaces the content of keyframe 5...

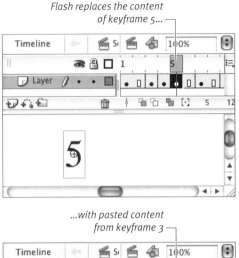

...with pasted content from keyframe 3

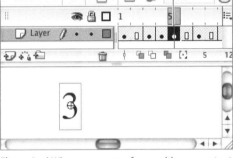

Figure 8.16 When you paste a frame with new content into a keyframe, Flash replaces the keyframe's content.

✔ Tips

- You can copy and paste multiple frames; in step 1 of the preceding task, select a range of frames.

- To copy and paste the content of a keyframe, you can also copy an in-between frame that displays that content. When you paste, Flash creates a new keyframe.

- Warning: Flash always replaces the content of the selected frame with the pasted frame (or, for multiple-frame pastes, with the first pasted frame). If you're not careful, you may eat up the content of keyframes you intended to keep. To be safe, always paste frames into in-between frames or blank keyframes. You can always delete an unwanted keyframe separately.

- You can't paste frames between back-to-back keyframes in a single step. You must first create an in-between frame (press F5) between the two, select the new in-between frame, and paste the copied frames.

To move frames using drag and drop:

1. In the Timeline of your practice document, select the keyframe span that starts with keyframe 5 and ends with frame 8.

2. Position the pointer over the selected frames.

   The pointer changes to an arrow with a square.

3. Click and drag the selected frames.

   Flash further highlights the selection with a rectangle of hatched lines. Flash uses this rectangle to preview the new location for the selected frames as you drag in the Timeline.

4. To move the selected frames to the end of your movie, drag the rectangle past the last defined frame and into the area of protoframes, and release the mouse button.

   Flash adds frames to the end of the movie; these frames display the content from frame 5. In frame-based selection style, Flash completely removes the content from frames 5–8 and adds those frames to the preceding span. In span-based selection style, Flash removes the content but keeps a keyframe at frame 5 (**Figure 8.17**).

5. To move the selected frames to the beginning of your movie, drag the selected frames to frame 1 and release the mouse button.

   The dragged frames replace the content of frames 1–4.

Select and drag: either selection style

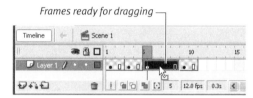

Frames ready for dragging

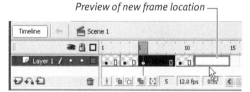

Preview of new frame location

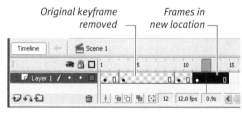

After drop: frame-based selection style

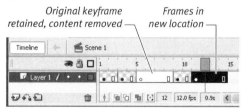

After drop: span-based selection style

Figure 8.17 The process of dragging and dropping frames in the Timeline to relocate them is the same in Flash's two frame-selection styles (top). The results, however, are quite different (bottom). The frame-based selection style removes selected keyframes from their original location, leaving only in-between frames. The span-based style retains the original keyframes but removes their content.

Flash replaces the content of keyframe 5...

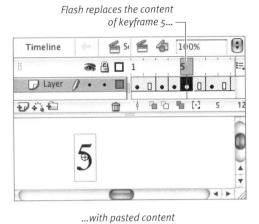

...with pasted content from keyframe 3

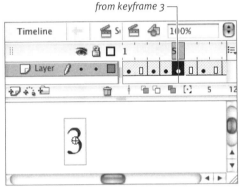

Figure 8.16 When you paste a frame with new content into a keyframe, Flash replaces the keyframe's content.

✔ Tips

■ You can copy and paste multiple frames; in step 1 of the preceding task, select a range of frames.

■ To copy and paste the content of a keyframe, you can also copy an in-between frame that displays that content. When you paste, Flash creates a new keyframe.

■ Warning: Flash always replaces the content of the selected frame with the pasted frame (or, for multiple-frame pastes, with the first pasted frame). If you're not careful, you may eat up the content of keyframes you intended to keep. To be safe, always paste frames into in-between frames or blank keyframes. You can always delete an unwanted keyframe separately.

■ You can't paste frames between back-to-back keyframes in a single step. You must first create an in-between frame (press F5) between the two, select the new in-between frame, and paste the copied frames.

To move frames using drag and drop:

1. In the Timeline of your practice document, select the keyframe span that starts with keyframe 5 and ends with frame 8.

2. Position the pointer over the selected frames.

   The pointer changes to an arrow with a square.

3. Click and drag the selected frames.

   Flash further highlights the selection with a rectangle of hatched lines. Flash uses this rectangle to preview the new location for the selected frames as you drag in the Timeline.

4. To move the selected frames to the end of your movie, drag the rectangle past the last defined frame and into the area of protoframes, and release the mouse button.

   Flash adds frames to the end of the movie; these frames display the content from frame 5. In frame-based selection style, Flash completely removes the content from frames 5–8 and adds those frames to the preceding span. In span-based selection style, Flash removes the content but keeps a keyframe at frame 5 (**Figure 8.17**).

5. To move the selected frames to the beginning of your movie, drag the selected frames to frame 1 and release the mouse button.

   The dragged frames replace the content of frames 1–4.

Select and drag: either selection style

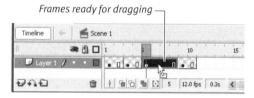

Selected frames

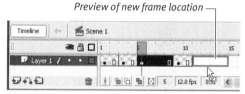

Frames ready for dragging

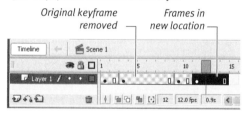

Preview of new frame location

After drop: frame-based selection style

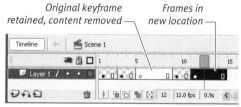

Original keyframe removed — Frames in new location

After drop: span-based selection style

Original keyframe retained, content removed — Frames in new location

Figure 8.17 The process of dragging and dropping frames in the Timeline to relocate them is the same in Flash's two frame-selection styles (top). The results, however, are quite different (bottom). The frame-based selection style removes selected keyframes from their original location, leaving only in-between frames. The span-based style retains the original keyframes but removes their content.

The Trick to Extending Keyframe Spans

In span-based selection style, the pointer becomes a double-headed arrow when it hovers over a keyframe or an end-of-span frame. Use this pointer to drag that frame to the right or the left to increase or decrease the length of the span.

Resizing a span in the middle of other spans gets a bit tricky. Flash won't let your expanding span eat up the content of other keyframes. Your expansion can reduce the length of a neighboring span, however. In your practice document, for example, using span-based selection, position the pointer over the end of the span that runs from frame 3 to frame 4 (the frame should not be selected). With the double-headed arrow pointer, drag frame 4 to the right. When you get to frame 7, you can drag no further. Release the mouse button. The span that starts at frame 3 now extends through frame 7. The content that was originally in keyframe 5 still exists, but Flash has pushed it into frame 8.

To increase the length of a span without affecting the length of neighboring spans, select the span or any frame within it; then choose Insert > Timeline > Frame or press F5. Flash adds an in-between frame to the selected span and pushes all subsequent spans to the right in the Timeline.

When you reduce the size of a span by dragging, Flash creates blank keyframe spans to cover any gaps between the end of the span you're resizing and the beginning of the neighboring span.

✔ Tips

■ To drag a copy of selected frames in the Timeline, hold down Option (Mac) or Alt (Windows) as you drag.

■ In span-based selection mode, if you select a span that consists of a keyframe and one in-between frame, you never get the arrow-with-square pointer; you only get the double-headed arrow. That means you can't drag the span to move it. To move such spans, switch to frame-based selection, or Option-drag (Mac) or Alt-drag (Windows) a copy of the span; then remove the original.

■ No matter which frame-selection style you use, pressing the ⌘ key (Mac) or Ctrl key (Windows) lets you access some of the functionality of the other style temporarily. In frame-based selection, the modifier lets you access the double-headed arrow pointer for extending keyframe spans. In span-based mode, the modifier gives you the arrow pointer for selecting individual frames.

■ If you make a mistake in modifying the frames in the Timeline, you can undo your steps by choosing Edit > Undo. Flash tracks the selection and deselection of frames as part of the undo history. Operations such as dragging frames to move them or to extend spans may require repeated Undo commands, because some of the steps involved are things Flash does behind the scenes.

MANIPULATING FRAMES IN ONE LAYER

Removing Frames

Flash has two commands for removing frames: Clear Keyframe and Remove Frames. To choose the correct command, ask yourself whether you want to eliminate the frame and reduce the length of the movie or just remove the frame's status as a keyframe, keeping the same total number of frames.

Flash's Clear Keyframe command removes keyframe status from a selected frame or range of frames. Clear Keyframe changes keyframes into in-between frames and deletes the keyframes' content from the movie. Clear Keyframe has no effect on the number of frames in the movie.

Remove Frames removes frames (and their content, if they're keyframes) from the movie. Remove Frames reduces the number of frames in the movie.

For the following tasks, use the same practice document you created for working with the tasks in "Manipulating Frames in One Layer."

To remove keyframe status from a frame:

1. In the Timeline, select keyframe 5.

2. Choose Modify > Timeline > Clear Keyframe, or press Shift-F6 on the keyboard.

   Flash removes the bullet from frame 5 in the Timeline (indicating that the frame is no longer a keyframe) and removes the graphic element it contained. Frame 5 becomes an in-between frame, displaying the contents of the keyframe at frame 3 (**Figure 8.18**). The total number of frames in the movie remains the same.

Before clearing the keyframe

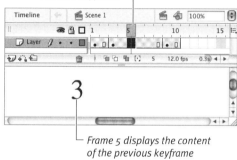

Selected keyframe is Frame 5

Content of selected keyframe

After clearing the keyframe

Frame 5 becomes an in-between keyframe

Frame 5 displays the content of the previous keyframe

Figure 8.18 The Modify > Timeline > Clear Keyframe command removes the contents of the selected keyframe from the Stage and converts the keyframe to an in-between frame. The Clear Keyframe command doesn't change the overall length of the movie.

The Indelible Keyframe

Even when you work in frame-based selection style, Flash is always dealing with keyframe spans behind the scenes. This fact may lead to initial confusion about how to delete the contents of a keyframe. If you select a keyframe that's followed by in-between frames and use the Remove Frames command, you shorten the span, but the keyframe and its contents remain (**Figure 8.19**).

To remove the content of a keyframe span, *do one of the following:*

◆ To remove the entire keyframe span, select the keyframe and its associated in-between frames, then use the Remove Frames command.

◆ To remove the content and keyframe, but add the leftover in-between frames to the preceding span, select the keyframe, delete the contents of the Stage, then use the Remove Frames command.

◆ To remove the content, convert the keyframe to an in-between frame, and add it and the leftover in-between frames to the preceding keyframe, select the keyframe and use the Clear Keyframe command. (Then use the Remove Frames command to reduce the number of in-between frames, if you want.)

Selection doesn't include associated in-between frames

The Remove Frames command retains keyframe and removes one in-between frame

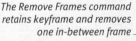
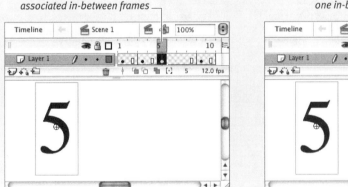
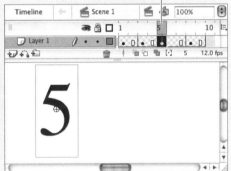

Figure 8.19 The Remove Frames command won't delete a keyframe's content fully unless you've selected all of its associated in-between frames.

To delete a single frame from a movie:

1. With your practice file in its original state (keyframes at 1, 3, 5, and 9), select frame 4 in the Timeline.

   Frame 4 is an in-between frame associated with keyframe 3.

2. Choose Edit > Timeline > Remove Frames, or press Shift-F5 on the keyboard.

   Flash deletes frame 4, reducing the overall length of the movie by one frame (**Figure 8.20**).

3. Select keyframe 3 and choose Edit > Timeline > Remove Frames again.

   Flash deletes the selected keyframe and its content, and reduces the length of the movie by one frame.

✔ Tip

- Flash doesn't allow you to use Clear Keyframe to remove keyframe status from the first frame of a movie, but you can delete it. If you select all the frames in the movie and choose Edit > Timeline > Remove Frames, Flash removes all the defined frames in the Timeline, leaving only protoframes. You must add back a keyframe at frame 1 to place any content in the movie.

Selected in-between frame —

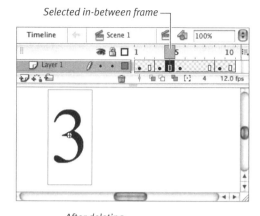

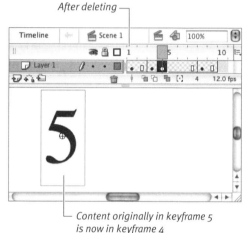

After deleting —

Content originally in keyframe 5 is now in keyframe 4

Figure 8.20 The Edit > Timeline > Remove Frames command removes frames from the movie and reduces its length.

REMOVING FRAMES

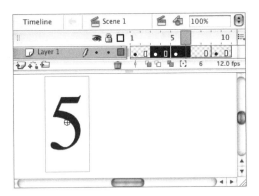

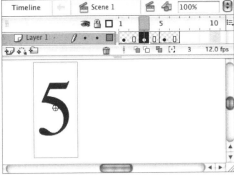

Figure 8.21 The Edit > Timeline > Remove Frames command can delete a selected range of frames. Because an entire keyframe span (frames 3 and 4) is included in the selection (top), Flash not only reduces the number of frames but also removes the content of that keyframe span (middle). Where only part of a span was selected (frames 5 and 6), the span gets shorter, but the content remains the same (bottom).

To delete a range of frames:

1. Using your practice file, in the Timeline, select frames 3–6.

2. Choose Edit > Timeline > Remove Frames.

   Flash removes all the selected frames (**Figure 8.21**).

✔ Tip

■ With the frame-based selection style active, you can replace the contents of one keyframe with those of another quickly. Select an in-between frame that displays the contents you want to copy. Drag that source frame over the keyframe whose contents you want to replace. Flash replaces the contents of the target keyframe with the contents of the source keyframe.

Making a Simple Frame-by-Frame Animation

In traditional cel animation or flip-book animation, you create the illusion of movement by showing a series of images, each slightly different from the rest, simulating snapshots of the movement. When you create each of these drawings and place them in a series of keyframes, that process is called *frame-by-frame animation*. When you create only the most crucial snapshots and allow Flash to interpolate the minor changes that take place between those snapshots, you're creating *tweened animation*. You learn more about tweening in Chapters 9 and 10.

A classic example of frame-by-frame animation is a bouncing ball. You can create a crude bouncing ball in just three frames.

To set up the initial keyframe:

1. Create a new Flash document, and name it something like Frame-by-Frame Bounce. By default, Flash creates a document with one layer and a keyframe at frame 1. Choose View > Grid > Show Grid to help you reposition your graphics in this task.

2. In the Timeline, select keyframe 1.

   Use the Frame View pop-up menu to set the Timeline to Preview in Context mode. This setting makes it easy to keep track of what you do in the example.

3. In the Tools panel, select the oval tool.

4. Set the stroke color to No Color.

5. Near the top of the Stage, draw a circle (**Figure 8.22**).

   This circle will be your ball. Make it fairly large. To make the most efficient use of your graphic, convert the circle to a symbol (see Chapter 7).

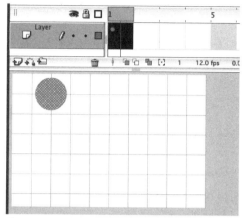

Figure 8.22 In keyframe 1, draw a circle near the top of the Stage. This circle will become a bouncing ball.

When to Use Frame-by-Frame Animation

With frame-by-frame animation, the more frames you add, the smaller you can make the differences between frames and the smoother the action is. Adding keyframes, however, also adds to your final movie's file size, which in turn affects the download time for people viewing your movie over the Web. Your goal is to strike a happy medium.

In the bouncing ball example, you could help keep file size down by making the ball a symbol so that adding another keyframe for the ball in a new position adds little to the size of the file. In the real world, however, if you can use a symbol, you might prefer to use a more labor-efficient animation technique, *motion tweening*. Reserve frame-by-frame techniqes for animations where shapes are constantly changing in subtle ways that you need to control precisely. Otherwise, use Flash's motion-tweening and shape-tweening tools (see chapters 9 and 10).

Selected frame 2

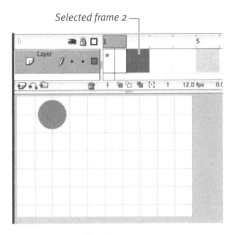

To create the second keyframe:

1. In the Timeline, select frame 2.

2. Choose Insert > Timeline > Keyframe. Flash creates a keyframe in frame 2 that duplicates your ball from keyframe 1.

3. In keyframe 2, select the ball and reposition it at the bottom of the Stage (**Figure 8.23**).

Inserted keyframe

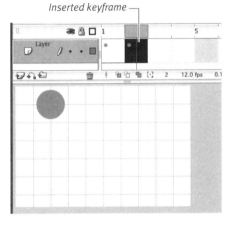

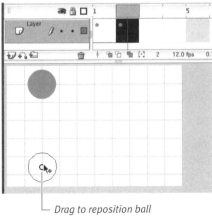

Drag to reposition ball

Figure 8.23 Use the Insert > Timeline > Keyframe command to duplicate the ball from keyframe 1 in keyframe 2. Then drag the ball to reposition it.

To create the third keyframe:

1. In the Timeline, select frame 3.

2. Choose Insert > Timeline > Keyframe.

   Flash creates a keyframe in frame 3 that duplicates your ball from keyframe 2.

3. In keyframe 3, select the ball and reposition it in the middle of the Stage (**Figure 8.24**).

   That's it. Believe it or not, you have just created all the content you need to animate a bouncing ball. To see how it works, in the Timeline, click keyframes 1, 2, and 3 in turn. As Flash changes the content of the Stage at each click, you see a very crude animation.

Selected Frame 3

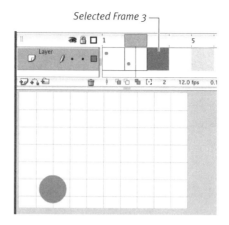

Inserted keyframe

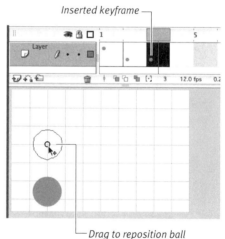

Drag to reposition ball

Figure 8.24 Use the Insert > Timeline > Keyframe command to duplicate the ball from keyframe 2 in keyframe 3. Drag the ball to reposition it again.

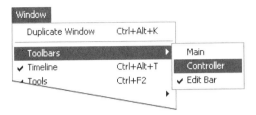

Figure 8.25 To access the Controller, choose Window > Toolbars > Controller.

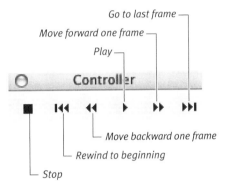

Figure 8.26 The Controller window contains VCR-style buttons for controlling playback of Flash movies.

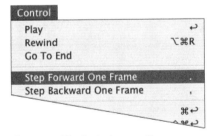

Figure 8.27 The Control menu offers commands for playing the whole Flash movie or stepping through it frame by frame.

Previewing the Action

Although you can click each frame to preview a movie, Flash provides more sophisticated ways to see your animation. The Controller window offers VCR-style playback buttons. The Control menu has commands for playback. You can also have Flash export the file and open it for you in Flash Player.

To use the Controller:

1. Choose Window > Toolbars > Controller (**Figure 8.25**).

   Flash opens a window containing standard VCR-style buttons.

2. In the Controller window, click the button for the command you want to use (**Figure 8.26**).

✔ Tip

- For those who prefer not to clutter the desktop with more floating windows, the Control menu in the main menu bar duplicates the Controller's functions.

To step sequentially through frames:

1. In the Timeline, select frame 1.

2. From the Control menu (**Figure 8.27**), choose Step Forward One Frame, or press the period (.) key.

   Flash moves to the following frame.

3. Choose Control > Step Backward One Frame, or press the comma (,) key.

   Flash moves to the preceding frame.

✔ Tip

- You can *scrub* (scroll quickly back and forth) through the movie. Drag the playhead backward or forward through the frames in the Timeline. Flash displays the content of each frame as the playhead moves through it.

To play through all frames in the Flash editor:

◆ To play through the frames once, choose Control > Play, or press Enter.

Flash displays each frame in turn, starting with the current frame and running through the end of the movie. The Play command in the Control menu changes to a Stop command, which you can use to stop playback at any time.

✔ Tip

■ To play through the frames repeatedly, choose Control > Loop Playback (**Figure 8.28**). Now, whenever you issue a Play command, Flash plays the movie repeatedly until you issue a Stop command.

To play frames in Flash Player:

◆ Choose Control > Test Movie (**Figure 8.29**).

Flash exports your movie to a Flash Player (SWF) file and opens it in a separate window. Flash stores the SWF file at the same hierarchical level of your system as the original Flash file. The SWF file has the same name as the original, except that Flash appends the .swf extension.

✔ Tip

■ If you'd prefer to have your Flash Player tests open in the tabbed window set with your Flash documents, you can set that as a preference. From the Flash (Mac) or Edit (Windows) menu, choose Preferences. In the Preferences dialog, from the Category list, select General. In the main window, select the Open Test Movie in Tabs check box.

Figure 8.28 Choosing Control > Loop Playback sets Flash to show your movie repeatedly when you subsequently issue a play command from the Controller, the Control menu, or the keyboard.

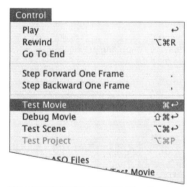

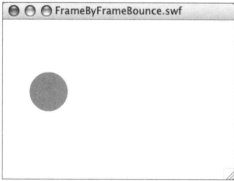

Figure 8.29 Choose Control > Test Movie (top) to see your movie in action in Flash Player (bottom).

PREVIEWING THE ACTION

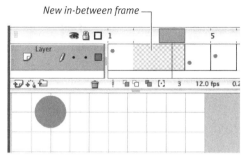

New in-between frame

Figure 8.30 With keyframe 1 selected, invoking the Insert > Timeline > Frame command twice inserts two new in-between frames after the first keyframe and pushes the original keyframe 2 (the ball at the bottom of the Stage) to frame 4.

Smoothing the Animation by Adding Keyframes

The three-frame bouncing ball you created in the preceding task is crude; it's herky-jerky and much too fast. To smooth out the movement, you need to create more snapshots that define the ball's position in the air as it moves up and down. This means adding more keyframes and repositioning the ball slightly in each one.

In the preceding task, the ball moves from the top of the stage to the bottom in one step. In the following task, you expand that first bounce movement to three steps.

To add keyframes within an existing animation:

1. In the Timeline of the three-frame bouncing ball animation, select keyframe 1.

2. Choose Insert > Timeline > Frame; then choose Insert > Timeline > Frame again.

   Flash creates new in-between frames at frames 2 and 3, and relocates the keyframes that show the ball at the bottom and middle of the Stage to frames 4 and 5 (**Figure 8.30**).

3. In the Timeline, select frames 2 and 3.

continues on next page

PREVIEWING THE ACTION

4. Choose Modify > Timeline > Convert to Keyframes.

Flash converts the in-between frames to keyframes that duplicate the content of keyframe 1 (**Figure 8.31**).

5. In the Timeline, select keyframe 2, and then reposition the ball on the Stage.

You can use the grid line to help you visualize where to place the ball; position it about a third of the distance between the top and bottom of the Stage.

6. In the Timeline, select keyframe 3, and then reposition the ball on the Stage (**Figure 8.32**).

Position the ball about two-thirds of the distance between the top and bottom of the Stage.

7. Preview the animation using any of the methods described in the preceding section.

The initial bounce movement is smoother. Repeat these steps to add even more frames with incremental movement to the first half of the bounce. You can also add frames to make the second half of the bounce smoother.

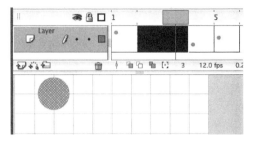

Duplicates of Keyframe 1

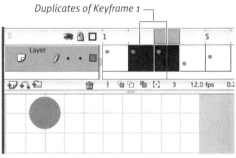

Figure 8.31 Modify > Timeline > Convert to Keyframes changes the selected in-between frames to keyframes containing the content of the preceding keyframe.

Frames previewed in context

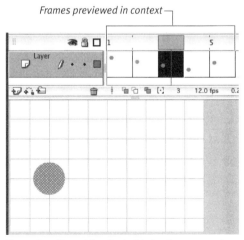

Figure 8.32 Reposition the ball in keyframes 2 and 3 to make the first bounce smoother.

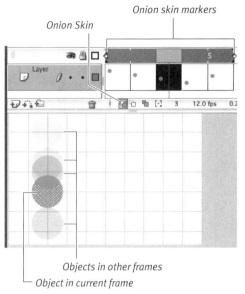

Onion Skin

Onion skin markers

Layer

3   12.0 fps   0.2

Objects in other frames

Object in current frame

Figure 8.33 In Onion Skin mode, Flash displays the content of multiple frames but dims everything that's not on the current frame. The onion-skin markers in the Timeline indicate how many frames appear at the same time.

Using Onion Skinning

In the preceding section, you repositioned a circle to try to create smooth incremental movement for a bouncing ball. To make this task easier, Flash's onion-skinning feature lets you see the circle in context with the circles in surrounding frames.

Onion skinning displays dimmed or outline versions of the content of surrounding frames. You determine how many of the surrounding frames Flash displays. The buttons for turning on and off the various types of onion skinning appear at the bottom of the Timeline, in the Timeline's Status bar.

To turn on onion skinning:

◆ In the Status bar of the Timeline, click the Onion Skin button.

The content of all the frames included in the onion-skin markers appears in a dimmed form (**Figure 8.33**). You can't edit the dimmed graphics—only the full-color graphics in the current frame.

To turn on outline onion skinning:

◆ In the Status bar of the Timeline, click the Onion Skin Outlines button.

The content of all the frames included in the onion-skin markers appears in outline form (**Figure 8.34**). You can't edit the outline graphics—only the solid graphics that appear in the current frame.

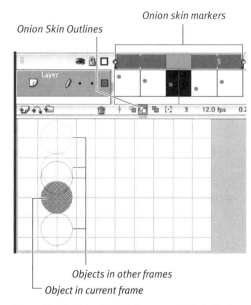

Onion skin markers

Onion Skin Outlines

Objects in other frames

Object in current frame

Figure 8.34 In Onion Skin Outlines mode, Flash displays the content of multiple frames, but it uses outlines for everything that's not in the current frame. Notice that two of the outlines appear very close together in this example of the bouncing ball. Using that visual cue, you can reposition the ball in keyframe 4 to make the spacing (and, thereby, the movement) more even.

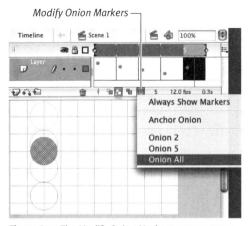

Modify Onion Markers

Figure 8.35 The Modify Onion Markers pop-up menu gives you control over the number of frames that appear as onion skins.

To adjust the number of frames included in onion skinning:

1. In the Timeline, click the Modify Onion Markers button.

   A pop-up menu appears, containing commands for setting the way the onion-skin markers work (**Figure 8.35**).

2. To see frames on either side of the current frame, *do one of the following:*

   ▲ To see two frames on either side of the current frame, choose Onion 2.

   ▲ To see five frames on either side of the current frame, choose Onion 5.

   ▲ To see all the frames in the movie, choose Onion All.

   Flash moves the onion-skin markers around in the Timeline as you move the playhead. Flash always includes onion skins (either solid or outline) for graphics in the selected number of frames before the current frame and after it.

✔ Tips

- Flash doesn't show the contents of locked layers in onion-skin views.

- Drag onion-skin markers in the Timeline to include more frames or fewer frames in the onion-skin view.

- You can prevent the onion-skin markers from moving each time you select a new frame in the Timeline. Set the markers to encompass the frames you want to see together. From the Modify Onion Markers menu, choose Anchor Onion. As long as you keep selecting frames inside the anchored range, the anchored set of frames stays in Onion Skin mode.

Editing Multiple Frames

If you decide to change the location of an animated element, you must change the element's location in every keyframe in which it appears. Repositioning the items one frame at a time is not only tedious but also dangerous. You may forget one frame, and you can easily get the animated elements out of alignment. Flash solves this problem by letting you move elements in multiple frames simultaneously. The same markers that indicate the frames to include in onion skinning indicate the frames you're allowed to edit simultaneously in Edit Multiple Frames mode.

To relocate animated graphics on the Stage:

1. Open your frame-by-frame animation of a bouncing ball.

2. In the Status bar, choose Edit Multiple Frames (**Figure 8.36**).

   Flash displays all graphics in all frames within the onion-skin markers and makes them editable.

3. From the Modify Onion Markers menu, choose Onion All.

   Now you can see the ball at each stage of its bounce, and you can edit each of these stages.

4. Using the selection tool, draw a selection rectangle that includes all the visible balls on the Stage (**Figure 8.37**).

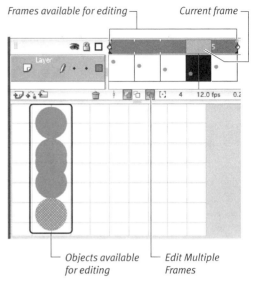

Frames available for editing — Current frame —

Objects available for editing — Edit Multiple Frames

Figure 8.36 In Edit Multiple Frames mode, Flash displays and makes editable all the graphics in the frames that the onion-skin markers indicate. This feature makes it possible to move an animated graphic to a new location in every keyframe at the same time.

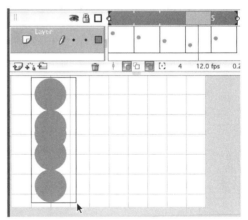

Figure 8.37 In Edit Multiple Frames mode, you can use a selection rectangle to select graphics in any of the frames enclosed in the onion-skin markers.

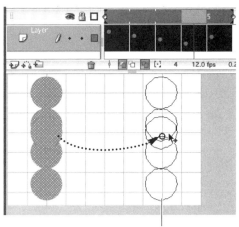

*Outline previews the new location
as you drag selected graphics*

Figure 8.38 In Edit Multiple Frames mode, you can relocate an animated graphic completely, moving it in every keyframe with one action.

*Outline-mode
toggle*

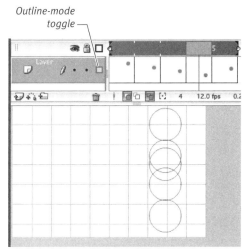

Figure 8.39 Select Outline mode to make it easier to work with graphics in multiple frames.

5. Drag the selection to the opposite side of the Stage (**Figure 8.38**).

With just a few steps, you've relocated the bouncing ball. (Imagine how much more work it would have been to select each keyframe separately, move the circle for that frame, select the next keyframe, line the circles up precisely in the new location, and so on.)

✔ Tip

■ When you select Edit Multiple Frames, Flash no longer displays onion skinning for keyframes; onion skinning does appear for in-between frames with tweened content. If you find it confusing to view solid graphics in multiple keyframes, turn on Outline view in the layer-properties section of the Timeline (**Figure 8.39**).

EDITING MULTIPLE FRAMES

267

Setting the Frame Rate

In Flash, you can set only one frame rate for the entire movie. You set the frame rate in the Document Properties dialog.

To set the frame rate:

1. To access the Document Properties dialog, *do either of the following:*

   ▲ Choose Modify > Document, or press ⌘-J (Mac) or Ctrl-J (Windows).

   ▲ In the Timeline's Status bar, double-click the frame-rate number (**Figure 8.40**).

2. In the Document Properties dialog, enter a value in the Frame Rate field (**Figure 8.41**).

3. Click OK.

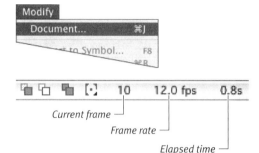

Current frame ⌐
Frame rate ⌐
Elapsed time ⌐

Figure 8.40 To call up the Document Properties dialog, choose Modify > Document (top) or double-click the frame-rate number in the Timeline's Status bar (bottom).

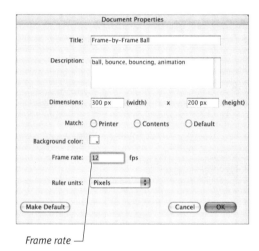

Frame rate ⌐

Figure 8.41 Enter a new value in the Frame Rate field. Flash's default frame rate is 12 fps.

Understanding Frame Rate

The illusion of animation relies on the human brain's ability to fill in gaps in continuity. When you see a series of images in very quick succession, your brain perceives a continuous moving image. In animation, you must display the sequence of images fast enough to convince the brain that it's looking at a single image.

Frame rate controls how fast Flash delivers the images. If the images come too fast, the movie turns into a blur. Slow delivery too much, and your viewers start perceiving each frame as a separate image; then the movement seems jerky. In addition, when you're working in Flash, you're most likely planning to deliver the movie over the Internet, and you don't always know what types of systems your viewers will be using. That means you won't necessarily be able to deliver a fast frame rate.

The standard rate for film is 24 frames per second (fps). For graphic animation that's going out over the Internet, 12 fps (Flash's default) is a good lowest-common-denominator setting. If you know your target audience uses low-bandwidth connections, consider lowering that to 10 fps; if your target uses high-bandwidth connections, try 15 fps. Today's high-bandwidth connections and Flash Player 8's capabilities, however, make higher frame rates a possibility. If you're confident that your target audience has the capability to handle it, try for something closer to film's rate. Flash creators who like to deliver even smoother animations or whose creations contain video may want to use a frame rate of 30 fps.

Varying the Speed of Animations

Although the frame rate for a movie is constant, you can make any particular bit of animation go faster or slower by changing the number of frames it takes to complete the action. You can lengthen a portion of an animation by adding more keyframes or by adding in-between frames. In the bouncing-ball example, the ball may drop down slowly (say, over five frames) but rebound more quickly (over three frames). The smoothest frame-by-frame animation has many keyframes, each showing the ball in a slightly different position. Adding keyframes, however, increases file size. Sometimes, you can get away with adding in-between frames to slow the action. In-between frames add little to the exported movie's file size.

To add in-between frames:

1. Open (or create) a five-frame bouncing-ball movie.

   Keyframe 1 shows the ball at the top of the Stage, keyframes 2 and 3 show the ball at two places in its descent, keyframe 4 shows the ball at the bottom of the Stage, and keyframe 5 shows the ball bouncing halfway back up. (For step-by-step instructions, see the tasks in "Smoothing the Animation by Adding Keyframes," earlier in this chapter.)

2. Choose File > Save As, and make a copy of the file.

   Give the file a distinguishing name, such as BounceSlower.

3. In the copy's Timeline, select frame 1.

4. Control-click (Mac) or right-click (Win) to access the contextual menu for frames.

continues on next page

5. Choose Insert Frame.

Flash inserts an in-between frame at frame 2 and pushes the keyframe that was there to frame 3 (**Figure 8.42**).

6. Repeat steps 3–5 for the second and third keyframes in the movie.

You wind up with keyframes in frames 1, 3, 5, 7, and 8 (**Figure 8.43**).

7. Choose Control > Test Movie.

Flash exports the movie to an SWF file and opens it in Flash Player. Play through the regular 5-frame bouncing ball, and then play through the one you just created (the one named BounceSlower). You can see that the action in the movie with added in-between frames feels different from the action in the movie in which one keyframe directly follows another. The added frames slow the motion.

✔ Tip

■ Keep in mind that this example serves to illustrate a process. In most animations, you shouldn't overuse this technique. If you simply add many in-between frames, you'll slow the action too much and destroy the illusion of movement.

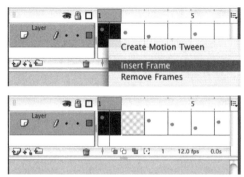

Figure 8.42 Select a frame; Ctrl-click (Mac) or right-click (Win), and choose Insert Frame from the context menu (top); Flash inserts an in-between frame directly after the selected frame (bottom).

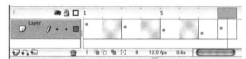

Figure 8.43 With in-between frames separating the initial keyframes, the first part of the animation moves at a slower pace than the second.

ANIMATION WITH MOTION TWEENING

Animating movement and changes to shapes by hand (frame-by-frame) is labor-intensive. Macromedia Flash 8 reduces the number of frames you must draw when you use a process called *tweening*. In Chapter 8, you created a three-frame animation of a bouncing ball by changing the position of the ball graphic in each of the three keyframes. Then you learned how to stretch out the animation by adding in-between frames that repeated the contents of the preceding keyframe. With tweening, you create similar keyframes, but Flash breaks the keyframe changes into multiple steps and displays them in the in-between frames.

To tween a graphic, Flash creates a series of incremental changes to that graphic; these changes are simple enough that Flash can describe them mathematically. Flash performs two types of tweening: motion tweening and shape tweening. This chapter covers motion tweening; Chapter 10 covers shape tweening.

Both types of tweening follow the same basic pattern. You give Flash the beginning and end of the sequence by placing graphic elements in keyframes. Then you tell Flash to spread the change out over a certain number of steps by placing that number of frames between the keyframes. Flash creates a series of images with incremental changes that accomplish the movement in the desired number of frames.

Drawing-Objects and Motion Tweening

Motion tweens require graphics that are in some form of container. In previous versions of Flash, to create a motion tween, the only graphic-container options were groups, symbols, or text boxes. Flash 8 gives you another choice: drawing-objects. When a drawing tool is set to Object Drawing mode, each shape it creates automatically winds up in a container. That means you can use a drawing-object directly in a motion tween without first converting the shape to a group or symbol.

Creating a Bouncing Ball with Motion Tweening

To create a motion tween, you must place the appropriate type of content in the beginning and end of a keyframe span and then set the span's Tween property to Motion. The graphic element in a motion tween must be a graphic-object (a drawing-object, group, symbol, or text box). You set the Tween property in the Frame Properties tab of the Property inspector. You can get assistance in making motion tweens from the Create Motion Tween command, which you'll learn about later in this chapter.

You can use motion tweening to create the same bouncing ball you made in Chapter 8, but in a slightly different way.

To prepare keyframes for motion tweening:

1. Create a new Flash document, and name it something like MotionTweenBounce.

   Flash creates a document with one layer and a keyframe at frame 1.

2. In the Timeline, select keyframe 1.

3. In the Tools panel, choose the oval tool, and set the stroke to No Color.

4. Near the top of the Stage, draw a circle. This circle will be the ball. Make it fairly large.

5. Select the circle, and choose Modify > Convert to Symbol.

   The Convert to Symbol dialog appears. The symbol can be any type, but for this task, choose Graphic.

Which Frames Contain Tweening?

As your road map of the movie, the Timeline provides visual cues about which frames contain tweens. Flash draws an arrow across a series of frames to indicate that those frames contain a tween.

Flash color-codes frames in the Timeline to distinguish motion tweens from shape tweens. With Tinted Frames active (choose it from the Frame View pop-up menu at the right end of the Timeline), Flash applies a shade of light bluish-purple (Mac) or bluish-gray (Win) to the frames that contain a motion tween. If Tinted Frames is inactive, the frames are white (Mac) or patterned (Windows), and Flash changes the arrow that indicates the presence of a tween from black to red. Flash indicates shape tweens by tinting frames light green (if Tinted Frames is active) or by changing the tweening arrow to light green (if Tinted Frames is inactive).

Frames containing a dotted line are set to contain a tween (either Motion or Shape), but something is wrong and Flash can't complete the tween. Such tweens are called *broken* tweens.

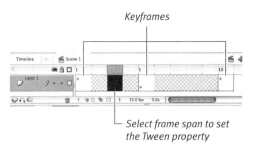

Keyframes

Select frame span to set the Tween property

Figure 9.1 The initial keyframes for a motion tween are similar to those of a frame-by-frame animation. The difference is that you must use a graphic-object (a drawing-object, symbol, group, or text box) and set the keyframe span's Tween property to Motion.

6. Enter a name for your symbol—for example, Ball—and click OK.

7. In the Timeline, select frame 5, and choose Insert > Timeline > Keyframe.

   The Insert > Timeline > Keyframe command makes a new keyframe that duplicates the contents of the preceding keyframe.

8. Select frame 10, and choose Insert > Timeline > Keyframe.

9. Select keyframe 5, and drag the ball to the bottom of the Stage.

   You have just set up a frame-by-frame animation quite like the one you did in Chapter 8. In keyframe 1, the ball is at the top of its bounce; in keyframe 5, the ball is at the bottom of its bounce; and in keyframe 10, the ball is back up at the top (**Figure 9.1**). To complete a tweened animation, you must set the tween property for the in-between frames in each keyframe span.

✔ Tip

- You could create the oval for this task as a drawing-object (or create it as a merge-shape and then group it) and then skip steps 5 and 6. The most efficient practice for creating graphic elements for motion tweens, however, is to use symbols. Symbols help to keep final file sizes small; you can name the symbols, reuse them, find them in the library to modify, and so on. You can also animate changes in color when you use symbols, whereas with drawing-objects and groups, you can't (see "Animating Color Effects," later in this chapter).

CREATING A MOTION TWEEN

To set the span's property to Motion Tween:

1. To define a motion tween for the first half of the ball's bounce, in the Timeline, select any of the frames in the first keyframe span (1, 2, 3, or 4).

   Note that Flash automatically selects the ball symbol. When you define a motion tween, the item to be tweened must be selected.

2. In the Frame Properties tab of the Property inspector, from the Tween pop-up menu, choose Motion (**Figure 9.2**).

   The settings for motion tweens appear. You learn more about using these settings in the following tasks.

   Flash defines frames 1–4 as a motion tween, updating the Timeline to give you information about the tween (see the sidebar "Which Frames Contain Tweening?") (**Figure 9.3**). These in-between frames no longer display the content of the preceding keyframe, instead they display the incrementally changed content that Flash creates. This tween content is shielded so you can't select it (clicking a graphic-object on an in-between frame set to tween is just like clicking a blank area of the Stage). You can, however, drag tween content, but doing so transforms the in-between frame into a keyframe.

3. To define the motion tween for the second half of the ball's bounce, in the Timeline, select any of the frames in the second keyframe span (5, 6, 7, 8, or 9).

4. Repeat step 2.

   Flash creates the second half of the ball's bounce with another motion tween (**Figure 9.4**).

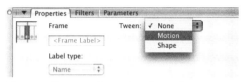

Figure 9.2 To access the settings for motion tweens, in the Frame Properties tab of the Property inspector, choose Motion from Tween pop-up menu.

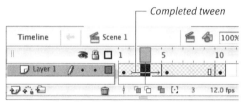

Figure 9.3 Flash adds information to the Timeline to indicate when frames contain motion tweens. Here, a blue tint and an arrow mean a completed motion tween.

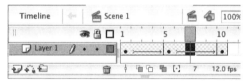

Figure 9.4 With two motion-tween sequences, you can create a bouncing ball: One sequence shows the downward motion, and the other shows the rebound.

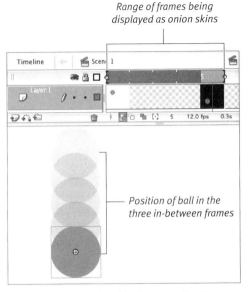

Range of frames being displayed as onion skins

Position of ball in the three in-between frames

Figure 9.5 Turn on onion skinning to preview the positions of a tweened object on the Stage.

✔ Tips

■ When you choose Preview or Preview in Context from the Frame View pop-up menu (at the right end of the Timeline), you can't see the incremental steps Flash creates for the tween. But if you turn on onion skinning, you can see all the in-between frames in position on the Stage (**Figure 9.5**).

■ Oddly enough, although you can't select a symbol on an in-between frame, you can edit it. Double-clicking a symbol on an in-between frame opens that symbol in symbol-editing mode. This trick doesn't work for drawing-objects or groups, however; you must be in a keyframe to edit those graphic-objects. And you must be careful when you double-click; if you drag the symbol even a tiny bit, Flash creates a new keyframe.

Adding Keyframes to Motion Tweens

After you have set up a motion tween, Flash creates new keyframes for you when you reposition a tweened graphic on an in-between frame. You can also add new keyframes by choosing Insert > Timeline > Keyframe.

To add keyframes by repositioning a tweened graphic:

1. Create a 10-frame motion tween of a bouncing ball, following the steps in the preceding task.

2. In the Timeline, select frame 3.

   On the Stage, you see the ball symbol in one of the in-between positions Flash created.

3. In the Tools panel, select the selection tool.

4. Drag the ball to a new position—slightly to the right of its current position, for example.

   Flash inserts a new keyframe at frame 3 and splits the preceding five-frame tween into separate tweens (**Figure 9.6**). The new keyframe contains another instance of the ball symbol.

To add keyframes by command:

1. Continuing with the document from the preceding task, select frame 7 in the Timeline.

2. Choose Insert > Timeline > Keyframe.

   Flash creates a new keyframe in frame 7. A new instance of your symbol appears on the Stage in the position Flash created for it in that in-between frame. You can now reposition the symbol.

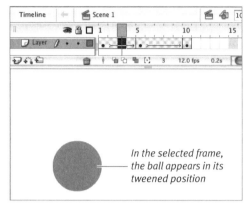

In the selected frame, the ball appears in its tweened position

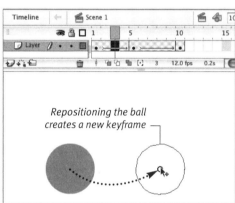

Repositioning the ball creates a new keyframe

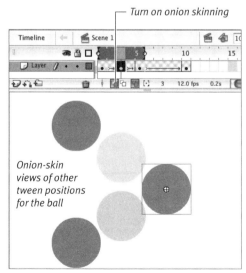

Turn on onion skinning

Onion-skin views of other tween positions for the ball

Figure 9.6 Repositioning the ball in an in-between frame that's part of a tween creates a new keyframe and a revision of the tweened frames.

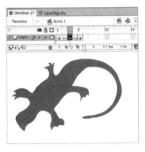

Figure 9.7 You can change the color of a symbol, as well as its position, in a motion tween. Flash creates transitional colors for each in-between frame.

Animating Color Effects

Tweening isn't just about changing the position of an item on the Stage. When you use motion tweening with symbol instances, you can also tween changes in color.

To change a symbol's color over time:

1. In a new Flash document, or in a new layer of an existing document, in keyframe 1, place a symbol instance on the Stage.

2. In the Timeline, select frame 5, and choose Insert > Timeline > Keyframe.

   Flash duplicates the contents of keyframe 1 in a new keyframe.

3. With keyframe 5 as the current frame, select the symbol.

4. To change the symbol's color, in the Properties tab of the Property inspector, from the Color menu, choose new settings. (For detailed instructions on modifying symbol color, see Chapter 7.)

5. Select any of the frames in the first keyframe span (1, 2, 3, or 4).

6. In the Properties tab of the Property inspector, from the Tween pop-up menu, choose Motion.

   Flash recolors the graphic-object in three transitional steps—one for each in-between frame (**Figure 9.7**).

✔ Tip

■ You can motion-tween a change in a graphic-object's transparency (Alpha) to make that graphic appear to fade in or out.

Animating Graphics That Change Size

Flash can tween changes in the size of a graphic. To tween graphics that grow or shrink, you must select the Scale check box in the Frame Properties tab of the Property inspector.

To tween a growing and shrinking graphic:

1. In a new Flash document, or in a new layer of an existing document, in keyframe 1, place a symbol instance on the Stage.

   (To review the creation and use of symbols, see Chapter 7.)

2. To create a keyframe that defines the end of a growing sequence, in the Timeline, select frame 5; then choose Insert > Timeline > Keyframe.

   Flash duplicates the symbol from keyframe 1 in the new keyframe.

3. Select any of the frames in the keyframe span (1, 2, 3, or 4).

4. Set the Tween property for the span to Motion.

   To do so, in the Frame Properties tab of the Property inspector, from the Tween pop-up menu, choose Motion. The motion-tween arrow and color coding now appear in frames 2–4.

5. With the playhead in keyframe 5, select your graphic and make it bigger.

   (For detailed instructions on resizing graphics, see Chapter 4.)

6. In the Timeline, select any of the frames in the first keyframe span (1, 2, 3, or 4).

7. In the Properties tab of the Property inspector, make sure the Scale check box is selected (it is selected by default).

   Flash increases the size of your graphic in equal steps from keyframe 1 to keyframe 5 (**Figure 9.8**).

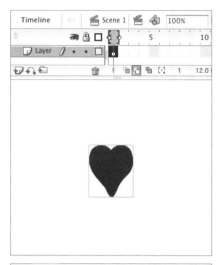

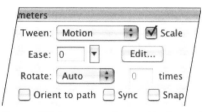

Figure 9.8 To tween a growing graphic, the graphic in the first keyframe of the sequence (top) must be smaller than the graphic in the end keyframe of the sequence (middle). To make the graphic grow in equal steps, set the Tween property of the frames in the tweened span to Motion, and choose the Scale property. You set the properties for a selected frame in the Frame Properties tab of the Property inspector (bottom).

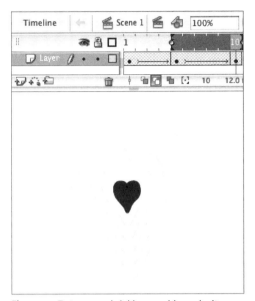

Figure 9.9 To tween a shrinking graphic, make it smaller in the end keyframe of the sequence. Turn on Onion Skin mode to see the size of the graphic Flash creates for each in-between frame.

8. To add the ending keyframe for a shrinking sequence, in the Timeline, select frame 10; then press F6.

Flash duplicates the symbol from keyframe 5 in the new keyframe.

9. Select any of the frames in the keyframe span (5, 6, 7, 8, or 9).

10. Set the Tween property for the span to Motion (see step 4).

The motion-tween arrow and color coding now appear in frames 6–9. The Scale property is already selected.

11. With the playhead in keyframe 10, select your graphic and make it smaller.

Flash creates a tween that shrinks your graphic in five equal steps (**Figure 9.9**).

✔ Tip

- As long as you don't change the settings in the Frame Properties tab of the Property inspector, the Scale check box remains selected, and Flash updates the tween any time you change the content in one of the keyframes in this series. You don't have to have the Frame Properties tab of the Property inspector open to fine-tune the size of your scaling graphic.

ANIMATING GRAPHICS THAT CHANGE SIZE

Rotating and Spinning Graphics

When you create motion tweens that involve spinning your graphic elements, creating beginning and ending keyframes isn't enough. You need to specify the direction in which the element should spin, and the number of times.

To rotate a graphic less than 360 degrees:

1. In a new Flash document, or on a new layer, in keyframe 1, place a symbol instance on the Stage.

   You can create a new symbol or use an existing one; use a graphic that looks different at various stages of its rotation (for example, a triangle or an arrow). (To review symbol creation, see Chapter 7.)

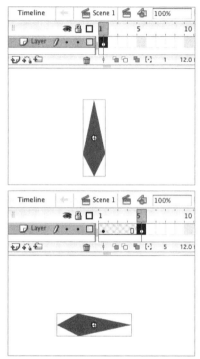

Figure 9.10 To prepare a rotational tween, in the keyframe that ends the tween, rotate the item to its ending position.

Creating Rotation with Just Two Keyframes

You can't create tweens of rotating and spinning graphics quite as easily as you create the types of motion tweens presented in the preceding tasks, because you can't describe rotation accurately with just two keyframes.

Imagine, for example, trying to rotate the pointer of a compass 180 degrees so that it turns from pointing north to pointing south. The initial keyframe contains the pointer pointing up; the ending keyframe contains the pointer pointing down. But how should the pointer move to reach that position?

Flash gives you three choices: rotate the pointer clockwise, rotate it counterclockwise, or flip it upside down. Trying to describe the pointer spinning all the way around the compass in just two keyframes would be even less informative, because the beginning and ending keyframes would be identical.

To clarify the motion, you could create a series of keyframes, rotating the pointer a few degrees in each one. That method is tedious, however. Fortunately, the Frame Properties tab of the Property inspector lets you provide extra information about tweens so that Flash can create rotational tweens with just two keyframes.

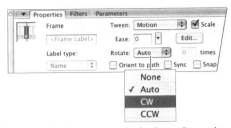

Figure 9.11 The Rotate menu in the Frame Properties tab of the Property inspector lets you tell Flash the direction in which to rotate a tweened object.

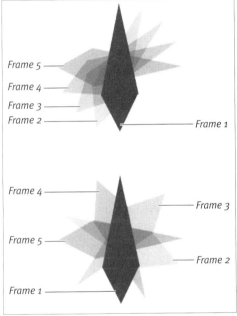

Figure 9.12 To create a tween that involves rotation, you can specify the direction of the rotation as clockwise or counterclockwise. You can also choose Auto to let Flash pick the direction that involves the smallest change, which allows Flash to create the smoothest motion. Compare the degree of change in each frame between rotating an arrow clockwise from 12 o'clock to 3 o'clock (top) versus rotating the arrow counterclockwise to reach the same position (bottom).

2. In the Timeline, select frame 5, and choose Insert > Timeline > Keyframe.

Flash duplicates the symbol from keyframe 1 in the new keyframe.

3. On the Stage, in keyframe 5, rotate your graphic 90 degrees clockwise (**Figure 9.10**). (For detailed instructions on rotating elements, see Chapter 4.)

4. In the Timeline, select any of the frames in the first keyframe span (1, 2, 3, or 4).

5. In the Frame Properties tab of the Property inspector, from the Tween pop-up menu, choose Motion.

The settings for motion tweening appear in the panel.

6. From the Rotate menu (**Figure 9.11**), *choose one of the following options:*

▲ To rotate the graphic in the direction that requires the smallest movement, choose Auto (**Figure 9.12**).

▲ To rotate the graphic clockwise, choose CW.

▲ To rotate the graphic counterclockwise, choose CCW.

Flash tweens the graphic so that it rotates around its transformation point. Each in-between frame shows the graphic rotated a little more.

To spin a graphic 360 degrees:

1. Follow steps 1 and 2 of the preceding task to create a five-frame sequence with identical keyframes in frame 1 and frame 5.

   You don't need to reposition your graphic, because the beginning frame and ending frame of a 360-degree spin should look exactly the same.

2. In the Timeline, select any of the frames in the first keyframe span (1, 2, 3, or 4).

3. Set the Tween property to Motion (see step 5 of the preceding task).

4. From the Rotate menu, choose a direction of rotation.

5. In the Rotate field, to the right of the Rotate menu, enter the number of rotations that you want to use (**Figure 9.13**).

   The value that you enter in the Rotate field determines how Flash tweens the graphic. Flash creates new positions for the graphic to rotate it completely the given number times in the span of frames. Flash tweens the graphic differently depending on the number of rotations you choose (**Figure 9.14**).

   Flash tweens the item so that it spins the number of times you indicated over the span of frames that you defined as the motion tween.

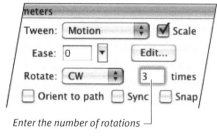

Enter the number of rotations ⌐

Figure 9.13 In the Frame Properties tab of the Property inspector, you can set the number of times a tweened item should spin.

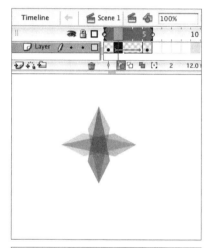

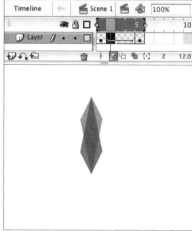

Figure 9.14 Compare a single rotation (top) with a double rotation (bottom) in the same number of frames.

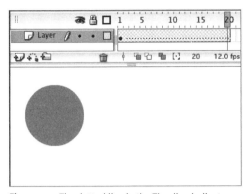

Figure 9.15 The dotted line in the Timeline indicates that these 20 frames contain a motion tween, but a broken one. The final keyframe is missing.

Moving Graphics in Straight Lines

In the preceding tasks, you created a well-behaved bouncing ball—one that moves up and down. To make one that bounces around like a crazy Ping-Pong ball, just add more keyframes and position the ball in various locations. The ball moves in a straight line from one position to the next, but the whole effect is livelier. To get frenetic bouncing, move the ball a great distance in a small number of in-between frames. To slow the action, move the ball a short distance or use a larger number of in-between frames.

To move an item from point to point:

1. In a new Flash document, or on a new layer, on the Stage, in keyframe 1, place an instance of a symbol containing a graphic of a ball.

(To review symbol creation, see Chapter 7.)

2. In the Timeline, select frame 20, and choose Insert >Timeline > Frame.

Flash creates 19 in-between frames.

3. In the Timeline, select any frame in the keyframe span (frames 1–20).

4. In the Frame Properties tab of the Property inspector, from the Tween pop-up menu, choose Motion.

Flash defines frames 1–20 as a motion tween but with a dotted line in the Timeline, indicating that the tween isn't yet complete (**Figure 9.15**). You need to create keyframes that describe the ball's motion.

continues on next page

5. In the Timeline, position the playhead in frame 5.

6. On the Stage, drag the ball to a new position.

Flash creates a new keyframe in frame 5 and completes a tween for frames 1–5 (**Figure 9.16**).

7. In the Timeline, position the playhead in frame 10.

8. On the Stage, drag the ball to a new position.

Flash creates a new keyframe in frame 10 and completes a tween for frames 5–10.

*Broken tween,
no ending keyframe*

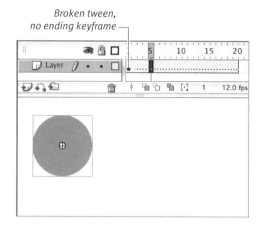

*Moving the graphic
adds a keyframe*

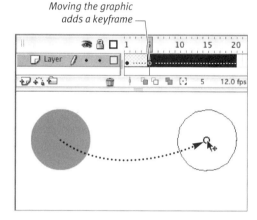

*Completed tween
segment*

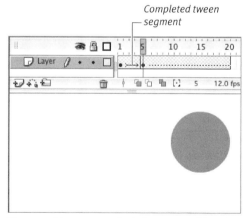

Figure 9.16 As you move the ball to new positions in different frames within the motion tween, Flash creates keyframes and completes the tween between one keyframe and the next.

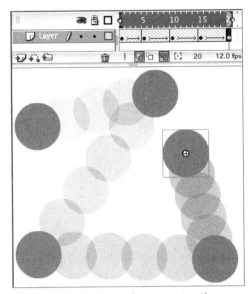

Figure 9.17 By stringing motion tweens together, you can animate a graphic-object that moves from point to point.

9. Repeat this repositioning process for frames 15 and 20.

You now have a ball that bounces around wildly (**Figure 9.17**).

10. To add more frames, select frame 30 or frame 40 and then choose Insert > Timeline > Frame.

Flash applies the motion tween property to all the newly defined frames. Now you can add keyframes by following the procedure described earlier in this task. Just be sure you end up with a keyframe as the last frame in the series. If you have more frames than you need, you can remove them.

11. To end the tween, select the last keyframe in the series.

12. In the Frame Properties tab of the Property inspector, from the Tween menu, choose None.

If you don't change the last frame's Tween property to None, any frames that you add after that will also be set to Motion Tween, which may create unexpected results.

MOVING GRAPHICS IN STRAIGHT LINES

Moving Graphics Along a Path

In the preceding task, you made the ball move all over the Stage in short, point-to-point hops. A ball does sometimes behave this way, but other things may require movements that are softer—trajectories that are arcs, not straight lines. You could achieve this effect by stringing together many point-to-point keyframes, but Flash offers a more efficient method: the motion guide. Several items can follow the same path, but they must be on separate layers linked to the same motion-guide layer. If you want different items to follow different paths, you need to create multiple motion-guide layers, each with its own set of guided layers.

To add a motion-guide layer:

1. Create a new Flash document containing a 10-frame motion tween.

   In the first keyframe, place the graphic to be tweened (it must be a graphic-object) in the top-left corner of the Stage. In the last frame, place the graphic in the bottom-right corner of the Stage. Your document should resemble **Figure 9.18**.

2. Select the layer that contains the graphic you want to move along a path.

3. At the bottom of the Timeline, click the Add Motion Guide button.

   Flash adds the motion-guide layer directly above the layer you selected and gives it a default name of Guide, followed by the name of the layer you selected (**Figure 9.19**). The motion-guide icon appears next to the layer name. Flash also indents the layer linked to the motion-guide layer.

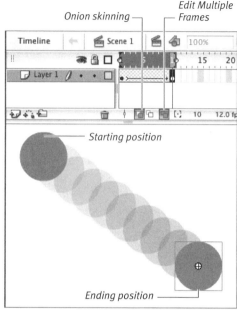

Figure 9.18 The first step in creating a tweened graphic that follows a path is defining a motion tween with the graphic in the beginning and ending positions you want to use. Here, the graphic moves from the beginning to the end in a straight line. (Onion Skin mode and Edit Multiple Frames are selected to show all the tween's components.)

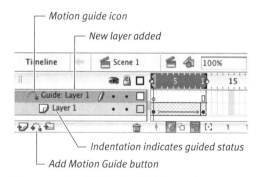

Figure 9.19 The Add Motion Guide button inserts a new layer, defined as a *motion-guide* layer, above the selected layer in the Timeline. The default name for the motion-guide layer includes the name of the layer selected when you created the motion-guide layer. The layer containing the tweened graphic is indented and linked to the motion-guide layer. Flash defines the linked layer as a *guided layer*.

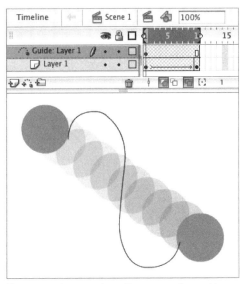

Figure 9.20 A merge-shape line on a motion-guide layer acts as a path that guides the motion of a tweened graphic on a linked layer.

The Mystery of Motion Guides

A *motion guide* is a graphic you create on a special separate layer. The motion guide defines the path for a tweened graphic to follow. One motion-guide layer can control items on several layers. The motion-guide layer governs any layers linked to it. The linked layers are defined as guided layers in the Layer Properties dialog.

If you want different elements to follow different paths, create several motion-guide layers within a single Flash document. Each motion guide governs the actions of graphic-objects on its own set of linked layers.

4. In the Tools panel, select the pencil tool; make sure that Object Drawing mode is deselected.

5. In the Timeline, select the motion-guide layer.

6. Draw a line on the Stage showing the path you want the graphic to take (**Figure 9.20**).

Merge-shape lines on a motion-guide layer create motion paths for graphic-objects on linked layers.

7. Choose View > Snapping > Snap to Objects.

For Flash to move an item along a motion path, the transformation point of the item (a small white circle within the symbol or group) must be centered on the path. The Snap to Objects setting will help you position the tween graphic correctly.

8. In keyframe 1, using the selection tool, drag the tween graphic by its transformation point to position it directly over the beginning of the motion path.

As you drag, the snapping ring enlarges slightly when it approaches any snapping elements you have set. For example, with Snap to Objects active, the ring grows larger when the point you're dragging is centered over the motion guide.

continues on next page

MOVING GRAPHICS ALONG A PATH

9. In keyframe 10, drag the tween graphic to position its transformation point directly over the end of the motion path.

Flash redraws the in-between frames so that the graphic follows the motion path (**Figure 9.21**). Flash centers the tweened graphic over the motion path in each in-between frame. In the final movie, Flash hides the path.

✔ Tips

■ After you draw the motion path, lock the motion-guide layer to prevent yourself from editing the path accidentally as you snap the graphic to the path.

■ In the Frame Properties tab of the Property inspector for the keyframes containing the tweened graphics, select the Snap check box to have Flash assist you in centering keyframe graphics over the end of the guide line (**Figure 9.22**).

■ You can use any of Flash's drawing tools—line, pencil, pen, oval, rectangle, polygon, polystar, and brush—to create a motion path. But the tools must be set to Merge Drawing mode.

■ If you accidentally create a drawing-object when creating a guide, select it and choose Modify > Break Apart to turn it into a merge-shape.

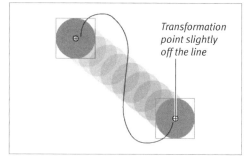

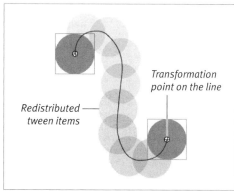

Figure 9.21 To follow the path, tweened items must have their transformation point (indicated by a small white circle within the selected graphic) sitting directly on the motion-guide line.

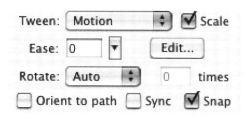

Figure 9.22 When a frame's Tween property is set to Motion, the Frame Properties tab of the Property inspector contains a Snap check box. Select Snap when the layer is linked to a motion-guide layer, and Flash automatically centers the transformation point of any graphic-object on that layer over the motion guide. Forced snapping ensures correct tweening along the motion-guide path.

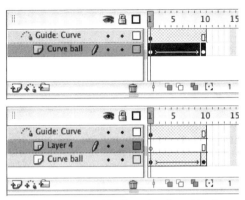

Figure 9.23 When a guided layer is selected (top), clicking the Insert Layer button creates another guided layer below the motion-guide layer (bottom).

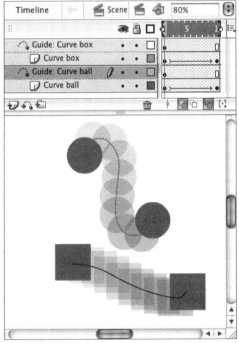

Figure 9.24 Add multiple guide layers to move graphic-objects along separate paths simultaneously.

To create a second guided layer:

1. In the Flash document you created in the preceding task, select the guided layer (the one containing the circle).

2. To add a new layer, *do either of the following:*
   - ▲ Choose Insert > Timeline > Layer.
   - ▲ In the Timeline, click the Insert Layer button.

   Flash adds a new indented (guided) layer above the selected layer (**Figure 9.23**). Tweened items on this layer follow the motion guide when you position them correctly.

To add a second motion-guide layer:

1. Create a Flash document with at least one normal layer containing a motion tween and one motion-guide layer with a linked guided layer containing a motion tween.

2. In the Timeline, select the normal layer containing the motion tween.

3. Click the Add Motion Guide button.

   Flash adds a motion-guide layer above the selected layer and links the selected layer to it. Follow the steps in the preceding tasks to draw the second motion path and position the tweened item.

4. Play the movie.

   The two tweened graphics follow their own motion paths simultaneously (**Figure 9.24**).

✔ Tip

- ■ To convert an existing layer to a guided layer quickly, drag it below the motion-guide layer or any of its linked layers.

MOVING GRAPHICS ALONG A PATH

Orienting Graphics to a Motion Path

As a default, tweened graphics keep a fixed orientation (they don't rotate) even when they follow a motion path. To create more natural movement, you can force a tweened graphic to rotate to preserve its orientation to the path in each frame of a tween.

To orient a graphic to the path:

1. Create a 10-frame motion tween of an item that follows a motion guide, using the steps in the first task in "Moving Graphics Along a Path" earlier in this chapter.

   This time, don't use a circle; draw an arrow or triangle or an animal.

2. Turn on onion skinning to see how the item moves along the path without orientation.

3. In the Timeline, in the layer containing the tweened graphic, select keyframe 1.

4. In the Frame Properties tab of the Property inspector, select the Orient to Path check box (**Figure 9.25**).

   Flash redraws the tween. In the in-between frames, Flash rotates the tweened item to align it with the path more naturally (**Figure 9.26**).

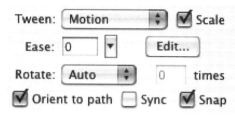

Figure 9.25 With Motion tweening selected in the Frame Properties tab of the Property inspector, select Orient to Path to make Flash rotate a tweened item to face the direction of movement.

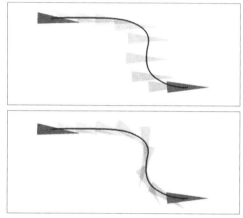

Figure 9.26 The arrow in the top tween isn't oriented to the path; it stays parallel to the bottom of the Stage and moves to various points along the path. The bottom tween is oriented to the path. The arrow rotates to align better with the path.

Why Orient to Path?

Imagine a waiter carrying a full tray through a crowded room, raising and lowering the tray to avoid various obstacles but always keeping the tray level to avoid spilling anything. That's how tweened animation works if you don't orient the tweened graphic to the motion guide. The transformation point of the tweened graphic snaps to a new spot on the motion guide in each frame, but the graphic never rotates. With a ball, that procedure may result in natural-looking motion, but with other graphic-objects, the result is often unnatural. You might want a living creature to face in the direction it's moving, rotating slightly to match the twists and turns of its path. You might want an airplane doing loops to trace the loop tightly with its nose, not stay perpendicular to the curve. Orienting the graphic to the motion path forces a tweened graphic to rotate as the motion path curves. This rotation creates the illusion that graphic-object is always facing the direction it's going along the path.

Orient to Path doing a poor job

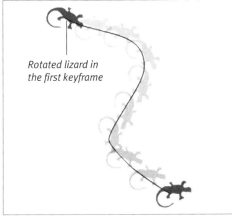

Rotated lizard in the first keyframe

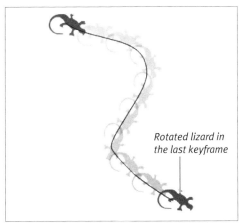

Rotated lizard in the last keyframe

Figure 9.27 Here, Flash could be doing a better job of aligning this lizard with the path (top). Rotating the lizard in the first keyframe (middle) and last keyframe (bottom) helps the Orient to Path feature do its job.

✔ Tips

■ To help the Orient to Path option create the most natural positions for your graphic, you may need to rotate the graphic in the first and/or last keyframe of a tween so that the graphic is facing the direction it's supposed to move in (**Figure 9.27**).

■ If, after following the preceding tip, the orientation still looks odd in spots, step through the tween one frame at a time. When you get to a frame where Flash positions the graphic poorly, you can fix it. In the Timeline, select the in-between frame, and choose Insert > Timeline > Keyframe. In the new keyframe that Flash creates, select the graphic and rotate it manually to align it with the motion guide. Flash redraws the in-between frames.

■ Turn on onion skinning as you follow the preceding tip. That way, you can see how your adjustments affect the orientation of your graphic in each frame of the tween.

■ Sometimes, moving the transformation point of your graphic helps it orient to the path in a more lifelike manner. The default transformation point of the lizard in Figure 9.27 is at the center of the graphic's bounding box. Because the lizard has a huge curved tail, that point isn't even inside the lizard body. Moving the transformation point to the middle of the lizard's body lets the Orient to Path setting create more lifelike movement. (Use the free-transform tool to reposition the transformation point of a graphic or symbol instance.)

Changing Tween Speed

In Chapter 8, you learned to make an animated item appear to move slowly or quickly by adjusting the number of in-between frames. When you create an animation with tweening, that method no longer works, because Flash distributes the motion evenly over whatever number of in-between frames you create. You can, however, make an animation slower at the beginning or end of a tween sequence by setting an Ease value. In Flash Professional 8, you can customize the Ease value, creating separate easing values for different aspects of your tween. Imagine animating a setting sun, for example. You may want the sun to change position quickly at first and slowly at the end; but you may want the sun's size and color to change slowly at first and then speed up at the end. Custom easing gives you that control.

To make the animation start slowly and accelerate (ease in):

1. Create a 10-frame motion tween of a graphic that follows a motion guide, using the steps in the first task in "Moving Graphics Along a Path," earlier in this chapter.

2. In the Timeline, select any of the frames in the keyframe span (frames 1–9).

3. In the Frame Properties tab of the Property inspector, enter a negative number in the Ease field (**Figure 9.28**).

4. Press Enter.

   The word *in* appears next to the field. Easing in makes the animation start slowly and speed up toward the end. The lower the Ease value, the greater the rate of acceleration.

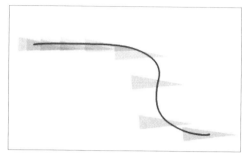

Figure 9.28 A negative Ease value (top) makes changes in the initial frames of the tween smaller and changes toward the end larger (bottom). The animation seems to start slowly and then speed up.

Why Use Easing?

Easing can create more natural-looking movement for items that gravity affects. In an animation of a rolling ball, for example, you may want the ball to start rolling quickly but slow toward the end to simulate the way that entropy in the real world slows the ball's movement.

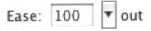

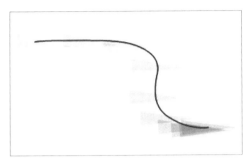

Figure 9.29 A positive Ease value (top) makes changes at the end of the animation smaller and changes in the initial frames larger (bottom). The animation seems to start quickly and then slow down.

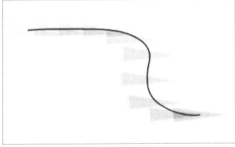

Figure 9.30 With an Ease value of 0 (top), Flash distributes the tweening changes evenly across the in-between frames (bottom). The effect is that of animation at a constant rate.

Figure 9.31 In Flash Professional 8, keyframe spans whose Tween property is set to Motion can have custom easing applied. In the Frame Properties tab for the span, click the Edit button to access a dialog for setting custom easing.

To make the animation start quickly and decelerate (ease out):

1. Follow steps 1 and 2 of the preceding task.

2. In the Frame Properties tab of the Property inspector, enter a positive number in the Ease field.

3. Press Enter.

   The word *out* appears next to the field. Easing out makes the animation start quickly and slow toward the end (**Figure 9.29**). The higher the Ease value, the greater the rate of deceleration.

✔ Tip

- An Ease value of 0 causes Flash to display the whole animation at a constant rate (**Figure 9.30**).

To create custom easing (Flash Professional 8 Only):

1. Create a motion tween in which several properties of the tweened graphic change over time.

   For example, use the oval tool to draw a yellow circle and convert it to a symbol named Sun. Use the Sun symbol to create a 30-frame motion tween. In keyframe 1, place an instance of the Sun at the top of the Stage. In keyframe 30, place an instance at the bottom of the Stage; resize it to be twice as large; and use the Color setting in the Properties tab of the Property inspector to change the color to dark orange.

2. Select any frame in the keyframe span (frames 1–29).

3. To access custom easing settings, in the Frame Properties tab of the Property inspector, click the Edit button (to the right of the Ease field) (**Figure 9.31**).

continues on next page

CHANGING TWEEN SPEED

The Custom Ease In/Ease Out dialog appears (**Figure 9.32**). The dialog shows the selected tween's changes over time on a graph; the horizontal axis represents each frame in the tween; the vertical axis represents the amount of change. When no easing values have been set, the graph begins as a straight line between a control point representing the tween's first frame (with 0 percent change) and a control point representing the tween's last frame (100 percent change). You can edit the graph to set specific easing values, frame-by-frame, for five properties of a tweened graphic-object (Position, Rotation, Scale, Color, and Filters).

4. To set easing for all five properties simultaneously, select the "Use one setting for all properties" check box.

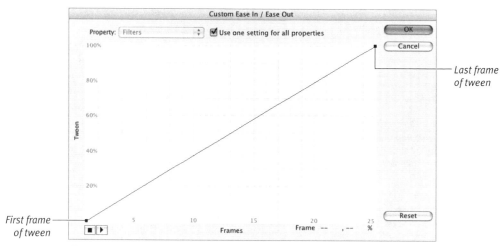

Figure 9.32 The Custom Ease In/Ease Out dialog allows you to control easing precisely, frame by frame, by creating a curve that defines the rate of change in each frame. Without easing, the rate is constant, starting at 0 percent in the first frame of the tween and reaching 100 percent in the last frame of the tween.

5. To modify the rate of change, click the graph's line at the frame where you want to the modification to start.

Flash adds a control point with tangent-point handles; these work similarly to anchor points and Bézier handles, allowing you to adjust the shape of the graph's line (**Figure 9.33**).

6. Drag a control point vertically to determine the amount of change that should occur by the current frame; adjust the tangent handles to fine-tune the rate of change in the frames on either side of the control point.

Dragging a control point toward the top of the graph makes the curve steeper (changes happen more quickly); dragging a control point to the bottom makes the curve flatter (changes happen more slowly). You can also manipulate the first and last control points' tangent handles to flatten or deepen the curve.

7. Repeat steps 5 and 6 as needed to speed or slow the rate of change in the desired frames of the tween.

8. Click OK.

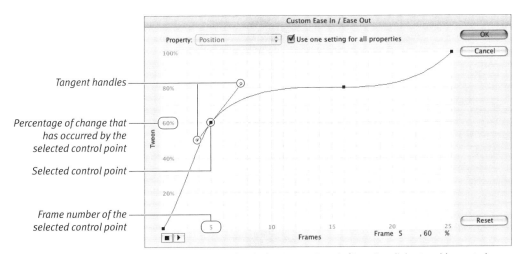

Figure 9.33 Click the line in the Custom Ease In/Ease Out dialog to add a control point. Changing a control point's vertical position makes more (or less) of a change take place by the current frame. Adjusting the tangent handles changes the shape of the curve: a steeper curve segment translates to a quicker rate of change; a flatter segment, to a slower one.

CHANGING TWEEN SPEED

✔ Tips

- To preview your settings, click the Play button in the lower-left corner of the Custom Ease In/Ease Out dialog. The tween plays in the Flash document window. You may need to move the custom-easing dialog to see the document window.

- If you have already set a regular Ease value in the Frame Properties tab of the Property inspector, the easing graph in the Custom Ease In/Ease Out dialog reflects that setting. You can use the regular Ease value as a starting place for your custom settings. But be warned: If you've set custom easing, and you enter a value in the regular Ease field, that new setting is applied to the custom-easing curve, wiping out your custom adjustments.

- You can use easing values to create variations on the general motion of your tween—for example, making a graphic move back and forth several times even though its tween sequence consists of just two keyframes that move the graphic in a straight line from one position to another. Imagine a 20-frame tween; in the first keyframe, the graphic sits on the left side of the Stage, and in the second, the graphic sits on the right side. Now, set custom easing values for Position in the keyframe span for this tween. Add a control point at frame 5, and position it vertically so that 50 percent of the change is made by that frame. Next, add a control point at frame 10, and position it so that 25 percent of the change has been made. The rectangle moves forward to the middle of the Stage by frame 5, moves backward between frames 5 and 10, and then moves forward again until it reaches the right side of the Stage in frame 20.

Figure 9.34 Deselecting the "Use one setting for all properties" check box activates the Property menu. Choose a property to create custom easing settings for that specific change.

To ease changes for different properties separately (Flash Professional 8 Only):

1. Follow steps 1–3 of the preceding task.

2. Deselect the "Use one setting for all properties" check box.

3. From the Property menu (**Figure 9.34**), select *one of the following:*

   Position controls the rate at which a tweened object moves around the Stage.

   Rotation controls the rate at which a tweened object spins (using the Rotation property set in the Frame Properties tab of the Property inspector).

   Scale controls the rate at which a tweened object changes size.

   Color controls the rate at which a tweened symbol instance's Color property changes.

   Filters controls the rate at which filter effects (Flash Professional 8 only) take place.

4. Adjust the settings by following steps 5–7 in the preceding task.

5. Repeat steps 3 and 4 of this task for each property you wish to control.

6. Click OK.

✔ Tips

- If you add keyframes within a span that has custom easing, Flash keeps the custom settings for those frames. Click the Edit button in the Frame Properties tab of the Property inspector to see and further edit those settings.

- To apply the same curve to several, but not all, of the properties, use the standard copy and paste commands. Set the curve for the first property, press ⌘-C (Mac) or Ctrl-C (Windows) to copy the curve, select a new property from the Property menu, press ⌘-V (Mac) or Ctrl-V (Windows) to paste the curve.

Getting Help with Motion Tweens

When you define a motion tween as you learned to do earlier in this chapter, you must convert any raw shapes to a symbol or group and set the Tween property of the frames involved. Flash assists you with those tasks when you use the Create Motion Tween command.

To use the Create Motion Tween command:

1. Open a new Flash document.

   The document has one layer and one keyframe by default. (Starting with a new document makes it easier to see what happens when you use the Create Motion Tween command.)

2. Using the drawing tools, create a shape on the Stage.

   The shape winds up in keyframe 1 of layer 1.

3. In the Timeline, select keyframe 1.

4. Choose Insert > Timeline > Create Motion Tween.

   Flash selects your shape and converts it to a symbol, giving it a default name. Flash sets the Tween property of keyframe 1 to Motion in the Frame Properties tab of the Property inspector.

5. In the Timeline, select frame 10.

6. Choose Insert > Timeline > Frame.

   Flash adds frames containing a dotted line, indicating a broken tween (**Figure 9.35**). The tween sequence requires an ending keyframe.

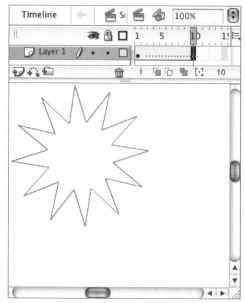

Figure 9.35 Adding frames after choosing Create Motion Tween results in a temporarily broken tween, indicated by the dotted line in the Timeline.

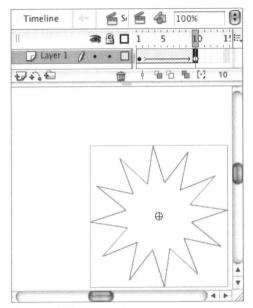

Figure 9.36 After you create a motion tween over a range of frames, reposition the frame's content in the last frame to convert that frame to a keyframe and complete the tween.

7. In frame 10, reposition the graphic on the Stage.

Flash creates a keyframe in frame 10, with the symbol in its new position. The tween arrow now appears in the keyframe span (**Figure 9.36**). Note that frame 10's Tween property is set to Motion in the Properties tab of the Property inspector. If you want subsequent frames to be tween frames, leave the property as is; otherwise, you must change it.

8. To end the tweening sequence, select keyframe 10.

9. In the Properties tab of the Property inspector, from the Tween pop-up menu, choose None.

✔ Tips

- If you choose Insert > Timeline > Keyframe in step 6 of the preceding task, you won't see the broken-tween line in the Timeline, because that command duplicates the content of the preceding keyframe. Flash considers the tween to be complete when it finds an ending keyframe with content. Nevertheless, your tween will still seem to be broken (it won't *do* anything) until you go into the ending keyframe of the sequence and make a change to its content—for example, reposition it or change its color or size.

- If the Properties tab of the Property inspector isn't active, you can remove tweening status from a selected frame by choosing Insert > Timeline > Remove Tween.

GETTING HELP WITH MOTION TWEENS

Dissecting Flash-Created Motion Tweens

When you choose Insert > Timeline > Create Motion Tween, Flash selects all the graphic elements in the active layer and converts them into one big symbol named Tween 1, Tween 2, and so on, based on the number of tweening symbols already created in the Flash document (**Figure 9.37**). It's a good idea to rename the tween symbol more meaningfully using the techniques described in Chapter 7. If the layer contains a single symbol, the Create Motion Tween command sets the Tween property for the keyframe span but doesn't rename the symbol or make a new copy in the library.

In addition, the Create Motion Tween command sets the Tween property of frames in the currently selected keyframe span to Motion.

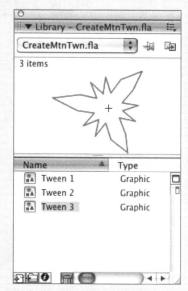

Figure 9.37 The Create Motion Tween command turns graphic elements in the selected frame on the currently active layer into a symbol and names the symbol Tween 1, Tween 2, and so on.

ANIMATION WITH SHAPE TWEENING

10

In shape tweening, as in motion tweening, you define the beginning and ending graphics in keyframes. Macromedia Flash 8 creates the in-between frames, redrawing the graphic with incremental changes that transform it. The important difference between motion tweening and shape tweening is that motion tweening requires graphics that are in containers (drawing-objects, groups, symbols, or text boxes qualify), and shape tweening requires editable graphics (merge-shapes and drawing-objects qualify).

You can use shape tweens to change properties of graphics—size, color, location, and so on. Shape-tweened graphics can move in straight lines, but they can't automatically follow a motion path or rotate a certain number of times.

Flash can shape-tween more than one graphic on a layer, but the results can be unpredictable. When you have several shapes on a layer, there is no way to tell Flash which starting shape goes with which ending shape. By limiting yourself to a single shape tween on each layer, you tell Flash exactly what to change.

You define shape tweens by setting the tweening property in the Properties tab of the Property inspector. For the tasks in this chapter, keep the Properties tab of the Property inspector open.

Creating a Bouncing Ball with Shape Tweening

Although shape tweens can animate changes in many properties of graphics—color, size, location—the distinguishing function of shape tweening is to transform one shape into another. You could use a shape tween to replicate the simple bouncing-ball animation you created in Chapters 8 and 9, but the beauty of shape tweening is that it lets you change the shape of the ball. A better use of shape tweening for a bouncing ball is to flatten the ball as it strikes the ground.

To define shape tweens via the Frame Properties tab of the Property inspector:

1. In a new Flash document, or in a new layer of an existing document, position the playhead in frame 1.

2. In the Tools panel, choose the oval tool.

3. Set the stroke to No Color.

4. Near the top of the Stage, draw a circle. This circle will be the ball. Make it fairly large.

5. In the Timeline, select frame 5, and choose Insert > Timeline > Keyframe.

   The Insert > Timeline > Keyframe command makes a new keyframe that duplicates the contents of the preceding keyframe.

6. Select frame 10, and choose Insert > Timeline > Keyframe.

Drawing-Objects and Shape Tweening

In the previous chapter, you learned that you can use drawing-objects to make motion tweens. That's because they fulfill the motion-tween requirement that shapes be isolated in a container and unable to interact with other shapes on the same layer. However, drawing-objects are also editable directly on the Stage. You can change their shape without drilling down to the individual merge-shapes. This makes them flexible enough to work in shape tweens as well. Drawing-objects are the only type of objects that can be used with either tweening method.

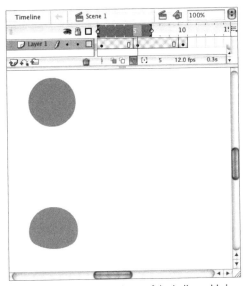

Figure 10.1 Changing the shape of the ball graphic in the keyframe representing the bottom of the bounce makes the movement appear more natural. The ball seems to respond to gravity by flattening on contact with something solid—say, the floor. (Turn on onion skinning to see the beginning and ending keyframes.)

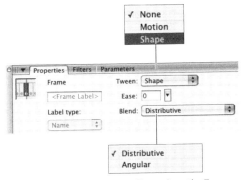

Figure 10.2 When you choose Shape from the Tween pop-up menu, the Frame Properties tab of the Property inspector displays the shape-tween settings.

7. In frame 5, select the ball, and drag it to the bottom of the Stage.

   Now you have the keyframes necessary to make a simple bouncing ball like the one in the motion-tween task. In frame 1, the ball is at the top of its bounce; in frame 5, the ball is at the bottom of its bounce; and in frame 10, the ball is back up at the top.

8. Use the drawing tools to reshape the oval in frame 5, flattening the bottom and elongating it a bit sideways (**Figure 10.1**).

   By changing the shape at the bottom of the bounce, you make it look like the ball really contacts something solid, such as a floor.

9. To define the shape tween for the first half of the ball's bounce, in the Timeline, select any of the frames in the first keyframe span (1, 2, 3, or 4).

   Note that the ball is selected automatically. When you define a shape tween, the element to be tweened must be selected.

10. In the Frame Properties tab of the Property inspector, from the Tween pop-up menu, choose Shape.

    The settings for the shape tween appear (**Figure 10.2**).

    Flash creates a shape tween in frames 1–4 and color-codes those frames in the Timeline. With Tinted Frames active (choose it from the Frame View pop-up menu at the end of the Edit Bar), Flash applies a light green shade to the frames containing a shape tween. If Tinted Frames is inactive, the frames are white (Mac) or patterned (Windows), but Flash changes the arrow that indicates the presence of a tween from black to green.

continues on next page

CREATING A BOUNCING BALL WITH SHAPE TWEENING

11. In the Ease field, *do one of the following:*

▲ To make the bounce start slowly and speed up, enter a negative value.

▲ To make the bounce start quickly and slow down, enter a positive value.

▲ To keep the bounce constant, enter 0.

12. From the Blend menu, *choose either of the following options:*

▲ To preserve sharp corners and straight lines as one shape transforms into another, choose Angular.

▲ To smooth out the in-between shapes, choose Distributive.

13. To define the shape tween for the second half of the ball's bounce, in the Timeline, select any of the frames in the second keyframe span (5, 6, 7, 8, or 9).

14. Repeat steps 10–12.

Flash creates the second half of the ball's bounce with another shape tween (**Figure 10.3**).

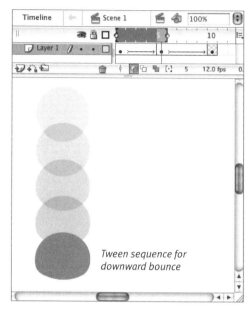

Tween sequence for downward bounce

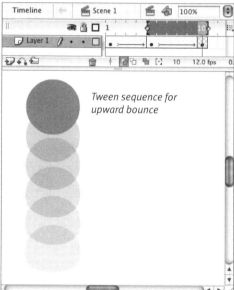

Tween sequence for upward bounce

Figure 10.3 With onion skinning turned on, you can see the in-between frames Flash creates for the shape tween. This animation looks similar to the bouncing ball created with a motion tween. In this case, the change in the object's shape creates the illusion of impact.

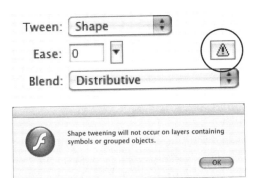

Figure 10.4 A warning button appears in the Frame Properties tab of the Property inspector when there are groups or symbols in frames you're defining as shape tweens (top). Click the exclamation-sign button to see the warning dialog (bottom).

Shape-Tween Requirements

To have a working shape tween, you need three things: a beginning keyframe containing one or more editable shapes (they can be merge-shapes or drawing-objects), in-between frames defined as shape tweens, and an ending keyframe containing the new editable shape.

For motion tweens, the Create Motion Tween command can help you combine those ingredients correctly. No equivalent command is available for shape tweens. You must create all shape tweens manually by creating the beginning and ending keyframes and then setting the keyframe span's Tween property to Shape in the Frame Properties tab of the Property inspector.

✔ Tips

- Flash doesn't prevent you from defining shape tweens for frames that contain grouped shapes or symbols, but those tweens won't work. Flash does warn you by placing the broken-tween dotted line in the relevant frames in the Timeline. When you select such frames, a warning button appears in the Frame Properties tab of the Property inspector (**Figure 10.4**). When you see these warnings, go back to the Stage and reevaluate what's there. If the item you want to tween is a group or symbol, you can use motion tweening. Or, to use shape tweening, you can break the group or symbol apart (select the shape or symbol, and then choose Modify > Break Apart). If there's a symbol or group on the same layer as the editable shape you want to tween, move the extra item to its own layer (select it and choose Modify > Timeline > Distribute to Layers).

- Note that Flash Professional 8's custom-easing settings aren't available for shape tweens; they're strictly for motion tweens.

Motion Tweening or Shape Tweening?

The key to deciding whether to use motion tweening or shape tweening is to ask yourself whether you need to change the outline (shape) of the graphic-object you're animating. If the answer is yes, then you need shape tweening. If you are animating a change to a property of the graphic-object (its location on the Stage, its color, its size, or rotation), Flash can make the change with motion tweening.

Another important distinction between motion tweening and shape tweening is that motion tweening requires that shapes be in some kind of container (drawing-objects, groups, symbols, and text boxes all qualify), whereas shape tweening requires shapes whose outlines can be modified directly on the Stage (merge-shapes and drawing-objects qualify). Note that drawing-objects qualify for both types of tweens; pay attention when applying the tween property to a keyframe span containing a drawing-object to make sure you create the animation style you intend.

Although you can sometimes arrive at the same tweening effect with either a motion tween or a shape tween, it's best to reserve shape tweens for the shape-changing animations that you can't achieve with motion tweens.

Motion tweens don't work if you apply them to a layer containing more than one graphic-object. If you want to tween a multipart graphic—say, a robot constructed of many shapes—you can place each shape on a separate layer and tween the shapes separately, or you can unify the shapes by turning them into a symbol or group. Symbols and groups can only be tweened with motion tweening. To create morphing effects—transforming a pumpkin into a magic coach, for example—you must use shape tweening. In addition, if you want Flash to move a tweened graphic around the Stage along a curving path (as opposed to a straight line), you must use motion tweening.

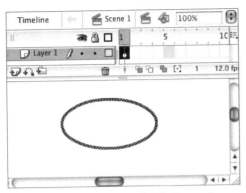

Figure 10.5 Draw an oval in the first keyframe of your shape tween.

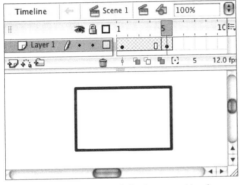

Figure 10.6 Draw a rectangle in the second keyframe of your shape tween.

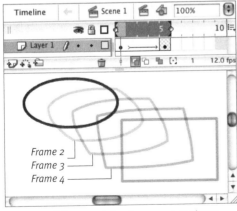

Frame 2
Frame 3
Frame 4

Figure 10.7 When you define frames 1–4 as shape tweens, Flash creates the three intermediate shapes that transform the oval into a square. Turn on onion skinning to see the shapes for the in-between frames.

Morphing Simple Lines and Fills

Flash can transform both fill shapes and lines (strokes). In this section, you try some shape-changing tasks with both types of shapes.

To transform an oval into a rectangle:

1. In a new Flash document, or in a new layer, in frame 1, draw an outline oval on the Stage (**Figure 10.5**).

2. In the Timeline, select frame 5, and choose Insert > Timeline > Blank Keyframe.

   Flash creates a keyframe but removes all content from the Stage.

3. On the Stage, in frame 5, draw an outline rectangle (**Figure 10.6**).

   Don't worry about placing the rectangle in exactly the same location on the Stage as the oval; you'll adjust the position later.

4. In the Timeline, select any of the frames in the keyframe span (1, 2, 3, or 4).

5. In the Frame Properties tab of the Property inspector, from the Tween pop-up menu, choose Shape.

   Flash transforms the oval into the rectangle in three equal steps—one for each in-between frame (**Figure 10.7**).

continues on next page

6. To align the oval and rectangle, in the Timeline status bar, click the Onion Skin or Onion Skin Outlines button.

Flash displays all the in-between frames.

7. In the Timeline, position the playhead in frame 1.

8. On the Stage, reposition the oval so that it aligns with the rectangle (**Figure 10.8**).

The oval transforms into a rectangle, remaining in one spot on the Stage.

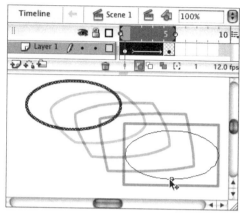

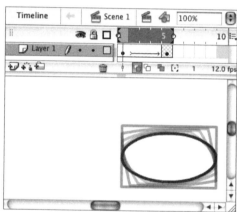

Figure 10.8 Use onion skinning to help position your keyframe shapes. Here, with frame 1 selected, you can drag the oval to center it within the rectangle (top). That makes the oval grow into a rectangle without moving anywhere else on the Stage (bottom).

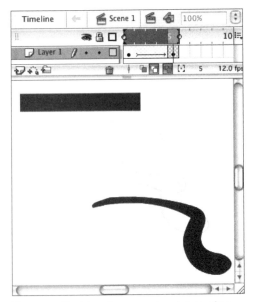

Figure 10.9 Flash transforms a rectangle into a free-form brush stroke with shape tweening.

To transform a rectangle into a free-form shape:

1. In a new Flash document, or on a new layer, in frame 1, draw a rectangular fill on the Stage.

2. In the Timeline, select frame 5, and choose Insert > Timeline > Blank Keyframe.

3. On the Stage, in frame 5, use the brush tool to paint a free-form fill.

   Don't make the fill too complex—just a blob or brush stroke with gentle curves.

4. In the Timeline, select any of the frames in the keyframe span (1, 2, 3, or 4).

5. Set the Tween property to Shape (see step 5 of the preceding task).

   Flash transforms the rectangle into the free-form fill in three equal steps—one for each in-between frame (**Figure 10.9**).

Shape-Tweening Multiple Shapes

In motion tweening, Flash limits you to one item per tween, meaning just one item per layer. In shape tweening, however, Flash can handle more than one shape on a layer. The drawback is that you may get some strange results. The simpler and fewer the shapes you use, the more reliable your multishape tweens will be. For the most predictable results, limit yourself to one shape per layer.

You may want to keep both shapes on the same layer for a fill with an outline (stroke), however. As long as the transformation isn't too complicated, Flash can handle the two together.

To shape-tween fills with strokes (outlines):

1. Follow the steps in the preceding tasks to create a shape tween of an outline oval transforming into a rectangle.

2. Fill each shape with a different color.

   Flash tweens the fill and the stroke together and tweens the change in color (**Figure 10.10**).

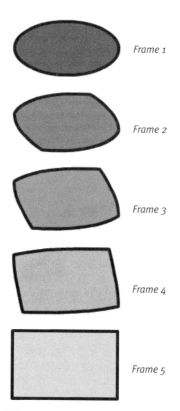

Frame 1

Frame 2

Frame 3

Frame 4

Frame 5

Figure 10.10 Here, Flash transforms a shape with a stroke in five frames. The shape tween changes not only the graphic's shape, but also its color (from dark to light).

✔ Tips

- You can tween a disappearing act: Make the stroke around a shape (or the shape, or both) get gradually lighter and lighter, until it finally disappears. Make the color of the final stroke (and/or shape) in the tween match the color of the background, or give it a fully transparent color (one with an alpha setting of 0%).

- To ensure that the item in the preceding tip does fully disappear (some low-color monitors may not display tint and alpha changes accurately), select the frame following the last keyframe of the tween sequence. Choose Insert > Timeline > Keyframe to duplicate the previous keyframe; then delete your disappearing stroke (or shape). If you want both the shape and its stroke to disappear together, choose Insert > Timeline > Blank Keyframe.

When Multiple Shape Tweens on a Single Layer Go Bad

If you're shape-tweening stationary elements, you probably can get away with having several on the same layer. But if the elements move around much, Flash can get confused about which shape goes where. Although you may intend the paths of two shapes to cross, Flash creates the most direct route between the starting shape and the ending one. **Figure 10.11** illustrates the problem.

All objects on one layer

All objects on one layer

Light circle and arrow on one layer

Dark circle and arrow on another layer

Figure 10.11 Tweening multiple shapes whose paths don't cross in a single layer works fine. In the left-hand image, both objects are on the same layer, and the light circle transforms into the light arrow without a hitch. In the middle image, both objects are on the same layer, but Flash transforms the light circle into the dark arrow and the dark circle into the light arrow because that's the most direct path. If you want to create diagonal paths that cross, you must put each object on its own layer, as in the right-hand image.

Transforming a Simple Shape into a Complex Shape

The more complex the shape you tween, the more difficult it is for Flash to create the expected result. You can help Flash tween better by using *shape hints*—markers that let you identify points on the original shape's outline that correspond to points on the final shape's outline.

To shape-tween a more complex shape:

1. In a new Flash document, or on a new layer, in frame 1, draw an oval with no stroke on the Stage.

2. In the Timeline, select frame 5, and choose Insert > Timeline > Keyframe.

   Flash duplicates the contents of keyframe 1 in keyframe 5.

3. In the Timeline, select any of the frames in the keyframe span (1, 2, 3, or 4).

4. In the Frame Properties tab of the Property inspector, from the Tween pop-up menu, choose Shape.

5. In the Timeline, position the playhead in frame 5.

6. Using the selection tool or the pen and subselection tools, drag four corner points in toward the center of the oval to create a flower shape.

   (For more detailed instructions on editing shapes, see Chapter 4.)

7. Play the movie to see the shape tween.

   Flash handles the tweening for this change well (**Figure 10.12**). It's fairly obvious which points of the oval should move in to create the petal shapes. If you modify the shape further, however, it becomes more difficult for Flash to know how to create the new shape. That's when you need to use shape hints.

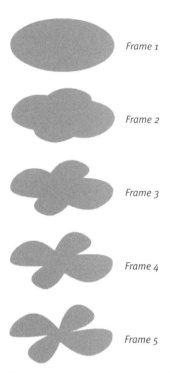

Frame 1

Frame 2

Frame 3

Frame 4

Frame 5

Figure 10.12 Flash handles the tween from an oval to a simple flower shape without requiring shape hints.

Frame 5

Frame 6

Frame 7

Frame 8

Frame 9

Frame 10

Figure 10.13 The addition of a stem to the flower overloads Flash's capability to create a smooth shape tween. Frames 7 and 8 are particularly bad.

Figure 10.14 Choose Modify > Shape > Add Shape Hint to activate markers that help Flash make connections between the original shape and the final shape of the tween.

To use shape hints:

1. Using the animation you created in the preceding task, in the Timeline, select frame 10, and choose Insert > Timeline > Keyframe.

   Flash duplicates the flower shape in a new keyframe.

2. In keyframe 10, edit the flower to add a stem.

   Reshape the outline with the selection tool or the pen and subselection tools, or add a stem with a brush stroke in the same color as the flower.

3. Define a shape tween for frames 5–9.

4. Play the movie.

   The addition of the stem to the flower makes it difficult for Flash to create a smooth tween that looks right (**Figure 10.13**).

5. To begin adding shape hints, position the playhead in keyframe 5 (the initial keyframe of this tweening sequence).

6. Choose Modify > Shape > Add Shape Hint, or press Shift-⌘-H (Mac) or Ctrl-Shift-H (Windows) (**Figure 10.14**).

   Flash places a shape hint—a small red circle labeled with a letter, starting with *a*—in the center of the object in the current frame. You need to reposition the shape hint to place it on a problem point on the shape's outline.

7. With the selection tool, drag the shape hint to a problem point on the edge of the shape.

   Don't worry about getting the shape hint in exactly the right spot; you can fine-tune it later.

   continues on next page

8. Repeat steps 6 and 7 until you have placed shape hints on all the problem points of your shape in keyframe 5 (**Figure 10.15**).

   Each time you add a shape hint, you get another small red circle labeled with a letter. You can't place the hints at random; you must place them so they go in alphabetical order around the edge of the shape. (Flash does the best job when you place shape hints in counterclockwise order, but you can also place them in clockwise order.)

9. In the Timeline, position the playhead in keyframe 10.

   Flash has already added shape hints to this frame; they all stack up in the center of the shape.

10. With the selection tool, drag each shape hint to its position on the new shape.

    Keep them in the same order (counterclockwise or clockwise) you chose in step 8 (**Figure 10.16**).

11. To evaluate the improvement in tweening, play the movie.

Areas of change

Figure 10.15 Start adding shape hints in the first keyframe of a tween sequence. Flash places the hints in the center of the tweened object (top). You must drag the hints into position (middle). Distribute the hints in alphabetical order around the outline of the object, placing them on crucial points of change (bottom). Here, the three points with hints a, b, and c define the points from which the stem of the flower will grow.

Figure 10.16 To complete the placement of shape hints, select the second keyframe of your tween sequence. Flash stacks up hints corresponding to the ones you placed in the preceding keyframe (top). You must drag them into the correct final position (bottom).

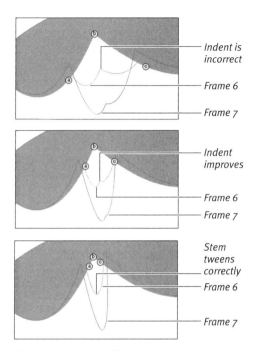

Indent is
incorrect

Frame 6

Frame 7

Indent
improves

Frame 6

Frame 7

Stem
tweens
correctly

Frame 6

Frame 7

Figure 10.17 It can be difficult to match up points in the two keyframes exactly when you first place the shape hints. When you've positioned the hints in the beginning and ending keyframes of a sequence, turn on onion skinning to see where you need to adjust the placement of your hints. With the initial placement, Flash starts the stem growing with an indent at the bottom (top). Moving the points closer together improves the tween (middle). When the onion skins reveal a smooth tween, you're done (bottom).

12. To fine-tune the shape hints' positions, select one of the tween's keyframes, and turn on Onion Skin mode.

Set the onion markers to include all the frames of the tween. Where the onion skins reveal rough spots in the tween, you may need to match the hint position better from the first keyframe to the last one (**Figure 10.17**). Repositioning the shape hints changes the in-between frames. You may need to adjust the shape hints in both keyframes. If you still can't get a smooth tween, try adding more shape hints.

✔ Tips

■ To remove a single shape hint, make the initial keyframe the current frame. Select the shape hint you want to remove, and drag it off the Stage, onto the Pasteboard. Or, Control-click (Mac) or right-click (Windows) the shape hint, and choose Remove Hint.

■ To remove all the hints at the same time, with the initial keyframe current, choose Modify > Shape > Remove All Hints. Or ⌘-click (Mac) or Ctrl-click (Windows) any shape hint, and choose Remove All Hints.

■ Onion skins don't always update correctly when you reposition shape hints. Clicking a blank area of the Stage forces Flash to redraw the onion skins.

■ If you can't create a smooth tween using shape hints alone, break the tween into smaller pieces by adding keyframes where the morphing gets off track. Then redraw the shapes for those frames yourself.

SIMPLE SHAPE INTO A COMPLEX SHAPE

Creating Shapes That Move as They Change

You can't create shape tweens that follow a path, but you can move shapes around the Stage in straight lines. To do so, reposition the elements on the Stage from one keyframe to the next.

To shape-tween a moving graphic:

1. In a new Flash document, or on a new layer, select frame 20, and choose Insert > Timeline > Frame.

   Flash adds blank in-between frames 2 through 20.

2. In the Timeline, select any frame in the span (frames 1–20).

   Note that you must click the frame to select it; you can't just position the play-head in the frame.

3. In the Frame Properties tab of the Property inspector, from the Tween pop-up menu, choose Shape.

   Even though you have no shapes on the Stage to tween yet, Flash gives the frames the shape-tween property. In the Timeline, the frames contain a dotted line, indicating that the tween is incomplete (**Figure 10.18**). Now you can add keyframes and shapes.

4. In the Timeline, insert a blank keyframe at frames 5, 10, 15, and 20.

   Flash creates four shape-tween sequences (**Figure 10.19**). For the moment, they're broken tweens because the keyframes are empty.

5. To complete the tween sequences, in each keyframe, draw a different shape; place each one in a different corner of the Stage.

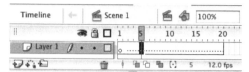

Figure 10.18 To save yourself numerous trips to the Tween pop-up menu in the Frame Properties tab of the Property inspector, you can assign the shape-tween property to a range of frames and add keyframes and shapes later. Flash defines a shape tween even though there's no content to tween yet.

Figure 10.19 When you insert keyframes into a long tween sequence, Flash breaks it into smaller tween sequences. Until you place content in the keyframes, the Timeline displays the dotted line in each span to indicate a broken tween.

Onion skinning on — — *Edit Multiple Frames*

First half of the full tween sequence

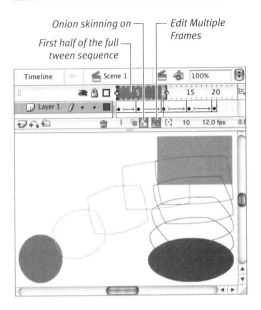

Second half of the full tween sequence —

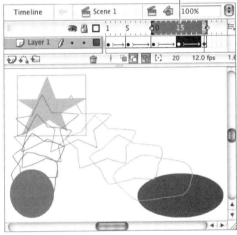

Figure 10.20 Place a different shape in a different location in each keyframe. Flash creates the intermediate steps necessary to transform the shapes and move them across the Stage. Play the movie or turn on onion skinning to examine the motion and shape changes on the in-between frames. (Here, Edit Multiple Frames is also on, making it easy to see the keyframe shapes.)

In frame 1, for example, draw a circular fill in the bottom-left corner of the Stage. In keyframe 5, draw a rectangular fill in the top-right corner of the Stage. In keyframe 10, draw a flattened oval in the bottom-right corner of the Stage. In keyframe 15, draw a star in the top-left corner of the Stage. And in keyframe 20, duplicate keyframe 1's circle in the bottom-left corner of the Stage. For extra variety, give each object a different color. As you add content to keyframes, Flash fills in the spans in the Timeline with tween arrows.

6. Play the movie.

    You see a graphic that bounces around the Stage, morphing from one shape to the next (**Figure 10.20**).

✔ **Tip**

■ Although shape-tweened objects can't follow a path the way motion-tweened objects can, you can make Flash do the work of creating the separate keyframes you need to animate shape tweens that move on curved paths. First, create your shape tween. In the Timeline, select the full range of frames in the tween sequence. Choose Modify > Timeline > Convert to Keyframes. Flash converts each in-between frame (with its transitional content) into a keyframe. Now you can position each keyframe object anywhere you like. To simulate a motion guide, create a regular guide layer (see Chapter 6), and draw the path you want your morphing shape to follow. Choose View > Snapping > Snap to Objects. Reposition the shape in each keyframe. When you drag a shape close to the line on the guide layer, Flash snaps the shape to the line.

MORE-
COMPLEX
ANIMATION TASKS

11

You've learned to manipulate shapes and animate them one at a time, in a single layer, but Macromedia Flash 8 is capable of handling much more complicated animation tasks. To create complex animated movies, you'll need to work with multiple shapes and multiple layers. You may even want to use multiple scenes to organize long animations. In this chapter, you learn to work with multiple layers in the Timeline, stack animations on the various layers to create more-complex movement, and save animations as reusable elements for easy manipulation—either as animated graphic symbols or as movie-clip symbols. With these techniques, you can really start to bring your animations to life.

Understanding Scenes

If the Timeline is the table of contents for the "book" of your movie, scenes are the chapters. A Flash project requiring lots of animation may include hundreds of frames. You can break the animation into smaller chunks by creating scenes. When you publish a movie from a regular Flash document, the scenes play back in order unless you use the interactivity features to provide instructions for playing the scenes in a different order. (To learn more about interactivity in Flash movies, see Chapters 12 and 13.) Flash's Scene panel makes it easy to see what scenes exist in your movie, create new scenes, delete scenes, and reorganize them.

To access the Scene panel:

◆ If the Scene panel isn't open, choose Window > Other Panels > Scene.

The Scene panel appears. In a new Flash document, the Scene panel lists only the default Scene 1. When you add scenes to a movie, the Scene panel lists all the movie's scenes in order (**Figure 11.1**).

To add a scene:

Do either of the following:

◆ Choose Insert > Scene (**Figure 11.2**).

◆ In the Scene panel, click the Add Scene button.

Flash adds another scene, giving it the default name Scene 2.

Duplicate scene —
Add scene —
Delete scene —

Figure 11.1 The Scene panel lists all the scenes in a movie. It also provides buttons for adding, duplicating, and deleting scenes.

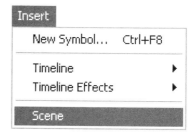

Scene panel's
Add Scene button

Figure 11.2 To add a new scene to your Flash document, choose Insert > Scene (top) or, in the Scene panel, click the Add Scene button (bottom).

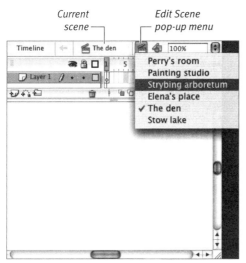

Current scene — *Edit Scene pop-up menu*

Figure 11.3 The Edit Bar displays the name of the current scene. Choose a scene from the Edit Scene pop-up menu to switch scenes quickly.

Click to delete selected scene —

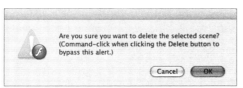

Figure 11.4 When you delete a scene (top), Flash asks you to confirm the deletion (bottom).

To select a scene to edit:

Do either of the following:

◆ Click the Edit Scene button in the Edit Bar above the Timeline.

A pop-up menu of scenes appears; select a scene from the list.

◆ From the scrolling list in the Scene panel, select a scene.

Flash displays the selected scene on the Stage, puts the scene name in the current-scene box in the Edit Bar, and places a check next to that scene's name in the Edit Scene pop-up menu (**Figure 11.3**).

To delete a selected scene:

1. In the Scene panel, click the Delete Scene button.

A dialog appears, asking you to confirm that you want to delete the selected scene (**Figure 11.4**).

2. Click OK.

Flash deletes the scene, removing it from the Edit Scene pop-up menu in the Edit Bar as well as from the scrolling list in the Scene panel.

✔ Tip

■ If you don't want to see the warning dialog when you delete a scene, ⌘-click (Mac) or Ctrl-click (Windows) the Delete Scene button in the Scene panel.

UNDERSTANDING SCENES

To change the scene order:

◆ In the Scene panel, drag a selected scene name up or down in the list.

Flash moves the clapper icon and scene name. In Windows, a highlighted line previews the new location for the scene; on the Mac, the highlight line underscores the name of the scene that will *follow* the scene you're repositioning (**Figure 11.5**).

To rename a scene:

1. In the Scene panel, double-click the name of the scene that you want to rename.

   The Name field activates for entering text.

2. Type the new name in the Name field.

3. Press Enter.

   or

   Click outside the text-entry field.

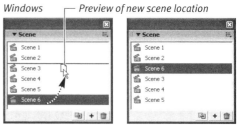

Windows ⎯ *Preview of new scene location*

Drag to reposition scene   *Reordered scenes*

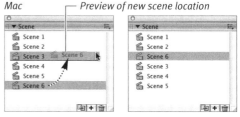

Mac ⎯ *Preview of new scene location*

Drag to reposition scene   *Reordered scenes*

Figure 11.5 Dragging a scene name in the Scene panel changes the order of scenes. In Windows, a horizontal bar previews the new location for the scene; on the Mac, the bar underlines the scene that will follow the scene you're dragging. When the scene is in the correct location, release the mouse button.

The Pitfalls of Using Scenes

Scenes in Flash are tools for organizing content during authoring; they don't exist at runtime. When you create a Flash document, each scene is like a self-contained movie, but when you publish the file, Flash links the scenes into one continuous set of frames. (Imagine a document with two scenes: scene 1 has frames numbered 1–10, and scene two has frames numbered 1–10. The published file winds up with frames numbered 1–20.)

The fact that each scene is, in a sense, a new beginning can make it difficult to keep the continuity of actions between scenes. For movies with interactivity that requires variables, scenes may be inappropriate. In such cases, you may need to stick to a single long movie or use separate movies or separate movie clips within one movie to organize your animation.

The fact that scenes don't exist in the published movie presents other problems. For example, you must be careful to avoid using identical frame labels in multiple scenes. Otherwise interactivities that rely on those frame labels to locate and display the appropriate frame will not work.

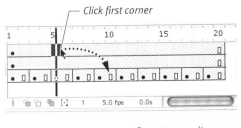

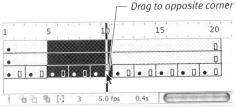

Figure 11.6 In frame-based selection mode, click and drag across frames and layers (top) to select frames in those layers (bottom).

Manipulating Frames in Multiple Layers

As your animation gets more complex, you'll need to add layers to your document. You can perform editing operations on selected frames and layers, for example, by copying, cutting, and pasting frames across multiple layers. You can also insert frames, keyframes, and blank keyframes into selected frame spans and layers.

To select and copy frames in several layers:

1. Create a Flash document that contains 3 layers, each with 20 frames.

   Place content in the layers to help you see what's going on as you work with the various frames and layers. Use the text tool, for example, to place the frame number in every other frame of layer 1 and to place a text block with the name of the layer in layers 2 and 3.

2. In the Timeline in layer 3, to make frame selections, *do either of the following:*

   ▲ In frame-based selection mode, click and drag as though you were drawing a selection rectangle from frame 5 through frame 10 in all three layers.

   ▲ In span-based selection mode, ⌘-click (Mac) or Ctrl-click (Windows), and drag to select a range of frames.

   Flash highlights the selected frames (**Figure 11.6**).

3. Choose Edit > Timeline > Copy Frames.

   Flash copies the frames and layer information to the Clipboard.

✔ Tip

- To select a block of frames that spans several layers without dragging, in frame-based selection mode, click a frame at one of the four corners of the block. Then Shift-click the frame at the opposite corner. Flash selects all the frames in the rectangle that you've defined (**Figure 11.7**). In span-based selection style, ⌘-click (Mac) or Ctrl-click (Windows) one corner, and then Shift-⌘-click (Mac) or Ctrl-Shift-click (Windows) the opposite corner to make your selection.

To replace the content of frames with a multilayer selection:

1. Continuing with the document you created in the preceding task, select frames 15–20 on all three layers.

2. Choose Edit > Timeline > Paste Frames.

   Flash pastes the copied frames 5–10 into frames 15–20 in each of the three layers. The numbers on the Stage in layer 1 now start over with 5 at frame 15, 7 at frame 17, and 9 at frame 19.

To paste a multiple-layer selection into blank frames:

1. Continuing with the document you created in the preceding task, select frame 21 on all three layers.

2. Choose Edit > Timeline > Paste Frames.

   Flash pastes the copied frames 5–10 into protoframes 21–26 in each of the three layers (**Figure 11.8**). Layer 1 now displays the number 5 at frame 21, 7 at frame 23, and 9 at frame 25.

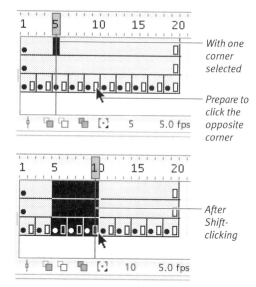

With one corner selected

Prepare to click the opposite corner

After Shift-clicking

Figure 11.7 To select a block of frames without dragging, in frame-based selection mode, click one corner of the block; then Shift-click the opposite corner to define the block. In span-based selection mode, ⌘-click (Mac) or Ctrl-click (Windows) the first corner, and then Shift-⌘-click (Mac) or Ctrl-Shift-click (Windows) the opposite corner of your selection block.

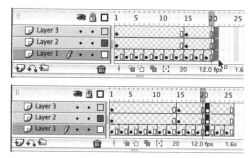

Figure 11.8 Pasting a multiple-layer, multiple-frame selection at the end of a set of defined frames (top) extends the Timeline to accommodate the new frames and layers (bottom).

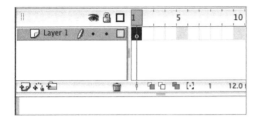

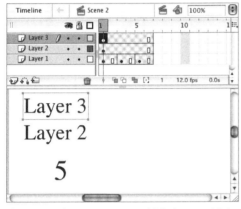

Figure 11.9 When you paste a multiple-layer, multiple-frame selection into the first frame of a new scene (top), Flash creates new layers and frames to hold the contents of the Clipboard (bottom).

To paste a multiple-layer selection into a new scene:

1. Continuing with the document you created in the preceding task, insert a new scene, following the instructions in the first section of this chapter.

   By default, the new scene has one layer and one keyframe.

2. Select keyframe 1.

3. Choose Edit > Timeline > Paste Frames.

   Flash pastes the copied selection from the first scene (frames 5–10 on layers 1–3) into the new scene. Flash adds layers 2 and 3 and creates frames 1–6 in each layer (**Figure 11.9**). Layer 1 now displays the number 5 at frame 1, 7 at frame 3, and 9 at frame 5.

MANIPULATING FRAMES IN MULTIPLE LAYERS

325

Animating Multiple Motion Tweens

As you learned in Chapter 9, Flash can motion-tween only one item per layer. You can tween multiple items simultaneously; you just have to put each one on a separate layer. You can use Onion Skin and Edit Multiple Frame modes to make sure all the elements line up in the right place at the right time. To get a feel for tweening multiple items, try combining three simple motion tweens to create a game of Ping-Pong. One layer contains the ball; the other layers each contain a paddle.

To set up the three graphics in separate layers:

1. Open a new Flash document, and add two new layers.

2. Rename the layers.

   Name the top layer *Ball,* the next layer *1st Paddle,* and the bottom layer *2nd Paddle.* Naming the layers helps you keep track of the elements and their locations.

3. Create the graphics.

   On the Stage, in the Ball layer, use the oval tool to create a ball; in the layer named 1st Paddle, use the rectangle tool to create a paddle; and then copy the paddle and paste the copy into the layer named 2nd Paddle. Give each shape a different color. Your file should look something like **Figure 11.10**.

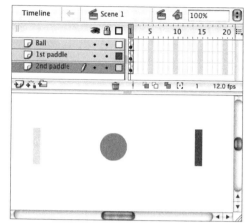

Figure 11.10 To have several graphics motion-tween simultaneously, you must place each one on a separate layer. Here, each item is on a separate layer. The descriptive layer names help you keep track of what goes where.

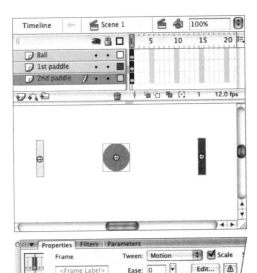

Figure 11.11 By using the Create Motion Tween command with frames selected on all three layers (top), you create three motion tweens with one command. The Frame Properties tab of the Property inspector reveals their status as motion tweens (bottom).

Figure 11.12 Using the Create Motion Tween command in keyframe 1, sets the Tween property for all the frames that follow (to end the tween sequence, you must change that property). The added frames contain broken tweens; you must add keyframes and content.

To set up the tween in all layers with one command:

1. Using the document you created in the preceding task, in the Timeline, select keyframe 1 in all three layers.

2. Choose Insert > Timeline > Create Motion Tween.

   Flash turns each shape into a symbol (naming the symbols Tween 1, Tween 2, and Tween 3) and gives all the frames the motion-tween property (**Figure 11.11**). It's a good idea to rename your tween symbols in the library.

3. In the Timeline, select frame 20 in all three layers.

4. Choose Insert > Timeline > Frame.

   Flash extends the motion tween through frame 20 on all three layers. A dotted line across the frames indicates an incomplete motion tween. Reposition the symbols and create keyframes to complete the tweens (**Figure 11.12**).

✔ Tips

- The Create Motion Tween command helps you create symbols and set the tween property, but it has drawbacks: You have no control over the symbol's type or registration point. If you use the command a lot, the generic names can be difficult to deal with. Rename the symbols meaningfully.

- You can create the graphics as symbols from the beginning, placing instances of each symbol in the appropriate layer in step 3 of the first task in this section. If you start with symbols, skip the Create Motion Tween command. In step 2 of the preceding task, set the Frame property to Motion in the Frame Properties tab of the Property inspector (see Chapter 9).

To adjust the positions of the tweened items:

1. Using the document you created in the preceding task, in the Timeline, position the playhead in frame 5.

2. On the Stage, drag the ball to the approximate location where it should connect with one of the paddles for the first hit.

   Flash makes Ball the active layer and creates a keyframe (in frame 5) for the ball in its new location (**Figure 11.13**). Flash completes the motion tween between keyframe 1 and keyframe 5 of the Ball layer and leaves the broken-tween line in all the other frames.

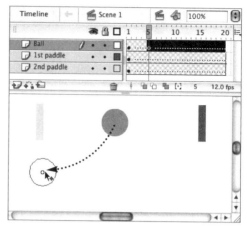

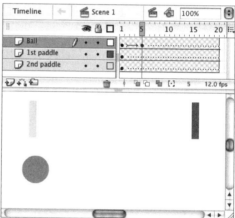

Figure 11.13 Moving a graphic in a frame that's defined as part of a motion tween causes Flash to make the layer containing the graphic the active layer (top). Flash creates a keyframe in that layer for the graphic's new position, completing one tween sequence (bottom).

Frames selected

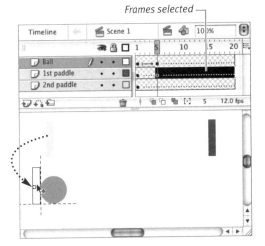

Tween in the correct location

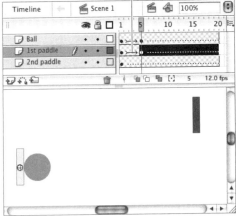

Figure 11.14 As you reposition the paddle (top), Flash appears to be selecting the wrong set of frames; but when you release the mouse button, Flash correctly tweens frames 1–4 (bottom).

3. On the Stage, reposition the first paddle graphic so that the paddle connects with the ball for the first hit.

Flash makes 1st Paddle the active layer and creates a keyframe (in frame 5) for the paddle in its new location (**Figure 11.14**).

4. In the Timeline, position the playhead in frame 10.

5. On the Stage, drag the ball to the approximate location where you want it to connect with a paddle for the second hit.

Flash makes Ball the active layer and creates a keyframe (in frame 10) for the ball in its new location. Flash completes the motion tween between keyframe 5 and keyframe 10 of the Ball layer.

continues on next page

ANIMATING MULTIPLE MOTION TWEENS

6. On the Stage, reposition the second paddle so that it connects with the ball for the second hit.

Flash makes 2nd Paddle the active layer and creates a keyframe (in frame 10) for the paddle in its new location (**Figure 11.15**).

7. Repeat steps 1–6, creating keyframes 15 and 20, to make the ball connect with each paddle one more time.

8. Play the movie to see the animation in action.

9. Select Onion Skin Outlines and Edit Multiple Frames, and then reposition objects as necessary to fine-tune the motion (**Figure 11.16**).

Although Edit Multiple Frames doesn't show onion skins for keyframes, it does show them for tween graphics.

✔ Tips

■ After you define a set of frames as tweens, any slight change you make to an object causes Flash to create a new keyframe. Even clicking and holding more than a second or two causes Flash to insert a keyframe. So that you don't change objects' positions or create new keyframes accidentally, lock or hide the layers that you're not working on.

■ To position items on the Stage with greater precision than dragging allows, select an item and use the Properties tab of the Property inspector or the Info panel to set the item's x and y coordinates.

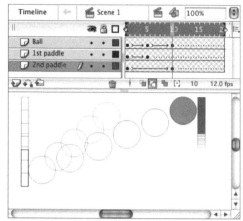

Figure 11.15 Moving an element in another frame creates another tween. Here, the paddle on the right side appears to move more slowly than the paddle on the left side, because Flash is creating a 10-frame tween for the right paddle, whereas the left paddle tweens in 5 frames. (Here onion skinning is turned on to make the tweened shapes visible.)

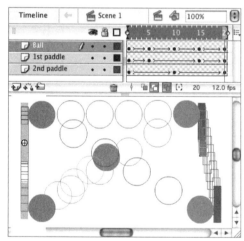

Figure 11.16 Selecting Onion Skin Outlines and Edit Multiple Frames makes fine-tuning the location of objects easier. Here, the paddle on the right doesn't move in a straight line. If you want it to do so, reposition the paddle graphics in the first and final frames so that one lies directly above the other; and then reposition the ball so that it comes into contact with both paddles.

- If you like to use Snap Align, Flash's default setting, to help you position items, you'll notice that sometimes in the preceding task, the snapping guides don't appear as you drag graphic elements in in-between frames whose Tween property is set to Motion. These guides work best when all objects involved are in keyframes. If the guides aren't appearing for you, drag items to approximate locations initially. Once Flash has created the new keyframes, you can drag your elements, and the guidelines will appear.

Tweening Text

You can use the multiple-motion tween idea to animate individual characters within a piece of text. After you create the text that you want to animate, select it and choose Modify > Break Apart. That command places each character in its own text box. Next, with each character of the text selected, choose Modify > Timeline > Distribute to Layers. Each character winds up on its own layer. Now use any of the animating techniques you learned in Chapters 8 and 9, or in earlier tasks in this chapter, to animate the individual text characters (**Figure 11.17**).

To transform the shapes of the letters, you need to use shape tweening. That means converting the letters from editable text elements to editable graphics. Select one or more text boxes containing individual letters, and choose Modify > Break Apart. The letterforms look the same, but now they're raw shapes that you can modify with the drawing tools and use in shape tweens. Shape tweening letters can get pretty complex. Remember to use shape hints (see Chapter 10) to help Flash make the transition between shapes correctly.

Text distributed to layers

Broken-apart text; one character per text box

Each letter is a separate motion tween

Figure 11.17 Using Flash's Modify > Break Apart command in conjunction with the Modify > Timeline > Distribute to Layers command, you can set up tweens quickly to animate individual text characters. Each letter in this animated text is a motion tween.

Animating Shape Tweens in Multiple-Shape Graphics

An important thing to remember about complex shape tweens is that Flash deals most reliably with a single shape tween on a layer. In the following tasks, you create a multipart, multilayer graphic and shape-tween the whole package simultaneously.

To create shape tweens on separate layers:

1. Open a Flash document, and add two new layers.

2. Rename the layers *Top Flame, Middle Flame,* and *Bottom Flame.*

   Naming the layers helps you keep track of the objects and their locations.

3. Create the shapes.

   On the Stage, use the oval tool to create three concentric oval shapes without strokes. In the Bottom Flame layer, create a large oval; in the Middle Flame layer, create a medium oval (center it over the first oval); in the Top Flame layer, create a small oval (center it over the medium oval). Give each oval a different color. Your file should look something like **Figure 11.18**.

4. Select frame 5 in all three layers.

5. Choose Insert > Timeline > Keyframe.

   Flash creates a keyframe with the same content as keyframe 1 for each layer.

6. In the Timeline, select any of the frames in the keyframe 1 span (1, 2, 3, or 4) in all three layers.

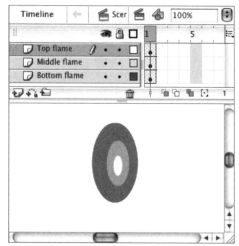

Figure 11.18 Create each part of a multiple-element shape tween on a separate layer. Name the layers to help you track what goes where.

When Should One Element Span Several Layers?

Often, an element that you think of as a single entity consists of several shapes in Flash. A candle flame is a good example. To simulate the flickering of a lighted candle, you might create a flame with three shades of orange and then animate changes in the flame shape and colors.

It's natural to keep drawing each piece of the flame in one layer, especially if you're creating merge-shapes and want to see the interaction of the shapes immediately. Unfortunately, Flash has trouble tween-ing multiple shapes (both merge-shapes and drawing-objects) on a single layer. You're better off creating a rough version of each piece in a separate layer and then fine-tuning that version. Or, create your shapes in one layer, but then select them and choose Insert > Timeline > Distribute to Layers to place them on separate layers. That way, Flash has to tween only one shape per layer, and the result will be cleaner.

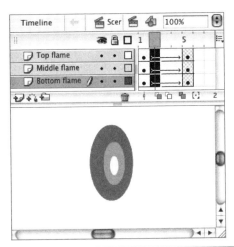

Figure 11.19 When you select multiple frames, you can set the tweening property for those frames simultaneously by choosing a property from the Tween pop-up menu in the Properties tab of the Property inspector.

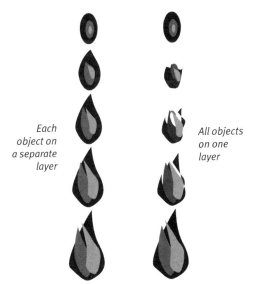

Each object on a separate layer

All objects on one layer

Figure 11.20 No matter whether you use merge-shapes or drawing objects, if you put the three flames on separate layers (left), Flash does a reasonable job of tweening even when you don't add shape hints. With the three flame shapes on a single layer (right), Flash has great difficulty creating the tweens.

7. In the Frame Properties tab of the Property inspector, from the Tween menu, choose Shape.

   Flash gives the shape-tween property to frames 1–4 on all three layers (**Figure 11.19**). To create flickering flames, you need to reshape the ovals in keyframe 5.

8. In the Timeline, position the playhead in keyframe 5.

9. On the Stage, edit the ovals to create flame shapes.

10. Play the movie to see the animation in action.

    Flash handles the shape-tweening of each layer separately. For comparison, try creating the oval and flame shapes on a single layer and then shape-tweening them (**Figure 11.20**).

11. Select Onion Skin Outlines and Edit Multiple Frames; then reposition the flame objects as necessary to fine-tune the motion.

Reversing Frames

Sometimes, you can save effort by creating just half the animation that you need and letting Flash do the rest of the work. Think of the candle flame you created in the preceding section. You might want the flame to grow larger and then shrink back to its original size. The shrinking phase is the reverse of the growing phase. You can make a copy of the growing-flame animation and then have Flash reverse the order of the frames.

To reverse the order of frames:

1. Open the document you created in the preceding section.

   This movie spans five frames on three layers. The first keyframe shows the flame as three concentric oval shapes; the final keyframe shows the flame in a taller, flickering configuration.

2. In the Timeline, select all five frames on all three layers.

3. In one of the selected frames, Control-click (Mac) or right-click (Windows) to access the frame-editing contextual menu; then choose Copy Frames (**Figure 11.21**).

4. In the Timeline, select frame 6 in all three layers.

5. In one of the selected frames, Control-click (Mac) or right-click (Windows) to access the frame-editing contextual menu, and choose Paste Frames.

   Your movie now contains two back-to-back animation sequences of the growing flame (**Figure 11.22**).

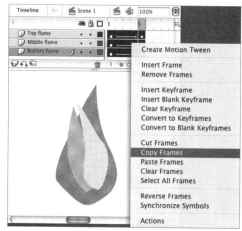

Figure 11.21 The contextual menu for frames lets you copy all selected frames with a single command.

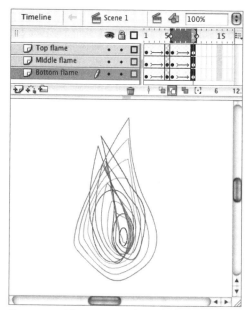

Figure 11.22 After you paste the copied selection, you have two tween sequences ending with the tall, flickering flame.

REVERSING FRAMES

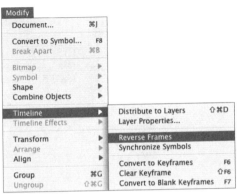

Figure 11.23 Choosing Modify > Timeline > Reverse Frames rearranges the order of selected frames. Use this command to make a selected tween run backward.

6. In the Timeline, select frames 6–10 on all three layers.

7. Choose Modify > Timeline > Reverse Frames (**Figure 11.23**).

Flash reverses the tween in the second sequence so that the flame starts out tall and flickery, and winds up in its original oval configuration in the final keyframe (**Figure 11.24**).

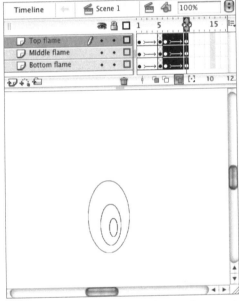

Figure 11.24 After you reverse the frames, the second tween sequence ends with the oval flame.

Combining Tweening with Frame-by-Frame Techniques

Especially with shape tweening, you can't always rely on Flash to create in-between frames that capture the exact movement you want. You can combine Flash's tweening with your own frame-by-frame efforts, however, letting Flash do the work whenever it can. Or, let Flash create the broad outlines of your animation, and then add keyframes to refine the movement. Flash helps with the process by allowing you to convert those intangible in-between frames to keyframes that you can edit and refine yourself.

In the preceding section, you created a crude version of a flickering flame. In the following tasks, you refine it.

To convert in-between frames to keyframes:

1. Open the Flash document you created in the preceding section.

2. In the Timeline, position the playhead in frame 2.

   The first step in this tween isn't particularly effective: The central flame portion seems to be a bit too far to the side (**Figure 11.25**). Because frame 2 is an in-between frame, however, you can't edit it. You can try to improve the motion by adding shape hints, or you can create a new keyframe to refine the animation.

3. To convert the in-between frame to a keyframe, in the Timeline, select frame 2 in all three layers.

4. Choose Modify > Timeline > Convert to Keyframes, or press F6 (**Figure 11.26**).

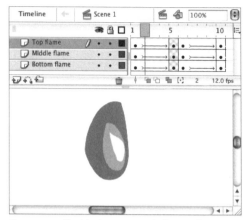

Figure 11.25 Flash's shape tween in frame 2 leaves something to be desired.

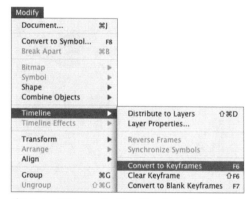

Figure 11.26 Choose Modify > Timeline > Convert to Keyframes to create a keyframe you can use to adjust your multilayer tween.

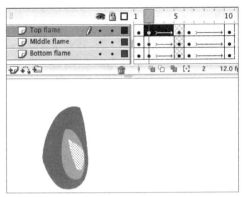

Figure 11.27 After you convert frame 2 from an in-between frame (part of a tween) to a keyframe, you can edit the flame shapes.

Flash converts frame 2 from an in-between frame to a keyframe; then it creates the contents of keyframe 2 from the transitional shapes it created for the shape tween at that frame. Now you're free to edit the contents to improve the tweening action (**Figure 11.27**). If you want to create a smoother motion, expand the tween between keyframe 1 and keyframe 2.

5. To add more in-between frames, position the playhead in keyframe 1 by clicking the number 1 above the layers or by dragging the playhead.

6. Choose Insert > Timeline > Frame, or press F5.

Flash adds new in-between frames in all layers. You can repeat the Insert > Timeline > Frame command to add as many frames as you like. These frames inherit the shape-tween property that you defined for keyframe 1. Now you can examine Flash's tweening for the new frames and repeat the process of converting any awkward tween frames to keyframes and editing them.

✔ Tips

■ In step 4 of the preceding task, when converting in-between frames of a shape tween to keyframes, Flash always creates the new shapes as merge-shapes (even if the shapes in the preceding keyframe are drawing-objects). This could result in unexpected consequences if your shapes are on a single layer. It's another reason to make sure your shapes are on separate layers for tweened animation.

■ Flash limits you to one color change per tween sequence. To speed the process of making several color changes, set up one long tween (either motion or shape) that goes from the initial color to the final color. Then selectively convert in-between frames to keyframes so that you can make additional color changes.

Saving Animations As Graphic Symbols

In Chapter 7, you learned to save work for reuse and keep file sizes small by using symbols. Flash lets you do the same thing with entire multiple-frame, multiple-layer animation sequences. You can save such sequences either as an animated graphic symbol or as a movie-clip symbol. You can use these symbols repeatedly with a much smaller hit on file size than if you simply re-create the animation by using graphic-symbol instances within separate animations. Additionally, for complex animations, symbols help keep down the number of frames and layers that you have to deal with at any time.

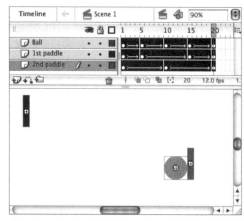

Figure 11.28 To convert an existing animation to a symbol, first select all the frames and layers that make up the animation sequence.

To convert an animation to a graphic symbol:

1. Open the document you created to make the Ping-Pong animation in "Animating Multiple Motion Tweens," earlier in this chapter, or create your own multiple-layer animation.

   The Ping-Pong animation is a 3-layer, 20-frame animation.

2. In the Timeline, select all 20 frames in all 3 layers (**Figure 11.28**).

3. Choose Edit > Timeline > Copy Frames.

4. Choose Insert > New Symbol, or press ⌘-F8 (Mac) or Ctrl-F8 (Windows).

   The Create New Symbol dialog appears (**Figure 11.29**).

5. In the Create New Symbol dialog, type a name for your symbol (for example, Ping-PongAnimation).

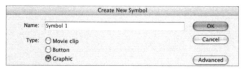

Figure 11.29 You set a new symbol's type in the Create New Symbol dialog. Movie clips operate from their own independent Timeline. Animated graphic symbols play in sync with the main movie that contains them. One frame in the main movie's Timeline displays one frame of the graphic symbol's Timeline.

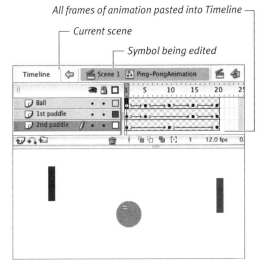

All frames of animation pasted into Timeline

Current scene

Symbol being edited

Figure 11.30 When you create a new symbol, Flash switches to symbol-editing mode, making the new symbol's Timeline available for editing. You must paste all the frames of your animation into the symbol's Timeline to create the animated symbol.

6. Choose Graphic as the symbol type.

7. Click OK.

Flash creates a new symbol in the library and switches you to symbol-editing mode for that symbol.

The name of your symbol appears in the Edit Bar above the Timeline. The default Timeline for your new symbol consists of one layer and a blank keyframe at frame 1.

8. In the symbol Timeline, select keyframe 1, and choose Edit > Timeline > Paste Frames.

Flash pastes the 20 frames and 3 layers that you copied from the original Ping-Pong movie into the Timeline for the Ping-PongAnimation symbol (**Figure 11.30**). If you want to make any adjustments in the animation sequence, you can do so at this point.

9. To return to document-editing mode, choose Edit > Edit Document.

Symbols Reduce Layer Buildup

In general, for tweened animations, you need to place each shape on a separate layer. To animate a person, for example, create separate layers for the head, the torso, each arm, and each leg. For complex motion, you might even create separate layers for the eyes, mouth, fingers, and toes. Add some other elements to this character's environment, and you wind up dealing with many layers.

Turning an animation sequence into a symbol in effect collapses all those layers into one object. The process is a bit like grouping. On the Stage, the symbol exists on a single layer, but that layer contains all the layers of the original animation.

✔ Tips

- In the list of symbols in the Library panel, an animated graphic symbol looks the same as a static graphic symbol; both have the same icon, and both are listed as Graphic in the Type column. An animated graphic symbol, however, has Play and Stop buttons in the top-right corner of the preview window; a static graphic symbol doesn't (**Figure 11.31**). You can preview an animated symbol by clicking the Play button.

- When you paste multiple frames and layers into the Timeline in symbol-editing mode, the registration crosshair may be in a strange position for the symbol as a whole. To reposition the items making up the symbol, in the Status bar, click the Edit Multiple Frames button; from the Modify Onion Markers pop-up menu, choose Onion All; finally, choose Edit > Select All to select the contents of each keyframe in each layer. Now you can position the symbol as a whole in relation to the crosshair.

Saving Animations As Graphic Symbols

Animated graphic symbol

Stop and Play buttons

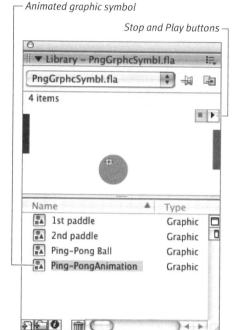

Static graphic symbol

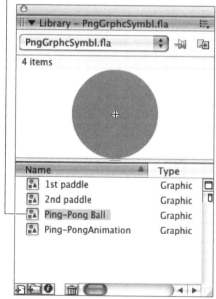

Figure 11.31 An animated graphic symbol (top) in the Library panel has Stop and Play buttons as part of its preview; otherwise, it's indistinguishable from a static graphic symbol (bottom).

How Do Animated Graphic Symbols Differ from Movie-Clip Symbols?

Flash provides for two kinds of animated symbols: graphic symbols and movie clips. The difference is a bit subtle and hard to grasp at first. An animated graphic symbol is tied to the Timeline of any movie in which you place the symbol, whereas a movie-clip symbol runs on its own independent Timeline. When the playhead stops moving in the main Timeline, an animated graphic symbol stops playing, but a movie-clip symbol continues to play.

Think of the frames of an animated graphic symbol as a tray of slides and a movie-clip symbol as a film loop. The animated graphic symbol projects its slides, one per frame, in lock step with the frames of its hosting movie: to see the next frame of the symbol, you move to the next frame in the hosting movie. Like a tray of slides, an animated graphic symbol has no sound track. If you have sounds in a movie and you convert that movie to a graphic symbol, you lose those sounds. If you have attached ActionScript to buttons, that interactivity survives the conversion to a graphic symbol (though any actions that control the Timeline affect the Timeline of the hosting movie, not the graphic symbol itself, potentially creating confusion). Other types of interactivity do not survive the conversion.

A movie-clip symbol can project all its frames one after another, over and over, in a single frame of the hosting movie. Movie clips do have a sound track and do retain their interactivity. (To learn more about sound, see Chapter 15. For interactivity, see Chapters 12 and 13.)

One more thing to know about the two symbol types is that movie clips, because they run on their own Timeline, don't appear as animations in the Flash authoring environment. You see only the first frame of the movie as a static element on the Stage. Animated graphic symbols, which use the same Timeline as the main movie, display their animation in the authoring environment.

Using Animated Graphic Symbols

To put an animated graphic symbol to work, you must place an instance of it in your main movie. The layer of the movie where you place the symbol must have enough frames to display the symbol. You can use instances of an animated graphic symbol just as you would any other symbol—combine it with other graphics on a layer; motion-tween it; modify its color, size, and rotation; and so on.

To place an instance of an animated graphic symbol:

1. In the movie you created in the preceding section, choose Insert > Scene to create a new scene.

   Flash displays the new scene's Timeline—a single layer with a blank keyframe in frame 1. The Stage is empty.

   Adding a new scene gives you a blank Stage to work with and makes it easy to compare the two animations: the original (created directly in the main movie Timeline) and the instance of the graphic symbol placed in the movie.

2. Access the Library panel.

   If it's not open, choose Window > Library.

3. In the Library panel for your document, select the Ping-PongAnimation symbol.

   The first frame of the animation appears in the preview window (**Figure 11.32**).

4. Drag a copy of the selected symbol to the Stage.

   Flash places the symbol in keyframe 1. At this point, you can see only the first frame of the animation (**Figure 11.33**). The animation is 20 frames long, so you need to add least 20 frames to view the symbol in its entirety.

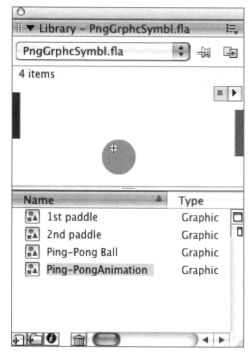

Figure 11.32 Select the graphic symbol you want to use, and then drag a copy to your Flash document to place an instance on the Stage.

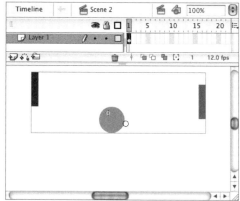

Figure 11.33 When you drag an instance of the animated graphic to the Stage, you see the symbol's first frame with its graphics selected. You must add frames to allow the full animation of the symbol to play in the main movie.

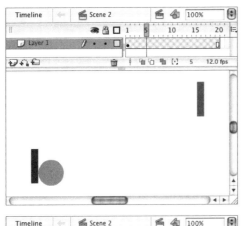

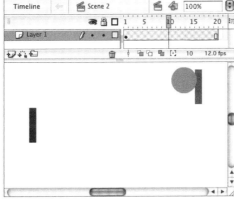

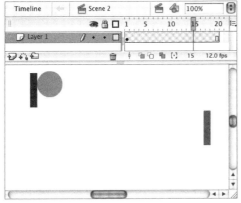

Figure 11.34 Frames 1–20 have a tweening property of None, but they still display animation. Flash displays the 20 tween frames of the graphic symbol that you placed in keyframe 1. It's as though the symbol is a tray of slides, and Flash is projecting one image per frame in the main movie. If the main movie is longer than the slide show, Flash starts the slide show over.

5. In the Timeline, select frame 20, and choose Insert > Timeline > Frame.

Flash adds in-between frames 2–20.

6. Play the movie.

Now Flash can display each frame of the animated graphic symbol in a frame of the movie. Frame 2 of the symbol appears in frame 2 of the movie, frame 5 of the symbol appears in frame 5 of the movie, and so on (**Figure 11.34**). If you place fewer than 20 frames in the movie, Flash truncates the symbol and displays only as many frames of the symbol as there are frames in the movie.

✔ Tips

- By default, Flash loops the animation of graphic symbols. If the layer containing the animated symbol instance in the main Timeline has more frames than the symbol requires, Flash starts playing the graphic symbol over again to fill those extra frames. You can prevent such looping. Select the symbol instance on the Stage. In the Properties tab of the Property inspector, from the Options for Graphics menu, choose Play Once (**Figure 11.35**). The options settings also let you choose to start the symbol's animation with a frame other than 1. Enter the desired frame number in the First field. (You can even choose to display just one frame of the animated graphic symbol. From the Options for Graphics menu, choose Single Frame, and then enter the desired frame number in the First field. You can use this technique to pause the animation of the symbol for a certain number of frames in the main movie. At the frame where the symbol should start running, add another keyframe and another copy of the symbol and set it to loop.)

Figure 11.35 By default, animated graphic symbols move in lock step with the Timeline of the main movie. If the symbol's animation contains fewer frames than does the layer containing the symbol instance in the main Timeline, the animated graphic symbol loops. To stop the selected symbol instance from looping, in the Properties tab of the Property inspector, from the Options for Graphics menu, choose Play Once.

Animated Graphic Symbols Increase File Size

Although symbols are used to keep file size down, animated graphic symbols don't do as good a job at that as movie-clip symbols. For each in-between frame that displays part of an animated graphic, Flash exports roughly 12-15 bytes of data. That's true even if you're just adding extra in-between frames and looping the animated graphic. You don't need any in-between frames to display the movie-clip symbol's animation

If you nest animated graphic symbols inside animated graphic symbols, you compound the problem because each in-between frame in the nested copy of the symbol adds its 12 bytes of data too. Reusing and nesting movie-clip symbols adds little extra data to your file. To test for yourself, nest an animated graphic symbol inside a copy of that symbol and place an instance of the symbol on the stage in a 20-frame keyspan. Test the movie (choose Control > Test Movie). Check the amount of data in each frame using the Bandwidth Profiler (see Chapter 16). Go back to the Flash document and change the symbols' type to movie-clip and test again.

A Note about Timeline Effects

In the previous version of Flash, Macromedia initiated a feature called *Timeline Effects*. The goal was to help less-experienced Flash users create a few special effects (such as a drop shadow and blur) and perform a few common animation tasks (such as moving an element in a straight line or breaking it apart as if it explodes) quickly and easily. To create Timeline Effects, you choose settings in an Effects dialog; Flash uses those settings to create symbols and animation for you. (Some of the symbols Flash creates are static, like the ones you learned about in Chapter 7; others are animated, like the ones you're learning about in this chapter.) Unfortunately, Flash names its effect symbols in confusing ways; adds a new folder to your Library panel to hold some, but not all, of the new symbols; and makes changes to the Timeline, renaming the active layer and adding frames to accommodate the animation. You may find these changes confusing. An even greater problem is that once the symbols and Timeline changes have been made, you're not free to use standard techniques to reuse and edit them; if you do, you risk breaking the effect. You must use a special command to access the Effects dialog to edit an effect; you must use another special command to remove the effect and all the changes to the Timeline and Library panel. Flash 8 continues to offer the eight Timeline Effects, but nothing has been done to improve the pitfalls of using them.

USING ANIMATED GRAPHIC SYMBOLS

Using Timeline Effects

Timeline Effects are easy to create but difficult to work with and they're not recommended (see the sidebar "A Note about Timeline Effects"). For anyone who would like to try them, as a quick-and-dirty solution, the procedures for creating the various effects are similar, though the precise settings vary. Here's a quick rundown for one effect.

To create a Timeline Effect:

1. Select one or more graphic-objects on the stage and convert them to a symbol.

You don't have to apply Timeline Effects to symbols, but it's a good idea. That way, you'll have a copy of the original graphic should the effect go wrong and you want to start again.

2. Select the symbol instance on the Stage.

3. Choose Insert > Timeline Effects > *Effect Category* > *Effect Name* (**Figure 11. 36**).

The Effect Setting dialog appears. The dialog bears the name of the effect you're creating (**Figure 11. 37**).

Figure 11. 36 Choose Insert > Timeline Effects > *Effect Category* > *Effect Name* to apply effect to a selected object.

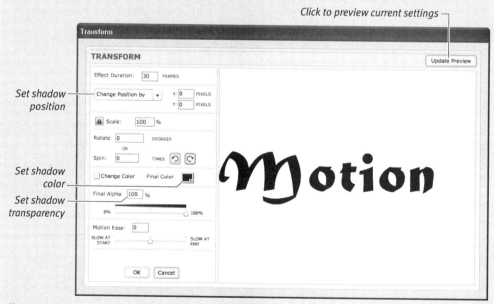

Click to preview current settings

Set shadow position

Set shadow color

Set shadow transparency

Figure 11. 37 The Effect Setting dialog's name and settings change for each effect. The Transform effect contains settings for changing the color, transparency, size, and/or location of an object over the specified number of frames. To preview changes to your settings, click the Update Preview button.

4. Use any of the dialog's menus, color controls, sliders, or entry fields to adjust the settings for the selected effect.

5. To see how the new settings look, click the Update Preview button.

   The resulting effect plays in the preview area of the dialog.

6. To apply the settings to your selected symbol, click OK.

   Flash creates special effects symbols and a folder named Effects Folder in the Library panel, renames the Timeline layer containing your original symbol (or graphic-object), and adds layers and frames as needed to create the effect (**Figure 11. 38**).

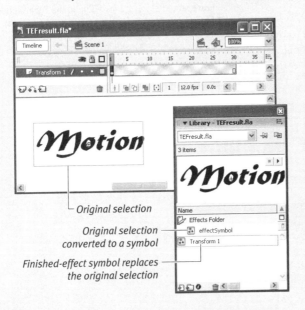

Figure 11. 38 When you apply an effect to a selected graphic on the Stage, Flash replaces your original selection with an instance of the finished-effect symbol.

Original selection

Original selection converted to a symbol

Finished-effect symbol replaces the original selection

To edit an existing Timeline Effect:

1. Select the Effect symbol on the Stage or select its keyframe span in the Timeline.

2. Choose Modify > Timeline Effect > Edit Effect.

   The Effect dialog appears and you can change the effect's settings. When you do, Flash re-creates the effect symbol, and yet again renames items in the library and Timeline.

To delete an existing Timeline Effect:

1. Select the Effect symbol on the Stage or select its keyframe span in the Timeline.

2. Choose Modify > Timeline Effects > Remove Effect.

   Flash restores your original symbol instance (or graphic-object) on the Stage, removes the effects symbols and folder from the Library panel, removes any layers and frames added to the Timeline, and restores the orignal layer name.

Saving Animations as Movie-Clip Symbols

The procedure you use to save an animation as a movie-clip symbol is the same as for saving an animated graphic symbol, except that you define the symbol as a movie clip in the Create New Symbol dialog.

To convert an animation to a movie-clip symbol:

1. Open the document you created to make the Ping-Pong animation in "Animating Multiple Motion Tweens" earlier in this chapter.

   The Ping-Pong animation is a 3-layer, 20-frame animation.

2. In the Timeline, select all 20 frames in all 3 layers.

3. Choose Edit > Timeline > Copy Frames.

4. Choose Insert > New Symbol, or press ⌘-F8 (Mac) or Ctrl-F8 (Windows).

   The Create New Symbol dialog appears.

5. In the Name field, type a name for your symbol—for example, Ping-PongClip.

   Flash remembers the symbol type you selected for the last symbol you created and selects that type for you again when you choose Insert > New Symbol.

6. Select Movie Clip as the symbol type (**Figure 11.39**).

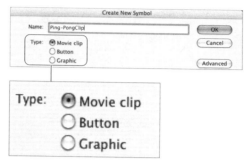

Figure 11.39 Selecting Movie Clip in the Type section of the Create New Symbol dialog defines a symbol that has an independent Timeline. The entire movie-clip symbol runs in a single frame of the main movie.

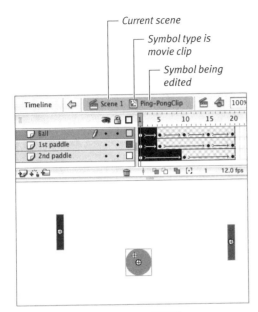

Current scene

Symbol type is movie clip

Symbol being edited

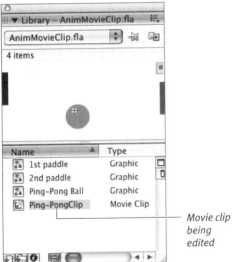

Movie clip being edited

Figure 11.40 After you name the symbol and define its type in the Create New Symbol dialog, Flash switches to symbol-editing mode. The icon that precedes the name of the symbol indicates that this symbol is a movie-clip. Now you can paste the animation frames into the symbol's Timeline.

7. Click OK.

Flash creates a new symbol in the Library panel and switches you to symbol-editing mode, with that symbol selected.

The name of your symbol appears in the Edit Bar. The default Timeline for your new symbol consists of one layer and a blank keyframe at frame 1.

8. In the symbol Timeline, select keyframe 1, and choose Edit > Timeline > Paste Frames.

Flash pastes all 20 frames and 3 layers that you copied from the original Ping-Pong animation into the Timeline for the Ping-PongClip symbol (**Figure 11.40**). If you want to make any adjustments in the animation sequence, you can do so at this point.

9. To return to document-editing mode, click the current scene name in the Edit Bar.

✔ Tip

- To make a movie clip that contains exactly the same frames as an existing animated graphic symbol (as you did in the preceding task), you can duplicate that symbol and change its type. Select the animated graphic symbol in the Library panel. From the Library panel's Options menu, choose Duplicate. The Duplicate Symbol dialog appears, allowing you to rename the symbol and set its type to movie clip.

SAVING ANIMATIONS AS MOVIE-CLIP SYMBOLS

The Mystery of 9-Slice Scaling

One of the beauties of Flash is the way it lets you reuse elements. One of the frustrations of reusing elements is that resizing can distort them. Imagine creating a rounded rectangle that you'll resize for various situations; it could be the graphic for an interface element, such as a button, or it could be a building block for an artistic animation. You would expect the amount of rounding in the corners to remain the same when you make the rectangle larger or smaller. In fact, the corners can change, sometimes distorting horizontally, sometimes vertically.

This distortion can occur in the Flash document, as you create your content, or at runtime when people view your movie. Runtime resizing happens if you create scripts that scale elements dynamically; it can also happen if people resize the browser window displaying your movie. You have some control over the second type of scaling when you set options for publishing a movie (see Chapter 16).

In Flash 8, when publishing for Flash Player 8, you can impose conditions on the way one type of graphic element—a movie-clip symbol—scales at runtime by invoking 9-slice scaling guides. When you activate the 9-slice guides, Flash superimposes a grid over your movie-clip symbol. The corner sections defined by the grid don't scale at all; the other sections of the grid scale up or down as required, and then the corners are pasted back on. This method allows you to keep the corners of an element uniform at all sizes.

To activate 9-slice scaling when you originally create a movie-clip symbol, open the Advanced section of the Symbol Properties dialog, and select the "Enable guides for 9-slice scaling" check box (**Figure 11.41**) To enable the guides later, select a symbol in the Library panel, choose Properties from the Library panel's Options menu to open the Symbol Properties dialog, and then select the "Enable guides for 9-slice scaling" check box. (You can also enable 9-slice scaling through ActionScript.)

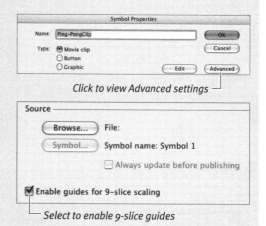

Click to view Advanced settings

Select to enable 9-slice guides

Figure 11.41 To enable 9-slice scaling for movie-clip symbols, in the Symbol Properties dialog, click the Advanced button to access the advanced settings (top). In the Source section, select the "Enable guides for 9-slice scaling" check box (bottom).

When the 9-slice guides are enabled, grid-lines appear in the symbol preview window in the Library panel and also when you edit the symbol (**Figure 11.42**). In symbol-editing mode, you can drag the guide lines to define the non-scaling corner areas appropriate to the graphic content of the movie-clip symbol you're creating.

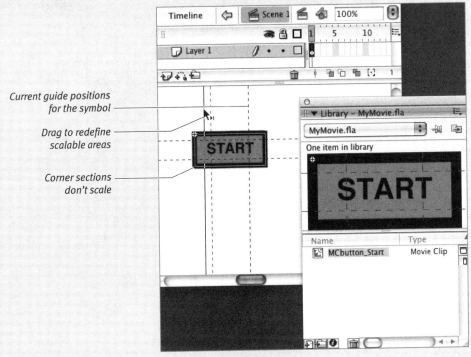

Current guide positions for the symbol

Drag to redefine scalable areas

Corner sections don't scale

Figure 11.42 With 9-slice scaling enabled, a symbol shows its scaling guides in the Library panel. In symbol-editing mode, the guides appear on the Stage and are adjustable. Drag a guide to reposition it.

Using Movie-Clip Symbols

You put movie-clip symbols to work by placing an instance of a symbol on the Stage in your Flash document. Unlike animated graphic symbols, movie-clip symbols have their own Timeline. A movie clip plays continuously, like a little film loop, in a single frame of the main movie. As long as the movie contains no other instructions that stop the clip from playing—a blank keyframe in the Timeline for the layer containing the movie clip, for example—the clip continues to loop.

As you work on your Flash document, you can see only the first frame of a movie clip. To view the animation of the movie-clip symbol in context with all the other elements of your movie, you must export the movie (by choosing one of the test modes, for example). You can preview the animation of the movie-clip symbol by itself in the Library panel.

To place an instance of a movie clip:

1. Continuing with the movie you created in the preceding task, choose Insert > Scene.

Flash creates a new scene and displays its Timeline: a single layer with a blank keyframe in frame 1. The Stage is empty.

2. Access the Library panel.

If it's not open, choose Window > Library.

3. Select the Ping-PongClip symbol.

The first frame of the animation appears in the preview window.

4. Drag a copy of the selected symbol to the Stage.

Flash places the symbol in keyframe 1 (**Figure 11.43**). You don't need to add any more frames to accommodate the animation, but you must export the movie to see the animation.

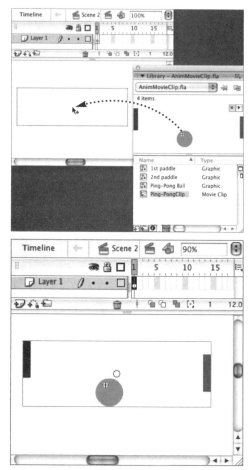

Figure 11.43 Drag an instance of your movie clip from the Library panel to the Stage (top). Flash places the instance in keyframe 1 (bottom).

Figure 11.44 Choose Control > Test Scene to preview the animation of just one scene in a movie.

Figure 11.45 The Exporting Flash Movie dialog contains a progress bar and a button for canceling the export.

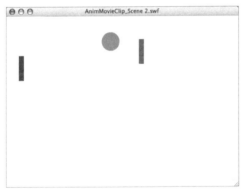

Figure 11.46 Flash Player displays your movie in a regular window. To exit the Player, close the window.

To view the movie-clip animation in context:

1. Continuing with the movie you created in the preceding task, choose Control > Test Scene (**Figure 11.44**).

   Flash exports the movie to a Flash Player format file, adding the .swf extension to the filename and using the current publishing settings for all the export options. (For more information on Publish Settings, see Chapter 16.) During export, Flash displays the Exporting Flash Movie dialog, which contains a progress bar and a Stop (Mac) or Cancel (Windows) button for canceling the operation (**Figure 11.45**).

   When it finishes exporting the movie, Flash opens the .swf file in Flash Player so you can see the movie in action (**Figure 11.46**).

2. When you've seen enough of the movie in test mode, click the movie window's Close box (Windows) or Close button (Mac) to exit Flash Player.

USING MOVIE-CLIP SYMBOLS

The Mystery of Bitmap Caching

Flash's original impact on the World Wide Web was due in large part to its ability to send vector graphics rather than bitmaps over the Internet. If you send multiple bitmap images for animation, the process bogs down. However, when the image is complex but doesn't change much over time, especially when most of the changes that do take place involve positioning within a frame rather than redrawing shapes, it's less processor intensive to work with bitmaps than with vectors.

An easy example to imagine is a cartoon background—say, a forest thick with trees and flowers, bushes and vines, over which you animate the creatures that move through the forest. If the background remains still, you can create a bitmap background layer that extends the length of your movie and doesn't require redrawing in each frame.

But there are drawbacks to that method. You can't create or edit the bitmap inside Flash; you must use a program such as Macromedia Fireworks or Adobe Photoshop and import the image. (You must edit the image externally and reimport it each time you do.)

And what if you want the background to move from time to time? Let's say you want to create a backdrop that's much wider than the screen and then shift it to the right periodically to show a bit of the scenery that's been hidden. Nothing changes but the position of the background. If you use a bitmap image, Flash can move it pixel by pixel without too much slowdown of the movie, but you still have the inconvenience of creating the image outside Flash. If you use a vector image, Flash must recalculate all the vectors in that background for each move, bogging things down. Flash 8 can give you the best of both worlds by, turning a vector image into a bitmap at runtime.

This technique is called *bitmap caching*. To enable it, you must create your complex element as a movie-clip symbol. Select the symbol instance on the Stage. In the Properties tab of the Property inspector, for that symbol instance, select the "Use runtime bitmap caching" check box (**Figure 11.47**). At runtime, Flash captures a snapshot of the vector image by turning it into a bitmap; then Flash moves that bitmap pixel by pixel as needed, thus avoiding recalculating all those vectors.

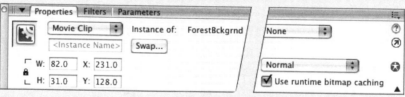

Figure 11.47 If a movie clip contains complex graphics, but they don't animate in complex ways, you can ask Flash to cache a bitmap of the symbols' image at runtime. Flash creates a sort of bitmap snapshot, redrawing the vector graphics only when something changes. Bitmap caching can speed processing during playback of your Flash creations. Select the movie-clip symbol on the Stage; then, in the Properties tab of the Property inspector, select "Enable runtime bitmap caching".

Figure 11.48 An easy way to create a rainbow is to fill a circle with a multiple-color radial gradient and then delete the bottom half of the circle. Here, bisecting a merge-shape circle by drawing a line through it (middle) makes deletion easy; select the line and the bottom half of the circle (bottom), and press Delete.

Using Animated Masks

In Chapter 6, you learned about Flash's ability to create mask layers that hide and reveal objects on lower layers. Sometimes, the best way to create the illusion of movement is to animate a mask so that it gradually hides or reveals objects.

Imagine a line that starts at the left edge of the Stage and goes all the way to the right edge. If you create a mask that reveals the line bit by bit, you create the illusion of a line that draws itself. Reverse the process, and you have a line that gradually erases itself.

Creating rotating and shape-tweened mask graphics can give you some interesting effects. The more familiar you are with using animated masks to reveal stationary items, the better sense you'll have of when to use this technique. For practice, try animating a mask that creates a growing rainbow.

To create a stationary graphic and a moving mask that reveals it:

1. Create a Flash document that has two layers.

   Name the bottom layer Rainbow and the top layer Rotating Rectangle.

2. In keyframe 1 of the Rainbow layer, on the Stage, use the drawing tools to create a rainbow graphic.

   One way to create the rainbow is to use the oval tool in Merge Drawing mode to draw a perfect circle. Give the circle a radial-gradient fill that has distinct bands of color. Then erase the bottom half of the circle (**Figure 11.48**).

   What's left is your rainbow shape. For safety, convert the rainbow to a symbol (select the rainbow on the Stage, choose Modify > Convert to Symbol, choose

continues on next page

Graphic as the type, name the symbol, and click OK) so you'll have a copy of the rainbow in case you accidentally delete the original.

3. In the Timeline, Control-click (Mac) or right-click (Windows) the Rotating Rectangle layer.

The contextual menu for layers appears.

4. Choose Mask.

Flash converts the layer to a mask, links the Rainbow layer to the mask, and locks both layers (**Figure 11.49**).

5. In the Timeline, click the padlock icons in the Rotating Rectangle and Rainbow layers to unlock them.

6. On the Stage, in keyframe 1 of the Rotating Rectangle layer, use the rectangle tool to draw a rectangle just below the bottom of the rainbow (**Figure 11.50**).

The rectangle is your mask. Any items that lie directly below the rectangle on a linked layer appear; everything else is hidden.

Make the rectangle a bit larger than the rainbow so the mask can cover the whole rainbow. Using a transparent fill color lets you see the rainbow through the mask rectangle and helps you verify the mask's position. (To make the rectangle's fill color transparent, select it and then, in the Color Mixer panel, assign it a low Alpha percentage.)

✔ Tip

■ You can use any of the three types of animation on a mask layer: frame-by-frame, motion tweening, or shape tweening. You can also use an animated graphic symbol or movie-clip symbol. Advanced ActionScripters can also use ActionScript to tell one movie-clip symbol to mask another and to create transparent masks.

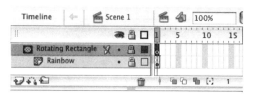

Figure 11.49 When you create a mask layer, Flash automatically links the layer directly below the mask layer in the Timeline and locks both layers.

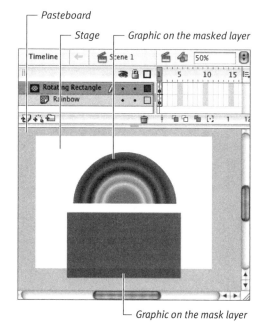

Figure 11.50 To create a mask that reveals the entire rainbow, draw a rectangle that's wider and taller than the rainbow. Positioning the rectangle below the rainbow hides the rainbow completely.

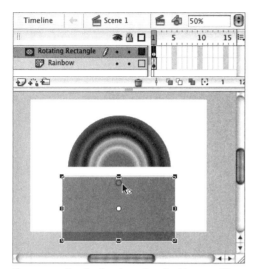

Figure 11.51 Use the free-transform tool to reposition the point around which a symbol (or grouped item) rotates. Drag the circle that indicates the transformation point to a new position. A small circle previews the new transformation-point location.

To prepare the mask for rotational animation:

1. Select the rectangle, and choose Modify > Convert to Symbol.

   Because you want to create rotational animation, you must use a motion tween for the mask, which means the mask graphic must be a graphic-object. You could use a drawing-object or a grouped element, but it's a good idea to use a symbol so that you can easily reuse the mask.

   The Convert to Symbol dialog appears.

2. In the Name field, enter a name for the symbol, choose Graphic as the symbol type, and click OK.

3. Using the free-transform tool, select the rectangle on the Stage, and position the pointer over the white circle that indicates the transformation point of the object.

   A small white circle appears next to the arrow pointer, indicating that you can move the selected object's transformation point.

4. Drag the transformation-point circle straight up until it rests in the middle of the top edge of the rectangle (**Figure 11.51**).

   Now you can rotate the rectangle so that it swings up and over the rainbow.

To complete the rotating-mask animation:

1. In the Timeline, in the Rainbow layer, select frame 15, and choose Insert > Timeline > Frame.

2. In the Timeline, in the Rotating Rectangle layer, select frame 15, and choose Insert > Timeline > Keyframe.

3. In keyframe 15, with the rectangle selected on the Stage, use the free-transform tool's Rotate and Skew modifier to reposition the rectangle; click and drag the bottom-left corner of the rectangle and rotate it so that the rectangle covers the rainbow (**Figure 11.52**).

   The mask that covers the rainbow in authoring mode will reveal the rainbow in the final movie.

4. In the Timeline, in the Rotating Rectangle layer, select any of the frames in the keyframe 1 span (frames 1–14).

5. In the Frame Properties tab of the Property inspector, from the Tween pop-up menu, choose Motion.

6. From the Rotate pop-up menu, choose CW.

7. Enter 0 in the Times field.

   This step sets up the motion tween that rotates the rectangle 180 degrees, swinging it up and over the rainbow until it fully covers the rainbow (**Figure 11.53**).

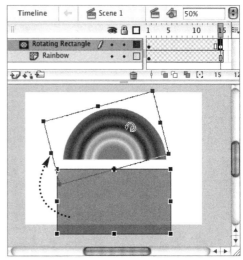

Figure 11.52 In the final keyframe of your sequence, position the mask to cover the item(s) it should reveal. Here the free-transform tool rotates the rectangle mask over the rainbow graphic.

Figure 11.53 In the final keyframe with the completed motion tween for the mask object, the mask covers the rainbow completely. Giving the mask a transparent fill lets you see the objects to be revealed through it as you work. The transparency of objects on the mask layer doesn't appear in the final movie.

Play movie,
layers unlocked

Play movie;
layers locked

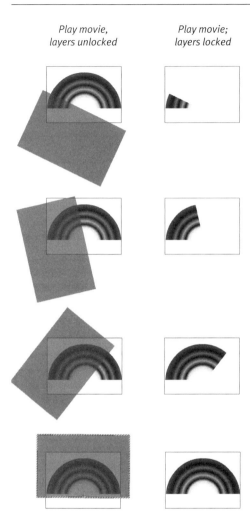

Figure 11.54 As you play the movie with the layers unlocked (left), you can see the in-between positions of the mask graphic. When you lock the layers (right), you see the masking as it will appear in the final exported movie.

To preview the animation:

◆ Choose Control > Test Movie, or choose Control > Test Scene.

or

◆ In the Timeline, click the lock icon to lock both layers to see the masked rainbow; then play the movie to see the mask reveal the rainbow.

If the rainbow isn't fully revealed during the tween, you may need to enlarge or reposition the rectangle. Unlock both layers, and move the playhead through the movie to see where the rectangle is in each in-between frame (**Figure 11.54**).

✔ Tips

■ To make the rainbow appear to fade in gradually, tween a change in its transparency. Select frame 15 of the Rainbow layer and press F6, duplicating the rainbow symbol instance in a new keyframe. In keyframe 1, select the rainbow symbol instance; in the Properties tab of the Property inspector, from the Color menu, choose Alpha; in the Value field, enter a low percentage; from the Tween pop-up menu, choose Motion.

A Note about Flash Professional 8's Blend Modes and Filters

One of Macromedia's goals in Flash 8 is to give designers greater control over the graphics in Flash. Two special new graphics features—blend modes and filters—are available only in Flash 8 Professional. The specifics of creating special graphic effects with blends and filters are beyond the scope of this *QuickStart Guide*, but here's a brief overview to give you a glimpse of the possibilities for these tools.

Blends: Anyone familiar with using blends in Macromedia Fireworks or Adobe Photoshop already has an idea about what Flash's blend modes can do, because they work similarly. Blends let you force overlapping images to interact in ways that create new colors and interesting effects. Artists often use blend modes for *compositing*, overlapping multiple images so that parts of each appear in one combined image (for example, superimposing an image of a child's face on an image of a balloon to make a balloon with a face). Photographers use blend modes to enhance or correct flaws in digital photos (for example, using a blend to lighten the areas of a photo where there is too much shadow).

You apply a blend to an instance of a movie clip on the Stage. Flash calculates new colors pixel by pixel, modifying the RGB values of each pixel in the movie clip according to a formula dictated by the chosen blend mode. Whether a particular pixel changes color depends on the type of blend, the color of the pixel in the movie clip, and the color of the pixel that lies on the layer below the movie clip. The pixels on lower layers may be other movie clips, graphic elements, or the background color of the Stage. You apply blends to selected movie-clip instances through the Properties tab of the Property inspector (**Figure 11.55**).

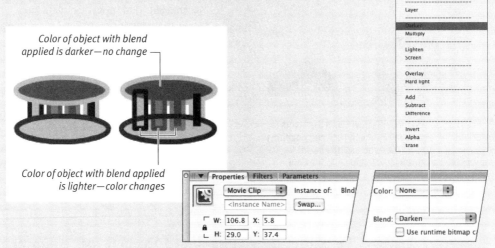

Color of object with blend applied is darker—no change

Color of object with blend applied is lighter—color changes

Figure 11.55 On the Stage, select a movie clip to which you would like to apply a blend; then choose a mode from the Blend menu in the Properties tab of the Property inspector. These two ovals are movie clips lying on a layer above the bar graphics. On the left, the ovals have a Blend property of Normal; they don't interact with the layer below. On the right, the ovals have a Blend property of Darken. Flash evaluates each pixel. Where the pixels in the object to which the blend is applied (the ovals) are lighter than the pixels in the underlying layer, Flash changes the pixels to the darker color.

USING ANIMATED MASKS

Filters: You can apply filters to instances of movie-clip symbols, button symbols, or text boxes. Filters modify the filtered item to create special effects such as drop shadows, beveled edges, and glows. Because Flash applies filters directly to a symbol instance, filters can be easier to use and modify (and have less effect on file size) than the Timeline effects that Macromedia provides. (Timeline effects create multiple symbols to make drop shadows and blurs.) You apply filters to selected text boxes or button or movie-clip instances through the Filters tab of the Property inspector (**Figure 11.56**). You can apply multiple filters to the same object, rearrange the order in which they're applied, and create presets to apply the same filter settings to other objects.

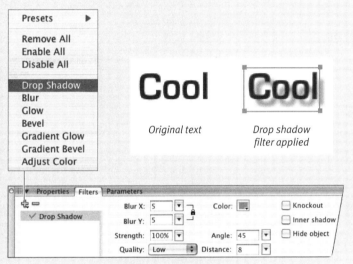

Original text   Drop shadow
filter applied

Figure 11.56 To apply filters (Flash Professional 8 only), select a movie clip, button, or text box on the Stage. In the Filters tab of the Property inspector, click the Add Filter menu and choose a filter effect. The settings for the effect appear on the Filters tab.

BUILDING BUTTONS FOR INTERACTIVITY

After you master the drawing and animating tools in Flash 8, you can create movies that play from beginning to end. But Flash is more than a tool for making animated movies. You can use it to create interactive environments that transform viewers into users. To move your Flash movie into the realm of interactive experience, you need to create interface elements that allow users to control and interact with your application. The most common interface element is a button. Buttons have two levels of interactivity. First, a button can respond to a user with visual feedback—for example, changing color when the pointer enters the button area. Second, the button can carry out tasks—for example, switching to a new scene when the user clicks the button.

Flash comes with a number of predefined interface elements, including button symbols and button components. For these elements, built-in coding takes care of the first level of button interactivity, responding to mouse movements with visual feedback. For example, when a user positions the pointer over a button symbol or component's hot area, built-in coding tells Flash to change the pointer to the hand cursor and alter the look of the button.

In this chapter, you learn to set up the first level of interactivity by working with button symbols and button components. You also learn to set up a movie clip symbol that can act as a visually responsive button.

To achieve the second level of interactivity, you attach scripts to individual button instances to make buttons respond in new ways and carry out tasks. You'll learn some simple ways to do that in Chapter 13.

The Mystery of Button Symbols

In Flash, you can make a button by creating a symbol and then assigning it button behavior. Buttons are actually short—four frames, to be precise—interactive movies. When you select button behavior for a symbol, Flash sets up a Timeline with four keyframes. You create graphics for the first three keyframes to display the button in three common states: Up, Over, and Down. The fourth keyframe (never shown to the viewer) defines the active area of the button.

In the Up state, you create a graphic that looks like a static, unused button. This graphic appears whenever the pointer lies outside the active area of the button. In the Over state, create the graphic as it should look when the pointer rolls over the button. Flash automatically changes the pointer to the hand cursor for the Over state; but often, you want additional visual changes to alert the viewer that the pointer is now on a live button. In the Down state, create the graphic as it should look when someone clicks the button. In the fourth frame, the Hit frame, create a graphic that defines the boundary of the button. Any filled shape in this frame becomes a place where mouse movements trigger the button during movie playback.

Any changes you make in the appearance of the graphic elements in the keyframes create the illusion of movement. In other Flash animation sequences, changes occur over time as the playhead moves through the frames. In button symbols, however, changes occur when the user moves the pointer over a specific area of the screen.

You can include movie clips within each frame of a button to create buttons that are fully animated, and you can attach actions to buttons to give your viewers more control of the movie.

Figure 12.1 Choosing Insert > New Symbol is the first step in creating a button.

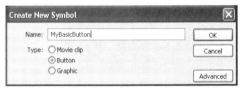

Figure 12.2 To make a button, create a new symbol and assign it Button behavior in the Create New Symbol dialog. You can also name the button there.

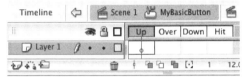

Figure 12.3 The Timeline for every button symbol contains four frames: Up, Over, Down, and Hit. Flash automatically puts a keyframe in the Up frame of a new button symbol.

Creating a Basic Button Symbol

A button is a Flash movie clip with different frames that represent the button in all its possible states. The button symbol has three button-state frames—Up, Over, Down—plus one frame that defines the active button area. To create the most basic button symbol, choose a simple shape and use it for each frame; change its color or add or modify internal elements for the various states. When you complete all four frames, your button is ready to use. Return to document-editing mode, and drag an instance of the button symbol from the Library panel to the Stage.

To create a button symbol:

1. Open a Flash document to which you want to add buttons.

2. Choose Insert > New Symbol, or press ⌘-F8 (Mac) or Ctrl-F8 (Windows) (**Figure 12.1**).

   The Create New Symbol dialog appears.

3. Type a name in the Name field (for example, MyBasicButton), choose Button in the Behavior section, and click OK (**Figure 12.2**).

   Flash creates a new symbol in the Library panel and returns you to the Timeline and Stage in symbol-editing mode. The Timeline for a button symbol contains the four frames that you need to define the button: Up, Over, Down, and Hit.

   By default, the Up frame contains a keyframe (**Figure 12.3**). You must add keyframes to the Over, Down, and Hit frames and place the graphic elements in each frame of the button. To give users feedback about the button—so they can tell when they're on a live button and sense the difference when they click it—use a different graphic in each frame.

To create the Up state:

1. Using the file from the preceding task, in the Timeline, select the Up frame.

2. On the Stage, create a new graphic or place a graphic symbol (**Figure 12.4**).

   This graphic element becomes the button as it's sitting onstage in your movie, waiting for someone to click it. The crosshair in the middle of the Stage in symbol-editing mode will become both the center point of the symbol and the point for registering the symbol in document-editing mode.

To create the Over state:

1. Using the file from the preceding task, in the Timeline, select the Over frame.

2. Choose Insert > Timeline > Keyframe.

   Flash inserts a keyframe that duplicates the contents of the Up keyframe. Now you can make minor changes in the Up graphic to convert it to an Over graphic. Enlarge an element within the button, for example (**Figure 12.5**). Duplicating the preceding keyframe makes it easy to align all your button elements so they don't appear to jump around as they change states.

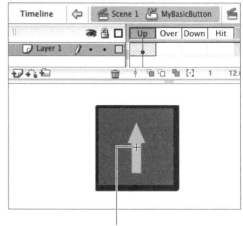

Registration crosshair marks the center of the symbol's Stage

Figure 12.4 When a button is waiting for your viewer to notice and interact with it, Flash displays the contents of the Up frame.

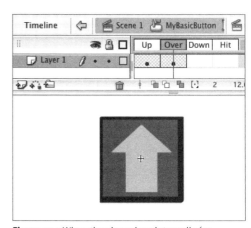

Figure 12.5 When the viewer's pointer rolls (or pauses) over the button, Flash displays the contents of the Over frame.

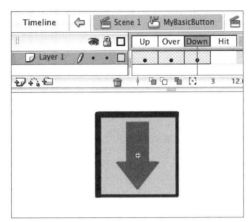

Figure 12.6 When the viewer clicks the button, Flash displays the contents of the Down frame.

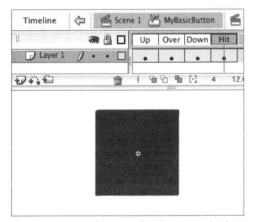

Figure 12.7 The Hit-frame graphic doesn't need to be a fully detailed image of the button in any state; it just needs to be a silhouette of the button shape. Flash uses that shape to define the active button area. This Hit frame contains a copy of the Down frame that has been filled with dark gray.

To create the Down state:

1. Using the file from the preceding task, in the Timeline, select the Down frame.

2. Choose Insert > Timeline > Keyframe.

   Flash inserts a keyframe that duplicates the contents of the Over keyframe. Now you can make minor changes to convert the Over graphic to a Down graphic. Change the button color, for example, and reverse the shadow effect so the button looks indented (**Figure 12.6**).

   After you create graphics for the three states of your button, you need to define the active area of the button.

To create the Hit state:

1. Using the file from the preceding task, in the Timeline, select the Hit frame.

2. Choose Insert > Timeline > Keyframe to duplicate the contents of the Down keyframe.

   When you use a graphic with the same shape and size for all three phases of your button, you can safely use a copy of any previous frame as the Hit-frame graphic.

3. If you want, use the paint bucket and ink bottle tools to fill the Hit-frame graphic with a single color (**Figure 12.7**).

   This step isn't required, but it helps remind you that this graphic isn't the one that viewers of your movie will see.

continues on next page

CREATING A BASIC BUTTON SYMBOL

4. Choose Edit > Edit Document, or click the Back button in the Edit Bar.

Flash returns you to the main Timeline. Now you can use the button symbol in your movie just as you would use any other symbol.

✔ Tip

■ If you use a copy of the Up, Over, or Down graphic in the Hit frame, try enlarging that copy slightly. Using a larger image ensures that users activate the button easily as soon as they get near it. To enlarge the graphic by a small amount quickly, select the graphic. Choose Modify > Shape > Expand Fill. In the Expand Fill dialog, enter a small value (say, 2 pixels). Choose Expand, and click OK.

The Mystery of Hit-Frame Graphics

Although it never appears in a Flash movie, the Hit frame's graphic content is vital to a button's operation. The sole purpose of the Hit-frame graphic is to define the button's boundaries. This graphic doesn't need to be detailed; it's just a silhouette that defines the button shape. Any fill or line in the Hit frame becomes an active part of the button. During playback, when the viewer moves the pointer into that area, the Over frame of the button appears; when the user clicks that area, the Down frame appears.

For the clearest, most user-friendly buttons, make sure your Hit-frame graphic is large enough to cover all the graphics in the first three frames of the button. To be safe, make your Hit-frame graphic a little larger than the other graphics.

If the Up, Over, and Down states of your button contain something delicate, such as type or a line drawing, don't use the Up, Over, and Down images for the Hit frame. Make the Hit-frame graphic a geometric shape—say, a filled rectangle or oval—that completely covers the Up, Over, and Down graphics. That way, your viewers won't have to position the pointer directly over a letter form or line to activate the button.

To place the newly created button in your movie:

◆ Continuing with the file from the preceding task, drag an instance of the button MyBasicButton from the Library panel to the Stage.

You can modify the instance to change its size, rotation, and color. (For more information on modifying symbol instances, see Chapter 7.)

✔ Tips

■ To create a consistent look on a Web site, you may want to use a set of buttons over and over. You can even reuse buttons in several projects with only slight changes. To save time, devote one whole document to buttons, and always create your button symbols there. Then you can copy a button from this master button file to your current Flash document and tweak the button there.

■ Always fill your Hit-frame silhouette with the same color—say, neon blue or another bright color that you won't use elsewhere in your movie. That way, the silhouette becomes another visual cue that you're in the Hit frame of a button, in symbol-editing mode.

■ You can preview the Up, Over, and Down states of your button by selecting the button in the Library panel and then clicking the Play button in the preview window. Flash displays each frame in turn.

■ Choose Control > Enable Simple Buttons to evoke the different states for a button instance on the Stage in authoring mode. Flash displays the Up, Over, and Down states as you move the pointer over the button and click. Remember, with buttons enabled, you can't select them or work with them. To turn off Enable Simple Button mode, choose Control > Enable Simple Buttons again.

CREATING A BASIC BUTTON SYMBOL

Creating Shape-Changing Button Symbols

Button graphics can emulate real-world switches or toggles. In a game, you can disguise buttons as part of the scenery—making the blinking eye of a character a button, for example. Finding the hot spots or buttons is part of the fun. When the Up, Over, and Down frames of your button symbol contain graphics of different shapes and sizes, however, creating an effective Hit-frame graphic can be tricky. You need to create a graphic for the Hit state that covers all of the other states.

To create Up, Over, and Down states with various graphics:

1. Open a Flash document to which you want to add buttons.

2. Choose Insert > New Symbol.
   The Create New Symbol dialog appears.

3. Enter a name in the Name field (for example, AnimatedBtn), choose Button in the Behavior section, and click OK.
   Flash creates a new symbol in the Library panel and returns you to the Timeline and Stage in symbol-editing mode. The Timeline for a button symbol contains the four frames necessary for defining the button: Up, Over, Down, and Hit.

4. In the Timeline, select the Over, Down, and Hit frames.

5. Choose Modify > Timeline > Convert to Blank Keyframes.
   Now you have a blank keyframe in every frame of your button, and you're ready to place various graphics in each frame (**Figure 12.8**).

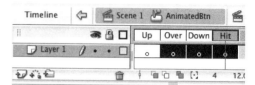

Figure 12.8 In a button symbol's Timeline, as in the main Timeline, choosing Modify > Timeline > Convert to Blank Keyframes places a blank keyframe in each selected frame.

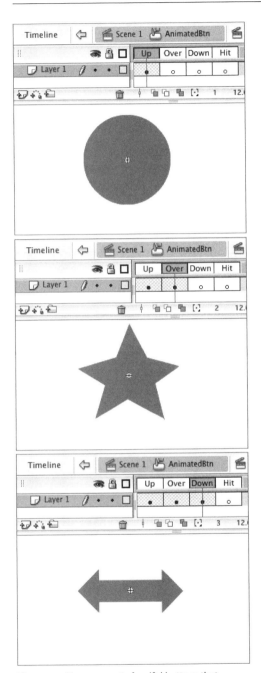

6. With the Up frame selected in the Timeline, on the Stage, create a new graphic, or place the graphic symbol that you want to use for the button's Up state.

7. Repeat step 6 for the Over and Down frames.

For this task, use graphics that have different shapes—a circle, a star, and a double-headed arrow, for example (**Figure 12.9**).

Figure 12.9 You can create fanciful buttons that change shape when a user rolls over or clicks them. In this example, the inactive button is a circle (top). When the pointer rolls over the button, the circle changes to a star (middle). When the user clicks the button, it changes to a double-headed arrow (bottom).

To create the Hit state for graphics of various shapes:

1. Using the file you created in the preceding task, in the Timeline, select the Hit frame.

2. To create the Hit-frame graphic, *do either of the following:*

   ▲ Draw a simple geometric shape large enough to cover all areas of the button. Turn on onion skinning so you can see exactly what you need to cover (**Figure 12.10**).

   ▲ Use Flash's Edit > Copy and Edit > Paste in Place commands to copy the graphic elements from the first three frames of the button and paste them into the Hit frame of the button one by one. The graphics stack up in the Hit frame, occupying the exact area needed to cover the button in any phase of its operation (**Figure 12.11**).

3. Return to editing the document, for example, by choosing Edit > Edit Document.

   You're ready to place an instance of the button on the Stage and test it out by choosing Control > Test Movie.

✔ Tips

■ When you use the copy-and-paste-in-place technique to create your Hit-frame graphic, it's a good idea to expand the resulting graphic slightly—by using the Modify > Shape > Expand Fill command, for example. Making the Hit graphic slop over the edges of the active button areas ensures that your viewers can easily activate the button.

■ Use a transparent color (one with an alpha value less than 100 percent) for your Hit-frame graphic. The other graphics will show through the Hit-frame graphic in onion-skin mode, making it easy to see how to position or size the Hit-frame graphic to cover the graphics in the other frames.

Onion- skin outlines

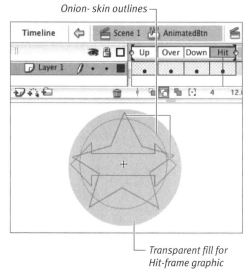

Transparent fill for Hit-frame graphic

Figure 12.10 The Hit-frame silhouette needs to encompass all possible button areas in all three button modes. For example, if you duplicate only the circle as your Hit frame for this button, you exclude the tips of the star. As the user moves the pointer over the tips, the the button returns to its Over phase; the user can't ever click the tips to activate the button. If you duplicate only the star, the user may roll over several areas of the circle and never discover that it's a button.

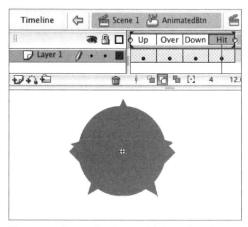

Figure 12.11 By copying the graphic in each of the button states and using the Paste in Place command to place them in the Hit frame, you wind up with a perfectly positioned silhouette that incorporates all the possible button areas.

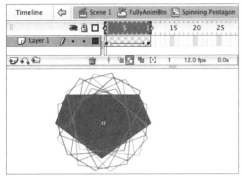

Figure 12.12 Placing an animated symbol in the Up frame of a button symbol makes that animation appear when the button is in the Up state. Here, onion skinning in symbol-editing mode reveals all the frames of the spinning pentagon symbol's animation.

Figure 12.13 With an animated symbol in the Over frame of a button, that animation appears when the pointer rolls or rests over the button area. Here, the Preview mode of the Timeline shows the animation of the symbol that turns a pentagon shape into a star.

Creating Fully Animated Button Symbols

The button symbols you created in the preceding tasks are animated in the sense that they change as the user interacts with them. Flash also lets you create button symbols that are fully animated—a glowing light bulb, for example, or a little ladybug that jumps up and down, saying, "Click me!" The trick to making fully animated buttons is placing movie clips in the frames of your button. Because the movie clips play in their own Timeline, animated buttons remain animated even when you pause the movie.

To animate a rollover button:

1. Open a Flash document to which you want to add buttons.

2. Choose Insert > New Symbol.
   The Create New Symbol dialog appears.

3. Name your button (for example, FullyAnimBtn), choose Button in the Behavior section, and click OK.

4. In the Timeline, select the Over, Down, and Hit frames of the button, and choose Modify > Timeline > Convert to Blank Keyframes.
   Flash creates blank keyframes for the button's Over, Down, and Hit frames.

5. In the Timeline, select the Up frame, and place an instance of a movie-clip symbol on the Stage. For this example, the Up-frame clip contains a spinning pentagon (**Figure 12.12**).

6. In the Timeline, select the Over frame, and place an instance of a movie-clip symbol on the Stage.
   In this example, the Over-frame clip contains a pentagon that turns into a star (**Figure 12.13**).

continues on next page

7. In the Timeline, select the Down frame, and create a movie-clip symbol or import one from another file.

   For this example, the Down-frame clip contains a star that flies apart (**Figure 12.14**).

8. In the Timeline, select the Hit frame, and create a graphic that covers all the button areas for the three button states (Up, Over, and Down).

   A large oval works well for this purpose (**Figure 12.15**). This graphic creates an active button area that's larger than the spinning pentagon. As your viewer's pointer nears the spinning graphic during playback, the button switches to Over mode. In Over mode, the oval is big enough to encompass all points of the star, and in Down mode, the user can let the pointer drift a fair amount and still be within the confines of the button.

9. Return to document-editing mode by clicking the name of the current scene in the Edit Bar at the top of the Stage.

10. Drag a copy of the FullyAnimBtn symbol from the Library panel to the Stage.

✔ Tips

■ You can place a movie clip in the Hit frame of your button, but only the visible graphic from the clip's first frame determines the hit area.

■ With buttons enabled, in document-editing mode, Flash previews the Up, Over, and Down frames of your button symbol but not its complete animation. For each frame, you see only the first frame of the movie clip. To view the fully animated button, you must export the movie and view it in Flash Player (by choosing Control > Test Movie, for example).

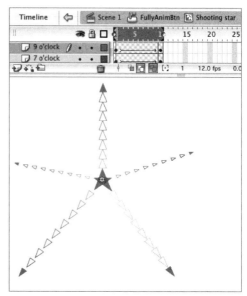

Figure 12.14 With an animated symbol in the Down frame of a button, the animation plays when the viewer clicks inside the button area. Here, onion skinning in symbol-editing mode reveals all the frames of the shooting star symbol's animation.

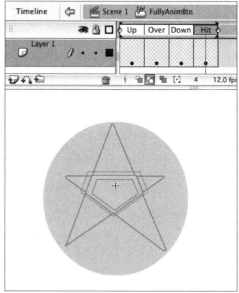

Figure 12.15 When you're creating a Hit-frame graphic, use onion skinning to see the first frame of the movie clip in each button frame. Here, the Hit-frame graphic is a transparent fill, which also helps you position the graphic to cover the graphics in the other frames.

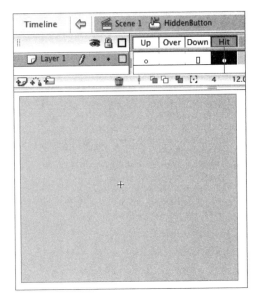

Figure 12.16 To make an invisible button, create a button symbol that has nothing in the Up, Over, and Down frames. Here, the Hit frame contains a filled rectangle large enough to cover the Stage.

Creating Invisible Button Symbols

The only frame of a button that must have content is the Hit frame, because it describes the active button area. Buttons without content in the Up, Over, and Down frames are invisible in the final movie. An invisible button with a Hit-frame graphic that covers the Stage allows users to click anywhere in the frame to trigger a button's actions.

To create an invisible button:

1. Open a new Flash document to which you want to add an invisible button.

2. Choose Insert > New Symbol.
   The Create New Symbol dialog appears.

3. Name your button (for example, HiddenButton), choose Button in the Behavior section, and click OK.

4. In symbol-editing mode, in the Timeline, select the Hit frame of the button, and choose Insert > Timeline > Blank Keyframe.
   Flash creates a blank keyframe for the button's Hit frame.

5. On the Stage, create a graphic element to represent the active button area.
   To create an invisible button that allows users to click anywhere to trigger an action, draw a filled rectangle large enough to cover the Stage (**Figure 12.16**). The solid rectangle turns the whole Stage into an active button, but because no graphics are associated with the button, it will be invisible to the user.

continues on next page

6. Return to document-editing mode, and drag a copy of the HiddenButton symbol to the Stage.

Flash displays a transparent version of the Hit-frame graphic, which indicates the hot-spot area of the invisible button (**Figure 12.17**). If necessary, you can reposition (or resize) the button so it covers the Stage fully.

✔ Tip

- In symbol-editing mode, the Stage is a fixed size (roughly 25.5 inches by 27.5 inches or 1990 pixels by 1990 pixels), and it's not necessarily the same size as the Stage in your current movie. To ensure that the Hit-frame rectangle of an invisible button covers the whole Stage, select the rectangle; then, in the Info panel or the Properties tab of the Property inspector, enter values in the Width and Height fields that are slightly larger than the dimensions of your document. Or, once you've created the invisible button, place an instance on the Stage, select it, and choose Edit > Edit in Place. You'll see the Stage in relation to the button's preview; you can then use the free-transform tool to resize the button, checking its coverage of the Stage by eye.

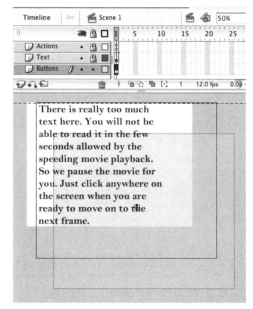

Figure 12.17 When the Up frame of a symbol is empty, Flash displays a transparent version of the Hit-frame graphic to help you position your invisible button in document-editing mode.

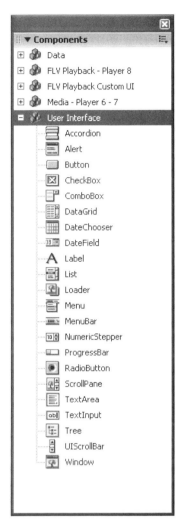

Figure 12.18 The Components panel lists all the default components that come with Flash. In Flash Professional (shown) there are five categories of components. Buttons are found under User Interface. To expand or collapse the list click the plus sign (Windows) or triangle (Mac) to the left of the title User Interface. Flash Basic's Components panel only offers the user-interface components.

Using Button Components

Button symbols handle the scripting necessary for displaying the common button states, but they also allow you to define the graphic look of a button. Using button symbols, you can create infinite interface looks for your projects. Flash also provides a different type of button—the *button component*—that has a predefined graphic look. A component is a special type of movie clip called a *.swc file,* or compiled clip. Although it's possible to change the graphic elements of a component, the techniques for doing so are beyond the scope of this book (see the sidebar "The Mystery of Components," later in this chapter). Each component has certain parameters that you can modify via the Component inspector panel or the Property inspector. To put a component to use, you place an instance of it in your Flash document.

To place an instance of the button component:

1. Open a Flash document to which you'd like to add a button component.

2. Access the following panels: Components, Component inspector, Library, and the Parameters tab of the Property inspector. These panels are all found under the Window menu. To access the Parameters tab, choose Window > Properties > Parameters; or, if the Property inspector is open, click the Parameters tab.

3. If necessary, in the Components panel, expand the list of user interface components (**Figure 12.18**). Click the triangle (Mac) or plus sign (Windows) to the left of the name User Interface to toggle between the expanded and collapsed views of the list.

continues on next page

USING BUTTON COMPONENTS

4. Drag an instance of the button component to the Stage.

Flash adds the button component to the document's library as a compiled-clip symbol (**Figure 12.19**).

✔ Tip

■ In many ways, compiled clips work just like other library assets (for more about working with library assets, see Chapter 7). In other ways they are different (see the sidebar "The Mystery of Components"). A confusing seeming similarity is that you can rename a component in the Library panel by double-clicking the compiled clip's name (Button) to activate the text field, and typing a new name. It's unadvisable to do so, however. You can change the name of the master compiled-clip symbol, but the symbol itself still bears the label Button. Moreover, if you bring another copy of the button component into the same document the two components will have the same linkage ID which may create problems in using the components in your published movie.

Figure 12.19 A button component is a special form of movie clip. When you drag a component from the Components panel to your document, the component symbol appears in the Library panel of that document, with its Type listed as Compiled Clip.

Control	
Play	Enter
Rewind	Ctrl+Alt+R
Go To End	
Step Forward One Frame	.
Step Backward One Frame	,
Test Movie	Ctrl+Enter
Debug Movie	Ctrl+Shift+Enter
Test Scene	Ctrl+Alt+Enter
Test Project	Ctrl+Alt+P
Delete ASO Files	
Delete ASO Files and Test Movie	
Loop Playback	
Play All Scenes	
Enable Simple Frame Actions	Ctrl+Alt+F
Enable Simple Buttons	Ctrl+Alt+B
✓ Enable Live Preview	
Mute Sounds	Ctrl+Alt+M

Figure 12.20 Choose Control > Enable Live Preview to see the basic look of a component as you edit your Flash document.

Figure 12.21 With Enable Live Preview active (Flash's default setting), you can see the parameters for component instances on the Stage while authoring (top). With Enable Live Preview inactive, Flash previews components with simple rectangular outlines that give no hint about what kind of element they represent (bottom).

To preview the component instance:

◆ To view a limited component preview during authoring, choose Control > Enable Live Preview (**Figure 12.20**).

As a default, the Enable Live Preview setting is active. If you're working with many components, this setting can slow things down; you may prefer to turn it off for a time. Whereas the Enable Simple Buttons setting lets you preview a button symbol's Up, Over, and Down states; Enable Live Preview reveals the button's parameter settings in the Up state (**Figure 12.21**). To view a fully enabled button component, you must view it in Flash Player. When Enable Live Preview is inactive, Flash previews component instances as simple outline rectangles on the Stage.

◆ To view all the parameters and button states of a component, choose Control > Test Movie.

Modifying Button Components

You can change a button component's dimensions, change its label text, add an icon to customize the button, set the button's visibility, and set the button to act as a toggle.

To modify button-component dimensions:

1. Continuing with the file you used in the preceding task, on the Stage, select the instance of MyBtnComponent.

2. In the Parameters tab of the Property inspector, in the W and H fields, enter new values for width and height (**Figure 12.22**).

   By default, the W and H fields are locked, so Flash preserves the component's *aspect ratio* (the ratio of width to height) when you enter new values. For this task, click the lock icon to deactivate the locked-aspect-ratio mode. Then enter the same value in both the W and H fields to create a square button.

3. Press Enter to confirm the new value(s).

   The button's dimensions change according to the value(s) you enter (**Figure 12.23**). The bounding box of the button defines the active area of the button. As you change the dimensions, Flash automatically changes the hit area for the button component to match.

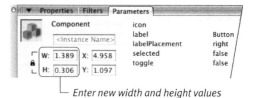

Enter new width and height values

Figure 12.22 To change the dimensions of a button component instance, access the Parameters tab of the Property inspector and enter new width and height values in the W and H fields.

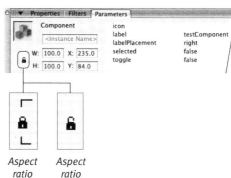

| Aspect ratio locked | Aspect ratio unlocked |

Figure 12.23 You can change the rectangular Button component to a square by entering the same value for width and height (here it's 100 pixels). You must first deactivate the component's locked-aspect-ratio mode. In the Parameters tab of the Property inspector, click the lock icon to put the width and height fields in the unlocked mode.

✔ Tips

- There are other ways to resize the button component. You can select the component instance and resize it using the Transform panel or the free-transform tool. Alternately, you can enter new width and height values in the Info panel.

- You can also rotate or skew a button component with the free-transform tool or Info panel. You should know, however, that Flash creates the button's label text using device fonts, which can't be rotated or skewed. If you rotate or skew a button component, its label text disappears.

- You can position your button precisely by entering values in the x- and y-coordinate fields of the Info panel or the Properties or Parameters tab of the Property inspector.

- Don't be confused by the minHeight and minWidth parameters in the Component inspector. Flash uses these parameters behind the scenes to resize the component as needed at runtime. More advanced Flash users who create their own applications can access these parameters via ActionScript to set up behind-the-scenes resizing rules.

The Mystery of Components

The Button is just one element in Flash's set of user interface components. These components contain built-in coding that makes them easy to use. Macromedia designed them to work together to give an application or Web site a consistent look and feel.

Components are sophisticated, scripted movie-clip symbols whose scripts have been compiled to save time during publishing. Unlike regular symbols, compiled symbols (also called .swc files) aren't directly editable within the authoring environment. Each component has its own editable parameters, however. Flash assists you in modifying these parameters through the Component inspector panel.

More experienced Flash developers can change the look of components by editing the underlying theme, style, and skin files on which components are based. Advanced scripters can change the look of components during playback via ActionScript. These modification techniques are beyond the scope of this book.

Although many of the advantages of components belong to advanced Flash authors who can use ActionScript to make components communicate with one another and to change them on the fly at runtime, even someone unfamiliar with scripting can use simple components to add interactivity to a project.

All the components that come with Flash appear in the Components panel. One of the beauties of components is that advanced scripters can create their own components and share them with other Flash authors. One source for new components is the Macromedia Exchange portion of the Macromedia Web site. As third-party components become available, you can add them to your Components panel for easy access.

To modify button-component labels:

1. Continuing with the file you used in the preceding task, on the Stage, select the instance of MyBtnComponent.

2. Access the Component inspector.

   In Flash Professional, the panel has three sections: Parameters, Bindings, and Schema. In Flash Basic, only the Parameters section appears.

3. If Parameters isn't active, click the Parameters button (Mac) or tab (Windows) to view the component's parameters.

   The panel displays a two-column table (**Figure 12.24**). The first column contains the parameter names; the second column contains the value for each parameter.

4. To modify the text that appears on your button instance, in the row for label, click the value Button.

   Flash activates the text field and selects the name; enter a new name, such as testComponent (**Figure 12.25**).

5. Press Enter, or click outside the active text field.

   With Flash's default settings, the new label text appears within the button-component instance (**Figure 12.26**). If you don't see the new text, choose Control > Enable Live Preview. Be forewarned, if your text is wider than the button instance, Flash will truncate the text to make it fit within the visible button area.

✔ Tip

- You can also modify most of the button component's parameters from the Property inspector. With an instance of the button component selected on the Stage, access the Parameters tab of the Property inspector; parameter fields for the button component instance appear in the tab.

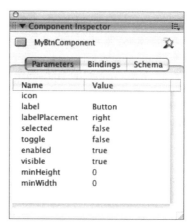

Figure 12.24 The Component inspector (Flash Professional shown here) displays all the parameters of the button component that you can modify during authoring.

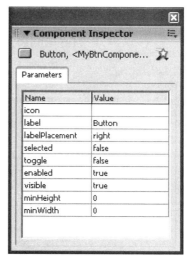

Figure 12.25 In the Component inspector (Flash Basic shown here) click the value field in the label row to activate text entry. Type your new label text. Press Enter to confirm the new label.

Figure 12.26 With Live Preview Enabled active, Flash previews your new label text in the button instance on the Stage.

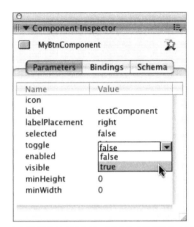

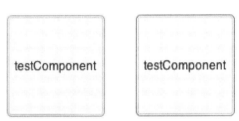

Figure 12.27 When you select the Toggle value in the Parameters section of the Component inspector (top) or in the Parameters tab of the Property inspector (bottom), you can access a menu for choosing a value of true or false.

testComponent   testComponent

Figure 12.28 When the button component instance has a toggle value of true, it acts as a toggle button. Here the button component instances are viewed on the Stage with live preview enabled. The button on the left is selected, and the one on the right is deselected. When printed in grayscale, the difference is subtle. The border is slightly darker in the deselected button. In color, the border of the selected button is neon-green, and the deselected border is gray.

To set the button to act as a toggle:

1. Select an instance of a button component on the Stage.

2. In the Component inspector or in the Parameters tab of the Property inspector, set the toggle value to true (**Figure 12.27**). Click anywhere in the row labeled Toggle, to activate the value pop-up menu. Click the value field to open the menu and select true. The button now acts as a toggle, so repeated clicks turn the button on and off (**Figure 12.28**).

✔ Tips

- The Parameters tab of the Property inspector and Parameters section of the Component inspector also contain a field for the button component's selected value (the choices are true and false). Use the selected value to set a toggle button's initial state (true sets the button to be selected initially; false sets the button to be deselected initially).

- To open the value pop-up menu quickly, double-click the value in the toggle row.

Creating Movie-Clip Buttons

Flash's button symbols and button components have built-in rules about how the button displays its three states in response to the user's mouse movements. You can take control of that functionality yourself and also create a button that has more than three states by making your own movie-clip button. In the following tasks, you learn to assemble artwork in the Timeline of the movie-clip to create a button with four states: _up, _over, _down, and Disabled. To give the movie-clip button even the first level of interactivity, to make the movie clip respond to mouse movements by displaying different states, you must attach ActionScript. You learn to do that in Chapter 13.

To create the button states:

1. In a Flash document where you'd like to use movie-clip symbols, Choose Insert > New Symbol.

   The Create New Symbol dialog appears.

2. Type a name for your symbol, MovieClipBtn; choose Movie Clip behavior; and click OK.

   Flash switches to symbol-editing mode. In the Timeline you see one layer, with a keyframe in frame 1.

3. Add two new layers to the Timeline, for a total of three layers.

   Each layer will hold a different type of information for your button. The top layer will hold ActionScript that tells the movie-clip button what to do; name this layer Actions. The second layer will hold text identifying each keyframe that represents a button state; name this layer Labels. The bottom layer will hold the graphic elements that give the button its look in each state; name this layer ButtonGraphics.

Figure 12.29 Your movie-clip button needs a keyframe for each button state. It's a good idea to create a separate layer for the actions, text, and graphic elements in the movie clip's Timeline.

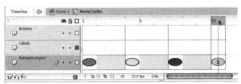

Figure 12.30 With Preview selected as your frame-viewing mode, the Timeline displays all the button-state graphics you've placed in the keyframes of the movie-clip button symbol. Use shades of gray for the graphics in the frame that represents the disabled state. (For clarity, since this book can't show you colors, the disabled-state graphic also contains an *X*.)

4. In the Timeline, for all three layers, insert keyframes in frames 4, 7, and 10 (**Figure 12.29**).

The layers that you added already had keyframes at frame 1. You need to add three more keyframes to accommodate all four button states: _up, _over, _down, and Disabled. Spacing the keyframes out makes them easier to deal with and lets you view the frame labels that you create in the following task.

5. In the ButtonGraphics layer, select keyframe 1; using the oval tool, draw an oval centered over the registration mark on the Stage.

This graphic represents the button's _up state. Give the oval a red fill and a black stroke. Make the stroke fairly wide to make the graphic look more button-like.

6. Select the oval, and choose Edit > Copy.

7. Select keyframe 4 in the ButtonGraphics layer, and choose Edit > Paste in Place.

This graphic represents the button's _over state. Change the fill color to green.

8. Repeat step 7 for keyframes 7 and 10.

In keyframe 7, change the oval fill to blue to represent the _down state. In keyframe 10, change the fill to a light gray and the stroke to a dark gray to represent the button in its Disabled state (**Figure 12.30**).

✔ Tip

■ There is no need to create a Hit-state keyframe for a movie-clip button. When you add the appropriate ActionScript (see Chapter 13), Flash uses the graphic element(s) in the frames of your movie clip that are displayed as button states to define the hit area.

To assign frame labels to button-state keyframes:

1. Continuing with the file you created in the preceding task, access the Properties tab of the Property inspector.

   If the Property inspector isn't open, choose Window > Properties > Properties.

2. In the Labels layer of the Timeline, select keyframe 1.

3. Click in the Frame Label field in the Frame Properties tab of the Property inspector to activate the field, and then type the name of this button state: _up (**Figure 12.31**).

   Flash places a red flag icon in any keyframe that has a label. If there's enough room in that keyframe span, Flash also displays the label name (**Figure 12.32**).

4. Repeat steps 2 and 3 for keyframes 4, 7, and 10, entering the names _over, _down, and Disabled.

   There are two reasons to assign labels to keyframes: First, the label reminds you what is in the keyframe; second, and more important, you can use ActionScript to find a frame with a particular label name and then display that frame. You'll use this technique to create the button's visual feedback in response to mouse movements.

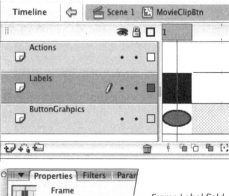

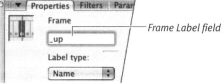

Figure 12.31 Enter a label for a selected keyframe in the Frame Label field of the Property inspector.

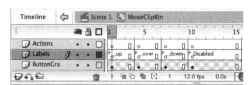

Figure 12.32 A red flag in a keyframe indicates that the frame has a label. If there are enough in-between frames following the keyframe, Flash displays the frame label as well as the flag (here frames have been added at the end of the sequence so the Disabled label is visible). The labeled keyframes in this movie-clip symbol indicate which button state the keyframe represents.

CREATING MOVIE-CLIP BUTTONS

5. Return to document-editing mode; for example, click the Back button in the Edit Bar.

6. Drag an instance of the MovieClipBtn symbol to the Stage.

   This movie clip is ready to be scripted to act like a button and to carry out whatever tasks you set for it with ActionScript. You'll learn to complete the button's interactivity in Chapter 13. To check out your button states, click the Play button in the symbol preview in the Library panel, or choose Control > Test Movie to play the symbol instance. Flash moves through the keyframes and displays each button state in turn.

7. Save this document for use in Chapter 13. Call it MyOwnBtn.fla.

Why Make Movie-Clip Buttons?

Flash's button symbols make it easy to create buttons quickly, but they limit you to just three states: Up, Over, and Down. Sometimes you'd like a button to have more states than that. Think of a typical slide show, for example, that has one button for moving to the next slide and another button for returning to the previous slide. The best interface designs use elements consistently. That way, users know what options are available to them and always know where to find the interface elements for carrying out a task. Still, on the last page of a slide show, there's no next slide to go to. In that case, it's common to display the Next button in a state indicating that the button doesn't function right now. When you make your own movie-clip buttons, you can create as many states as you like.

✔ Tips

■ When you use the labels _up, _down, and _over in your movie clip, ActionScript recognizes these labels as button states and you will have to do minimal scripting to get the button to work (see Chapter 13). To make a more flexible button (for example, one that responds differently to different mouse movements), use other labels. You can use MyUp, MyOver, MyDown, MyDragOut, and so on.

■ Another way to add a reminder about what a keyframe does is to add a comment. To enter a frame comment, select the keyframe; in the Frame Label field in the Property inspector, type two slashes (//) followed by your comment text (**Figure 12.33**). Frame labels and frame comments are mutually exclusive: Each keyframe can have one or the other. To work around that limitation, add separate layers for comments and labels. Place keyframes in both layers, and then add comments to one layer and labels to the other, as needed.

■ Instead of typing two slashes, you can choose Comment from the Label Type menu. Flash adds the slashes for you.

■ Because ActionScript may use frame labels to create interactivity, Flash exports frame-label text with the other movie data when you publish a Flash Player file. Keeping frame labels short helps keep files sizes small. Comments aren't exported with the final movie. You can make comments as long as you like, but remember that the next keyframe in the layer cuts off the comment text. Size your comments to fit the span containing them.

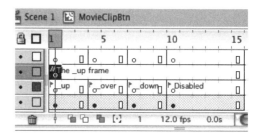

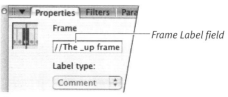

Figure 12.33 The Frame Label field in the Frame Properties tab of the Property inspector can also be used to create comments for a selected keyframe. Type two slashes in the field to begin comment text or choose Comment from the Label Type menu. Comments appear in the Timeline in the keyframe span; long comments are cut off by the next keyframe in the layer.

The Mystery of Frame Label Naming

Flash is sensitive about names. Frame label names become part of target paths in ActionScripting; therefore, certain characters that have special meaning in scripting—slashes, equal signs, plus signs, and so on—are off limits for labeling frames. To be safe, use only letters, numbers, and underscore characters; don't even use spaces to make word divisions in frame labels. Use capitalization and the underscore character instead.

BASIC INTERACTIVITY

Macromedia Flash 8 isn't just a tool for creating animated cartoons or blinking ad banners. You can use Flash to create complex, interactive Websites for e-learning, e-commerce, and other internet applications. To make your Flash content interactive, you need to add scripts to your Flash documents. Flash includes a complete scripting language, ActionScript, for developing interactivity. Scripting and the ActionScript language are both complex topics, and teaching them is beyond the scope of this book. However, Flash provides two tools that can help inexperienced scripters: The Actions panel's Script Assist mode helps you to input ActionScript code accurately, and the Behaviors panel generates scripts for common interactivity tasks. In this chapter, you'll use these tools to create very basic scripts. This is just a taste of scripting to get you started thinking about the ways you might use interactivity in your Flash creations.

Touring the Actions Panel

The Actions panel is a whole scripting environment in a box. It has three separate work areas: the Script pane, the Actions Toolbox, and the Script Navigator. To access the panel, choose Window > Actions or press Option-F9 (Mac) or F9 (Windows).

The *Script pane* is a text window where you assemble scripts. You can enter actions into the pane manually (it acts like a text editor); you can also add actions from the Actions Toolbox or the Add pop-up menu. You can import scripts or pieces of script from an external file, such as one created with a stand-alone text editor. When you use behaviors, Flash adds the script directly to the Script pane of the Actions panel. When you activate Script Assist mode (it's on by default in Flash Basic 8), the area above the Script pane enlarges and becomes the *Script Assist window*, which displays information and input tools that help you create scripts.

The *Actions Toolbox* contains most of the words (actions) that make up the ActionScript language. These pieces of code appear in hierarchical lists; click one of the folder-like icons to view the contents of a category. Double-click an action to add it to the Script pane. You can also drag items from the Actions Toolbox to the Script pane. (The list of ActionScript actions also appears in the Add menu. To access the menu, click the plus sign in the toolbar above the Script pane. Selecting an action from the Add menu adds it to the Script pane.)

What Is Interactivity?

By default, a published Flash file plays through its scenes and frames sequentially. The movie opens with scene 1, plays all those frames in order, moves to scene 2, plays those frames, and so on. Sometimes, that's appropriate; sometimes it's not.

Imagine an online training course where you want the same five frames of general instructions to appear before each section of the course. You can make those frames a separate scene and then duplicate the scene so it appears repeatedly between other scenes containing the training sections. Duplicating scenes increases file size, however, slows the performance of your published course, and makes it more difficult to edit later. A more efficient method is to create one scene containing the instructions and direct Flash to repeat that scene when each training section ends. In addition, you may want the users taking your course to interact with the content: clicking buttons, dragging elements, or entering text to answer quiz questions, for example. And you may want the course to interact with the user, summarizing the quiz score. These are examples of interactivity in Flash.

To achieve this type of interactivity, you must create a script that directs the playback of your published Flash content. You can do that with Flash's own scripting language, ActionScript (see "The Mystery of ActionScripting").

The *Script Navigator* helps you to locate and maneuver through the scripts in your movie. This feature is especially useful when you've attached scripts to objects, because there is no special indication that an object has an attached script.

Figure 13.1 shows the elements of the Actions panel.

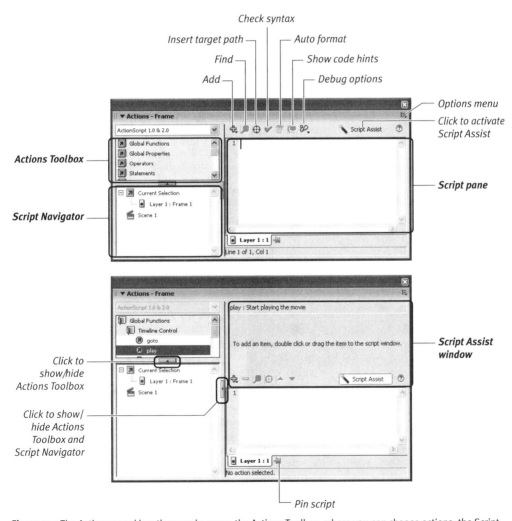

Figure 13.1 The Actions panel has three main areas: the Actions Toolbox, where you can choose actions; the Script Navigator, where Flash displays the elements in your movie that have scripts attached; and the Script pane, where Flash assembles the ActionScript. When Script Assist is active, information and scripting aids appear above the Script pane in an area called the Script Assist window.

The Mystery of ActionScripting

Flash Basic 8 and Flash Professional 8 both come with a full-fledged scripting language—ActionScript—that lets you add interactivity to Flash content. A *script* is a series of commands, or statements, that make Flash perform tasks at run time—that is, when a published Flash (.swf) file runs in Flash Player for viewing by your end users (see Chapter 16).

You can create ActionScript scripts in various ways: Enter text in the Script pane of the Actions panel, create the text in an external text editor and copy the text into the Script pane, create the text in an ActionScript file (an external file separate from your Flash document) and have Flash pull the script in when you publish your movie.

The Actions panel's Script Assist mode helps you enter code in the Script pane. For beginners, the word *assist* sounds attractive, and Script Assist can be helpful, but it isn't designed for someone who has no knowledge of scripting. With Script Assist, you create code by choosing radio buttons, check boxes, or menu offerings and entering text in special fields. Script Assist ensures that your ActionScript code has the correct syntax (see "The Mystery of ActionScript Syntax"). To use Script Assist, however, you must be familiar with the concept of scripting and with the specifics of ActionScript classes. If you know the kind of statements you need to create an interactivity, Script Assist will make sure you write them correctly; but Script Assist won't help you figure out what statements you need in the first place.

Scripting novices and people who don't want to learn scripting can use the Behaviors panel. This panel lists a set of common actions you might want in your movie, makes it easy to enter information about how those actions should work in your movie, and then creates a script for you. The drawback to the Behaviors panel is that it creates scripts that don't follow the best practices of ActionScripting. The best scripts are continuous instructions that govern large chunks, if not all, of a Flash movie. Behaviors ask you to select an object on the Stage or a keyframe in the Timeline and attach instructions to that object or keyframe. When you use behaviors, you wind up with snippets of script throughout your Flash document; these can be difficult to locate and coordinate as you refine your Flash content. In addition the scripts for complex behaviors contain behind-the-scenes coding. You may find it difficult to recognize the correlation with your entries.

Creating an ideal Flash script works something like creating a script for a play: A playwright creates a document containing all the dialogue for all the characters and all the stage instructions. Creating a script by using behaviors works more like putting together a skit, with individual actors developing dialogue and stage movements as they go. Anyone can go to the full script of a play to see what's happening when. To get the full picture of the skit, you have to interview each actor to find out who says what, where, and when, or watch the skit being performed. Although it would be a nightmare to develop a full-length, three-act drama using the skit model, plays and skits both have a place in the entertainment world.

The scripting techniques in this book are inappropriate for developing an interactive online store or a complex e-learning course. But these simple techniques may be all you need to let your end users start, stop, and replay an animated cartoon; select a favorite scene to view; or link to a Web page. With any luck, they'll whet your appetite for learning more about ActionScript as well.

Customizing the Actions Panel

The Actions panel takes up a good deal of room on your screen. You can resize the panel and its panes or collapse panes completely. You can customize the way scripts appear in the Script pane to view them in the smallest typeface you can read, for example (or, if you've spent long hours staring at tiny onscreen type, you can make scripts display in nice large letters). You can choose settings for font and type size; you can set Flash to highlight different types of script elements in different colors; you can control the number of spaces Flash uses to indent with each tab you type; and you can turn code hints on or off.

Two Types of Actions

This book uses two types of scripts: scripts that attach to keyframes and scripts that attach to objects. You can create both types by entering code directly in the Script pane of the Actions panel or by using Script Assist or the Behaviors panel. Before entering a script or choosing a behavior to create a script for you, first select the keyframe or object to which the script belongs.

Frame-based scripts are sets of actions attached to a keyframe. In the final exported movie, when the playhead reaches a keyframe that contains a script, Flash carries out the script's instructions. More advanced ActionScripters can create frame-based scripts that control all interactivity in the movie, responding not only to frame-based cues but also to object-based events, for example, a user clicking a button.

Object-based scripts are sets of actions attached to buttons, movie clips, or components (compiled clips). Actions attached to buttons usually require input from someone who is viewing the movie. In a text-heavy frame, for example, you can make the movie pause until the user clicks a button that instructs Flash to resume playback. Actions attached to movie clips and components can also respond to user input.

More advanced scripters can use ActionScript to trigger movie-clip actions without user intervention—for example, to make all sounds stop playing when a movie clip first appears. In addition, advanced ActionScripters can create scripts that target text fields, performing operations that modify them or retrieve information from them. Text fields on their own, however, can't have attached scripts.

To set preferences for the Actions panel:

1. From the Edit menu (Windows) or from the Flash application menu (Mac), choose Preferences.

or

From the Options menu in the top-right corner of the Actions panel, choose Preferences.

The Preferences dialog appears.

2. In the Category list, select ActionScript.

The settings for working with statements in the Script pane of the Actions panel appear in the main window of the Preferences dialog (**Figure 13.2**).

3. To get scripting help from code hints, in the Editing section, select the Code Hints check box.

Move the lever of the Delay slider to set the amount of time Flash waits before displaying the hint as you type directly in the Script pane.

4. To choose the font for writing scripts, in the Font section, *do the following:*

▲ From the pop-up menu of installed fonts, choose a font.

▲ From the pop-up menu of sizes, choose a type size.

The Actions panel can display scripts in text as small as 8 points and as large as 72 points.

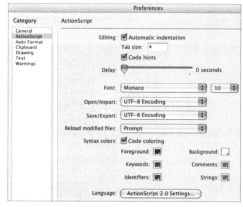

Figure 13.2 In the Preferences dialog, choose the ActionScript category to access settings for customizing the way Flash displays your scripts.

CUSTOMIZING THE ACTIONS PANEL

Figure 13.3 Activate syntax coloring by selecting the "Syntax colors: Code coloring" check box in the ActionScript category of the Preferences dialog. Change the colors to make more of a distinction between scripting "words" to begin getting a feel for ActionScript's parts of speech.

5. To color-code script items, in the Syntax Colors section, select the Code Coloring check box (**Figure 13.3**).

Using the color controls to access a pop-up set of swatches, *choose new colors for any of the following:*

Foreground. The basic text color for your scripts.

Keywords. Words reserved for special purposes in ActionScript.

Identifiers. The names of things, such as objects, variables, and functions, that are built into ActionScript. Identifiers are also used for custom classes for which you've defined an .xml file for code hints.

Background. The color against which your script displays in the Script pane.

Comments. Text that Flash ignores when it reads the script, used to make notes about what's going on in the script.

Strings. Series of characters (letters, numbers, and punctuation marks). Strings generally appear inside quotation marks.

6. Click OK.

Flash applies your preferences settings immediately.

✔ Tips

- Flash's default settings for keywords and identifiers are similar shades of blue. Try setting them to wildly different colors— say, pink and orange. This technique will help you learn to recognize these different parts of ActionScript speech as they're used in the scripts you create.

- Code hints work like tool tips within the Actions panel when Script Assist isn't active. With code hints turned on, you can make the Actions panel display certain types of scripting information in a tool-tip-type box or drop-down menu. Position the insertion point to the right of a dot (a period character) or an opening parenthesis in the Script pane, and then click the Show Code Hints button. If you enable Code Hints in the ActionScript Preferences, the hints appear automatically whenever you type a period or opening parenthesis.

- You may want to color-code only certain parts of your scripts. If, for example, you want your comments to appear in a different color but nothing else, set the color controls for Keywords, Identifiers, and Strings to match the color you choose for Foreground.

Organizing Frame Actions

A little letter *a* in the Timeline indicates a keyframe that has actions attached (**Figure 13.4**). Can you imagine scrolling through dozens—or hundreds—of layers, looking for the letter *a* when you want to edit the actions in your document? That's a recipe for eyestrain. And more than that, it's a recipe for disaster if you (or someone else) need to change the ActionScript later; it's difficult to remember (or guess) where the frame actions are lurking. It's a good idea to put all your frame actions in their own layer.

Restricting frame actions to their own layer prevents you from accidentally putting actions in keyframes in two different layers for the same frame number, which can cause problems if you reorder the layers.

To create a separate layer for frame actions:

1. Open a Flash document.

2. In the Timeline, add a new layer.

   (For detailed instructions on adding layers, see Chapter 6.)

3. Rename the layer Actions.

4. Drag the layer to the top or bottom of the Timeline.

   With a separate Actions layer as the top or bottom layer, you'll always know where to find the keyframes that contain actions when you need to modify or add to them (**Figure 13.5**).

✔ Tip

■ To prevent yourself from adding graphic elements to the Actions layer accidentally, lock it (by clicking the bullet in the padlock column). Locking keeps you from making changes in the elements on the Stage for that layer, but it doesn't prevent you from adding actions to keyframes.

Figure 13.4 Keyframes that contain actions display the letter *a* in the Timeline.

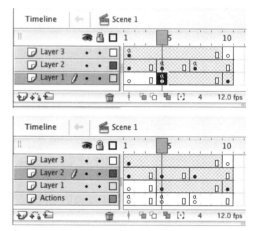

Figure 13.5 When you assign actions to many layers (top), it's harder to find them, and you may accidentally assign actions to the same frame number on different layers. Adding a separate layer for actions (bottom) makes it easy to find them all and to see whether a certain frame contains an action.

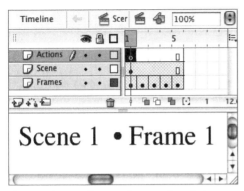

Figure 13.6 To test frame actions—actions that instruct Flash to move to a specific frame or to start and stop playback—it's useful to have a document that identifies each frame. That way, you can see the results of your scripts easily.

Adding Frame Actions

Some of the most basic scripting tasks involve controlling movie playback: making your movie stop and start and jump from place to place. By default, a movie begins running at playback; you can change that in the Publish Settings (see Chapter 16), but you can also do it more definitively with actions.

To make your first script in Flash, set up a multiframe document that has identifying text in each frame. Then add a `stop` action to keyframe 1, to make the movie start out paused at playback. As you create other scripts to navigate the movie, you can easily see their results. Save this file as a template for use in other scripting tasks.

To set up a document for testing frame actions:

1. Create a Flash document with three layers: Actions, Scene, and Frames.

2. In the Scene layer, add in-between frames in frames 2–5; there is a keyframe in the first frame by default.

3. On the Stage, for keyframe 1, create text that identifies the scene (Scene 1).

4. In the Frames layer, create keyframes in frames 1–5.

5. On the Stage, for each keyframe, add text that identifies the frame number (Frame 1, Frame 2, and so on).

   Your document should look like **Figure 13.6**.

The Pitfall of Placing Actions on Multiple Layers

At each point in the Timeline, Flash implements the actions in the highest-level keyframe that contains an action. Imagine a three-layer movie. Frame 2 of the top layer contains no actions. In frame 2 of the middle layer, a keyframe contains an action telling Flash to skip to frame 5. In frame 2 of the bottom layer, a keyframe contains an action telling Flash to skip to frame 10. When you play this movie, and the playhead hits frame 2, Flash looks in the top layer for actions and finds none, moves to the next layer down, finds an instruction and follows it, and so on, creating a queue of instructions. If you reorder layers Flash carries out the actions in the new order. This situation can cause havoc with your movie.

To begin scripting by adding comments:

1. Continuing with the document you created in the preceding task, in the Actions layer, select keyframe 1.

2. Access the Actions panel.

   The name Actions-Frame appears in the title bar of the Actions panel. If the panel isn't open, choose Window > Actions.

3. From the Options menu, in the upper right corner of the Actions-Frame panel, make sure Line Numbers is active (**Figure 13.7**).

   Visible line numbers make it easier to keep your place as you script. (Line Numbers is turned on by default; a check mark appears next to the name in the menu when it's active.)

4. From the Options menu, choose Word Wrap.

   Word Wrap forces the lines of your script to break to fit within the Script pane. Note that such line breaks aren't meaningful in the script itself; the ActionScript syntax tells Flash where the meaningful divisions in script text occur (see the sidebar "The Mystery of ActionScript Syntax").

5. In the toolbar of the Actions-Frame panel, check that Script Assist is active. If necessary, click the Script Assist button to open the Script Assist window (**Figure 13.8**).

Figure 13.7 Open the Options menu in the Actions panel to make sure that line numbering and word wrap are active (if not, select them to activate them). Visible line numbers make it easier to keep your place while scripting; word wrap makes it easier to view scripts as it forces them to stay within the visible Script pane area.

Click to activate Script Assist

Figure 13.8 Clicking the Script Assist button in the toolbar of the Actions panel opens a pane where information and settings appear to help you with scripting.

Figure 13.9 To view categories and subcategories in the Actions Toolbox, single-click the name or the book icon to its left; the item expands to reveal its contents. As you select items in the Actions Toolbox, Script Assist places the appropriate information and options in the Script Assist window.

6. In the Actions Toolbox, click the Global Functions category.

A list of subcategories appears in the Actions Toolbox; a description of the Global Functions category appears in the Script Assist window.

7. Click the Miscellaneous Functions subcategory.

A list of actions appears in the Actions Toolbox.

8. In the list of miscellaneous functions, click Comment.

A description of the comment action appears in the Script Assist window (**Figure 13.9**).

continues on next page

continues on next page

About Comment Lines

The double slash is known as a *comment delimiter;* the delimiter sets the boundaries of a comment within a script. Flash ignores any text between the two slashes and the next paragraph return for the purposes of scripting. When compiling the script for playback, Flash leaves that text out of the final file, so you don't need to worry that your comments will increase the .swf file size. It's a good idea to write notes about your script to remind yourself what you intend the script to do. Comments will also help anyone who needs to modify your script later.

For long comments, there's what's called a *multiline delimiter.* (Choose the Multiline check box in the Script Assist window to add a multiline comment to your script.) A multiline comment begins with /* and ends with */. Flash excludes everything in between the opening and closing delimiters from the script.

When you're testing long scripts or trying different ways to achieve your scripting task, it can be useful to temporarily remove part of the script to see what happens. Comment delimiters let you do this quickly without deleting any code. Script Assist won't help you with this, but you can turn off Script Assist and then manually insert double slashes at the front of a line or two of the script. If you want to block out a large section of the script temporarily, use the /* and */ delimiters.

9. To add the comment action to the script, *do either of the following.*

   ▲ Double-click the comment action in the Actions Toolbox.

   ▲ Drag the comment action from the Actions Toolbox to the Script pane.

   Instructions and a text field for entering comment text appear in the Script Assist window. Flash adds two slashes (//) to line 1 of the Script pane and selects them.

10. Click the Comment field in the Script Assist window to activate the field.

11. Type Pause the movie on frame 1 at runtime (**Figure 13.10**).

    Flash adds your comments to the Script pane. With word wrap turned on, Flash wraps your text to fit in the Script Pane; in the real script, the comment is just one line.

✔ Tip

■ Comments are so easy to enter that you may prefer to skip using Script Assist. With Script Assist inactive, click in the Script pane, type your comment delimiter, and then type your comment text. Turn on Script Assist when you're done to get help with the rest of your script.

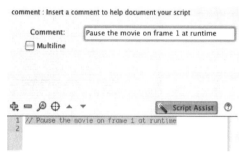

Figure 13.10 The two slashes indicate the beginning of a comment. When you add a comment action using Script Assist, Flash adds slashes to the script automatically. The text you enter in the Comment field is added to the script after the slashes.

Figure 13.11 With the comment code selected in Script Assist mode, Flash adds the next action you double-click (here it's stop) below the existing comment text.

To set the movie to pause at playback:

1. Continuing with the document you created in the preceding task, in the Actions Toolbox, click the Global Functions category to expand it, and then click the Timeline Control subcategory.

   A list of actions for controlling the play-back of the movie appears.

2. To add an action that pauses the Timeline, double-click the stop action (or drag it to the Script pane).

   Flash adds the new action below the comment line (**Figure 13.11**).

3. Save the document as a template for future use; name it FrameActionsTemplate.

   (For detailed instructions about saving documents as templates, see Chapter 1.)

4. Close the document.

   You don't want to inadvertently make more changes to your master template document, so close it at this point.

✔ Tip

■ Instead of using the Actions Toolbox to find and add actions, you can use the Add menu in the Actions panel. Click the plus sign located above the line numbers in the Script pane to view the menu. Choose *Category* > *Subcategory* > action (for example, Global Functions > Timeline Control > stop); Flash adds the selected action to your script.

The Mystery of ActionScript Syntax

ActionScript has its own rules, which are analogous to the rules of grammar and spelling in English. These rules, called *syntax,* govern such things as word order, capitalization, and punctuation of action statements. When you use Script Assist or the Behaviors panel, Flash handles all the details of syntax for you. When you start moving toward more independent scripting, you need to handle these details yourself. The following list briefly describes four crucial ActionScript punctuation marks that you'll see in those scripts.

Dot (.). ActionScript uses *dot syntax,* meaning that periods act as links between objects and the *properties* (characteristics) and *methods* (behaviors) applied to them. In the statement

```
clone_mc.duplicateMovieClip
```

the *dot* (the period) links the object (a movie clip named clone_mc) with the method (duplicatMovieClip) that creates a copy of the object.

ActionScript also uses the dot to indicate the hierarchy of files and folders in path names for targeting objects (such as movie-clip symbol instances) within one Flash file, similar to the way HTML syntax uses a slash. (Note that Flash 3 and 4 used slashes to indicate these types of path names. Flash 8 and Player 8 still recognize this *slash syntax,* but ActionScript 2.0 doesn't.) Macromedia recommends using dot syntax unless you're creating files for playback in Flash 3 or 4, and that's what you'll find in the scripts created by Script Assist and the Behaviors panel.

Semicolon (;). A semicolon indicates the end of a statement. The semicolon isn't required—Flash interprets the end of the line of statements correctly without it—but including it is good scripting practice. The semicolon also acts as a separator in some action statements.

Braces ({}). Braces set off ActionScript statements that belong together. A set of actions that are supposed to take place after on (release), for example, must be set off by braces.

Note that the action statements within braces can require their own beginning and ending braces. The opening and closing braces must pair up evenly. When you use Script Assist or the Behaviors panel to enter multiple actions in a script, Flash handles positioning of braces, ensuring that the pairs match. When you enter multiple actions without assistance, you must pay close attention to where you're adding statements and braces within the Script pane to ensure that you group the actions as you intend.

Parentheses (()). Parentheses group the arguments that apply to a particular statement—defining the scene and frame in a goto action, for example. Parentheses also allow you to group operations, such as mathematical calculations, so that they take place in the right order.

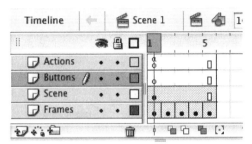

Figure 13.12 To practice with button actions, create a movie with identifying text, and separate layers for buttons and actions. Add in-between frames as needed so that all the layers are the same length.

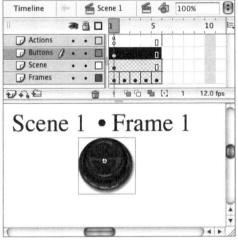

Figure 13.13 In-between frames extend the Buttons layer to the match the length of the other layers; the button symbol in keyframe 1 will be visible throughout the movie, although the identifying text from the Scene and Frames layers will change.

Adding Actions to Buttons

As you learned in the previous chapter, Flash's button symbols and button components have certain actions built in. By default, when you move the mouse into the button area, Flash jumps to the Over frame; when you click the button, Flash takes you to the Down frame. To make the button carry out a task or to refine the way a button responds to a user's mouse movements, you attach ActionScript to an instance of a button symbol or button component. You can use Script Assist or the Behaviors panel to get help creating the script.

To prepare a document for testing button scripts:

1. Open a new copy of the FrameActions-Template you created earlier in this chapter.

   This is a five-frame document with identifying text for each frame and a `stop` action in keyframe 1.

2. In the Timeline, add a new layer anywhere below the Actions layer; name the new layer *Buttons*.

   Frame 1 of the new layer is a keyframe; frames 2–5 are in-between frames. Any items you place on this layer will be visible throughout the five-frame movie (**Figure 13.12**).

3. With the Buttons layer selected, place an instance of a button symbol on the Stage (**Figure 13.13**).

   Follow the techniques in Chapter 12 to create a new button symbol, or use one from the Common Library of buttons. (To access this library of button symbols that comes with Flash, choose Window > Common Libraries > Buttons.) Drag a button-symbol instance from the library to the Stage.

continues on next page

4. To name the button instance, access the Properties tab of the Property inspector and type a name in the Instance name field (**Figure 13.14**).

It's a good idea to get into the habit of naming each instance of a symbol in your document. For ActionScript to be able to control a symbol, the symbol must have a unique instance name.

5. Save your document as a template for use throughout this chapter, and name it ObjectActionsTemplate.

(For detailed instructions about saving documents as templates, see Chapter 1.)

6. Close the document.

Choosing Save As doesn't close the file you're in. To avoid making further changes to the master template document, you must close it at this point.

To add an action to a button-symbol instance using Script Assist:

1. Open a new copy of the ObjectActions-Template that you created in the preceding task.

This is a five-frame document with identifying text, one button instance, and a stop action in keyframe 1.

2. On the Stage, select the button instance.

3. Access the Actions panel.

The Actions panel name changes to Actions - Button (**Figure 13.15**).

4. To get help scripting, click the Script Assist button.

The Script Assist window opens.

5. From the Add menu (the plus sign above the Script pane), choose an action (for this task, choose Global Functions > Timeline Control > goto) (**Figure 13.16**).

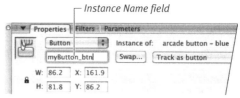

Instance Name field

Figure 13.14 Select the button symbol on the Stage, and enter a name in the Instance Name field in the Properties tab of the Property inspector. Ending the name with _btn makes it clear that the symbol is a button and allows code hints to give you more information as you create scripts.

Figure 13.15 The Actions panel name reflects the type of element you're about to script. When you select a frame or click a blank area of the Stage, you're about to create a frame action, and *Frame* is part of the panel's name (top). When you select a button symbol on the Stage, the panel name includes *Button* (bottom).

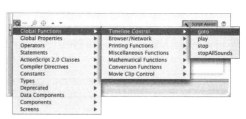

Figure 13.16 You can choose an action from the Add menu (the plus sign icon). Select the desired action from the hierarchical menu of categories and subcategories.

Description of the action selected in
the Actions Toolbox (or Add menu)

Settings appropriate to the action

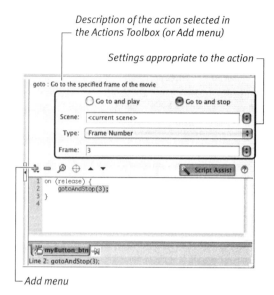

Add menu

Figure 13.17 When you add a goto command using Script Assist, Flash uses the settings in the Script Assist window to write a script that takes the playhead to a specific frame. The script appears in the Script pane.

Settings for the goto action appear in the Script Assist window.

6. To script the button to send the playhead to frame 3 and then stop movie playback, *do the following:*

   ▲ Select the "Go to and stop" radio button.

   ▲ Leave the Scene field at its default: <current scene>.

   ▲ Leave Type at its default: Frame Number.

   ▲ In the frame field, enter 3.

   Flash uses these settings to create a script in the Script pane (**Figure 13.17**). You're ready to test your button; see "Previewing Actions at Work," later in this chapter.

✔ Tip

■ In the preceding task, you made the playhead move to a specific frame and stop playback. You can also make the playhead jump to a new frame and resume playback from there. In step 6, select the "Go to and play" radio button.

The Mystery of Instance Names

The tasks in this section suggest that you end the name of a button instance with the suffix _btn. This practice has two purposes. First, it reminds you what type of object you're looking at; if you name objects consistently with Flash's suffixes, when you read through your scripts you'll be able to see what types of objects are involved. Additionally, the code-hint feature of the Actions panel can provide more information about scripting objects if the object type is identified by the proper suffix. With a movie-clip instance, you'd use the suffix _mc. (Advanced scripters can create scripts that work with text boxes; they use the suffix _txt. Sound objects use the suffix _sound; you'll learn to name instances for sound objects in Chapter 15.)

Because instance names may wind up as part of an ActionScript, you must avoid including spaces or characters that have special meaning in ActionScript: for example, slashes or the equals sign. To be safe, use only letters, numbers, and underscore characters. Ideally, instance names should start with a letter.

The Mystery of Event Handlers

Scripts attached to buttons and movie clips acting as buttons must start with a special piece of code—on ()—that tells Flash to make the scripted object respond like a button to mouse movements (changing the arrow pointer to a pointing hand, for example, when a user rolls over the button). That code is called an *event handler* because it responds to things that happen (events) and uses that incoming information to decide (handle) when and how to run a chunk of ActionScript.

What follows the handler in parentheses—(release), for example—indicates the condition under which the script will run (in this example, when the user clicks and releases the pointer over a button's hit area or within the graphic area of a movie clip. The statement inside the parentheses is the *event*. Both Script Assist and the Behaviors panel let you select which mouse-related event *(mouseEvent)* or keyboard-related event *(keypress)* will trigger the script.

To change the triggering event, select a new one in the Script Assist window of the Actions panel (or in the Behaviors panel) or delete the text between the parentheses and type a new event directly in the Script pane of the Actions panel.

When you use the Behaviors panel to attach an action to a button or a movie-clip symbol, Flash automatically adds the event handler on (release) to the script. When you use Script Assist to attach an action to a button, Flash also adds the on (release) handler to the script automatically. When you use Script Assist to attach an action to a movie-clip symbol, however, you must add the on () handler in a separate step (see "Adding Actions to Movie Clip Buttons," later in this chapter). Otherwise, Flash may add the onClipEvent () handler instead. The onClipEvent () handler responds to mouse events anywhere in a frame containing the scripted movie clip, not just when the mouse interacts with the movie-clip itself.

Button components have their own set of triggering events. The Behaviors panel inserts click as the default event in scripts attached to button components.

The other items that your script requires when you set up event handlers are curly braces.

{ indicates the beginning of the list of actions that are to be triggered by the specified event.

} indicates the end of the list of the actions that are to be triggered by the specified event.

All actions between the two braces take place when the triggering event occurs.

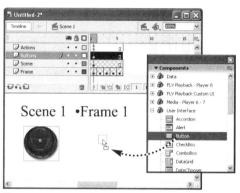

Figure 13.18 Drag an instance of the button component from the Components panel (Flash Professional 8 shown here) to the Stage to add it to your movie.

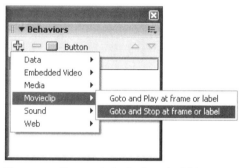

Figure 13.19 Choose a behavior from the Add Behaviors menu in the Behaviors panel.

Targeting Frame Labels

In setting up the target-frame parameter for the Goto behavior for a movie-clip button, you can enter a frame number or a frame label. There's an advantage to using frame labels. If you ever add or remove frames from the movie-clip button, the frame numbers for the states may change. If they do, you must go back into the Behaviors panel or script to update the frame numbers. It's a hassle, and you must *remember* that you need to do it. If you target the frame by label, you need never update the script to accommodate changes to frame numbers.

To add an action to a button component instance using the Behaviors panel:

1. Continuing with the copy of ObjectActions-Template that you created in the preceding task, access the Actions, Behaviors, and Components panels.

2. In the Components panel, expand the User Interface category, and drag an instance of the button component to the stage (**Figure 13.18**).

3. On the Stage, select the button-component instance.

   The Actions panel name changes to *Actions*. The Behaviors panel displays the button-component icon and the name of the selected component.

4. In the Behaviors panel, from the Add Behavior menu, choose Movieclip > Goto and Stop at frame or label (**Figure 13.19**).

5. In the Goto and Stop dialog that opens, to script the button to send the playhead to frame 4 and then stop movie playback, *do the following:*

▲ For pathname style, select the Relative radio button. A *relative pathname* identifies the target Timeline in terms of its relative position within the hierarchy of Timelines in a movie: for example, saying start where I am; the target is one level above me; or the target is within me, one level down. An *absolute pathname* describes the location more specifically, always starting with the top-level Timeline and working its way down to the target movie.

▲ In the target movie-clip pane, select _root. This pane lists the movie clips in your document. Flash refers to the main document as a movie clip named _root. To instruct Flash to move around in the main Timeline, choose _root as your target movie clip. Flash creates the appropriate pathname using the selected pathname style. (Flash enters the pathname in the field above the target movie-clip pane.)

▲ For the frame at which to stop playing, type 4 (**Figure 13.20**).

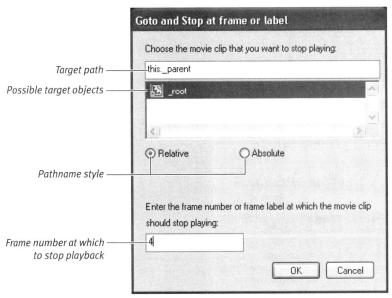

Target path

Possible target objects

Pathname style

Frame number at which to stop playback

Figure 13.20 Flash will use the settings in the Goto and Stop dialog to create the script for the behavior that takes the playhead to a specific frame and stops playback.

6. Click OK.

Flash adds the behavior to the Behaviors panel and adds comments and code to the Script pane of the Actions panel (**Figure 13.21**). Button components take their own special events; click is the default.

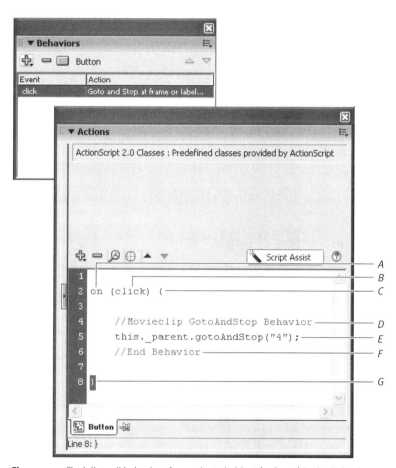

Figure 13.21 Flash lists all behaviors for a selected object (or frame) in the Behaviors panel (top). The script for the button component created by choosing Behavior > Movieclip > Goto and Stop instructs Flash to move to frame 4 and then pause playback (bottom). The script contains the following elements: A) an event handler (on); B) the event parameter (the triggering event—click); C) a curly brace marking the beginning of actions that take place in response to the event; D) a comment noting the beginning of the code specific to this behavior; E) a set of actions triggered by clicking and releasing the mouse button inside the active button area (in the main Timeline, go to frame 4 and pause); F) a comment noting the end of the code specific to this behavior; and G) a curly brace marking the end of the actions that take place in response to the event.

✔ Tips

- You can use the Behaviors panel to assign actions to button symbols. Follow the same steps as in the preceding task for a button component; Flash inserts the default event handler on (release) into the script instead of on (click).

- You can also use the Actions panel in Script Assist mode to assign actions to button components (or any movie-clip symbol acting as a button); but the steps are more complex (see "Adding Actions to Movie-Clip Buttons," later in this chapter).

- When you use behaviors to create a script, Flash leaves line 1 of the script blank. Use that line to add comments. Each behavior adds its own comments, but they're fairly cryptic general notes about which behavior the script is for— for example, //Movieclip GotoAndStop Behavior. A comment like //Go to the Company Address page may be more meaningful to your project.

The Mystery of Target Paths

Because a button component is a type of movie clip and thus has its own independent Timeline, it needs a pathname that identifies it that way. Behaviors help you deal with this. Place a button component and a button symbol in the same Flash document, and apply a behavior to each; choose the goto behavior to make the movie jump to a specific frame in the main Timeline.

If you choose Absolute as the pathname style, the behavior creates the same pathname for both button elements: _root. If you choose Relative for the pathname style, however, the behavior creates different pathnames: this for the button *symbol* targeting the main Timeline, and this._parent for the button *component* targeting the main Timeline. What's going on?

Think of translating *this* as *me* or *my*. Flash considers the button symbol to be controlled directly by the main Timeline. The symbol's pathname (this) means the target Timeline is *my Timeline*. Flash considers the button component to be a separate Timeline nested inside the main Timeline, so its pathname (this._parent) translates to *my parent's Timeline*.

When you use behaviors to create a goto script for a movie-clip symbol, you select the pathname style and the target. To use Script Assist to achieve the same result is more complex. You must first create the on (release) event handler, then enter a target path to tell Flash which object to control.

Figure 13.22 To make button symbols active, so that you see their Up, Over, and Down states in the authoring environment, choose Control > Enable Simple Buttons. (This command has no effect on button components.) To further enable them to carry out simple ActionScript tasks, choose Control > Enable Simple Frame Actions.

Previewing Actions at Work

To see the way simple scripts attached to button symbols work, you can enable them in the Flash authoring environment. To see button components or more complex scripts in action, you need to view the movie in Flash Player. You can do this by publishing the movie (see Chapter 16) or by using one of the test modes. *Test mode* is an abbreviated form of publishing a movie while still working in the authoring environment.

To enable simple buttons:

1. In the Flash document containing the button symbols you want to try out, choose Control > Enable Simple Buttons (**Figure 13.22**).

   Now when you position the pointer over a button object on the Stage, you see its Over frame; when you click the button, you see its Down frame.

2. Choose Control > Enable Simple Frame actions.

   When you click the button, it carries out its scripted task, provided that task is simple enough to carry out within the authoring environment.

To test fully enabled elements:

1. In the Flash document containing the elements you want to test, choose Control > Test Movie or Test Scene (**Figure 13.23**).

   Flash exports the movie or scene to a Flash Player file, adding the .swf extension to the filename and using the current Publish settings. (For more information on Publish Settings, see Chapter 16.) During export, Flash displays the Exporting Flash Movie dialog, which contains a progress bar and a button for canceling the operation.

   When it finishes exporting the movie, Flash opens the .swf file in Flash Player so you see the movie in action. The buttons and movie clips in the test window are all live, so you can see how they interact with the viewer's mouse actions. Any scripts you've created will run.

2. When you finish testing, click the movie window's close box (Windows) or close button (Mac) to exit the Player.

   Flash returns you to the document-editing environment.

✔ Tips

■ When you choose Control > Test Scene, Flash appends the name of the scene to the file, as well as .swf, when it creates the Player file. This situation can make the file name exceed the number of allowable characters. If Test Movie worked fine with your file, but Test Scene brings up the warning dialog, try shortening the scene name.

■ To test the interactivity of a symbol, for example, a movie clip, choose Control > Test Scene while you are working on the symbol in symbol-editing mode. Flash publishes just the symbol and the items nested within that symbol.

Figure 13.23 To test the full animation and interactivity of button components, you must export your movie—for example, by choosing Control > Test Movie (or Control >Test Scene).

Changing Events

When you preview the three states of a basic button symbol during authoring (choose Enable Simple Buttons), pressing the mouse button down triggers Flash to display the Down frame. You can use ActionScript to override a button's built-in actions. When you use Script Assist or behaviors to attach actions to a button-symbol instance, Flash automatically adds the default event handler, on (release), to the Script pane. That code makes the release of the mouse button trigger the actions attached to the button. You can select different triggering events in the Script Assist window. (If you created the script using behaviors, you can also choose a new event handler in the Behaviors panel.)

To choose a triggering event using Script Assist:

1. Open the document GoToButtons.fla, which you created earlier in this chapter.

   This is a five-frame movie with a button symbol and a button component that you scripted to take you to different frames when clicked.

2. On the Stage, select the button-symbol instance and duplicate it.

   Choose Edit > Duplicate or copy and paste to create a duplicate. To help you remember which button is which, place identifying text near each button. Label the original button Release; label the duplicate Press.

3. Select the Press button.

   Its script appears in the Script pane in the Actions panel.

4. Make sure Script Assist is active; if the Script Assist window isn't visible, click the Script Assist button.

continues on next page

5. In the Script pane of the Actions panel, click anywhere in line 1, the line containing the event handler on (release).

Flash highlights the line of script and displays a set of check boxes for assigning triggering events in the Script Assist window (**Figure 13.24**).

6. Deselect the Release check box.

7. Select the Press check box.

The Script pane updates to reflect the new event choice (**Figure 13.25**).

8. Choose Control > Test Movie to see these buttons in action.

Position the pointer over the original button (labeled Release); click and hold for a second or two, and then let go of the mouse button. Flash moves to frame 3 only after you release the mouse button. Now return to the first frame where your buttons are (choose Control > Rewind). Position the pointer over the Press button. Click and hold. Flash takes you to frame 3 immediately; you don't need to release to activate the script.

✔ Tip

■ If you want the button to respond the same way to multiple triggering events (for example, when the user rolls over or rolls out), select the event check boxes for those events. The triggering events all appear within the parentheses defining the event parameter of the action: for example, on (roll over, roll out).

Figure 13.24 When you select a line of script in the Script Pane, the Script Assist window displays other possible options for the selected action. With line 1 (the event handler) selected, the Script Assist window displays other possible triggering events.

Figure 13.25 The Script pane updates to reflect your choices in the Script Assist window. Here line 1 of the script now uses the on (press) event handler.

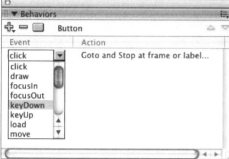

Figure 13.26 Click the entry in the Event column for a behavior to activate a list of events (top). Click the active field or the triangle to its right to expand the list (bottom).

Figure 13.27 Choose a new event to modify the selected behavior. Flash updates the script in the Actions panel accordingly. With on (keyDown) as the event handler, this component carries out its task when a user presses any keyboard key.

To choose a triggering event using the Behaviors panel:

1. Continuing with the document GoToButtons.fla, on the Stage, select the button-component instance and duplicate it.

   Place identifying text near each component instance. Label the original click; label the duplicate keyDown.

2. Select the button component labeled keyDown.

   Its script appears in the Script pane in the Actions panel. The component's behavior also appears as an entry in the Behaviors panel.

3. In the Behaviors panel, click the first line in the Event column (the word *click*).

   Flash activates a menu of events.

4. To view the event choices, click the triangle to the right of the word *click*.

   A menu of events appears (**Figure 13.26**).

5. From the menu of events, select keyDown.

   The value in the Events column of the Behaviors panel changes to keyDown, and the script in the Actions panel updates (**Figure 13.27**). (Note that keyDown is intended to be used with more advanced ActionScripting techniques, where you would write a listener script to capture the exact keys being pressed. But you can use keyDown here to practice changing an event through the Behaviors panel.)

   continues on next page

CHANGING EVENTS

6. Choose Control > Test Movie to see the two button components in action.

You must click the component labeled click to get it to carry out its task of taking you to a different frame. Clicking the component labeled keyDown does nothing; but press any key while that component is on Stage, and Flash whisks you off to frame 4.

✔ Tips

■ If you use the Behaviors panel to assign actions to button symbols, use the same steps as in the preceding task; the event choices in the menu in step 5 will be appropriate to whatever type of object you're working with.

■ Although you created the button-component script in the Behaviors panel, you can edit the script in the Actions panel using Script Assist. In the Script pane, select line 3, the line containing on (click) or on (keyDown). In the Script Assist window, make sure the Component check box is selected. This option tells Flash to treat the object as a component. Choose the desired event from the pop-up menu (**Figure 13.28**). At this level of editing, Flash keeps the link to the behavior, updating the Event column in the Behaviors panel. If you make substantial edits to a behavior-created script in the Actions Panel—especially if you edit the script directly—without Script Assist, you may lose the ability to edit the script via the Behaviors panel.

Figure 13.28 You can update behavior-created scripts in the Actions panel using Script Assist. In the Script pane, select the line of code containing the event; in the Script Assist window, select the Component check box; and then choose an event from the pop-up menu.

The Mystery of Mouse Events

For button symbols and movie clips, the event handler on() can respond to eight different events. Because most of these events involve user input with a mouse (or equivalent device), they're often called *mouse events*. You can choose which mouse event triggers your button or movie clip's script:

Press refers to the downward part of a click when the pointer is located within the hit area of a button.

Release refers to the upward part of a click (the user presses and then releases the mouse button) when the pointer is located within the hit area of a button. A Release event lets users click and then change their minds—and avoid activating the button—by dragging away before releasing the mouse button. This is the way most buttons in professional programs work.

Release Outside happens when the user clicks inside the button area, holds down the mouse button, and moves the mouse outside the active button area before releasing the mouse button.

Key Press happens any time the user presses the specified keyboard key while the Flash button is present on screen. The user doesn't have to use the mouse to interact with the button for this event to trigger an action.

Roll Over occurs any time the pointer rolls into the button's hit area when the mouse button hasn't been pressed.

Roll Out happens any time the pointer rolls out of the button's hit area when the mouse button hasn't been pressed.

Drag Over works in a slightly unexpected way. A Drag Over event occurs when the user clicks and holds down the mouse button within the button's hit area, rolls the pointer outside the hit area, and then rolls the pointer back into the hit area, all without releasing the mouse button.

Drag Out happens when the user clicks within the button's hit area, holds down the mouse button, and rolls the pointer out of the hit area.

There are ten events for components (click, focusIn, focusOut, keyDown, keyUp, resize, move, draw, load, and unload). The one that makes the most sense for a button component is click, which is the equivalent of Release for button symbols. The other events are meant for use with more-advanced ActionScripting, where the script gathers information about what transpires: for example, keeping track of which keys the user presses.

Triggering Actions from the Keyboard

The keyPress mouse event allows users to trigger actions from the keyboard by pressing a specified key. Although you assign it to a button, on (keyPress) affects the entire range of frames in which that button resides. A button symbol's Hit-frame graphic need not cover the whole Stage, and the user need not position the pointer over the button before pressing the specified key. Whenever the button appears in the currently displayed frame, pressing the specified key triggers the assigned actions.

To set up an action triggered by a key press:

1. Open a new copy of the ObjectActions-Template that you created earlier in this chapter.

2. Select the button on the Stage. Using Script Assist or behaviors, attach a script that makes the button take you to frame 3.

   (To review the required steps, see "Adding Actions to Buttons," earlier in this chapter.)

3. Select the button on the Stage.

4. In the Script pane of the Actions panel, select the event handler (the line of code that begins with on).

   The possible events appear in the Script Assist window.

5. Deselect the currently selected event check box (Release), and select the Key Press check box.

   The text field to the right of the check box activates.

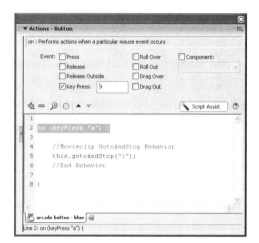

Figure 13.29 Selecting the Key Press check box activates a text field where you can enter a letter (or key). Flash adds the appropriate script for using the letter you enter as a trigger for actions whenever the button appears on screen.

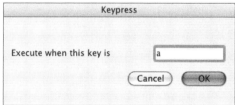

Figure 13.30 When you choose the On Key Press event in the Behaviors panel, the Keypress dialog opens; here you can enter the triggering character (or key).

6. In the dialog's text-entry field, type the letter *a* (or another letter or key that you want to act as a trigger).

In the Script pane, the event handler changes to on (keyPress "a") (**Figure 13.29**).

You're ready to test the movie. During playback, no matter where the pointer is in relation to the button, when the button is on screen and you press *a* on the keyboard, Flash jumps to frame 3 of the movie.

7. Save your file for use in a later task; name the file KeyPressBtn.fla.

✔ Tips

■ If you use a behavior to create the button script, you can also assign the triggering letter in the Behaviors panel. Select the button on the Stage. In the Event column of the Behaviors panel, double-click On Release to activate the list of events. Select On Key Press. The Keypress dialog opens, in which you can enter the triggering key (**Figure 13.30**). Click OK to close the dialog.

■ In some situations, assigned key-press actions fail to work in a published movie. (Browsers, for example, often intercept all key presses, assuming that the user wants to enter a new URL.) When a user clicks a button in a Flash movie, Flash grabs the key-press focus—the capability to intercept all key presses—for itself. To ensure that your key-press actions always work, include a button for users to click before they can enter a part of the movie that uses key presses.

■ If the triggering key is also a keyboard shortcut in Test Movie mode, such as the Enter key, choose Control > Disable Keyboard Shortcuts when you test your movie. Otherwise, Flash will interpret the keypress in its normal way.

Triggering Multiple Actions with One Event

Flash doesn't limit you to a single action for each button script; you can combine multiple actions to make a button carry out several tasks in response to one event. Script Assist and behaviors both help you to do this, but Script Assist is easier to use for this purpose.

To add multiple actions using Script Assist:

1. Open a new copy of the ObjectActions-Template that you created earlier in this chapter.

2. Attach a script to the button in keyframe 1 that uses the goto action to send the playhead to keyframe 3. (To review the process, see "To add an action to a button-symbol instance using Script Assist" in the section "Adding Actions to Buttons.")

3. Select the button instance on the Stage.
   The button's script appears in the Script pane of the Actions panel.

4. Make sure the Script Assist window is visible in the Actions panel.
   If the Actions panel isn't in Script Assist mode, click the Script Assist button.

5. To determine the order of the added action, *do either of the following,*

   ▲ To have the action be carried out *before* the goto action you added in step 2, select line 1 of the script by clicking anywhere in that line in the Script pane.

   ▲ To have the action be carried out *after* the goto action, select line 2 of the script by clicking anywhere in that line in the Script pane (**Figure 13.31**).

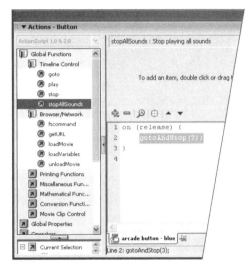

Figure 13.31 When using Script Assist, to prepare to add new actions, select the line containing the action that you want to happen first. To add an action that that takes place after the goto action in this script, select line 2.

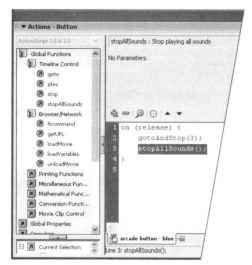

Figure 13.32 When you've selected an action statement in the Script pane, double-clicking an item in the Actions toolbox (or selecting an item from the Add menu) adds a new action statement after the selected line in the script. The actions that appear within the curly braces all take place, in order, in response to the triggering event.

6. Choose Add > Global Functions > Timeline Control > `stopAllSounds`.

Script Assist adds `stopAllSounds` () in the line following the one selected in step 5. For example, if you select line 2 in the Script Pane, Script Assist adds `stopAllSounds` to line 3 of the script (**Figure 13.32**). The script now contains two actions; both take place in response to the user's clicking the button. The actions happen in the order that they appear in the script. First the movie jumps to frame 3, and then all sounds currently playing stop. (You'll learn more about working with sounds in Chapter 15.) To revise the order in which the actions occur, rearrange them in the Script Pane.

✔ Tip

■ In the Actions panel, with Script Assist disabled, when you double-click an action in the Actions toolbox (or choose it from the Add menu), Flash inserts the code wherever the insertion point is in the Script pane and adds a return at the end of its insertion. Be sure to place the insertion point at the beginning of the line of code that should follow your addition.

To organize actions using Script Assist:

1. Continuing with the document from the preceding task, select line 3 in the Script pane.

2. To move the selected action up one line, click the upward triangle in the Script pane's toolbar.

   Flash rewrites the script to put the stopAllSounds action first (**Figure 13.33**). Now when you click the button, all sounds stop playing, and then the movie jumps to frame 3. You can also move a selected line of script down a line by clicking the downward triangle.

✔ Tip

■ When you use Script Assist to insert code into a script, Flash adds the inserted code in a new line after the line you've selected in the Script pane. When Script Assist is inactive, Flash inserts new code where the cursor is and then follows the insert with a return to go to a new line. If you select some text in the Script pane, Flash replaces that text with your new entry. To add a new line of code to your script, be sure to place the cursor at the start of the line you want to follow your new line. It may help you to add an extra return so you can place the cursor in a blank line to be sure your text winds up in the right spot.

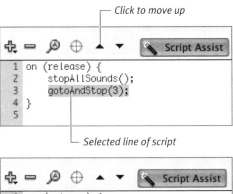

Click to move up

Selected line of script

Reordered actions

Figure 13.33 The up and down triangles in the Script Assist toolbar move selected lines of script up or down within the Script pane.

A) Click the Remove button when one
line within the braces is selected

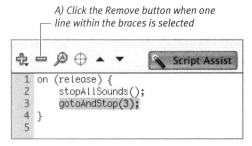

B) Selected line deleted

C) Click the Remove button when a
line containing a brace is selected

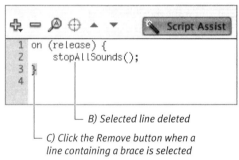

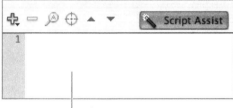

D) Entire action statement deleted

Figure 13.34 In the Script pane, select the line of code
containing the action you want to delete, and then
click the Remove button (the minus sign icon) in the
Script Assist toolbar (A). Script Assist deletes that line
from the script (B). If you select a line containing a
curly brace (C), clicking the Remove button removes
the whole action statement (D).

To delete actions using Script Assist:

1. Continuing with the document from the
   preceding task, to delete a single action
   within the block of code defined by the
   curly braces, *do the following:*

   ▲ Select line 3 in the Script pane.

   ▲ Click the Remove button (the minus
   sign in the Script Assist toolbar). Flash
   removes the selected line of code.

2. To delete the entire set of actions, *do
   the following:*

   ▲ Select a line that contains a curly
   brace, line 1 or line 3.

   ▲ Click the Remove button. Flash
   removes the entire action script—
   event handler, braces, actions, and all
   (**Figure 13.34**).

Working with Multiple Behaviors

You can script multiple actions for a button by adding multiple behaviors to the same object. Select an instance of a button symbol on the Stage. In the Behaviors panel, from the Add menu, choose Movieclip > `Goto and Stop at frame or label`. In the Goto and Stop dialog, enter the parameters to take you to a different frame. Flash creates the script in the Script pane. With the button instance selected on the Stage, in the Behaviors panel, from the Add menu, choose Sounds > `Stop All Sounds`. Flash puts the code for the `stopAllSounds` action at the head of the existing `goto` script (**Figure 13.35**). At runtime, Flash will first stop the current sounds and then jump to the specified frame. If you want the actions to take place in a different order, you must rearrange them.

Select a behavior in the Behaviors panel. Now use the Move Up and Move Down buttons (the triangle icons in the upper-right corner of the Behaviors panel) to move the selected behavior to a new place in the list. To delete a section of code created by a behavior, select the behavior in the Behaviors panel and then click the Delete Behavior button (the minus sign icon) (**Figure 13.36**).

You can use Script Assist to move behaviors up and down within the Script pane of the Actions panel or to delete them entirely, but the task is complex. When you use behaviors, Flash adds beginning and ending comments and extra lines of space in the script; you need to delete them or move them properly.

Manual alterations to scripts created by the Behaviors panel may introduce syntax errors that prevent Flash from recognizing a script as a behavior. In that case, you won't be able to use the Behaviors panel to modify or delete the script. Sometimes, using Script Assist to alter the behavior script makes the script unworkable for Flash's scripting assistants.

Once you are familiar with ActionScript syntax, you can cut and paste or drag and drop sections of code to reorganize a behavior-created script to make actions occur in any order you want. Until then, it's safest to modify the behaviors only through the Behaviors panel. Or, use Script Assist when you want to create multiple actions for one button.

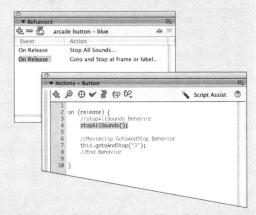

Figure 13.35 The Behaviors panel lists all the behaviors you've applied to the button. Click the text (in either the Event or Action column) to select the behavior. You can add new actions for the button from the Add menu. The Behaviors panel always adds a new action for the same handler at the beginning of the script, directly under the event handler line.

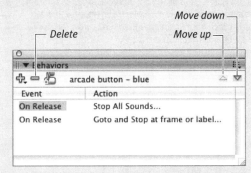

Figure 13.36 To change the order in which Flash carries out the actions created by behaviors, in the Behaviors panel, select an action and move it up or down in the list using the triangle buttons. To delete an action, click the minus sign.

TRIGGERING MULTIPLE ACTIONS WITH ONE EVENT

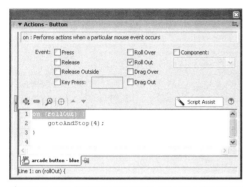

Figure 13.37 In Script Assist mode, selecting the event handler line in the script gives you access to other events. Deselect the default Release and select the Roll Out check box to make the button respond to a user's rolling out of the button area.

Using Multiple Handlers for One Button

You can make one button respond differently to different mouse events by placing several handlers in the button's script. You can, for example, create a button that jumps Flash to the next frame when the user clicks and then releases the mouse button within the active button area but that pops up the message "You must click the button to move to the next question" if the user presses a key on the keyboard.

To vary a button's response to different mouse events:

1. Open a new copy of the ObjectActionsTemplate that you created earlier in this chapter.

2. Select the button on the Stage.

3. In the Actions panel, with Script Assist active, from the Add menu (or the Actions Toolbox) choose Global Functions > Timeline Control > goto.

4. In the Script Assist window, *change the following parameters:*

   ▲ Select the Goto and Stop radio button.

   ▲ In the Frame field, enter 4.

   Flash adds the script to the Script pane.

5. In the Script pane, click line 1.

   The event handlers appear in the Script Assist window.

6. Deselect the Release check box, and select the Roll Out check box (**Figure 13.37**).

continues on next page

7. In the Script pane, click line 3.

Flash highlights the closing curly brace (**Figure 13.38**). This closing brace marks the end of the actions carried out by on (release).

8. Repeat step 3 to add another goto action.

Script Assist scripts a new action statement complete with its own event handler and set of braces; Script Assist automatically handles the syntax and placement of the two scripts in relation to one another in the Script pane (**Figure 13.39**).

9. Repeat step 4; but this time, in the Frame field, enter 5.

10. In the Script pane, select line 4 (the event handler for the second action statement).

The events appear in the Script Assist window.

Figure 13.38 To add a new action statement to your script in Script Assist mode, select the ending curly brace of the existing script. Then choose another action from the Add menu or Actions toolbox.

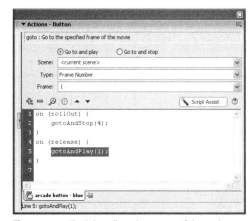

Figure 13.39 Flash handles placement of the scripts for multiple action statements. Here are two complete action statements starting with an event handler, followed by a set of braces enclosing the action that should take place when the triggering event occurs.

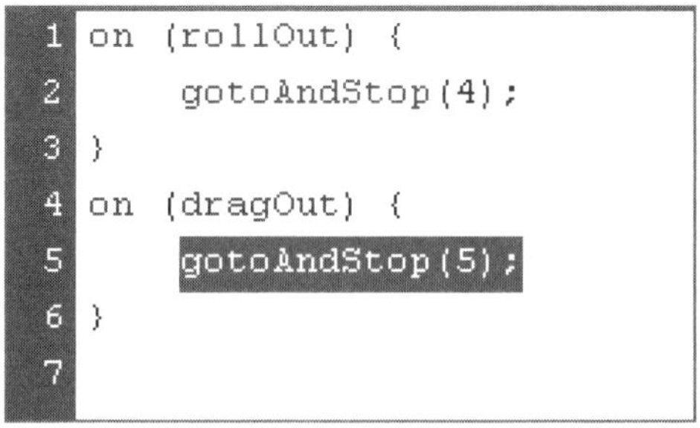

```
1  on (rollOut) {
2      gotoAndStop(4);
3  }
4  on (dragOut) {
5      gotoAndStop(5);
6  }
7
```

Figure 13.40 This script contains two different event handlers; the button will respond differently to different mouse movements. Contrast this script with the one you created earlier in **Figure 13.32** to carry out multiple actions. In that script, multiple action statements appear within one set of curly braces. In this script, multiple sets of curly braces appear, each containing one action.

11. Deselect the Release check box, and select the Drag Out check box.

Flash updates the Script pane to reflect the new event. Your script should look like **Figure 13.40**.

12. Choose Control > Test Movie.

Move the pointer so that it rolls into and then out of the button area without your pressing the mouse button; you jump to frame 4. Click the movie button, and then drag out of the button area without releasing the mouse button; you jump to frame 5. When you're done viewing the movie in test mode, close the Flash Player window.

13. Save your file for use in an upcoming task; name it MultiEventBtn.fla.

✔ Tips

- When you use the Behaviors panel to add to an existing behavior that uses the default event handler (see the sidebar "Working with Multiple Behaviors"), Flash adds the new action within the curly braces for the existing action statement; it doesn't matter what line of the script was selected initially in the Script pane. To use the Behaviors panel to add a separate action with a different triggering event, you must change the scripted behavior's triggering event before you add the new behavior (see "Changing Events," earlier in this chapter). When the script contains a behavior whose event isn't on (release), Flash adds a new behavior as a separate action statement.

- When the Behaviors panel contains multiple behaviors, you can control the order in which they're scripted by selecting one of the lines in the Behaviors panel. When you select a new behavior from the Add Behavior menu, Flash adds it to the list before the selected behavior.

USING MULTIPLE HANDLERS FOR ONE BUTTON

Editing Scripts

In previous tasks, you modified the parameters of an action as you used the Behaviors panel and Script Assist to create a script. You can use the same assistants to edit those scripts in the future.

To edit a behavior-based script using the Behaviors panel:

1. Open a document containing an object (or keyframe) with an attached behavior.

   For example, open a document containing a button with a behavior that sends the movie to a new frame.

2. Access the Behaviors and Actions panels.

3. Select the object (or keyframe) whose behavior you want to modify.

   The Behaviors panel displays the behavior assigned to the object (or keyframe); the script for this behavior appears in the Script pane of the Actions panel.

4. To change the triggering event, click it in the Event column of the Behaviors panel.

   A menu of events appears from which you can choose a new one (see "Changing Events," earlier in this chapter).

5. To change the parameters of a behavior, in the Action column of the Behaviors panel, double-click the action.

   The dialog containing the parameters for the behavior appears. You can change any of the parameters. In a Goto and Stop at frame or label behavior, for example, you can change the target movie clip, the pathname style, and/or the frame number (**Figure 13.41**).

6. Click OK.

   Flash updates the script.

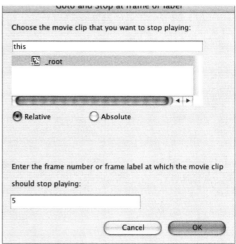

Figure 13.41 The goto action for the selected button symbol in this movie was created with a behavior (note the button icon at the top of the panel). To modify the behavior, double-click the action name in the Action column (top). The dialog containing parameters for that action appears (bottom). Changes you make to these parameters appear in the Script pane after you close the dialog.

Figure 13.42 The Script Assist window displays parameters for a selected line of script. Changing these parameters modifies the script. (Note that Script Assist gives you minimal direction. Script Assist gives you the Object field for entering the target path; Behaviors asks you to choose the movie clip. Where Script Assist displays a Parameters field; Behaviors describes what you must enter into the field (the frame number or label).

To edit a script using Script Assist:

1. Continuing with the document in the preceding task, access the Actions panel. The script for the selected button appears in the Script pane.

2. Activate Script Assist mode.

3. In the Script pane, click the line containing the goto action.

   Fields named Object and Parameters appear in the Script Assist window (**Figure 13.42**). These helpers are more cryptic than what you see in the parameters dialog for the behavior script in step 5 of the preceding task and more cryptic than what you'd see if you were creating a goto script from scratch using Script Assist. That's because the behavior uses a different technique to create the script than Script Assist does. When Script Assist works with that line of script, it assumes you must understand the ideas behind it.

   continues on next page

EDITING SCRIPTS

4. In the Script Assist window, enter new values for the parameters. For this example, *do the following:*

▲ In the Object field, enter the pathname of the target object. To get more assistance, select the text in the Object field and click the Insert Target Path button in the Script Assist toolbar; in the Insert Target Path dialog that appears, select the target object and a pathname style, and then click OK (**Figure 13.43**).

▲ In the Parameters field, enter a new frame number.

Flash updates the script. This kind of minor editing doesn't break the link to the Behaviors panel. If you double-click the Action column for this **goto** action, you'll see your new target object and frame number in the parameters dialog.

✔ Tips

■ If you used Script Assist originally to set up the same **goto** action for a button, clicking the **goto** line in the Script pane displays the same parameters you used in the original setup.

■ It's best to begin your edits using the same method you used to create the script initially. If you used the Behaviors panel, start there; if you used Script Assist, start there. You can use Script Assist to help you edit scripts created using behaviors, but doing so may break the link to the Behaviors panel. As you become more familiar with ActionScript scripting, you can also type directly in the Script Pane to edit scripts, but doing so may make it impossible to use Script Assist or behaviors on that script from then on. Flash displays a warning dialog and puts error messages in the Output panel if Script Assist is unable to work with your script.

Figure 13.43 When you use Script Assist to edit a script created by behaviors, you get less direction. To get help entering the target path for the scripted button, select the Object field, and then click the Insert Target Path button in the Script Assist toolbar (top). Flash opens the Insert Target Path dialog where you can choose your target visually (bottom).

EDITING SCRIPTS

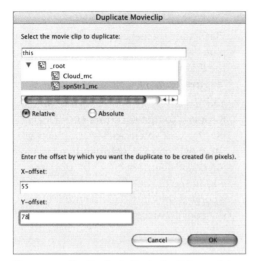

Figure 13.44 The Duplicate Movieclip dialog contains the parameters required for letting users make copies of movie clips by clicking a button symbol or movie clip. The offset values define the location of the duplicate.

Adding Actions to Movie Clips

With the right script attached, movie-clip symbols can act as if they're buttons. When you add the on (mouseEvent) handler to a movie clip, Flash creates a hit area for you from the graphic elements in the currently displayed frame of the movie clip. When a user positions the pointer over the scripted movie clip, Flash changes the pointer to the pointing hand cursor, indicating that this movie clip can respond to mouse movements. To get the most assistance with this type of script, use the Behaviors panel.

To add actions to make a movie clip duplicate itself:

1. Open a new Flash document, and open the Behaviors and Actions panels.

2. Place an instance of a movie-clip symbol on the Stage.

   Create a new movie-clip symbol (see Chapter 11) or bring one in from an existing document.

3. Select the movie-clip instance.

   The Actions panel name changes to Actions - Movie Clip. The Behaviors panel displays a movie-clip icon and the name of the selected movie clip.

4. In the Behaviors panel, from the Add Behavior menu (click the plus sign to access the menu), choose Movieclip > Duplicate Movieclip.

   The Duplicate Movieclip dialog appears. This dialog helps you to supply values for the required parameters of the duplicate MovieClip action (**Figure 13.44**).

continues on next page

5. In the dialog, *do the following:*

▲ In the target movie-clip pane, select the movie clip that you want to dupli-cate. Note that you can't duplicate the main movie, so don't select _root. Your movie-clip instance will appear indented beneath _root. If you haven't named the instances, the movie-clip name appears in parentheses.

▲ For the pathname style, select Relative.

▲ Enter values for X-offset and Y-offset. These tell Flash where to position the movie clip copy in relation to the original. To make the duplicate appear far away from its original, enter large values.

6. Click OK.

Flash adds the behavior to the Behaviors panel and adds comments and code to the Script pane of the Actions panel (**Figure 13.45**).

You're ready to try out the movie clip that responds to mouse movements. During playback, as you move the pointer over the movie clip, the pointing-hand cursor appears. When you click and release within the movie-clip area, Flash makes a copy of the clip. Click the original or the copy to make another duplicate.

— Target pathname

```
1
2  on (release) {
3
4      //Duplicate Movieclip Behavior
5      //Requires Flash Player 7 or later
6      var newdepth = this._parent.getNextHighestDepth();
7      var newname = "copy" + newdepth;
8      var prevname = "copy" + (newdepth-1);
9      if (this._parent[prevname] == undefined) this._parent[
   prevname] = this;
10     this.duplicateMovieClip(newname,newdepth);
11     this._parent[newname]._x = this._parent[prevname].x + 55          ——— Horizontal offset
12     this._parent[newname]._y = this._parent[prevname].y + 78          ——— Vertical offset
13     //End Behavior
14
15  }
```

Figure 13.45 The script for the Duplicate Movieclip behavior gives you some idea of the complexity of advanced ActionScripting. This script must account for naming each duplicate movie-clip instance and placing it on its own sublayer (or *level*) of the frame to ensure that all instances appear correctly and don't interfere with one another. Still, the basic parameters you set up in the dialog are there.

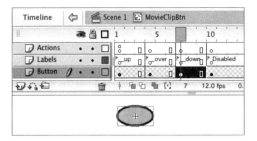

Figure 13.46 To pause the movie-clip button, edit the movie-clip master symbol to add a stop action to the first keyframe. The letter *a* (indicating the presence of an action) appears in the Timeline (top); the script should look like the figure at the bottom.

Adding Actions to Movie-Clip Buttons

In Chapter 12, you created a movie clip with four keyframes representing different button states. When you use ActionScript's default button-state names for the movie clip's frame labels, you can turn the movie clip into a responsive button element. You start by scripting the symbol to pause on its first frame, then add a mouse-event handler.

To pause the movie-clip button:

1. Open a new copy of the FrameActions-Template that you created earlier.

   Make sure the Properties tab of the Property inspector and the Actions panel (in Script Assist mode) are open.

2. In the Timeline, add a new layer beneath the Actions layer, name it mcButtons, and place an instance of a movie-clip button on the Stage.

   The movie clip should contain four labeled keyframes: _up, _over, _down, and Disabled. Open the library of the file MyOwnBtn.fla, which you created for the task "Creating Movie-Clip Buttons," in Chapter 12, and drag an instance of the movie-clip button symbol (MovieClipBtn) to the Stage; or create a new movie-clip symbol that contains those button states. For instructions for opening external library files, see Chapter 7.

3. Using the techniques you learned in "Adding Frame Actions," earlier in this chapter, edit the master button-style movie-clip symbol to add a stop action in keyframe 1.

   Your symbol and its script should look like **Figure 13.46**. For details about editing master symbols, see Chapter 7.

4. To return to the main Stage, choose Edit > Document.

To add the mouseEvent handler that displays the default button states:

1. Continuing with the file from the preceding task, select the instance of MovieClipBtn on the Stage.

   The Actions panel's title bar changes to Actions-Movie Clip.

2. In the Properties tab of the Property inspector, in the Instance Name field, enter a name, for example, MyBtn1_mc.

3. From the Actions panel's Add menu choose Global Functions > Movie Clip Control > on (**Figure 13.47**).

   Flash adds on (release) to the Script pane (**Figure 13.48**). This handler, in combination with the default button-state frame labels that you created for this symbol, allows the symbol to respond to a user's mouse movements the same way a standard Flash button symbol does.

   To make the movie-clip button carry out a task, you must attach actions to it, just as you did for the button. A good all-purpose action for testing is trace.

4. With the button instance selected on the Stage, select line 1 in the Script pane, the event handler on (release).

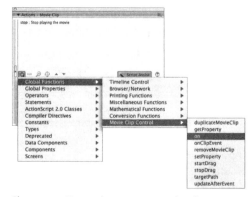

Figure 13.47 To attach a mouse-event handler to an instance of a movie-clip symbol, select the instance on the Stage; from the Actions panel's Add menu, choose Global Functions > Movie Clip Control > on.

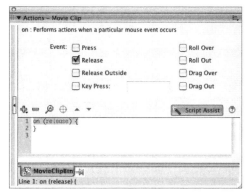

Figure 13.48 When you attach the on () handler to a movie-clip instance that has frame labels _up, _over, and _down, Flash uses those labels to make the movie-clip act like a button. To choose the triggering event(s) in Script Assist mode, select or deselect the Event check boxes. Select Release to make the movie-clip button carry out its action when the user clicks and releases the pointer inside the movie clip's graphic area.

5. From the Actions panel's Add menu, choose Global Functions > Miscellaneous Functions > `trace`.

The Message field and Expression check box appear in the Script Assist window.

6. With the Expression check box deselected, enter text in the Message field to remind you what the script just did.

Deselecting Expression tells Flash to treat the text you enter as text, not a mathematical formula or number. Flash enters the message label text into the script surrounded by quote marks (**Figure 13.49**).

continues on next page

Triggering event

Action to carry out

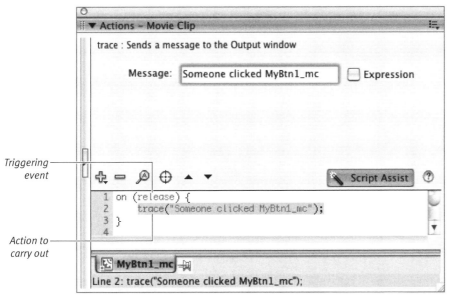

Figure 13.49 Flash carries out the action(s) that appear between the curly braces when the triggering event takes place. The `trace` action can stand in for as yet unspecified actions to speed testing as you develop movie-clip buttons.

ADDING ACTIONS TO MOVIE-CLIP BUTTONS

7. Choose Control > Test Movie to try out the first phase of your button-style movie clip.

In the Flash Player window, position the pointer over various areas of the Stage. Upon moving into the image area of the movie clip, the pointer changes from an arrow to a pointing hand, and the graphic for the _over state appears (**Figure 13.50**). When you click the button, the _down state appears; when you release, Flash opens the Output panel and types in your trace message (**Figure 13.51**). Flash automatically makes the graphics in the movie-clip symbol define the hit area of the button.

8. Save this file for use in the following task: name it ScriptAClipBtn.fla.

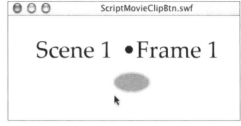

Figure 13.50 During playback, when the pointer is outside the graphic area of the movie-clip button that has an on () handler (top), Flash displays the symbol's _up frame and the pointer is an arrow. Upon entering the graphic area of the movie clip (bottom), the pointer changes to a pointing hand, and Flash displays the symbol's _over frame.

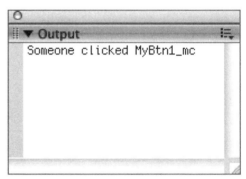

Figure 13.51 Each time you click the movie-clip button, Flash enters the trace message in the Output panel. If the panel is closed or hidden behind other windows, Flash opens it or brings it forward.

✔ Tip

■ The preceding task creates a movie-clip button that acts like a button symbol. You can also create movie-clip buttons that respond to mouse movements in a different way—perhaps showing one graphic when the user rolls the pointer over the movie-clip button and another when the user clicks the movie clip button, then drags and releases the mouse button outside the graphic area of the movie clip. When you use your own labels, however, you must do more scripting. To create a non-standard movie-clip button, label the frames for the different button states something other than the default names. The frame labels can be similar though, for example, MyUp, MyOver, and MyDown. Add keyframes and labels for the additional states you want to show, for example, RollOut or DragOut. Instead of attaching a single event handler to the symbol, you must attach multiple handlers that tell Flash which frame to show for each possible interaction. For example, attach on (release) with a goto action that displays the MyUp frame; attach on (rollOver) with a goto action that displays the MyOver frame, attach on (dragOut) with a goto action that displays the graphic for dragging outside the button area, and so on.

Making Frame Actions Control Objects

If you decide to do a lot of interactivity, you'll need to learn more about ActionScript. Ideally, you'll want to place less code directly on objects and put most of your code in frames. Using frame actions to control objects is a sophisticated technique that goes beyond the scope of this book. To give you a peek at the power of this type of scripting, the following tasks walk you through creating a simple frame action that controls a movie-clip instance. You'll use a mix of assisted and unassisted scripting methods.

In the preceding section, you scripted your movie-clip button to use the standard button states (showing the _up, _over, and _down frames) but made no use of its Disabled frame. You may want the disabled state to appear only in certain frames of your movie, not in response to a user's interaction. A Back button that takes users to the previous page may be disabled in frame 1, for example. You can use frame actions to disable (or enable) a movie-clip button.

To add frame actions to disable a movie-clip button using Script Assist:

1. Open the file you created in the preceding task, ScriptAClipBtn.fla.

   This is a document containing four 5-frame layers: Actions, mcButtons, Scene, and Frames. There is a **stop** action in keyframe 1 of the Actions layer.

   The Properties tab of the Property inspector and Actions panel (in Script Assist mode) should be open on your desktop. ActionScript preferences should be set to display code hints (see "Customizing the Actions Panel," earlier in this chapter).

Instance Name field

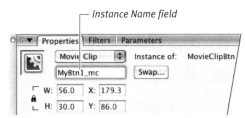

Figure 13.52 Give the movie-clip instance a name that can be used in the script. Enter the name in the Instance Name field in the Properties tab of the Property inspector.

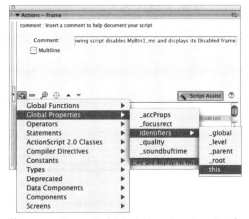

Figure 13.53 To use Script Assist to enter a target path for a movie-clip symbol instance, start by choosing the identifier this. Script Assist displays an Expression field where you can enter the pathname.

2. Select the movie-clip instance on the Stage.

The instance should already have the instance name MyBtn1_mc. If not, in the Properties tab of the Property inspector, enter the name in the Instance Name field, (**Figure 13.52**).

3. In the main Timeline, select keyframe 1 in the Actions layer.

The Actions panel title changes to Actions-Frame.

4. Click line 2 in the Script pane of the Actions panel,

Flash selects the code for the stop() action that you created earlier.

5. Add a comment to the Script to remind you what the script you're about to add does (see "To begin scripting by adding comments" in the section "Adding Frane Actions," earlier in this chapter).

For example, add The following script disables MyBtn1_mc and displays the Disabled frame.

6. Click the comment to select it in the Script pane.

7. From the Actions panel's Add menu choose Global Properties > Identifiers > this (**Figure 13.53**).

The Expression field appears in the Script Assist window. Use this field to enter code for the target symbol and its properties.

8. Select the contents of the Expressions field (the word *this*).

9. In the toolbar above the Script pane, click the Insert Target Path tool (the target-sight icon).

continues on next page

10. In the Insert Target Path dialog that appears, select the movie-clip instance that you want to control (MyBtn1_mc), choose the Relative radio button (for pathname style), and click OK.

Flash enters this.MyBtn1_mc in the Expressions field (**Figure 13.54**).

11. Click at the end of the text in the Expression field to position the insertion point and type a period character (.). With code hints active, the code hint menu appears.

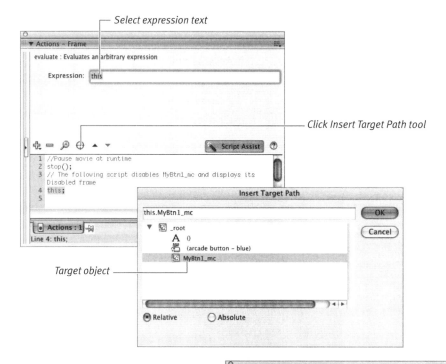

— *Select expression text*

— *Click Insert Target Path tool*

Target object ——

MAKING FRAME ACTIONS CONTROL OBJECTS

Figure 13.54 To enter the pathname for your movie-clip button, select the contents of the Expression field (top), click the Insert Target Path tool and choose your symbol in the dialog that appears (middle). Flash enters the path name for your movie-clip symbol into the script (bottom). Script Assist adds the semicolon that defines the end of an action statement; you don't need to add it in the Expressions field.

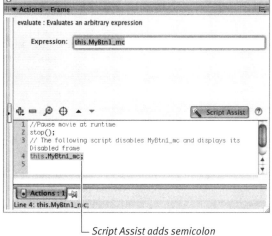

— *Script Assist adds semicolon*

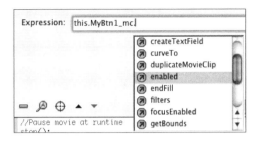

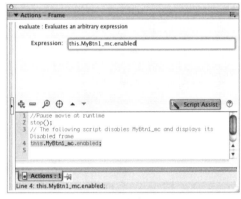

Figure 13.55 Items in the code-hint menu appear alphabetically (top). Select the property enabled and press Enter to add it to the Expression field and the script (bottom).

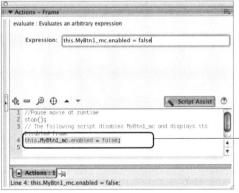

Figure 13.56 A script that sets the enabled property of the movie-clip button to false disables that movie-clip button.

12. Scroll the menu to find enabled, click it to select it, then press Enter.

Flash adds enabled to the Expression field and to the script in the Script pane. Items in the code-hint menu appear alphabetically, with underscore sorting before letters (**Figure 13.55**).

13. With the insertion point at the end of the text in the Expressions field, type a space character followed by the equals sign (=), then another space character, then the word false.

Flash updates the code in the script pane (**Figure 13.56**).

This code tells Flash not to carry out any script attached to the movie-clip button instance MyBtn1_mc. When you publish the movie, the button acts like a static graphic even though it has an event handler that would normally make it show its button states. You can test the movie at this point and see that the movie-clip button no longer responds when you roll over it or click it.

continues on next page

Object being controlled   Property   Value

14. Select line 4 in the script pane, the code that disables the button.

15. From the Add menu, choose ActionScript 2.0 Classes > Movie > MovieClip > Methods > gotoAndStop.

The fields Object and Frame appear in the Script Assist window.

16. Click the Object field, to activate it, and click the Insert Target Path tool.

17. In the Insert Target Path dialog that appears, select the movie clip that you want to control (MyBtn1_mc), choose the Relative radio button, and click OK.

Flash updates the Object field and the script pane.

18. Click the Frame field in the Script Assist window; type the frame label that you want to display, Disabled; then deselect the Expression check box.

Flash enters the frame label text, surrounded by quote marks, into the script (**Figure 13.57**).

19. Choose Control > Test Movie to try out your button.

Frame actions take place when the playhead enters the frame, not in response to mouse movements by the user. The Disabled frame (the grayed out version of the button) appears when playback starts; when you roll over the button or click it, nothing happens (**Figure 13.58**). In effect, the button is turned off in frame 1.

In a real-world application, this would be only a first step. You would script other frame actions to test what frame the user is in as they interact with MyBtn1_mc, turning it on again when appropriate. The following task shows one way to turn on the movie-clip button and make it responsive when the playhead enters frame 2.

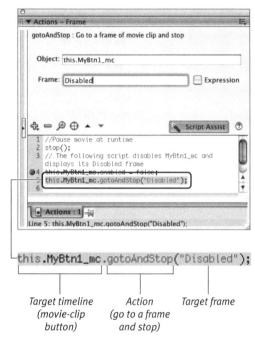

Target timeline | Action | Target frame
(movie-clip | (go to a frame |
button) | and stop) |

Figure 13.57 When you add the gotoAndStop action, the Object and Frame fields appear in the Script Assist window. Use the Insert Target Path tool to fill in the Object field. In the Frame field, type the name of the frame you want the button to display.

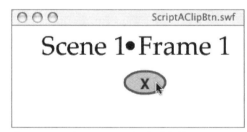

Figure 13.58 When you test the disabled button, it displays the graphic for the Disabled frame; the pointer doesn't change as you move it over the graphic.

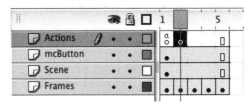

Figure 13.59 To enable the button in frame 2 of the main Timeline, add a keyframe to the Actions layer, then add an enabling script to that keyframe.

Figure 13.60 Add a comment describing your script. With word wrap active, Flash wraps your comment text to fit in the Script pane. When you finish typing the comment, press Enter to start the next numbered line of your script.

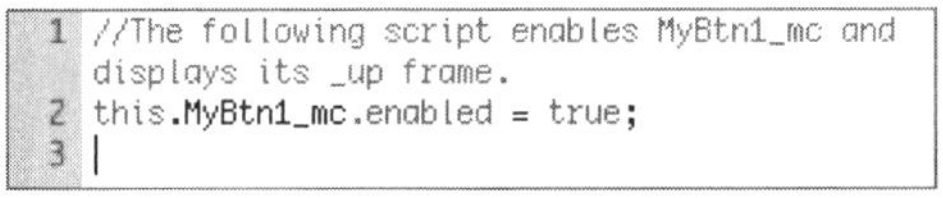

```
1  //The following script enables MyBtn1_mc and
   displays its _up frame.
2  this.MyBtn1_mc.enabled = true;
3  |
```

Figure 13.61 Setting the enabled property of the movie-clip instance to true makes the movie-clip button active again.

To add frame actions directly in the Script pane:

1. Continuing with the file from the preceding task, in the main Timeline, select frame 2 in the Actions layer.

2. Choose Insert > Timeline > Keyframe. Flash inserts keyframe 2 and selects it (**Figure 13.59**).

3. In the Actions panel, click the Script Assist button to turn off Script Assist mode. The insertion point appears in the Script pane, but the Script pane may not have focus.

4. Click line 1 in the Script pane to prepare to enter code.

5. To add a comment, type two slashes (//) followed by text that reminds you what the script does, for example, The following script enables MyBtn1_mc and displays its _up frame.

6. To begin the next line of script, press Enter. The insertion point moves to line 2 in the Script pane (**Figure 13.60**).

7. To enable the movie-clip button, click the Insert Target Path tool and in the Insert Target Path dialog that appears, select the instance MyBtn1_mc, select the Relative radio button, and click OK. Flash adds the target object to the script.

8. Type a period character (.); from the code-hint pop-up menu that appears, choose enabled; and press Enter.

9. Type a space character, an equal sign (=), a space character, the word true followed by a semicolon (;), and press Enter to start a new line.

   Your script should look like **Figure 13.61**. You must add a goto action to display the movie clip's _up frame again.

continues on next page

MAKING FRAME ACTIONS CONTROL OBJECTS

10. From the Actions panel's Add menu, choose ActionScript 2.0 classes > Movie > MovieClip > Methods > `gotoAndStop`.

Flash enters a line of code beginning with the text `not_set_yet` in red and ending in parentheses. The insertion point appears between the parentheses, ready for you to enter the correct parameter (**Figure 13.62**). With code hints active, a hint pops up reminding you to enter the frame number or label.

11. Type "`_up`" between the parentheses, and type a semicolon (;) following the closing parenthesis.

The red text (`not_set_yet`) indicates another parameter that you must define; here it's the object's target path.

12. To enter the path, select the red text (don't select the dot that follows it) (**Figure 13.63**).

When Script Assist is inactive, the Script pane works like any text editor; drag to select text, or click and Shift-click to make a selection.

13. Click the Insert Target Path tool.

In Script Assist mode, this tool is available only when you've selected a text field in the Script Assist window. When Script Assist is inactive, the tool is always available.

Figure 13.62 With Script Assist turned off, when you choose actions from the Add menu (or double-click them in the Actions Toolbox), Flash adds the script directly to the Script pane of the Actions panel. With code hints active, a hint appears reminding you about certain parameters that you must provide.

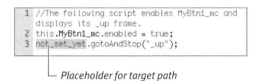

— *Placeholder for target path*

Figure 13.63 Select the red text (`not_set_yet`) and replace it with the pathname of the movie-clip instance. You can use the Insert Target Path tool to enter the pathname or type it in manually.

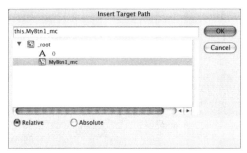

Figure 13.64 Click the Insert Target Path tool, select your movie-clip instance in the dialog, and click OK.

```
1  //The following script enables MyBtn1_mc and
   displays its _up frame.
2  this.MyBtn1_mc.enabled = true;
3  this.MyBtn1_mc.gotoAndStop("_up");
```

Figure 13.65 Flash replaces the selected placeholder text with the correct path to the movie clip instance; this script tells Flash to display the _up frame of the movie-clip instance as soon as the playhead enters frame 2 of the main Timeline.

14. In the Insert Target Path dialog that appears, select the movie clip instance MyBtn1_mc, select the Relative radio button (for pathname style), and click OK.

Flash replaces the red text you selected with the target path (**Figure 13.64**).

Line 3 of the script is complete (**Figure 13.65**); it tells Flash that when the playhead enters this frame (frame 2), Flash should display the _up frame of MyBtn1_mc.

15. To get the movie to move to frame 2 at run time, add a new button to frame 1; script it to jump to frame 2 and stop playback when the user clicks it (to review one technique, see "Adding Actions to Buttons," earlier in this chapter).

16. Save the file, and choose Control > Test Movie to try your script.

As the movie starts, the movie-clip button displays its Disabled frame. Click the second button to move to frame 2 of the main Timeline. The first line of code in the script for frame 2 tells Flash to enable the movie-clip button; the second line of code says to show the movie-clip button's _up frame. Click the button and it carries out the trace script you attached to it.

✔ Tip

■ If you don't have the ActionScript category of Preferences set to show code hints, you can still view them. When the insertion point is right after a period or between parentheses in the Script pane, click the Show Code Hint button in the toolbar to see a hint. The Show Code Hint button is available only when Script Assist is inactive.

Using Buttons to Control Movie Clips

Most Flash creations employ a mixture of interface objects: button symbols, button components, and movie clips. More advanced ActionScripters can add script to control other types of objects. Flash's assisted scripting modes aren't quite as open ended, but you can use them to create scripts that control the playback of movie clips. You can script a button to start and stop a movie clip, or script a button component to jump to a specific frame in a movie clip. The key is to specify the correct target path. As you saw in "Adding Actions to Buttons," earlier in this chapter, Script Assist can handle target paths for buttons but not for movie-clip symbols or components. For the following task, use the Behaviors panel.

To make a button symbol stop movie-clip playback:

1. Open a new Flash document, and access the Actions and Behaviors panels.

2. Place one instance of a button symbol, a button component, and an animated movie-clip symbol (for example, one containing a simple motion tween of a spinning star) on the Stage.

3. Select the button-symbol instance.

4. From the Add menu in the Behaviors panel, select Movieclip > `Goto and Stop at frame or label`.
   The Goto and Stop dialog appears.

5. In the target movie-clip pane, select the movie clip instance.
   For one object to control another, the object that is being controlled must have an instance name. Because you didn't name the movie-clip instance name in step 2, a warning dialog appears (**Figure 13.66**).

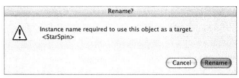

Figure 13.66 When you want to set up a button that controls playback of a movie clip, the target movie clip must have an instance name. Flash warns you if you select an instance that lacks an instance name. Click the Rename button to give the instance a name.

Tips for Naming Instances

A movie clip's instance name may wind up being part of the pathname in a script. Therefore, you must be careful how you name the instances of buttons and movie clips. Use letters and numbers; feel free to use the underscore character or capitalization to act as word dividers. Don't use spaces or other punctuation marks, because these may have special meanings in ActionScript and create errors in scripting.

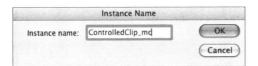

Figure 13.67 The Instance Name dialog allows you to name an instance while you're setting parameters in the Goto dialog. Otherwise, you would have to return to the Stage, select the instance, and enter a name for it in the Properties tab of the Property inspector.

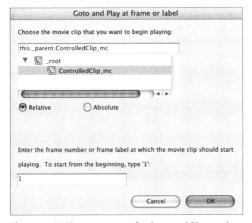

Figure 13.68 The parameters for Goto and Play are just like those for Goto and Stop. When you opt to control a movie clip with a button, the target frame is the frame in the movie clip that you want to jump to. To start the movie clip at the beginning, choose frame 1.

6. In the Rename dialog, click the Rename button.

The Instance Name dialog appears.

7. Enter an instance name for your movie clip—for example, ControlledClip_mc (**Figure 13.67**).

8. Click OK.

Flash returns you to the Goto and Stop dialog. Leave the other parameters at their default settings: Relative pathname, with frame 1 as the target frame on which to stop playback.

9. In the Goto and Stop dialog, click OK.

10. On the Stage, select the button-component instance.

11. From the Add menu in the Behaviors panel, select Movieclip > Goto and Play at frame or label.

Flash opens the Goto and Play dialog. (Because you already named the movie-clip instance, the Rename warning dialog doesn't appear.)

12. In the Goto and Play dialog, *set the following parameters.*

▲ Select ControlledClip_mc as the target movie clip.

▲ Select Relative as the pathname style.

▲ Type 1 in the target-frame field (**Figure 13.68**).

13. Click OK.

You're ready to test your buttons in Flash Player. When you click the button symbol, the animated movie clip goes back to its first frame and stops playing. Click the button component, and the movie clip resumes playing.

Linking to Other Web Pages

Flash gives you two ways to open new files by linking to URLs. You can select text on the Stage and turn it into a live link by entering a URL in the link field of the Text (Tool) Property inspector. You can also use ActionScript to instruct Flash Player to open a URL. Both techniques let you open the new file in a different browser window or different frame of the current window.

To script a button that opens a Web page:

1. In a Flash document, select or create a button instance.

2. Access the Actions panel, and choose Script Assist mode.

3. From the Add menu, choose Global Functions > Browser/Network > getURL (**Figure 13.69**).

   The parameters for getURL appear in the Script Assist window.

4. Enter the desired URL in the URL field.

5. From the Window pop-up menu (**Figure 13.70**), *choose one of the following:*

   _self opens the specified URL in same frame of the browser window as the content being currently viewed.

   _blank opens the specified URL in a new browser window.

   _parent opens the specified URL in the parent of the current frame.

   _top opens the specified URL in the top-level frame of the current browser window.

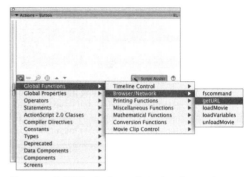

Figure 13.69 With a button selected on Stage, choose Global Functions > Browser/Network > getURL from the Actions panel's Add menu to script the button to open a new URL in the browser window.

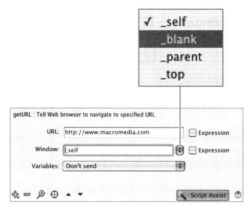

Figure 13.70 With Script Assist active, you can enter the URL and choose what window or frame the new URL opens in.

```
1  on (release) {
2      getURL("http://www.macromedia.com", "_blank");
3  }
4
```

Figure 13.71 Script Assist creates a script that opens the new URL when the end user interacts with the button.

6. Leave the Variables setting as Don't Send.

Flash adds the button's default handler on (release) and the getURL function to the script in the Script pane of the Actions panel (**Figure 13.71**). The send variables setting is of concern to more advanced ActionScripters who are setting up their own variables.

7. Choose Control > Test Movie or Control > Test Scene to try out your button.

When you're testing Flash content on your local system and asking to load a URL that is on the network, you can run into security issues. For testing purposes, you may need to change the security settings in the Flash section of the Publish Settings dialog or give special permissions to the file you're testing via Macromedia's Security Settings Manager (see Chapter 16).

To create a text link to a URL:

1. On the Stage, select the text that you want to be a link.

You can select individual letters or words using the text tool or select an entire text box using the selection tool.

2. Access the Property inspector, and enter the desired URL in the URL Link field (to the right of the chain-link icon).

3. From the Target pop-up menu, choose the method you want Flash Player to use when opening the URL.

The choices are the same as in step 5 of the preceding task. Flash creates the script for opening the new Web page in the manner you chose.

4. Choose Control > Test Movie or Control > Test Scene to try out your live link text.

The Mystery of URLs

The acronym URL stands for Uniform Resource Locator, which is a standardized way of handling the addresses of files so that they can be found on the Internet. The conventions of the URL make it possible to decipher the hierarchical structure of the *server* (or local computer) on which a file is stored, allowing you to maneuver through all the directories, folders, and subfolders to the specific file that you want.

URLs have two forms: absolute and relative.

An *absolute URL* is a complete address that specifies the protocol your browser should use to open the file (HTTP, or Hypertext Transfer Protocol, is one used to transfer the text and graphics of Web sites), the name of the server on which the file resides, the path name (the nested hierarchy of directories, volumes, folders, and so on), and the name of the file itself.

A relative URL is a shorthand version of the full address that lets you describe one file's location in relation to another. In essence, you tell Flash to move up and down the hierarchy of nested files, folders, and directories, starting from the file where you give Flash the `getURL` instruction. It's like saying, "Look in the folder you're in right now for a file called Fabulous.fla" or "Look in the folder you're in right now for a folder called OtherJunk, and then look inside that folder for the file Fabulous.fla," or "Go up one level to the folder that contains the folder containing the file you're in right now. In that higher-level folder, look for a folder called ThisJunk. Look in ThisJunk for a file called Abysmal.fla."

Using relative URLs in a script or link has the advantage of allowing you to test your movies on your computer without opening an Internet connection. Additionally, provided that you keep your files in the same relative positions in the hierarchy, you don't need to rename the files when you transfer them from your local computer to the server where you'll make them available to your viewers.

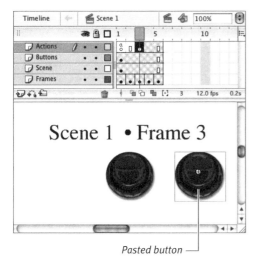

Pasted button

Script for the pasted button

Figure 13.72 When you copy and paste a button that has an attached script, the script is attached to the pasted copy.

Using the Script Navigator

The Script Navigator is a separate pane of the Actions panel that shows all the items in your document that have scripts attached. This tool is important when you're adding scripts to objects as well as frames. Clicking an item in the Script Navigator list selects that item in the document and, unless you've pinned a script, shows that item's script in the Script pane. To try it, create a document with various scripted items.

To select and view scripts via the Script Navigator:

1. Open the document named MultiEventBtn.fla, which you created in "Using Multiple Handlers for One Button," earlier in this chapter.

2. On the Stage, select and copy the button that responds differently to different mouse events. You can close the document now if you wish.

   When you copy a button instance that has script attached, you also copy that script.

3. Open the document named KeyPressBtn.fla, which you created and saved in the task "Triggering Actions from the Keyboard," earlier in this chapter.

4. In the Timeline, in the Buttons layer, select frame 3 and insert a blank keyframe (press F7).

5. Paste the button you copied in step 2 (**Figure 13.72**).

continues on next page

6. Access the Scenes panel, and click the Duplicate Scene button.

   If the panel isn't open, choose Window > Other Panels > Scene.

7. Access the Actions panel.

   If the panel isn't open, choose Window > Actions.

8. Resize the horizontal and vertical dividers of the Actions panel as needed to view the Script Navigator pane in the lower-left corner of the panel.

   For this task, you can close the Actions toolbox (see "Touring the Actions Panel," earlier in this chapter). The Script Navigator displays a list of items divided by category: Current Selection, Scene, Symbol Definition(s). These items are the frames and objects in this document that have scripts attached (**Figure 13.73**).

9. In the Script Navigator, under Scene 1, select the first item: Actions: Frame 1.

   Flash selects frame 1 of the Actions layer and displays the associated script in the Script pane of the Actions panel. In this case, the script is a single line with the action stop(); (**Figure 13.74**).

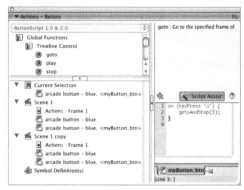

Figure 13.73 The Script Navigator pane of the Actions panel displays a hierarchical listing of all the elements in the current movie that have scripts attached.

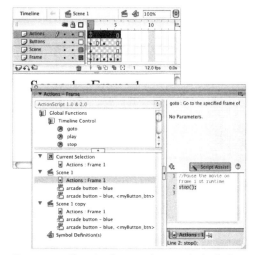

Figure 13.74 Choosing frame 1 of scene 1 in the Script Navigator selects that frame in the Timeline and displays the script for that frame in the Script pane of the Actions Panel.

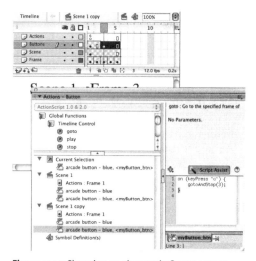

Figure 13.75 Choosing an element in Scene 1 copy causes Flash to move the playhead to that scene and select the frame that contains that element.

10. In the Script Navigator, under Scene 1, select the second item.

Flash displays that scene in the Timeline, moves the playhead to frame 1, selects the button instance on the Stage, and displays the associated script in the Script pane of the Actions panel.

11. In the Script Navigator, under Scene 1 copy, select the third item.

Flash displays that scene in the Timeline, moves the playhead to frame 3, and selects the button. The button script appears in the Script pane (**Figure 13.75**). Continue checking out the scripts in this document by choosing items in the Script Navigator. In more complex documents with more elements and scripts, you may need to expand or collapse sections of the Navigator to find the precise script you want. To do so, click the plus (or minus) signs (Windows) or triangles (Mac) to the left of the items in the list.

✔ Tips

- Double-clicking an item in the Script Navigator pins it in the Script pane. For more details about pinning scripts, see the sidebar "The Mystery of Pinned Scripts."

- If you'd like to examine a file with more complicated ActionScript, open a copy of one of the Quiz templates that come with Flash. These documents contain a number of scripted elements.

The Mystery of Pinned Scripts

To prevent Flash from displaying a different script as you select items on the stage, you can *pin* a script. Pinning forces Flash to continue displaying the same script even if you select a different frame in the Timeline or object on the Stage. Pinning allows you to examine a variety of elements and situations without losing your place in the script you're creating. To pin the script currently displayed in the Script pane, click the pushpin icon below the pane; the icon changes to a more upright version of a pushpin. You can pin multiple scripts. To display a new script to pin, select an item in the Script Navigator. Double-clicking the item pins its script. Flash adds tabs for pinned scripts to the area below the Script pane.

The item currently selected on the Stage or in the Timeline always appears in the leftmost tab below the Script pane. The tab for a pinned script currently on display is highlighted (in Windows, it's white; on the Mac, it's blue); tabs for other pinned scripts are gray. Click a gray tab to select that script. To unpin a script, display that script, and then click the upright-pushpin icon (**Figure 13.76**).

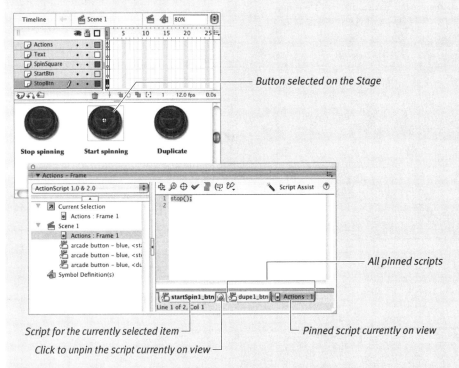

Button selected on the Stage

All pinned scripts

Script for the currently selected item

Click to unpin the script currently on view

Pinned script currently on view

Figure 13.76 The leftmost tab beneath the Script pane displays the name of the item currently selected in the document; the highlighted tab (blue on Macs, white in Windows) displays the name of the pinned script currently visible in the Script pane; the gray tabs indicate other pinned scripts. To select another pinned script, click its tab.

USING NON-FLASH GRAPHICS

14

With the addition of Object Drawing mode in version 8, Flash's set of drawing tools has new flexibility for graphic artists who are familiar with the vector-based tools in other graphics programs. Still, you don't have to abandon all other sources of graphic material. You may already be using another vector graphics program—Macromedia FreeHand or Adobe Illustrator, for example—and you may feel more comfortable with its tools or want to take advantage of advanced features it offers. You may want to include scanned photos or other bitmaps in your Flash document, or use a body of artwork that you created outside Flash. Don't despair; you can import those graphics into Flash.

Importing Non-Flash Graphics

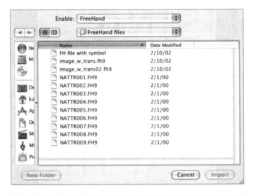

Flash imports vector art and bitmapped graphics either through the Clipboard or via the Import command. When you import graphics from FreeHand versions 7 through 10, and MX, you can also drag and drop elements directly between files.

If you use a program other than Flash to create a series of images that will be keyframes in a movie (a set of FreeHand files, for example), Flash can expedite the import process if the filenames end in a series of sequential numbers. (To learn more about keyframe animation, see Chapter 9.)

To import a FreeHand file to the Stage:

1. Open a Flash document.

2. Choose File > Import > Import to Stage. The Import dialog appears (**Figure 14.1**).

3. From the Enable (Mac) or Files of Type (Windows) menu, choose the format of the file you want to import: FreeHand.

4. Navigate to the file on your system.

5. Select the file.

Figure 14.1 Bring graphics created in other applications into your Flash document through the Import dialog: Mac (top), Windows (bottom).

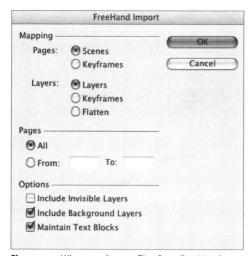

Figure 14.2 When you import files from FreeHand versions 7 through MX, you have control over how the elements appear in the Flash document.

The Flash/FreeHand Partnership

Although not all features of other vector programs translate directly into Flash, there are strong ties between Flash and Macromedia FreeHand versions 7 through MX. You can import the full FreeHand file, you can copy selected FreeHand content via the Clipboard then paste it on the Stage in Flash, and you can drag content from an open FreeHand file directly onto the Stage in Flash.

When you choose File > Import > Import to Stage, the FreeHand Import dialog appears, giving you a chance to control the way that content appears in the Flash document. In addition, if you're importing FreeHand 9, 10, or MX files that contain symbols, Flash automatically adds those symbols to the Flash document's library.

6. Click Import (Mac) or Open (Windows).

The Importing External File dialog appears, with a Stop button for canceling the operation. Then, the FreeHand Import dialog appears (**Figure 14.2**).

7. In the Mapping section, to convert the FreeHand file's pages and layers to Flash format, *do any of the following:*

▲ To create a new scene from each FreeHand page, in the Pages subsection, choose Scenes.

▲ To create a new keyframe from each FreeHand page, in the Pages subsection, choose Keyframes.

▲ To create a new layer from each FreeHand layer, in the Layers subsection, choose Layers.

▲ To create a new keyframe from each FreeHand layer, in the Layers subsection, choose Keyframes.

▲ To combine multiple FreeHand layers into one layer, in the Layers subsection, choose Flatten.

8. In the Pages section, to select the pages to import, *do either of the following:*

▲ To import the entire FreeHand file, choose All.

▲ To import a range of pages from the FreeHand file, choose From/To and then enter the first and last page number.

continues on next page

9. In the Options section, *do any of the following:*

▲ To import any hidden layers from the FreeHand file, choose Include Invisible Layers.

▲ To import the background layer of the FreeHand file, choose Include Background Layers.

▲ To have Flash create editable text blocks from any FreeHand text blocks, choose Maintain Text Blocks. Otherwise, Flash imports the text characters as grouped shapes.

10. Click OK.

The Importing External File dialog appears, with a Stop button for canceling the operation. Flash imports the FreeHand graphics and places them on the Stage creating layers and/or keyframes in the main Timeline of your document according to the import options you selected (**Figure 14.3**). Flash opens the Output panel and adds notes to it about how many objects it just imported or created from the import (**Figure 14.4**).

✔ Tips

■ In previous versions of Flash, if you imported a FreeHand file containing overlapping shapes on a single layer, those shapes segmented one another in Flash. Flash 8 imports the FreeHand shapes as drawing-objects; there's no problem with inadvertent segmenting.

■ If you import a FreeHand file containing objects that have transparent lens fills, Flash sets the imported objects' transparency to re-create the transparent effect.

Imported layers

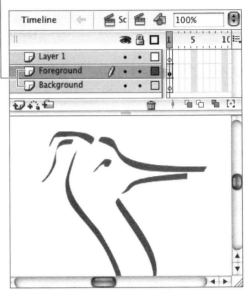

Figure 14.3 Flash imports FreeHand files according to the settings in the FreeHand Import dialog. Here, the import options were set to include the background layer.

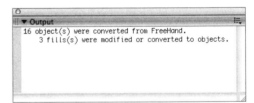

Figure 14.4 When you import FreeHand files, Flash gives you information about how many FreeHand objects the file contained and how many objects Flash had to create in the import process. Flash adds the information for each FreeHand file import to the Flash Output panel.

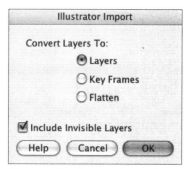

Figure 14.5 The Illustrator Import dialog offers options for dealing with the layers of an original AI file created in Illustrator 8 or earlier.

To import Adobe Illustrator (.AI, version 8 or earlier) files to the Stage:

1. With your Flash document open, choose File > Import > Import to Stage.

   The Import dialog appears.

2. From the Enable (Mac) or Files of Type (Windows) menu, choose Adobe Illustrator.

   This setting displays files with the extensions .ai and .eps.

3. Navigate to the file, select it, and Click Import (Mac) or Open (Windows).

   The Illustrator Import dialog appears (**Figure 14.5**).

4. In the Convert Layers To section, *do one of the following:*

   ▲ To re-create the layers in the original file, choose Layers.

   ▲ To convert the layers to keyframes, choose Key Frames.

   ▲ To place all the graphics on one layer, choose Flatten.

5. To import any invisible layers, select the Include Invisible Layers check box.

6. Click OK.

To import Adobe Illustrator (AI, version 9 or later), Portable Document Format (PDF) or Encapsulated PostScript (EPS) files to the Stage:

1. Follow steps 1–3 in the preceding exercise.

   The Import Options dialog appears (**Figure 14.6**). Note that to view PDF files, you should select All PostScript in step 3.

2. In the Convert Pages To section, *do either of the following:*

   ▲ To make each page a new scene, choose Scenes.

   ▲ To make each page a new keyframe, choose Keyframes.

3. In the Convert Layers To section, *do one of the following:*

   ▲ To re-create the layers in the original file, choose Layers.

   ▲ To convert the layers to keyframes, choose Keyframes.

   ▲ To place all the graphics on one layer, choose Flatten.

4. In the Which Pages to Import section, *do either of the following:*

   ▲ To import all pages, choose All.

   ▲ To import a selected page range, choose From/To, and enter the first and last page number.

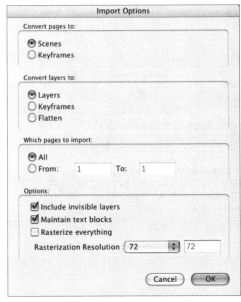

Figure 14.6 When you import an AI (created in Illustrator 9 or later), EPS or PDF file, you have more control over the import than with earlier AI files, choosing how to handle pages, layers, invisible layers, and text blocks. You can also rasterize the imported text and graphic elements and set the resolution of the resulting images.

5. In the Options section, *do the following:*

▲ To import any invisible layers, choose Include Invisible Layers.

▲ To import text into editable, static text boxes, choose Maintain Text Blocks.

▲ To convert all graphic and text elements into a bitmap, choose Rasterize Everything and enter the Rasterization Resolution, either by selecting a value from the pop-up menu or by typing the value into the field.

6. Click OK.

✔ Tip

■ You can have Flash import a file directly to the library instead of placing the graphic elements on the Stage. Choose File > Import > Import to Library. The import options for each file type are the same whether you import to the Stage or to the library. When you import a vector graphic to the library, Flash places the vector elements within a symbol. Any layers and keyframes that you request in the Import Options dialog appear in the symbol's Timeline.

What Graphics Formats Does Flash Import?

Flash imports a variety of bitmapped and vector-graphic file formats. For bitmaps, Flash accepts files in GIF, and animated GIF, PNG, JPEG, and BMP (Windows) formats. For vector graphics, Flash accepts files from FreeHand versions 7 through MX, Illustrator version 10.0 and earlier; EPS and PDF files in version 1.4 or earlier (Adobe Acrobat 5.0 for example, creates version 1.4 PDF files). Flash accepts files in PICT (Mac) and in WMF and EMF (Windows) formats. Flash also accepts files from Flash Player 6 through 8 (SWF), as well as from Future Splash Player (SPL files).

When Flash imports graphics in a format that includes transparency, Flash preserves the transparency. Transparent areas of a GIF image, for example, have an alpha value of 0 when imported into Flash. When importing PICTs or PNGs with alpha channels, Flash correctly reads the transparency values of the alpha channel.

Flash can also import AutoCAD DXF files from version 10.

Flash works with Apple's QuickTime 4 (or a later version) to import additional file formats. Both Mac and Windows users who have the Flash 8/QuickTime 4 combination can import files in Photoshop, QuickTime Image, QuickTime Movie, Silicon Graphics Image, TGA, TIFF, and MacPaint formats. In addition, Windows users can import PICT files as bitmaps, and Mac users can import BMP files.

To import bitmapped graphics to the Stage:

◆ Follow steps 1–6 of the first exercise in this section, choosing the bitmap format of your choice in step 3.

There are no special import options for bitmaps. Flash imports the file you selected into your document, storing a master bitmap asset in the library and placing an instance of the bitmap on the Stage in the active layer (**Figure 14.7**).

✔ Tip

■ You can edit an imported bitmap in its creator program, if that program is installed on your system; or you can use any installed bitmap-editing program. Select the bitmap in the Library panel, Control-click (Mac) or right-click (Windows) the bitmap icon, and choose Edit With from the contextual menu. (If the creator program is present, it appears as a separate menu choice.) In the window that opens, navigate to an editing program and click Open to launch it. The selected bitmap opens in the external program. When you save the bitmap file, Flash updates the imported image in your library.

To import a series of graphics files to the Stage:

1. Follow steps 1–6 of the first exercise in this section. In step 3, choose the appropriate format, and navigate to the first file in the series.

A dialog appears, asking whether you want to import what looks like a series of sequential images (**Figure 14.8**). Flash recognizes files that form a sequence if they're all within a single folder and have filenames that differ only in the number at the end of the filename—for example, bounce1, bounce2, and bounce3.

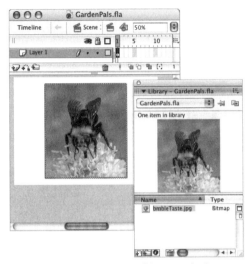

Figure 14.7 When you import a bitmap to the Stage, Flash also stores a master copy of the bitmap in the library.

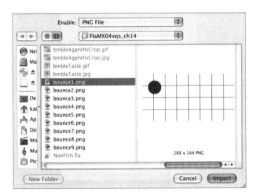

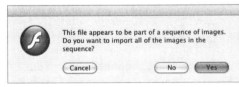

Figure 14.8 When you import one file in a series of numbered files (top), Flash asks whether you want to import the whole series (bottom).

2. In the dialog, click Yes.

Flash places each image in a separate keyframe in the active layer (**Figure 14.9**).

✔ Tips

■ You can also bring bitmaps and vector graphics into Flash via the Clipboard. Open the original graphic and copy it, using the procedures appropriate to the creator application. Open your Flash document, and choose Edit > Paste in Center. If the graphic is a bitmap, Flash pastes it on the Stage as a bitmap; Flash also places it in the Library panel. If the graphic is a vector, Flash places it on the Stage as a grouped element. When you copy and paste multiple vector shapes, Flash brings each one in as a separate group. Flash doesn't add these pasted vector shapes to the library. If you copy and paste symbols from FreeHand, Flash places the pasted symbols in the library as well as on the Stage.

■ To preserve individual text boxes from FreeHand versions 7 through MX as editable text when importing through the Clipboard, choose Flash > Preferences (Mac) or Edit > Preferences (Windows); in the Preferences dialog, select the Clipboard category; in the FreeHand Text section, choose Maintain as Blocks. Otherwise, Flash imports each character in a text block as a grouped shape and groups those groups.

■ Copy and paste isn't the most reliable process for importing graphics into Flash. Vector graphics in particular may lose something in translation when they go through the Clipboard. If you have trouble using the Clipboard with a particular item, try saving the file that contains the graphic in one of the formats that Flash imports and then bringing the whole file in with the Import command. You can always delete any portions of the file you don't want to use in Flash.

Preview mode shows images in keyframes

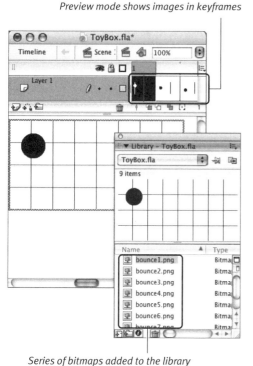

Series of bitmaps added to the library

Figure 14.9 When Flash imports a numbered series of files, it places each one in a separate keyframe in the Timeline of the current document.

Turning Bitmaps into Vector Graphics

After you import a bitmap into a Flash file, you can trace the bitmap to turn it into a set of vector shapes that looks like the bitmap. Flash offers several settings to help you strike a balance between the accurate rendering of the color areas in the bitmap and the creation of too many curves and small vectors within one object, which increases the file size.

To trace a bitmap:

1. Place a copy of the bitmap on the Stage.

2. Select the bitmap.

3. Choose Modify > Bitmap > Trace Bitmap (**Figure 14.10**).

   The Trace Bitmap dialog appears (**Figure 14.11**).

4. Enter values for the four settings in the dialog: Color Threshold, Minimum Area, Curve Fit, and Corner Threshold.

   The settings in this dialog control how closely the vector image matches the bitmapped image. Flash creates the vectors by examining the pixels that make up the bitmap, lumping together contiguous pixels that are the same color and making a vector shape out of that clump:

   Color Threshold (a number between 1 and 500) tells Flash how to decide when one pixel is the same color as its neighbor. The higher the threshold, the broader the range of colors Flash lumps together. A sky made up of light and dark blue pixels in three slightly different shades, for example, may wind up as one vector shape if you set a high-enough threshold but may wind up as dozens of separate shapes if you set a low threshold.

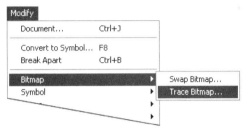

Figure 14.10 Choose Modify > Bitmap > Trace Bitmap to convert a bitmap to a group of vector shapes.

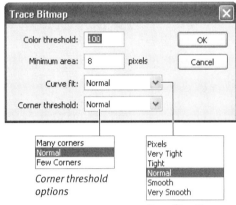

Figure 14.11 The Trace Bitmap dialog controls how Flash converts bitmaps to vectors.

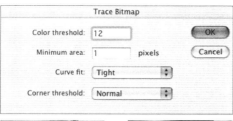

Figure 14.12 These tracings use different settings. The top one closely imitates the original bitmap; the bottom one has a posterized effect but ends up at a much smaller file size.

Minimum Area (a number between 1 and 1,000) determines how many neighbor pixels to include in calculating the color.

Curve Fit tells Flash how smoothly to draw the outlines around the vector shapes it creates.

Corner Threshold tells Flash whether to create sharp corners or smoother, more rounded ones.

5. Click OK.

The Tracing Bitmap dialog appears, with a progress bar and a Stop button. (To cancel the tracing process, click Stop.)

Flash replaces the bitmap with filled vector shapes that imitate the image (**Figure 14.12**).

✔ Tip

■ To translate a bitmap in vectors most closely (for example, to turn a digital photo into a set of vector graphics that still look like a photo), Macromedia recommends settings of 10 for Color Threshold, 1 for Minimum Area, Pixels for Curve Fit, and Many Corners for Corner Threshold. However, these settings can result in huge files, often larger than the original bitmap.

Editing Bitmaps in Flash

You can always edit bitmaps with an external bitmap editor, but Flash also lets you create a version of a bitmap that you can edit (to a certain degree) within Flash. First, you must break the image apart (select it and choose Modify > Break Apart). Flash converts the bitmap to a special type of graphic and selects it. Flash has no specific name for this type of graphic, but let's call it an *editable bitmap*.

An editable bitmap is no longer a collection of individual pixels, each with its own color value; neither is it a collection of tiny vector shapes. It acts more or less like a single vector shape with a gradient fill. (Macromedia describes this state as being a number of *discrete color areas*.) If you use the selection tool to click any area of the image now, you select the entire image.

To select just a region of color in the editable bitmap, you must use the lasso tool in Magic Wand mode. Select the lasso tool in the Tools panel, and then select the Magic Wand Settings modifier (the right-hand wand icon in the Options section of the Tools panel). In the dialog that appears, enter values for Threshold and Smoothing. The Threshold setting works the same way as the Color Threshold setting in the Trace Bitmap dialog (described earlier in this chapter). Smoothing works similarly to the Curve Fit setting of the Trace Bitmap dialog; it determines how smooth a vector path Flash draws when the magic wand makes a selection. Click OK. Select the lasso tool's Magic Wand modifier (the left-hand wand icon in the Options section of the Tools panel). Using the tool's hot spot, the transparent area in the center of the starburst, click the editable bitmap.

Flash selects the pixel you clicked and all surrounding pixels of the "same" color (determined by the threshold you chose). Now you can edit the selection. Try filling it with a single color by clicking the selection with the paint-bucket tool. Flash replaces all the pixels in the selection with the new color, creating a solid vector shape that you can edit with Flash's tools.

If the magic wand fails to grab the full range of colors you wanted, change Threshold to a higher number and try again. You can also add to the selection by clicking (or Shift-clicking, depending on your Preferences setting) the missed pixels.

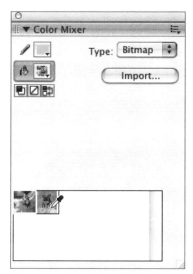

Figure 14.13 Select Bitmap in the Type menu of the Color Mixer panel to see bitmap thumbnails. Click a thumbnail to select it as the fill.

Using Bitmaps as Fills

You can create bitmap fills in two ways: by using the bitmaps that live in the library or by using editable bitmaps. When you select a bitmap as a fill, Flash turns it into a repeating, or *tiling*, pattern within the area it fills. You can use bitmap fills with any of the drawing tools that create fills: the oval, rectangle, polystar, pen, paintbrush, and paint bucket tools.

To apply a bitmap fill from the Color Mixer:

1. Open a Flash document that contains bitmap graphics.

2. On the Stage, create a shape with a solid fill, using the oval, rectangle, polystar, pen, or paintbrush tool.

3. Access the Color Mixer panel.

   If the panel isn't already open, choose Window > Color Mixer.

4. From the Fill Type menu, choose Bitmap.

   The panel's color-definition bar becomes a window displaying thumbnails of the bitmaps in the current document's library.

5. Position the pointer over one of the thumbnails.

   The pointer changes to the eyedropper tool (**Figure 14.13**).

continues on next page

6. Click the bitmap thumbnail you want to use.

The bitmap appears as the current fill selection in all the Fill Color controls (**Figure 14.14**). You're ready to use the bitmap fill as you would any other fill color.

7. In the Toolbar, select the paint bucket; position the paint bucket over the shape you created in step 2; then click.

Flash fills your shape with a tiling pattern made from the bitmap you selected (**Figure 14.15**). Each tile is 5 percent of the original image's size.

✔ Tips

- In step 4, if the document you're working in contains no bitmaps, Flash opens the Import to Library dialog so that you can import one.

- In step 7, it makes no difference if the fill is locked or unlocked.

Figure 14.14 When you select a bitmap for use as a fill, a miniature version of that bitmap appears in each of the Fill Color controls (this one is in the Color Mixer panel).

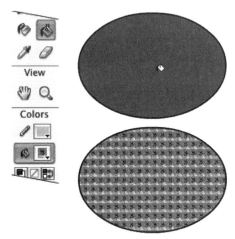

Figure 14.15 With the bitmap fill selected as the fill "color," click the item you want to fill with the bitmap pattern (top). Flash fills the shape with small repeating tiles of the bitmap (bottom).

Figure 14.16 Click an editable bitmap with the eyedropper tool to pick up the fill "color."

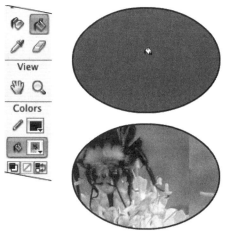

Figure 14.17 When you sample an editable bitmap with the eyedropper tool, Flash makes the bitmap the current fill color and selects the paint bucket tool. Click the item you want to fill with the bit-mapped pattern (top). Flash fills the shape with large repeating tiles of the editable bitmap (bottom).

To apply an editable bitmap as a fill:

1. On the Stage, create a shape with a solid fill using the oval, rectangle, polystar, pen, or paintbrush tool.

2. Create an editable bitmap (see the sidebar "Editing Bitmaps in Flash").

3. In the Toolbar, select the eyedropper tool.

4. Position the eyedropper over the editable bitmap on the Stage (**Figure 14.16**).

5. Click anywhere within the editable bitmap.

   In the Toolbar, Flash makes the bitmap the current fill selection and selects the paint bucket tool.

6. Position the paint bucket over the fill shape you created in step 1, and then click.

   Flash fills your shape with a tiling pattern made from the editable bitmap (**Figure 14.17**). Each tile shows the bitmap image at 100 percent. Depending on your shape, the tile may not be placed to show itself well.

✔ Tips

- To modify the tiles of a bitmap fill, in the Toolbar, select the gradient-transform tool (**Figure 14.18**) and position it over the filled shape. Click the fill. Transformation handles and a transformation-point circle appear around one tile of the fill (**Figure 14.19**). Drag the circle to change the way the tiling pattern fits within your shape. To scale, rotate, or skew the tiles, drag any of the other handles as you would when using the free-transform tool (see Chapter 4).

- If a drawing-object was ever part of a symbol that you broke apart, you may have trouble modifying its bitmap fill. If you're working on a drawing-object with a bitmap fill and find that the gradient-transform tool never changes to a transformative arrow, and you can't grab the tile's gradient-transform handles, this may be your problem. To restore the ability to use the gradient-transform tool on this drawing-object, double-click it to drill down to its underlying merge-shape. You can either use the gradient-transform tool on that shape or choose Edit > Edit Document to return to the main Stage. From now on, the gradient-transform tool will recognize the handles.

- Any of the tools that create fill shapes can create shapes with the bitmap fill as the chosen "color." For example, select the paintbrush tool in the Toolbar, and then select a bitmap as the fill following the steps in either of the preceding tasks. Paint a shape on the Stage. The brush-strokes you create fill with the tiling pattern. You can use the filled oval, rectangle, polystar, and pen tools this way, too.

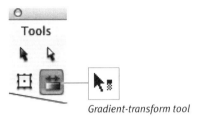

Gradient-transform tool

Figure 14.18 Select the gradient-transform tool to modify the tiles of a bitmap fill.

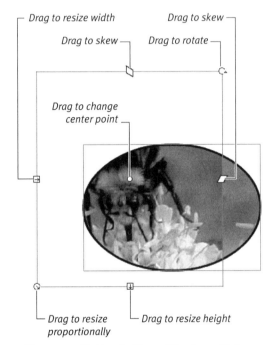

Drag to resize width — Drag to skew —
Drag to skew — Drag to rotate —
Drag to change center point —
Drag to resize proportionally — Drag to resize height

Figure 14.19 Clicking the bitmap fill pattern with the gradient-transform tool brings up handles for modifying the tiles.

15

ADDING SOUND

It's amazing how much a classic silent film conveys with just moving pictures and text, but that era is history. Audio is a vital feature of today's Web sites. In Macromedia Flash, you can incorporate sound in your projects, either as an ongoing background element or as a synchronized element that matches a particular piece of action—say, a slapping sound that accompanies a pair of hands clapping.

To add sound to Flash movies, you must import sound clips to the library and then attach instances of the sound clips to keyframes. You can access sounds and control synchronization of sounds via the Frame Properties tab of the Property inspector.

Flash offers a limited form of sound editing. You can clip the ends off a sound and adjust its volume, but you must do other kinds of sound editing outside Flash. When you publish your finished movie, pay attention to the sampling rate and compression of sounds to balance sound quality with the file size of your finished movie. You learn more about these considerations in Chapter 16.

Importing Sounds

The procedure for importing sounds is just like the procedure for importing bitmaps or other artwork: You use the File > Import > Import to Stage or File > Import > Import to Library command. Flash brings the sound file into the library for the current document, and you drag a copy of the sound from the Library panel into a specific keyframe.

To import a sound file:

1. Open the file to which you want to add sounds.

2. Choose File > Import > Import to Stage or press ⌘-R (Mac) or Ctrl-R (Windows) (**Figure 15.1**).

   You can also choose File > Import > Import to Library. The standard file-import dialog appears (**Figure 15.2**).

3. From the Enable pop-up menu (Mac) or the Files of Type pop-up menu (Windows), choose the format of the sound file you want to import.

   Choose All Sound Formats to see files in any sound format.

4. Navigate to the sound file on your system.

5. Select the file.

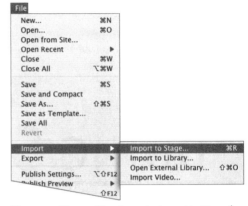

Figure 15.1 Choose File > Import > Import to Stage (or Import to Library) to bring sounds into your Flash document.

Figure 15.2 The Import dialog lets you import sound files into Flash. Choose a sound-file type that is appropriate for your platform from the pop-up menu of file types. You can also choose to see all sound formats.

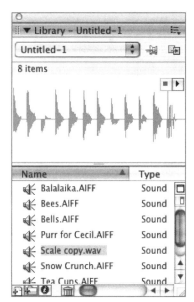

Figure 15.3 Flash keeps sound files in the library. You can see the waveform for a selected sound in the preview window. Click the Play button to hear the sound.

6. Click Import (Mac) or Open (Windows).

   Flash imports the sound file you selected, placing it in the library. The waveform of the sound appears in the library's preview window (**Figure 15.3**). Sound files can be quite large; as sounds import, a dialog named Working appears, showing a progress bar. You can stop the import by clicking the Stop button in the dialog.

✔ Tips

- For imported graphics, the File > Import > Import to Stage command places an instance on the Stage in the selected keyframe. For sounds imported to Flash, that's not true. Imported sounds wind up in the library; you must place them in the keyframe yourself.

- You can hear a sound without placing it in a movie. Select the sound in the Library panel. Flash displays the waveform in the preview window. To hear the sound, click the Play button in the preview window.

What Sound Formats Does Flash Import?

Flash deals only with *sampled sounds*—those that have been recorded digitally or converted to digital format. Flash imports AIFF-format files for the Mac OS, WAV-format files for Windows, and MP3-format files for both platforms. In addition, with the combination of Flash 8 and QuickTime 4 (or later versions), users on both platforms can import QuickTime movies containing just sounds and Sun AU files; Mac users can import WAV, Sound Designer II, and System 7 sounds; and Windows users can import AIFF sounds. Any sounds you import or copy into a Flash document reside in the file's library.

Adding Sounds to Frames

You can assign a sound to a keyframe the same way you place a symbol or bitmap: by selecting the keyframe and then dragging a copy of the sound from an open Library panel (either that document's or another's) to the Stage. You can also assign any sound that resides in a document's library to a selected keyframe in that document by choosing the sound from the Sound pop-up menu in the Frame Properties tab of the Property inspector.

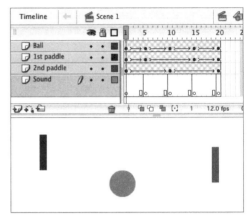

Figure 15.4 Create a separate layer for the sounds in your movie. In that layer, add a keyframe at each place where you want a sound to occur. Here, the keyframes in the Sound layer correspond to the keyframes in other layers where the ball makes contact with a paddle.

To assign a sound to a keyframe:

1. Open a Flash document to which you want to add sound.

   The Ping-Pong animation you created in Chapter 11 makes a good practice file. The document contains four keyframes in which a ball connects with a paddle. Adding sound can heighten the reality of that contact: You can make the sound realistic (say, a small *thwock*) or make it humorous, if the sound is unexpected (a *boing*, for example).

2. Add a new layer for the sounds in your document, and name it Sound.

   For more details on how to set up a sound layer, see the sidebar "Tips for Organizing Sounds."

3. In the Timeline, select the Sound layer, and add keyframes at frames 5, 10, 15, and 20.

   These four keyframes match the keyframes in which the ball hits one of the paddles in the animation (**Figure 15.4**).

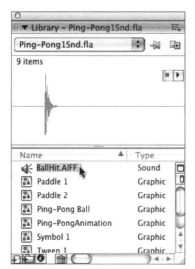

Figure 15.5 After you've imported a sound, it appears in the Library panel. Select the sound, and drag it to a keyframe.

4. Import the sound you want to hear when the paddle connects with the ball.

For more detailed instructions, follow the steps in "Importing Sounds" earlier in this chapter. If you don't have your own stock of sound clips, you can download a sound clip named BallHit from the companion Web site for this book. (Click the Files link at http://www.peachpit.com/vqs/flash8 to find the materials for this chapter.)

5. In the Timeline, select keyframe 5 of the Sound layer.

This is the first frame in which the ball and paddle connect.

6. Access the Library panel, and select your sound (**Figure 15.5**).

Its waveform appears in the preview window.

7. Drag a copy of the sound from the Library panel to the Stage.

Although sounds have no visible presence on the Stage, you must drag the sound copy to the Stage. As you drag the sound, you see the outline of a box on the Stage. When you release the mouse button, Flash puts the sound in the selected keyframe and displays the waveform in that keyframe and any in-between frames associated with it (**Figure 15.6**).

8. In the Timeline, select keyframe 10 of the Sound layer.

This is the second frame in which the ball and paddle connect.

9. Access the Frame Properties tab of the Property inspector.

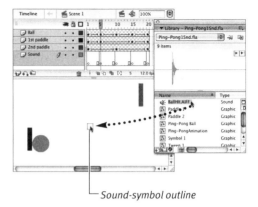

Sound-symbol outline

Waveform of the sound assigned to keyframe 5

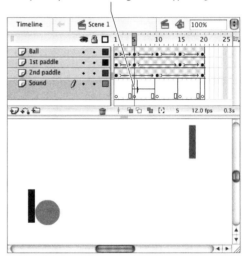

Figure 15.6 When you drag a sound from the Library panel to the Stage, you see the symbol outline (top). A sound has no visible presence on the Stage, but Flash displays the sound's waveform in the Timeline (bottom).

ADDING SOUNDS TO FRAMES

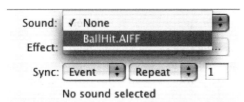

Figure 15.7 In the Frame Properties tab of the Property inspector, the Sound pop-up menu lists all the sounds that are in the library of the current document. From this menu, you can choose a sound that you want to assign to the keyframe that's selected in the Timeline.

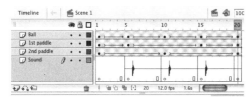

Figure 15.8 For each spot in the movie where a sound should occur, add a sound to a keyframe in the sound layer. A condensed image of the sound's waveform appears in the keyframe span. Within a single keyframe, you won't see much of the waveform; in keyframe 20, for example, just the initial line is visible.

10. From the Sound pop-up menu, choose your sound.

All the sounds in the document's library are available from the Frame Properties tab of the Property inspector's Sound pop-up menu (**Figure 15.7**). You don't have to drag a copy of the sound to the Stage each time you want to turn on that sound in a keyframe.

For now, leave the other settings in the Frame Properties tab of the Property inspector alone. You learn more about them in later tasks.

11. Repeat steps 6 and 7 (or 8, 9, and 10) for keyframes 15 and 20.

After adding the sound to the four keyframes, you're ready to play the movie and check out the sounds (**Figure 15.8**). As each paddle strikes the ball, Flash plays the assigned sound, adding a level of realism to your simple Ping-Pong animation.

✔ **Tip**

■ If you want to try adding sounds to your Flash projects, but you don't have the equipment to record your own, lots of copyright-free sounds are available. You can purchase CDs of sounds for use in projects; there are also online sites with downloadable sounds. Just make sure the sounds are copyright free before you download them for use in your own project.

Tips for Organizing Sounds

Nothing prevents you from placing sounds in layers that contain other content, but your document will be easier to handle—and sounds will be easier to find for updating and editing—if you always put sounds in separate layers reserved for your soundtrack. Here are some tips for working with layers for sounds:

◆ Name layers as a reminder of their content. For detailed instructions on working with layers, see Chapter 6.

◆ Place all your sound layers either at the bottom of the Timeline or at the top, so you can find them easily. The position of layers in the stacking order has no effect on the playback of sounds in the movie.

◆ Create a layer folder for sounds. Flash Player 8 (you'll learn about publishing for Flash Player in Chapter 16) can handle up to 32 sounds playing at one time (earlier Flash Player versions can handle up to 8 simultaneous sounds). If you put each sound on a separate layer, that's a lot to track. If you'll be working with lots of sound layers, create a layer folder, and name it SoundTracks. Placing all the sound layers in the SoundTracks folder makes it easier to track the sounds (**Figure 15.9**)

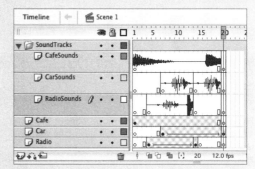

Figure 15.9 It's best to keep sounds in separate layers from the graphics and actions in your movie. To organize multiple sound layers, place them in a separate layer folder. Increasing layer height lets you see the sounds' waveforms more easily.

◆ Increase the height for sound layers to make it easier to see the *waveform* (a graphic image of the sound) for that layer. Choose Modify > Timeline > Layer (or double-click the layer icon of the selected layer) to access the Layer Properties dialog. From the Layer Height pop-up menu, choose 200% or 300% to make the layer taller. Click OK.

◆ After you've placed sounds in a layer, lock the layer—to prevent yourself from adding graphics to it accidentally—by clicking the bullet in the column below the padlock icon.

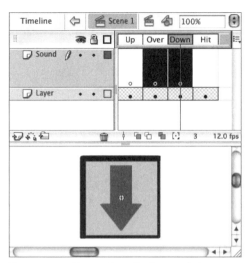

Figure 15.10 Add a new layer for the sounds in a button symbol. In that layer, create keyframes for the button states where you plan to assign sounds.

Adding Sounds to Buttons

Auditory feedback helps people who view your Flash creation interact with buttons correctly. For buttons that look like real-world buttons, adding a click sound to the Down frame provides a more realistic feel. For more fanciful buttons or ones disguised as part of the scenery of your movie, adding sound to the Over frame lets users know they've discovered a hot spot.

To enhance buttons with auditory feedback:

1. Open a Flash document containing a button symbol to which you want to add sound.

   (To learn about working with button symbols, see Chapter 12.)

2. Open the file's Library panel (choose Window > Library), and select the button symbol you want to modify.

3. From the Library panel's Options menu, choose Edit.

   Flash opens the button in symbol-editing mode.

4. In the button symbol's Timeline, add a new layer (click the Add Layer button), and name it Sound.

5. In the Sound layer, select the Over and Down frames, and choose Modify > Timeline > Convert to Blank Keyframes (**Figure 15.10**).

   continues on next page

6. Using the techniques described in "Adding Sounds to Frames," earlier in this chapter, assign a sound to the _over frame and a different sound to the _down frame.

Flash displays as much of the waveform as possible in each frame. When you add sounds to buttons, it makes sense to increase the height of the layer that contains sounds (**Figure 15.11**). Make sure that the sound's Sync property is set to Event (the default) in the Property inspector. (You'll learn more about setting the Sync property in the next section.)

7. Return to document-editing mode.

Every instance of the button symbol in the document now has sounds attached.

8. To hear the buttons in action, choose Control > Enable Simple Buttons.

When you move the pointer over the button, Flash plays the sound you assigned to the _over frame. When you click the button, you hear the sound you assigned to the _down frame.

✔ Tips

■ The most common frames to use for button feedback are the _over and _down frames, but you can add sounds to any of the button symbol's frames. Sounds added to the _up frame play when the pointer rolls out of the active button area. Sounds added to the Hit frame play when you release the mouse button within the active button area.

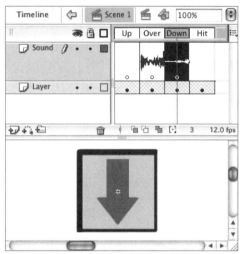

Figure 15.11 Flash displays the waveform of the assigned sound in the keyframe. Unlike movie Timelines, button symbol Timelines have no in-between frames that can contain part of the waveform. Increasing the layer height for a button symbol's Sound layer enlarges any waveforms in the button's frames, letting you see more detail.

■ You can also add sounds to movie-clip buttons, such as those you learned about in Chapters 12 and 13. As in this task, you add a sound layer to the symbol and then add sounds to the relevant keyframes in the movie-clip symbol. If you add a sound to the _up frame of a movie-clip button, the sound plays whenever the button first displays its _up frame—for example, when the playhead reaches the frame containing the movie-clip button.

Using Event Sounds

One of the sound settings available in the Frame Properties tab of the Property inspector is Sync. The Sync setting determines the way Flash synchronizes the sounds in your movie. Sync has four settings: Event, Start, Stop, and Stream. The default is Event.

Event sounds play independently of the main Timeline. Flash starts an event sound at a keyframe in a movie; the event sound plays until Flash reaches the end of the sound clip or encounters an instruction to stop playing that sound or all sounds. Long event sounds can continue to play after the playhead reaches the last frame in the movie. If your movie loops, every time the playhead passes a frame with an event sound, Flash starts another instance of that sound playing.

To understand how synchronization works, it's helpful to work in a file that has identifying text in keyframes.

To set up a file for testing sounds:

1. Create a 20-frame, 3-layer Flash document.

2. Label the layers Objects, Sound 1, and Sound 2.

3. In all layers, insert keyframes into frames 1, 5, 10, 15, and 20.

4. In the Objects layer, place identifying text on the Stage for each keyframe.

5. Import several sounds of different lengths into the file's library.

   This example uses a 15.8-second sound clip of a musical-scale passage, a water drop sound, a melodic passage, and some rhythm sounds.

6. Save the document as a template for use throughout this chapter, and name it SoundSyncTemplate.

   For detailed instructions on saving documents as templates, see Chapter 1.

Independent Sounds vs. Synchronized Sounds

Unsynchronized sound clips play independently of the frames in a movie and can even continue playing after the playhead reaches the last frame in the movie. Flash starts these *event sounds* at a specific frame, but thereafter, event sounds play without relation to specific frames. On one viewer's computer, the sound may take 10 frames to play; on a slower setup, the sound may finish when only 5 frames have appeared.

Flash can also synchronize entire sound clips with specific frames. Flash breaks these *stream sounds* or *streaming sounds* into smaller pieces and attaches each piece to a specific frame. For streaming sounds, Flash forces the animation to keep up with the sounds. On slower setups, Flash draws fewer frames so important actions and sounds stay together.

To make an assigned sound an event sound:

1. Open a new copy of SoundSyncTemplate, created in the preceding task.

2. In the Timeline, select keyframe 5 of the Sound 1 layer (**Figure 15.12**).

3. In the Frame Properties tab of the Property inspector, from the Sound pop-up menu, choose the sound named Scale.AIFF (**Figure 15.13**).

4. From the Sync pop-up menu, choose Event (**Figure 15.14**).

   The Scale.AIFF sound is assigned to keyframe 5 of the Sound 1 layer.

5. Position the playhead in keyframe 1, and play your movie (choose Control > Play).

   In a movie that has a standard frame rate of 12 frames per second (fps), the 15.8-second Scale sound continues to play after the playhead reaches the last frame of the movie.

✔ Tip

■ To understand better how Flash handles event sounds, choose Control > Loop Playback. Now play the movie again, and let it loop through a couple of times. Each time the playhead enters keyframe 5, Flash starts another instance of the Scale sound, and you begin to hear not one set of notes going up the scale, but a cacophony of bad harmonies. When you stop the playback, each sound instance plays out until its end—an effect sort of like people singing a round.

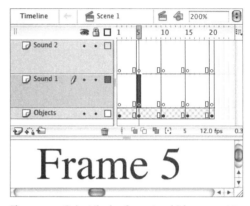

Figure 15.12 Select the keyframe to which you want to assign a sound. Settings that you create in the Frame Properties tab of the Property inspector are applied to the selected keyframe.

Figure 15.13 In the Frame Properties tab of the Property inspector, choose a sound from the Sound pop-up menu.

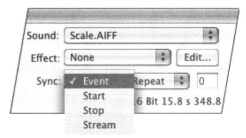

Figure 15.14 From the Sync pop-up menu, choose Event to make the assigned sound start in the selected keyframe and play to the end of the sound, without synchronizing to any subsequent frames of the movie.

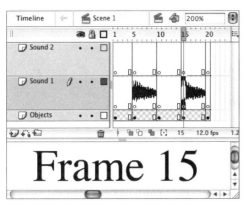

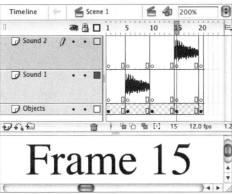

Figure 15.15 You can add a second instance of your sound and make it play on top of the first. Event sounds play independent of the main Timeline, so you're free to add the second sound to the same layer as the first (top). Alternatively, you can add the second sound to its own layer (bottom).

To play overlapping instances of the same sound:

1. Using the file you created in the preceding task, to assign a sound to a later point in the movie's Timeline, *do either of the following:*

   ▲ Select keyframe 15 of the Sound 1 layer.

   ▲ Select keyframe 15 of the Sound 2 layer.

   Because Flash starts a new instance of an event sound even if that sound is already playing, you have the choice of adding a second instance to the same layer as the first or adding it to a different layer.

2. In the Frame Properties tab of the Property inspector, from the Sound pop-up menu, choose the sound named Scale.AIFF.

3. From the Sync pop-up menu, choose Event.

   The Scale.AIFF sound is assigned to keyframe 15 of whichever layer you chose (**Figure 15.15**).

4. Position the playhead in keyframe 1, and play your movie one time.

   When the playhead reaches keyframe 5, the Scale.AIFF sound starts. When the playhead reaches keyframe 15, another instance of the Scale.AIFF sound starts, and the two sounds play together (you hear two voices). When the first instance ends, you again hear only one voice. Within a single layer, each frame can contain only one sound. To make Flash begin playing different sounds at the same point in a movie, you must put the sounds in separate layers.

5. Save this file for use in a later task; name it OverlapSnds.fla.

To start different sounds simultaneously:

1. Open a new copy of the SoundSync-Template you created earlier in this chapter.

2. In the Timeline, select keyframe 5 of the Sound 1 layer.

3. In the Frame Properties tab of the Property inspector, from the Sound pop-up menu, choose Scale.AIFF.

4. From the Sync pop-up menu, choose Event.

5. In the Timeline, select keyframe 5 of the Sound 2 layer.

6. In the Frame Properties tab of the Property inspector, from the Sound pop-up menu, choose a different sound.

   You can also import a new sound to your movie's library or open the Library panel of another movie containing the sound you want to use and then drag a copy of the sound to the Stage. This example uses a sound named Melody.AIFF.

   Flash places the waveform for the second sound in keyframe 5 of the Sound 2 layer (**Figure 15.16**).

7. In the Frame Properties tab of the Property inspector, from the Sync pop-up menu, choose Event.

8. Position the playhead in keyframe 1, and play your movie one time.

   When the playhead reaches keyframe 5, Flash starts playing the Scale.AIFF and Melody.AIFF sounds simultaneously.

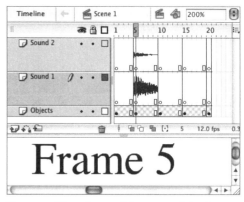

Figure 15.16 To make two different sounds begin playing simultaneously, you must put each sound in a different layer in a keyframe at the same spot in the Timeline—for example, keyframe 5.

✔ Tip

- All the information required to play an event sound lives in the keyframe to which you assigned that sound. When you play the movie, Flash pauses at that keyframe until all the information has downloaded. It's best to reserve event syncing for short sound clips; otherwise, your movie may be interrupted by long pauses for downloading sounds.

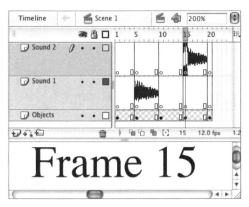

Figure 15.17 To change a sound's Sync setting, select the keyframe that contains the sound. Then, in the Frame Properties tab of the Property inspector, from the Sync pop-up menu, choose a new setting.

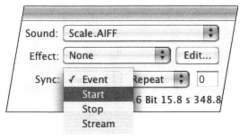

Figure 15.18 To prevent Flash from playing another instance of a sound if that sound is already playing, choose Start from the Sync pop-up menu in the Frame Properties tab of the Property inspector.

✔ Tip

- To avoid playing multiple instances of a sound when a movie loops, set the sound's Sync parameter to Start. If the sound is still playing when Flash starts the movie again, Flash lets the sound play, adding nothing new. If the sound has finished, Flash starts the sound again when the playhead enters a keyframe containing the sound.

Using Start Sounds

Start sounds behave just like event sounds, with one important difference: Flash doesn't play a new instance of a start sound if that sound is already playing.

To set an assigned sound's Sync parameter to Start:

1. Open OverlapSnds.fla, the file you created in "To play overlapping instances of the same sound" earlier in this chapter.

   You should have one instance of the Scale.AIFF sound in keyframe 5 and another in keyframe 15. The second instance is in the Sound 1 or Sound 2 layer, depending on what you did in the earlier task.

2. In the Timeline, select the keyframe 15 that contains the Scale.AIFF sound (**Figure 15.17**).

3. In the Frame Properties tab of the Property inspector, from the Sync pop-up menu, choose Start (**Figure 15.18**).

4. Position the playhead in keyframe 1, and play your movie one time.

   When the playhead reaches keyframe 5, the Scale.AIFF sound starts. When the playhead reaches keyframe 15, nothing changes; you continue to hear just one voice as the Scale.AIFF sound continues playing. When a sound is playing and Flash encounters another instance of the same sound, the Sync setting determines whether Flash plays that sound. When Sync is set to Start, Flash doesn't play another instance of the sound.

Using Stream Sounds

Stream sounds are specifically geared for playback over the Web. When Sync is set to Stream, Flash breaks a sound into smaller sound clips. Flash synchronizes these sub-clips with specific frames of the movie—as many frames as are required to play the sound. Flash stops streaming sounds when playback reaches a new keyframe or an instruction to stop playing either that specific sound or all sounds.

Unlike event sounds, which must download fully before they can play, stream sounds can start playing after a few frames have downloaded. This situation makes streaming the best choice for long sounds, especially if you'll be delivering your movie over the Web.

To make an assigned sound a stream sound:

1. Open a new copy of the SoundSync-Template that you created earlier in this chapter.

2. In the Timeline, in the Sound 1 layer, remove keyframe status from keyframe 10 (select it and choose Modify > Timeline > Clear Keyframe).

3. In the Timeline, in the Sound 1 layer, select keyframe 5.

4. In the Frame Properties tab of the Property inspector, from the Sound pop-up menu, choose Scale.AIFF.

5. From the Sync pop-up menu, choose Stream (**Figure 15.19**).

6. To see how the sound fits into the avail-able time in your movie, in the Sound section of the Frame Properties tab of the Property inspector, click the Edit button. The Edit Envelope window appears.

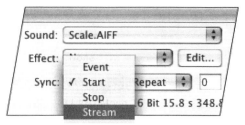

Figure 15.19 To make Flash force a sound to synchronize with specific frames of your movie, choose Stream from the Sync pop-up menu in the Frame Properties tab of the Property inspector.

The Mystery of Streaming Sound

When you choose Stream as the Sync set-ting for a sound, Flash divides that sound clip into smaller subclips and embeds them in individual frames. The movie's frame rate determines the subclips' size. In a movie with a frame rate of 10 frames per second (fps), for example, Flash divides stream-ing sounds into subclips that are a tenth of a second long. For every 10 frames, Flash plays 1 second of the sound.

Flash synchronizes the start of each sub-clip with a specific frame of the movie. If the sound plays back faster than the computer can draw frames, Flash sacri-fices some visuals (skips drawing some frames of the animation) so that sound and images match up as closely as possible. Setting a sound's Sync setting to Stream ensures, for example, that you hear the door slam when you see it swing shut— not a few seconds before. If the discrep-ancy between sound-playback speed and frame-drawing speed is big enough, how-ever, those dropped frames make the movie look jerky, just as it would if you set a low frame rate to begin with.

Edit button

Sound: Scale

Effect: None   Edit...

Sync: Stream | Repeat | 0

11 kHz Mono 16 Bit 15.7 s 345.6 kB

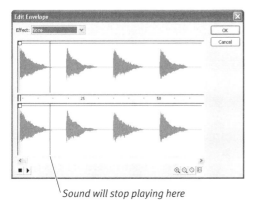

Sound will stop playing here

Figure 15.20 When you set a sound's Sync to Stream, you can check how much of the sound will play, given the number of in-between frames there are for the sound to play in. In the Frame Properties tab of the Property inspector, click the Edit button (top) to open the Edit Envelope window (bottom). This window displays a sound's full waveform in relation to time or to frame numbers.

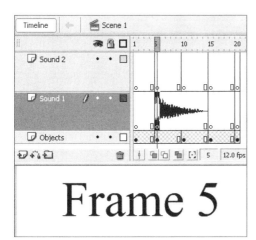

Figure 15.21 There is time enough in the 10-frame span from keyframe 5 to keyframe 15 to play only the first note of the Scale sound. Flash displays just that much of the full 15.8-second waveform in the Timeline.

At 15.8 seconds, the Scale.AIFF sound is too long to play completely in the frames between keyframe 5 and keyframe 15. When Sync is set to Stream, Flash plays only as much of the sound as can fit in the frames that are available to it—in this case, slightly less than a second. In the Edit Envelope window, a vertical line indicates where Flash truncates this instance of the sound (**Figure 15.20**).

7. To close the Edit Envelope window, click OK or Cancel.

   The truncated waveform appears in frames 5–15 (**Figure 15.21**).

8. Position the playhead in keyframe 1, and play your movie to hear the sound in action.

   When the playhead reaches keyframe 5, the Scale.AIFF sound starts. When the playhead reaches keyframe 15, the keyframe span ends, and Flash stops playback of the Scale.AIFF sound.

9. Choose Control > Loop Playback, and then play the movie to hear the sound in looping mode.

   Flash repeats the same snippet of sound, stopping it each time the playhead reaches keyframe 15.

✔ Tips

■ You can hear streaming sounds play as you drag the playhead through the Timeline (a technique called *scrubbing*). As the playhead moves over the waveform, you can see how the images and sounds fit together. You can then add or delete frames to better synchronize the sounds with the images onscreen.

- Try Shift-clicking the Timeline to take the playhead to a particular frame (or Shift-dragging the playhead to that frame). As long as you hold down the Shift key and the mouse button, Flash repeats the portion of sound that synchronizes with the frame where the playhead is.

- If your stream sound is getting cut off too soon, switch the units of measure in the Edit Envelope window to see how many frames you need to add to accommodate the sound (**Figure 15.22**).

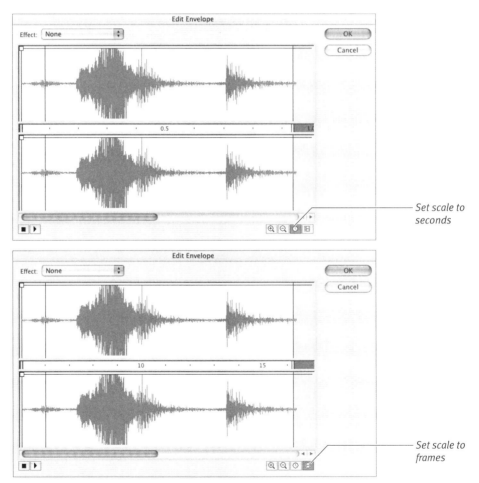

Set scale to seconds

Set scale to frames

Figure 15.22 The scale for the waveform in the Edit Envelope window can be set to seconds (top) or frames (bottom). If you set the scale to frames, you can see exactly how many frames you need to provide enough time for the major parts of the sound to finish. (For this sound, you would need 15 frames.) Usually, you want to make room for the segments of the wave that have the greatest amplitude.

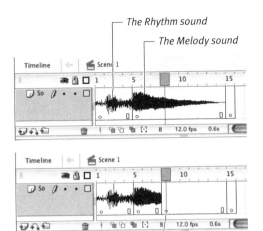

The Rhythm sound

The Melody sound

After adding blank keyframe

Figure 15.23 Inserting a new keyframe cuts off your view of the preceding sound's waveform in the Timeline. If the sound is an event sound, however, it continues playing even when the playhead moves past the keyframe.

Stopping Sounds

Although event sounds normally play to the end, you can force them to stop at a specific keyframe. To issue an instruction to stop a specific sound, set that sound's Sync parameter to Stop.

To stop playback of a sound:

1. Create a new 15-frame Flash document with two fairly long event sounds (at least 2 or 3 seconds each); place one sound in keyframe 1 and the other in keyframe 5.

   (For more detailed instructions, see "Adding Sounds to Frames" earlier in this chapter.) In this example, keyframe 1 contains the sound Rhythm.AIFF, and keyframe 5 contains the sound Melody.AIFF.

2. In the Timeline, at frame 8, insert a new blank keyframe (**Figure 15.23**).

   Flash cuts off the waveform at keyframe 8 because of the keyframe, but on playback, both event sounds continue to play after the playhead reaches keyframe 8.

3. Select keyframe 8.

4. In the Frame Properties tab of the Property inspector, from the Sound pop-up menu, choose Rhythm.AIFF.

continues on next page

5. From the Sync pop-up menu, choose Stop (**Figure 15.24**).

Flash uses this instruction to stop playback of the Rhythm.AIFF sound at keyframe 8.

Flash places a small square in the middle of keyframe 8 in the Timeline to indicate that the frame contains a stop-sound instruction (**Figure 15.25**).

6. Position the playhead in keyframe 1, and play your movie to hear the sounds in action.

The Rhythm.AIFF sound starts immediately; Melody.AIFF kicks in at keyframe 5. When the playhead reaches keyframe 8, Rhythm.AIFF cuts out, but Melody.AIFF plays on even after the playhead reaches the end of the movie.

✔ Tips

■ The Stop setting and the sound that it stops can be in different layers. The Stop setting stops playback of all instances of the specified sound that are currently playing in any layer.

■ To stop only one instance of a sound, set the Sync parameter of that instance to Stream; then, in the layer containing that instance, put a blank keyframe in the frame where you want that instance of the sound to stop.

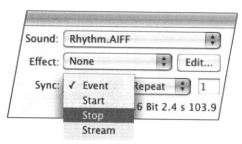

Figure 15.24 To stop a sound's playback at a specific point in a movie, create and then select the keyframe where the sound should stop. In the Frame Properties tab of the Property inspector, from the Sound pop-up menu, choose the sound you want to stop. From the Sync pop-up menu, choose Stop. Here, the Stop instruction refers to the Rhythm sound.

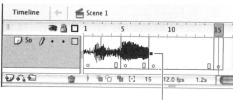

Sync is set to Stop for this keyframe

Figure 15.25 In the Timeline, a small square in the middle of a keyframe indicates the presence of the stop-sound instruction.

Figure 15.26 To prepare a sound to be targeted by ActionScript, you must set its Linkage properties. Select the sound in the Library panel; then, from the Options menu, choose Linkage to see a dialog with linkage settings.

Using Behaviors to Control Sounds

In the previous tasks, you control sound playback by adding and removing sound instances directly in the Timeline during authoring. ActionScript allows you to control sounds during playback—loading, playing, and stopping sounds as needed at runtime. Scripting sounds is a complex task, but Flash 8 provides a set of sound behaviors for common sound-related tasks. You can use these behaviors to attach ActionScript to button symbols, button components, or movie clips, setting them up to load and play a specific sound, to replay a loaded sound, or to stop all event sounds that are currently playing whether they were loaded with ActionScript or placed in the Timeline during authoring. To target a sound with a behavior, you must set the sound's Linkage properties so that ActionScript can locate and work with the sound.

To set a sound's Linkage properties:

1. Open a new copy of the SoundSync-Template you created earlier in this chapter.

   The document contains three Timeline layers (Sound 1, Sound 2, and Objects); identifying text in keyframes 1, 5, 10, 15, and 20; and several sounds in the library (Rhythm.AIFF, Melody.AIFF, Drip.AIFF, and Scale.AIFF).

2. Select Rhythm.AIFF in the Library panel.

3. From the Library panel's Options menu, choose Linkage (**Figure 15.26**).

   The Linkage Properties dialog appears.

   continues on next page

4. Select the Export for ActionScript check box.

Flash automatically enters the sound's name (here, Rhythm.AIFF) as the default Identifier and selects the "Export in first frame" check box. For this task, keep these default settings (**Figure 15.27**).

5. Click OK.

6. Repeat steps 2–4 for all the sounds that you plan to control with ActionScript.

For the following task, you need at least two sounds, Rhythm.AIFF and Melody.AIFF.

To load and play a sound with a button:

1. Continuing with the file you created in the preceding task, insert a new layer in the Timeline and name it Buttons.

2. With keyframe 1 of the Buttons layer selected, place an instance of a button symbol on the Stage.

For more detailed instructions about using button symbols, see Chapter 12. To keep the button visible throughout the entire movie during playback, make sure the Buttons layer extends the whole length of the movie (if it doesn't, select frame 20 in the Buttons layer and press F5 to insert in-between frames). Your document should look like **Figure 15.28**. It's a good idea to give the button an instance name—for example, Drum_btn (for details about naming button instances, see Chapter 13).

3. Access the Behaviors and Actions panels.

4. Select the button-symbol instance on the Stage.

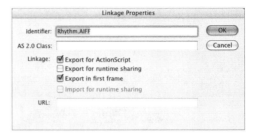

Figure 15.27 When you select Export for ActionScript in the Linkage Properties dialog, Flash assigns a default identifier. You can change the ID if you wish.

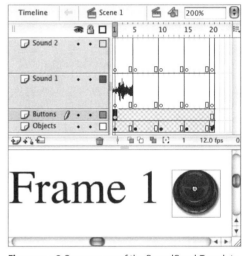

Figure 15.28 Open a copy of the SoundSynchTemplate you created; add a button symbol instance in its own layer. Now you can assign a behavior to the button to load and play a sound.

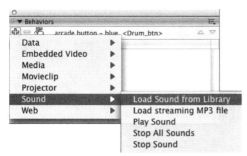

Figure 15.29 Choose Sound > Load Sound from Library to script a button that loads (and plays) a sound when a user clicks the button during playback of your movie.

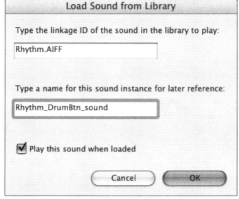

Figure 15.30 When the "Play this sound when loaded" check box is selected, clicking the button during playback both loads and plays the sound. Deselect the check box to load the sound now but play it later. In that case, you'll need another triggering object and event to play the sound.

5. From the Add Behavior menu (the plus sign) in the Behaviors panel, choose Sound > Load Sound from Library (**Figure 15.29**).

The Load Sound from Library dialog appears.

6. In the Load Sound from Library dialog, *do the following:*

▲ Type the linkage identifier in the first field. This is the name you assigned when you set the sound's Linkage properties in the preceding task. The Linkage ID tells ActionScript which master sound to use. In the preceding task, you used the default linkage ID, Rhythm.AIFF.

▲ Type an instance name in the second field; for this example, type Rhythm_DrumBtn_sound. You can only assign instance names to sound instances via ActionScript. The behavior will take care of the scripting for you, using the name you enter here.

▲ Leave the "Play this sound when loaded" check box selected (**Figure 15.30**). This setting tells Flash to load the sound and play it immediately when the user clicks the button during playback. To load a sound for future use, deselect this check box.

continues on next page

USING BEHAVIORS TO CONTROL SOUNDS

493

7. Click OK.

Flash adds the behavior to the Behaviors panel and adds the appropriate ActionScript to the Script pane of the Actions panel (**Figure 15.31**).

8. Repeat steps 2–7 for a second button.

Set this button to load and play a different sound—for example, Melody.AIFF. Give the button an instance name, such as SongBtn_sound (**Figure 15.32**). For clarity, add text boxes (to the Button layer or a separate Text layer) to indicate which button plays which sound.

9. Choose Control > Test Movie to try out your buttons.

The first time you click the Drum_btn button, Flash loads the Rhythm.AIFF sound and starts it playing; click the Song_btn button, and Flash loads and plays the Melody.AIFF sound. On subsequent clicks, Flash starts each sound playing again; there's no need to reload it.

Figure 15.31 The behavior-created script that loads a sound from the library is quite complex. Flash targets the instance name you created for your sound and issues a command for it to start playing.

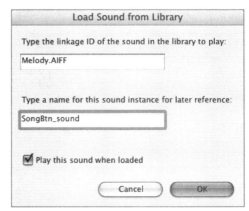

Figure 15.32 Set up a second sound to load from the library. In the Load Sound from Library dialog, enter the sound's identifier and give the sound an instance name.

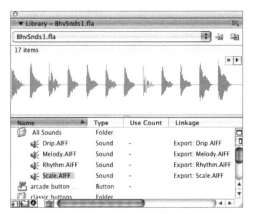

Figure 15.33 The Linkage column of the Library panel shows the linkage name of each sound asset. You can resize the panel to view the column.

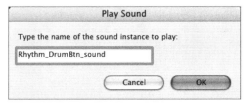

Figure 15.34 To replay a loaded sound, you need to tell Flash which precise sound instance to play. Use the instance name you assigned when you set up the behavior, Load Sound from Library.

✔ Tips

■ If you can't remember the Linkage ID for a sound, you can see it in the Library panel. Linkage is the fourth column in the window and often gets hidden when you size panels to take up as little screen real estate as possible. Resize the window, or scroll to see the Linkage column (**Figure 15.33**).

■ It's a good idea to add your own comments to a script created by a behavior. With ScriptAssist inactive, in the Script pane of the Actions panel, click the first line (which the behavior leaves blank). Type two slashes and your comment text: for example, `//This script makes the Drum button load and play the Rhythm sound.`

To replay loaded sounds:

1. Continuing with the file from the preceding task, add a third button to keyframe 1 of the Buttons layer.

   You can add a text box to label this button Play Rhythm.

2. With the Play Rhythm button selected on the Stage, from the Add Behavior menu in the Behaviors panel, choose Sound > Play Sound.

   The Play Sound dialog appears.

3. Type the sound's instance name that you created in step 6 of the preceding task: Rhythm_DrumBtn_sound (**Figure 15.34**).

4. Click OK.

5. Choose Control > Test Movie to try out your buttons.

   Click the Drum_btn and Song_btn buttons to load those sounds and start them playing. Now click the Play Rhythm button; Flash starts the Rhythm sound playing again.

To stop individual loaded sounds:

1. Continuing with the file from the preceding task, add a fourth button to keyframe 1 of the Buttons layer.

    You can add a text box to label this button Stop Rhythm.

2. With the Stop Rhythm button selected on the Stage, from the Add Behavior menu in the Behaviors panel, choose Sound > Stop Sound (**Figure 15.35**). The Stop Sound dialog appears.

3. Type the Linkage ID for the sound you want to stop: Rhythm.AIFF.

4. Type the sound's instance name that you created in the first task in this section (when you added the behavior for loading the sound): Rhythm_DrumBtn_sound (**Figure 15.36**).

5. Click OK.

    Flash adds the behavior to the Behaviors panel and the script to the Script pane (**Figure 15.37**).

6. Choose Control > Test Movie.

    Click the Drum_btn button to start the Rhythm sound playing, and then click the Stop Rhythm button. Flash stops playback of the Rhythm sound immediately.

To stop all sounds:

1. Open a new Flash document, and add layers, keyframes, and sounds.

    Place a few different sounds into different layers and keyframes. The sounds should be 1 or 2 seconds long so you'll have time to click a button while they're still playing. Make sure each keyframe containing a sound has Event as the Sync setting in the Properties tab of the Property inspector.

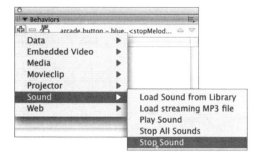

Figure 15.35 Choose Add Behavior > Stop Sound to target a specific loaded sound you want to control and stop.

Figure 15.36 In the Stop Sound dialog, enter the Linkage ID and instance name of the target sound.

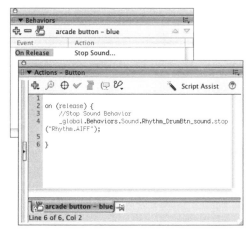

Figure 15.37 The behavior appears in the Behaviors panel, and its script appears in the Script pane of the Actions panel.

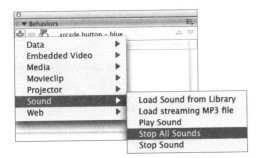

Figure 15.38 Choosing Add Behavior > Sound > Stop All Sounds (top) brings up a dialog explaining the behavior's function (middle). The resulting script (bottom) is much simpler than the behavior-created script for stopping a particular target sound.

2. Add a layer for buttons, and place an instance of a button symbol in keyframe 1 of that layer.

   Make sure the layer contains enough in-between frames to match the length of the other layers. That way, this button will be visible throughout the movie. To be methodical, name the layer and give the button an instance name as well.

3. Select the button.

4. From the Add Behavior menu in the Behaviors panel, choose Sound > Stop All Sounds.

   The Stop All Sounds dialog appears. This dialog reminds you that this behavior will cause all sounds to stop playing.

5. Click OK.

   Flash adds Stop All Sounds to the Behaviors panel and creates a script in the Script pane of the Actions panel for your button (**Figure 15.38**).

6. Choose Control > Test Movie to test your button.

   As the movie plays, the sounds you placed begin playing. When you click the button, all the sounds that are currently playing cease playing until the playhead reaches the next keyframe that contains a sound—for example, when the movie loops back to the beginning.

✔ Tip

■ The Stop All Sounds behavior stops sounds no matter how they were originally started in your movie. For fun, try adding buttons that load and play sounds from the library to this file. You'll see that the `stopAllSounds` action stops these loaded sounds as well.

USING BEHAVIORS TO CONTROL SOUNDS

Repeating Sounds

Flash's sound-repeating parameter allows you to play a sound several times in a row without adding other instances of the sound to a frame. Type a value in the Repeat field in the sound area (the right side) of the Frame Properties tab of the Property inspector. Flash plays the sound the specified number of times. You can repeat event sounds and streaming sounds. The sound's Sync parameter applies to the whole set of repeated sounds. You can also set sounds to loop until further instruction.

To set a Repeat value:

1. Create a 5-frame Flash document with a short event sound in keyframe 1.

   This task uses a sound called Drip.AIFF.

2. In the Timeline, select keyframe 1.

3. In the sound area of the Frame Properties tab of the Property inspector, from the Repeat pop-up menu, choose Repeat (the default setting).

4. Type 3 in the field to the right of the Repeat menu (**Figure 15.39**).

   Flash extends the sound's waveform by stringing together three copies of it. In the Timeline, Flash displays as much of the extended waveform as will fit in the available frames (**Figure 15.40**).

5. Save this document for use in the next task; name it RepeatSnds.fla.

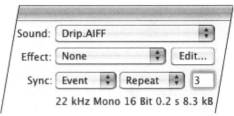

Figure 15.39 Typing a value in the Repeat field tells Flash how many times to play the selected sound.

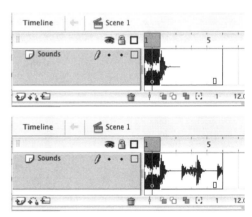

Figure 15.40 When Repeat is set to 0, Flash displays just the original waveform in the Timeline (top). When Repeat is set to 3, Flash displays as much of the repeated waveform as there is room for (bottom).

Figure 15.41 Choosing Loop from the Repeat menu in the Frame Properties tab of the Property inspector sets the sound for the selected keyframe to play over and over until there is an instruction to stop that sound (or stop all sounds).

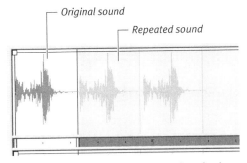

Original sound

Repeated sound

Figure 15.42 You can see a precise waveform for the repeated sound graphed against seconds or frames (shown here) of your movie in the Edit Envelope window. The grayed-out waveforms are the repeated portion of the sound.

✔ Tips

■ To make a sound repeat continuously until you issue an instruction to stop the sound, choose Loop from the Repeat menu (**Figure 15.41**).

■ Although you can use the Repeat parameter with sounds whose Sync parameter is Stream, doing so adds to the size of your exported file.

■ To see the extended waveform graphed against seconds or frames, click Edit in the Frame Properties tab of the Property inspector. The full sound appears in the Edit Envelope window (**Figure 15.42**).

■ Because Flash links the repeated sounds and displays them as a single sound in the Edit Envelope window, you can edit the repeating sound. You can change the volume so the sound gets louder with each repetition, for example. You learn about editing sounds in the following section of this chapter.

Editing Sounds

Flash allows you to make limited changes in each instance of a sound in the Edit Envelope window. You can change the start and end point of the sound (that is, cut a piece off the beginning or end of the waveform) and adjust the sound's volume.

Flash offers six predefined volume edits: Left Channel, Right Channel, Fade Left to Right, Fade Right to Left, Fade In, and Fade Out. These sound-editing templates create common sound effects, such as making a sound grow gradually louder (Fade In) or softer (Fade Out), or (for stereo sounds) making the sound move from one speaker channel to the other.

In addition to changing a sound's volume, you can make a sound shorter by instructing Flash to remove sound data from the beginning, the end, or both.

To assign packaged volume effects:

1. Open the document you created in the preceding task (RepeatSnds.fla).

   This is a 5-frame movie with an event sound that loops three times within those frames.

2. In the Timeline, select keyframe 1.

   This frame contains the sound Drip.AIFF.

3. In the sound area of the Frame Properties tab of the Property inspector, click the Edit button.

   The Edit Envelope window appears, displaying the waveform of the sound from keyframe 1 (**Figure 15.43**).

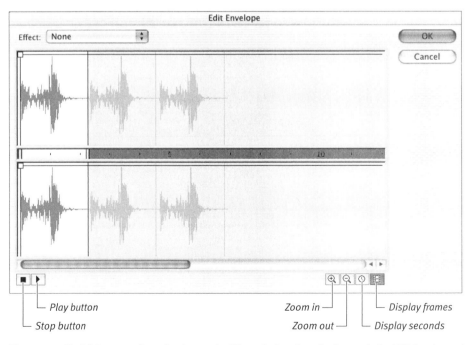

Figure 15.43 Flash lets you perform simple sound editing—for length and volume—in the Edit Envelope window.

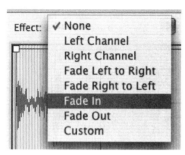

Figure 15.44 The Effect pop-up menu in the Edit Envelope window offers six templates for common sound effects that deal with volume. Choose Fade In to make the sound start soft and grow in volume.

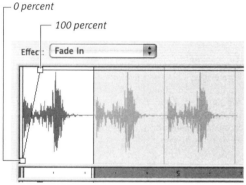

Figure 15.45 The Fade In effect brings the sound's envelope down to 0 percent (the bottom of the sound-editing window) at the start of the sound and quickly raises it to 100 percent (the top of the sound-editing window).

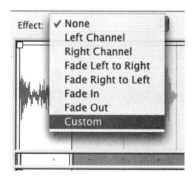

Figure 15.46 To edit the volume of a sound yourself, from the Effect pop-up menu in the Edit Envelope window, choose Custom.

4. In the Edit Envelop window, click the Display Frames button.

The window can measure the length of the sound in seconds or in frames. Clicking the film-strip icon in the lower-right corner of the window sets the units to frames; clicking the clock icon sets the units to seconds.

5. From the Effect pop-up menu, choose Fade In (**Figure 15.44**).

Flash adjusts the sound envelope (**Figure 15.45**). When the envelope line is at the top of the window, Flash plays 100 percent of the available sound. When the envelope line is at the bottom of the window, Flash plays 0 percent of the available sound.

6. Click the Play button to hear the sound with its fade-in effect.

The first iteration of the sound starts soft and grows louder. The repetitions play at full volume.

7. Click OK.

Flash returns you to document-editing mode.

✔ Tip

■ If you don't need to look at your sound's waveform, you can bypass the Edit Envelope window. Just choose an effect from the Effect pop-up menu in the sound area of the Frame Properties tab of the Property inspector.

To customize volume effects:

1. Follow steps 1–3 in the preceding task.

2. From the Effect pop-up menu, choose Custom (**Figure 15.46**).

continues on next page

EDITING SOUNDS

3. In the Edit Envelope window, drag the square envelope handles that appear at the beginning of the sound in both channels down to 0 percent.

4. In the right channel (the top section of the window), click the waveform at three places to set a different level for each repetition of the sound; for this sound, add handles near the marks for frames 2, 4, and 5.

Flash adds envelope handles so both channels have four handles.

5. In the right-channel window, drag the second handle up to the 50 percent volume level (**Figure 15.47**).

6. Repeat step 5 for the left channel.

7. In both channels, drag the third handle to the 50 percent level and the fourth handle to the 100 percent level (**Figure 15.48**).

You can use as many as eight handles to create a variety of volume changes within one sound.

8. Click the Play button to hear the sound with its fade-in effect.

Flash fades in the first iteration of the sound, plays the second iteration at half volume, and plays the third iteration at full volume.

9. Click OK.

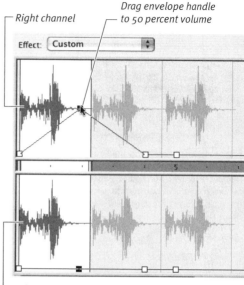

Figure 15.47 Click the waveform in the sound-editing window to add a handle. Drag the handle to adjust the sound envelope. You can make the sound envelope the same or different for both channels. For monaural sounds, both waveforms are identical.

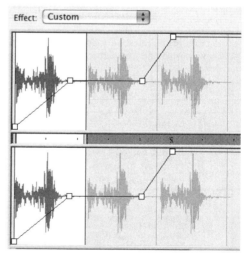

Figure 15.48 You can use up to eight handles to shape a sound's envelope. By using the zoom tools to view more of the sound in the Edit Envelope window, you can see the sound envelope for all three iterations of the sound. The first fades in, the second plays at 50 percent volume, and the third plays at full volume.

Time-in control   *Dead air*

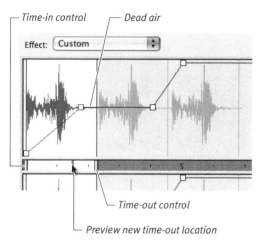

Time-out control

Preview new time-out location

Figure 15.49 Flash lets you trim the beginning and end of a sound in the Edit Envelope window. Here, dragging the time-out control clips off the end of the sound where the wave's amplitude is smaller, almost a flat line. (The small amplitude indicates very soft sound or silence).

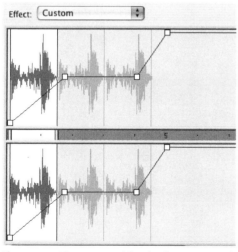

Figure 15.50 After you reposition the time-out control, the new, shorter waveform appears in the Edit Envelope window.

✔ Tips

■ To remove unwanted envelope handles, drag them out of the sound-editing window.

■ When you add a handle to one channel, Flash automatically adds another to the same location in the other channel. To create different volumes from the two channels, however, you can drag the handle to a different level in each channel.

■ You can start with one of the preset effects and build on it to create a custom effect. Choose the effect from the Effect menu in the Edit window; Flash sets the handles for that effect. Add envelope handles or reposition the existing handles; Flash switches the Effect menu to Custom and uses the new settings for the sound in this keyframe.

To edit sounds for length:

1. Using the movie you created in the preceding task, select keyframe 1.

2. To access the Edit Envelope window, in the Frame Properties tab of the Property inspector, click the Edit button.

3. In the Edit Envelope window, drag the time-out control to the place where the waveform goes flat (**Figure 15.49**).

   Flash shortens the sound in both channels (**Figure 15.50**).

continues on next page

EDITING SOUNDS

503

4. Click OK.

Flash returns you to document-editing mode. Now all three iterations of the repeating sound are visible in the Timeline (**Figure 15.51**).

✔ Tips

■ To remove dead air from the beginning of a sound, drag the time-in control. Flash dims the initial portion of the sound's waveform to indicate that it won't play.

■ Although you can change the start and end points of a sound in Flash, you still have the whole sound taking up room in your movie file. If you find yourself trimming many sounds in Flash, consider investing in a sound-editing program that allows you to leave the excess on the cutting-room floor rather than behind the curtains in Flash.

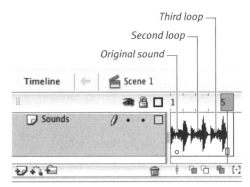

Figure 15.51 After you shorten the sound, all three iterations fit into the 5-frame movie.

EDITING SOUNDS

Delivering Movies to Your Audience

16

When you finish creating graphics, animation, and interactivity in Macromedia Flash 8, it's time to deliver the goods to your audience. You must export the Flash document to another format for playback. You have several formats to choose among. The one that guarantees viewers will see all your animations and take part in all your movie's interactivity is the Flash Player format. Player files end with the extension .swf.

When you install Flash 8, you can also install version 8 of the Flash Player application. You can view SWF files running directly in Flash Player on your computer. Other programs, such as Web browsers, can also control Flash Player.

You can export movies as a series of images in either bitmap format (GIF or PNG files, for example) or vector format (such as Adobe Illustrator files). Another option for movie delivery is a self-playing file called a *projector*. Users double-click the projector file to open and play the movie. And you can print your entire movie or individual frames, should you want to give someone a hard-copy version of the movie (for storyboarding, for example).

DELIVERING MOVIES TO YOUR AUDIENCE

Preparing Your Movie for Optimal Playback

When you create movies to show over the Web, you must face the issue of quality versus quantity. Higher quality (smoother animation and better, longer sounds) increases file size. The larger the file, the longer the download time and the slower your movie will be. Things that add to your file's size include lots of bitmaps (especially animated bitmaps), video clips, sounds, multiple areas of animation at one time, embedded fonts, gradients, and separate graphic elements instead of symbols and groups.

To help you find out where your movie is bogging down, Flash offers simulated streaming. The Size Report and Bandwidth Profiler reveal which frames will cause hang-ups. You can then rethink or optimize the problem areas.

To use the Bandwidth Profiler:

1. Open the Flash document that you want to test for playback over the Web.

2. Choose Control > Test Movie (or Test Scene).

   Flash exports the movie and opens it in Flash Player.

3. From Flash Player's View menu, choose Download Settings, and select the download speed you want to test.

   The menu lists eight speeds, all of which are customizable. To change them, choose View > Download Settings > Customize (**Figure 16.1**). By default, Flash lists five common connection speeds—14.4 Kbps, 28.8 Kbps, 56 Kbps, DSL, and T1—with settings that simulate real-world data-transfer rates. You can see the settings in the Custom Download Settings dialog (**Figure 16.2**). To create a custom setting, enter new values, and then click OK.

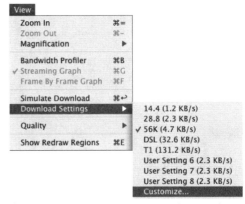

Figure 16. 1 To create a custom connection speed for simulating playback over the Web, from the test environment's View menu, choose Download Settings > Customize.

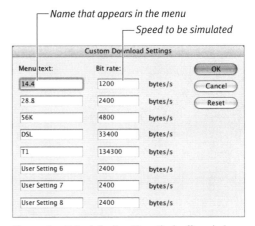

Figure 16.2 At its default setting, Flash offers choices for simulating five standard connection speeds. You can change the names and rates for these speeds in the Custom Download Settings dialog.

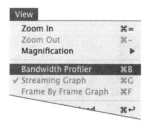

Figure 16.3 To view a graph of the amount of data in each frame, choose View > Bandwidth Profiler when a Flash Player window is open.

Downloads within the set frame rate ———

Causes a delay in playback ———

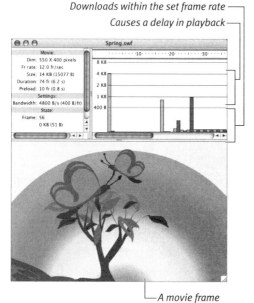

— A movie frame

Figure 16.4 The Bandwidth Profiler graph at the top of the Flash Player window shows how much data each movie frame contains. Each bar in this version of the graph represents a frame of the movie.

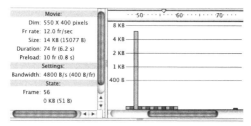

Figure 16.5 In Frame by Frame Graph mode, the height of each bar indicates how much data the frame holds.

4. From Flash Player's View menu, choose Bandwidth Profiler (**Figure 16.3**).

At the top of the Test Movie window, Flash graphs the amount of data that is being transmitted against the movie's Timeline (**Figure 16.4**). The bars represent the number of bytes of data per frame. The bottom line (highlighted in red) represents the amount of data that will safely download fast enough to keep up with the movie's frame rate. Any frame that contains a greater amount of data forces the movie to pause while the data downloads.

To view the contents of each frame separately:

1. From the Flash Player's View menu, choose Frame by Frame Graph, or press ⌘-F (Mac) or Ctrl-F (Windows).

Flash presents a single bar for each frame in the Bandwidth Profiler graph. The numbers along the top of the graph represent frames (**Figure 16.5**). The height of the bar represents the amount of data in that frame.

2. Select a bar.

Specifics about that frame and the movie in general appear in the profile window.

To see how frames stream:

1. Choose View > Streaming Graph, or press ⌘-G (Mac) or Ctrl-G (Windows).

   Flash displays the frames as alternating bars of light and dark gray, sized to reflect the time each one takes to download (**Figure 16.6**). The numbers along the top of the streaming graph represent frames as a unit of time based on the frame rate. (In a 12 fps movie, for example, each number represents $\frac{1}{12}$ second.) For frames that contain very little data, you may see several bars in a single time unit in the graph. Frames that have lots of data stretch out over several time units.

2. Select a bar.

   Specifics about that frame and the movie in general appear in the profile window (**Figure 16.7**).

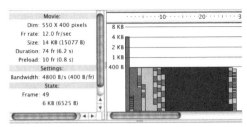

Figure 16.6 In Streaming Graph mode, the width of each bar indicates how long the frame takes to download at the given connection speed and frame rate. In this movie, frame 49 contains 6 KB of data and takes roughly 5 seconds to download at a frame rate of 12 fps over a 14.4 Kbps modem. Each number along the top of the graph is a frame, and at 12 fps, this equals $\frac{1}{12}$ second.

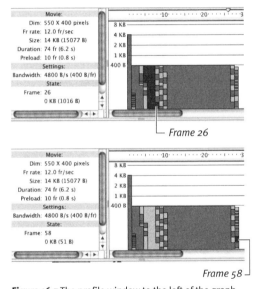

Frame 26

Frame 58

Figure 16.7 The profile window to the left of the graph displays information about the movie. The State section identifies the selected frame (the frame highlighted in red) and lists the amount of data in that frame. You can see that frame 26 (top) has 1016 bytes of information, whereas frame 58 (bottom) contains only 51 bytes.

To display a download-progress bar:

◆ With Bandwidth Profiler active, from Flash Player's View menu, choose Simulate Download, or press ⌘-Return (Mac) or Ctrl-Enter (Windows).

As the animation plays in the test window, Flash highlights the numbers of the Timeline in green to show where you are in the download process.

To exit Bandwidth Profiler:

◆ From Flash Player's View menu, choose Bandwidth Profiler again to deselect it.

✔ Tips

■ After you set up a test environment incorporating the Bandwidth Profiler, you can open any SWF file directly in test mode. Choose File > Open, navigate to the file you want to test, and then click Open. Flash opens the movie in a Flash Player window, using the Bandwidth Profiler and other viewing options you selected.

■ You can get a printed version of the information about the amount of data in each frame. Choose the Generate Size Report option in the Export Flash Player dialog or the Flash tab of the Publish Settings dialog (for more information, see "Exporting vs. Publishing," later in this chapter). During the export or publishing process, Flash simultaneously creates a text file documenting how many bytes of information each frame of the movie contains.

A Note About Accessibility

As you think about the best ways to deliver Flash movies to your audience, also consider the fact that some members of the audience may have physical conditions that affect the way they interact with your site. As the Web has become more visually interesting, it presents challenges to users with visual impairments who want to take advantage of the many resources available.

Our society is becoming more sensitive to the ways in which activities and resources exclude people with disabilities. Web designers need to use Flash not only to make eye-catching Web sites that dazzle with artwork, animation, interactivity, sound, and video, but also to make sites that can convey information to a wide range of people. Remember that some of your users are unable to view or hear a site's content; some need to navigate and explore the site strictly through an input device—for example, by tabbing to each element in turn.

Flash addresses the issue of accessible Web sites by allowing you to make Flash content available to screen-reading software that uses Microsoft Active Accessibility (MSAA) technology. (At the time Flash 8 was released, MSAA was available only for Windows.) Screen readers provide audio feedback about a variety of elements on a Web site, reading aloud the labels of buttons, for example, or reading the contents of text fields. Through Flash's accessibility features, you can create descriptions of objects for the screen reader; prevent the screen reader from attempting to describe certain objects (such as purely decorative movie clips); and assign keyboard commands that let the user manipulate objects by pressing keys or tabbing through text fields, for example.

The considerations that go into making an effective, accessible site are too numerous and complex to cover in this book. But you can check out the tools for defining accessible objects in the Accessibility panel. Choose Window > Other Panels > Accessibility to open the panel, or click the Accessibility icon in the bottom-right quadrant of the Properties tab of the Property inspector (**Figure 16.8**). The accessibility parameters for selected objects appear in the panel.

Macromedia outlines some of the basic concepts of accessible Web design in the Help panel (see the topic Using Flash > Creating Accessible Content). More information is available on Macromedia's Accessibility page (*http://www.macromedia.com/ resources/accessibility/*).

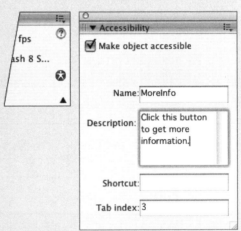

Figure 16.8 Clicking the Accessibility icon (left) in the Properties tab of the Property inspector opens the Accessibility panel (right). Use these settings to make selected objects in your movie available (or unavailable) to screen-reader software.

Figure 16.9 To access the settings for publishing a movie, choose File > Publish Settings.

Publishing

To make your movie available to the public, you must publish or export it. Flash's Publish function is geared toward presenting material on the Web and creating a range of formats for various viewers. The Export feature has similar settings but creates just one format at a time (see the sidebar "Exporting vs. Publishing"). The Publish command can create the Flash Player (SWF) file and an HTML document that puts your Flash Player file in a browser window. The Publish command can also create alternate file formats—GIF, JPEG, PNG, and QuickTime— and the HTML needed to display them in the browser window. Alternate formats let you make some of the animation and interactivity of your site available even to viewers who lack the Flash plug-in. Flash can also create stand-alone projector files.

To set the publishing format:

1. Open the Flash document you want to publish.

2. Choose File > Publish Settings, or press Option-Shift-F12 (Mac) or Ctrl-Shift-F12 (Windows) (**Figure 16.9**).

   The Publish Settings dialog appears. The top of the dialog displays a Current Profile and buttons for working with profiles. If you're working in a new document and have never created a profile, Default is your only option. If you open a file made with a previous version of Flash, the profile name reflects that version. A profile is the compilation of settings for the various publishing options. You can save settings in new profiles (see "Creating Publishing Profiles," later in this chapter). Leave the current profile in place.

   continues on next page

Exporting vs. Publishing

Flash's Export Movie command translates a Flash document directly into a single format. In general, the options for exporting from Flash—GIF, JPEG, PNG, and QuickTime—are the same as those for publishing to those formats. The arrangement of some options differs between the export and publish dialogs, and some formats have more options in the Publish Settings dialog. In the Publish Settings dialog, for example, you have the choice to remove gradients from GIFs (to keep the file size small), whereas in the Export GIF dialog, you don't have that option. Another difference between publishing and exporting is that Flash stores the publish settings with the movie file for reuse.

3. Click the Formats tab (Windows) or button (Mac) (**Figure 16.10**).

4. Choose one of the eight format options.

The options are Flash (.swf), HTML (.html), GIF Image (.gif), JPEG Image (.jpg), PNG Image (.png), Windows Projector (.exe), Macintosh Projector, and QuickTime (.mov).

5. To set the options for a selected format, choose the tab (Windows) or button (Mac) associated with that format (as outlined in separate tasks later in this chapter).

6. To save these settings with the current file, click OK.

Flash uses these settings each time you choose the Publish or Publish Preview command for this document. Flash also uses a file's current publish settings when you enter test mode (by choosing Control > Test Movie or Control > Test Scene).

✔ Tip

- If you have the Properties tab of the Property inspector open as you work on your Flash document, you can open the Publish Settings dialog quickly. In the Publish section of the tab, click the Settings button.

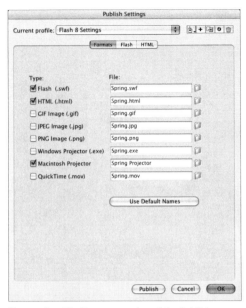

Figure 16.10 The Formats section of the Publish Settings dialog lets you publish your Flash content in as many as seven formats at the same time. An eighth format choice creates an HTML document for displaying the published files in a browser.

Figure 16.11 Click the Publish button in the Publish Settings dialog (left) or choose File > Publish (right) to publish your Flash files.

Figure 16.12 To cancel the publishing process, click the Stop (Mac) or Cancel (Windows) button in the Publishing dialog. If you've published the file before, the dialog may appear only briefly, making it difficult to cancel the operation.

Figure 16.13 The File > Publish Preview submenu displays all the formats selected in the Publish Settings dialog. Flash publishes your movie in the selected format and opens it in your browser.

To publish a movie:

1. Open the Flash file you want to publish.

2. To issue the Publish command, *do either of the following:*

   ▲ Choose File > Publish Settings. The Publish Settings dialog appears. You can follow the steps in the preceding task to set new format options or accept the current settings. Then click the Publish button (**Figure 16.11**).

   ▲ Choose File > Publish, or press Shift-F12.

   The Publishing dialog appears, displaying a progress bar and a button for canceling the procedure (**Figure 16.12**). Flash uses the publish settings stored with your Flash document, creating a new file for each format selected in the Publish Settings dialog.

✔ Tips

- By default, Flash places the published files in the same location as the original Flash file. You can choose a new location. In the formats section of the Publish Settings dialog, click the folder icon to the right of the filename. The Select Publish Destination dialog appears, allowing you to select a new location for the file.

- You can open your browser and preview a movie in one step. Choose File > Publish Preview. Flash offers a menu that contains all the formats selected in the Publish Settings dialog (**Figure 16.13**). Choose a format. Flash publishes the file in that format, using the current settings, and opens the movie in a browser window.

continues on next page

PUBLISHING

513

- You can use Publish Preview to test your Flash creation in a browser window. If you're testing SWF files that reside on your local system, and your Flash movie links to a URL on the network, you can run into security issues. For testing purposes, you may need to change the security settings in the Flash section of the Publish Settings dialog (setting the Local Playback Security setting to Access Network Only) or you may need to give special permissions to the file you're testing (see the sidebar "A Note about Flash Player 8's Security Settings").

- Flash makes one of the formats the default for Publish Preview. To publish in the default format, press Shift-F12. If you want to do lots of testing in a format other than SWF (to test your animated GIF versions, for example), set your publish settings in only that format. Then that format is the default, and you can choose it quickly by pressing Shift-F12.

- By default, Flash names the published files by adding the appropriate extension to the filename—adding .gif for a GIF file or .png for a PNG file, for example. Change the name by typing a different name in the File field in the Publish Settings dialog. To return to the default name, click the Use Default Names button (**Figure 16.14**).

- The Publish and Publish Preview commands don't give you a chance to name the published files; they take the names directly from the Publish Settings dialog. If you want to publish multiple versions of a movie, each with different settings, you must make sure that you don't overwrite the published file. Rename the published file, move that file to a new location, or type a different name in the Formats section of the Publish Settings dialog.

Figure 16.14 You can type your own filenames in the fields of the Publish Settings dialog box. Just be sure to end the name with the proper extension. To return to the default name, click the Use Default Names button.

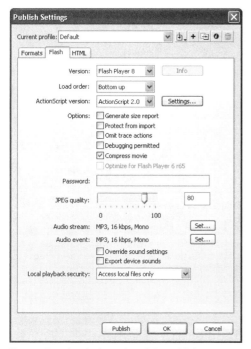

Figure 16.15 The Flash section of the Publish Settings dialog offers options for publishing your Flash movie as a Flash Player (SWF) file.

Working with Flash Player Settings

The stand-alone Flash Player is an application file that installs with Flash. The Player opens when you double-click the icon of a file that has the .swf extension. (From within Flash Player, you can use the File > Open command to open and play SWF files.) To prepare a Flash movie for playing in the stand-alone Player, choose either the Export or Publish command in the Flash editor. The options are basically the same for both commands.

To publish a Flash Player (SWF) file:

1. In the Flash editor, open the Flash (.fla) file you want to publish.

2. Choose File > Publish Settings.

   The Publish Settings dialog appears; choose a base publishing profile, or leave the current setting.

3. Click the Formats tab (Windows) or button (Mac).

4. In the Type section, select Flash (.swf).

   If you wish, type a new name in the File field for the Flash (SWF) file. Be sure to include the .swf extension.

5. Select the Flash tab (Windows) or button (Mac) (**Figure 16.15**).

6. Set Flash options as described in the following tasks.

7. Click Publish.

To choose a Flash Player version:

◆ From the Version pop-up menu, choose a version of Flash Player (**Figure 16.16**).

Your options are Flash Player 1 (formerly known as FutureSplash Animator) through 8. (Flash Professional 8 users can also choose to publish to Flash Lite 1.0 and 1.1: players that work in devices such as mobile phones.) If you publish your file as a version earlier than Flash Player 8, you lose some features specific to Flash 8.

✔ Tips

■ Before you start creating ActionScripts, set the Flash export options in the Publish Settings dialog to the earliest version of Flash Player to which you plan to export. Any Flash 8 actions that won't work in that version appear with yellow highlighting in the Actions Toolbox in the Actions panel.

■ When you choose Flash Player 6 from the Version pop-up menu, the Optimize for Flash Player 6 r65 check box becomes active. Select the check box to enable Flash to take advantage of performance improvements made to Flash Player 6 (these enhancements appear in release 65 and later of Flash Player 6).

To control how Flash draws the movie's frames:

◆ From the Load Order pop-up menu, choose the order in which Flash loads a movie's layers for display (**Figure 16.17**). When playback over the Web is slow, Flash starts displaying individual layers as they download. The Top Down setting tells Flash to send (and display) the top layer first and then work its way to the bottom layer. Bottom Up does just the opposite.

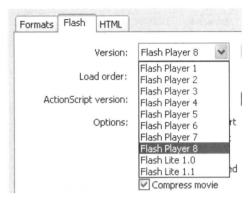

Figure 16.16 Choose a version of Flash Player to publish to. Publishing to earlier versions makes some features of Flash 8 unavailable but ensures that a wider audience will have the correct player. Users of Flash Professional 8 (shown here) can also choose a Flash Lite version.

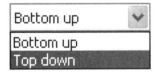

Figure 16.17 The Load Order pop-up menu determines the order in which Flash draws the layers of the frames of your movie.

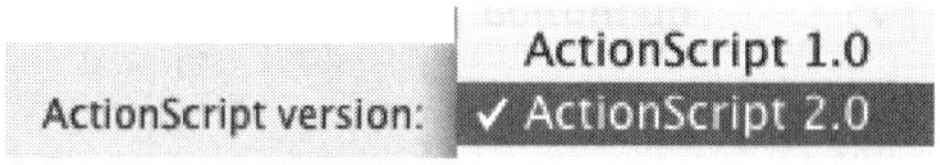

Figure 16.18 ActionScript 2.0 presents special tasks for the compiler when Flash publishes a SWF file. Be sure to select it if you use version 2.0 for scripting.

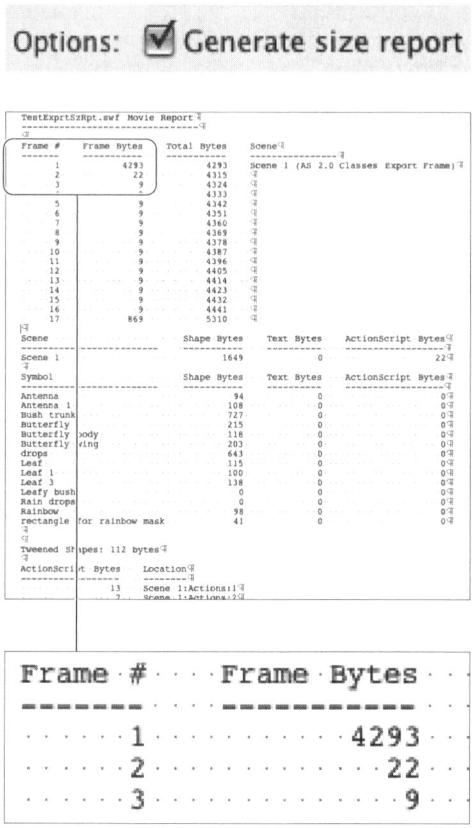

Figure 16.19 Choose Generate Size Report (top) to have Flash create a text file that lists the amount of data in your movie (bottom).

To choose the version of ActionScript used (Flash Player 6–8):

◆ From the pop-up menu, choose ActionScript version.1. 0 or ActionScript version 2.0 (**Figure 16.18**).

This setting tells Flash which version of the scripting language you've used in scripts in your document so the compiler treats the code appropriately. The menu becomes active only when you've chosen Player versions 6–8.

✔ Tip

■ The components found in Flash 8's Components panel rely on ActionScript 2.0. If you've used any of those components in the current document, you must choose ActionScript 2.0.

To list the amount of data in the movie by frame:

◆ Select the Generate Size Report check box (**Figure 16.19**).

Flash creates a separate text file listing the frames of the movie and how much data each frame contains. (The Size report text also appears in the Output panel.) This report helps you find frames that bog down the movie's playback. You can then optimize or eliminate some of the content in those frames.

✔ Tip

■ The Size report also details how much data is in each symbol used in the movie. Symbols that aren't used appear in the report, but they contain 0 bytes of data.

To protect your work:

◆ Select the Protect from Import check box (**Figure 16.20**).

This setting prevents viewers from obtaining the SWF file and converting it back to a Flash document (FLA).

✔ Tip

■ You can make the Protect from Import setting selective. Enter a password in the Password field. Only those who enter the correct password can import the SWF file.

To set trace and debug options:

◆ To tell Flash how to deal with `trace` actions and debugging (options that are useful for more advanced ActionScripters), *select either of the following check boxes:*

Omit trace actions prevents `trace` actions from appearing in the Output window during debugging. This option strips the `trace` actions from the published movie, allowing you to view only non-`trace` debugging items in the Output window. Omitting `trace` actions also reduces file size slightly if your scripts contain lots of `trace` actions.

Debugging permitted allows remote debugging of ActionScripts. This option allows you or other users to debug a Flash Player (SWF) file as it plays over the Internet.

✔ Tip

■ When the Debugging Permitted option is selected, you should always enter a password in the Password field (**Figure 16.21**). This password prohibits unauthorized individuals from accessing your script but allows authorized personnel to debug the file remotely.

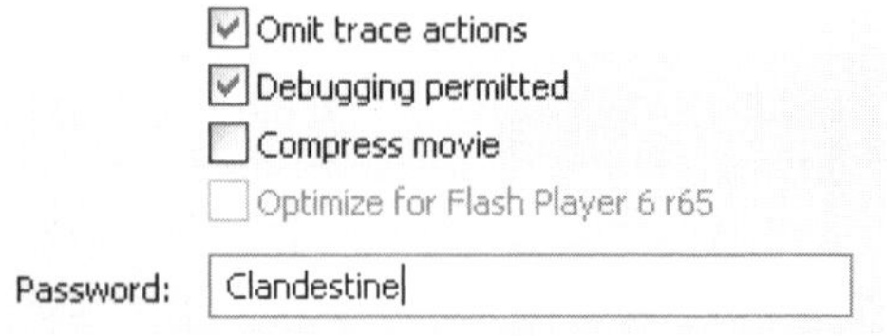

Figure 16.20 Choose Protect from Import to prevent viewers from converting a SWF file back into a FLA file.

Figure 16.21 When you select the Debugging Permitted check box, you should also enter a password to protect movies that are open to remote debugging.

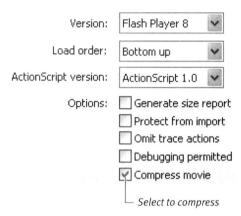

Select to compress

Figure 16.22 When you've chosen to publish to Flash Player versions 6–8, you can also choose to compress the movie. Compression helps to reduce the file size, especially for text-heavy movies or those with lots of ActionScript.

Figure 16.23 To set JPEG compression for any bitmaps in your movie, type a value in the JPEG Quality field or use the slider. A setting of 0 results in the most compression (worst quality); 100 results in the least compression (best quality).

To compress the SWF file (Flash Player 6–8):

1. Choose Flash Player 6–8 from the Version pop-up menu.

2. Select the Compress Movie option (**Figure 16.22**).

   Compress Movie is an option only when you publish for Flash Player versions 6–8. The setting has no effect on the JPEG-quality and audio-compression settings you choose in the following tasks.

To compress the bitmaps in your movie:

◆ To set JPEG compression, *do either of the following:*

   ▲ Adjust the JPEG Quality slider.

   ▲ Enter a specific value in the JPEG Quality field (**Figure 16.23**).

This setting controls how Flash applies JPEG compression as it exports the bitmaps in your movie. A setting of 0 provides the most compression (and the lowest quality, because that compression leads to loss of data).

✔ Tips

■ Flash doesn't apply JPEG compression to GIF images that you've imported into your movie, because Flash defaults to using lossless compression for GIFs.

■ You can also set compression for individual bitmaps in the library of your Flash document. Select the bitmap in the Library panel. From the panel's Options menu, choose Properties. The Compression pop-up menu in the Bitmap Properties dialog lets you choose lossy compression (JPEG) or lossless compression (PNG/GIF).

To control compression and sample rate for all movie sounds:

1. In the Audio Stream section (or the Audio Event section) of the Publish Settings dialog, click the Set button (**Figure 16.24**).

   The Sound Settings dialog appears. Flash divides sounds into two types: stream and event (for more details, see Chapter 15). You must set the compression for each type separately, but the process and options are the same for both.

2. To set compression parameters, from the Compression pop-up menu (**Figure 16.25**), *choose one of the following options:*

   Disable makes Flash omit sound from the published file.

   ADPCM sets compression for movies containing mostly short event sounds, such as handclaps or button clicks. (Generally, you'll use this setting in the Audio Event section.) The ADPCM options appear. From the ADPCM Bits pop-up menu, choose 2-Bit for the greatest degree of compression (resulting in the lowest-quality sound); choose 5-Bit for the least compression (resulting in the highest-quality sound). With the ADPCM setting, you can also set a sample rate and convert stereo sound to mono sound.

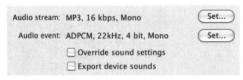

Figure 16.24 You must set the sample rate and compression options for stream sounds and event sounds separately. Click the Set button to access the options for each type of sound.

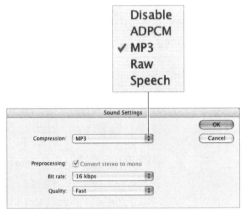

Figure 16.25 Choose a compression method from the Compression pop-up menu. Other options appropriate to the selected method appear. Choose Disable to turn off sound.

Sample-Rate Rule of Thumb

Sample rates are measured in kHz or frequency. Recording for music CDs is done at 44 kHz. For multimedia CD-ROMs, 22 kHz is a standard rate. For music clips in Flash movies played on the Web, 11 kHz is often sufficient. For shorter sounds, including spoken words, you may be able to get away with even lower sampling rates.

MP3 sets compression for movies containing mostly longer stream sounds. (Generally, you'll use this setting in the Audio Stream section.) The MP3 options appear. From the Bit Rate pop-up menu, choose one of 12 bit rates for the published sounds. At a Bit Rate setting of less than 20 Kbps, Flash converts sounds from stereo to mono; at settings of 20 Kbps and above, you can publish stereo sounds or convert them to mono sounds. From the Quality pop-up menu, choose Fast when you are testing your movie; choose Medium or Best when you publish for your target audience as they provide better quality.

Raw omits sound compression. Raw does allow you to control file size by choosing a sample rate and converting stereo sound to mono.

Speech sets compression for sounds consisting of spoken words. Choose a sample rate from the pop-up menu of options that appears.

Digitally Recorded Sounds

As motion pictures are to movement, digital recordings are to sound. Both media capture slices of a continuous event. By playing the captured slices back in order, you re-create the event. In a movie, the slices are frames of film; in a digital recording, they're snippets of sound.

You can think of the recording process as capturing a sound wave by laying a grid over it and copying a piece of the wave at each intersection on the grid. The lines across the horizontal axis are the *sample rate*—how often you capture the sound. The lines up and down the vertical axis are the *bit rate*—how much of detail of the sound wave's amplitude you capture. The greater the frequency and bit rate (the finer the mesh of your recording grid), the greater the realism of your recording during playback. Unfortunately, greater realism translates into larger files.

The sound options in the Publish Settings dialog give you the flexibility to create different versions of your movie with different sample rates and bit rates without actually changing the sounds embedded in the movie. You might allow yourself larger file sizes and higher-quality sounds for a version being delivered on CD-ROM than for a version being distributed on the Web. As you try different sound options, be sure to listen to your published sounds to determine the best balance between sound quality and file size.

To control access to local and network files for security:

◆ To determine which types of files the SWF file can copy data from or write data to, in the Local playback security section, from the pop-up menu (**Figure 16.26**), *choose either of the following options:*

Access local files only. With local-only access, the SWF file can share information with files located on the local system where the SWF file resides, but not with files located on the Internet. Local-only access prevents a SWF file from loading XML files from the Internet or posting data from an entry form to the Internet, for example.

Access network only. With network-only access, the SWF file can share information only with files located on the Internet, not with local files.

Figure 16.26 Flash 8 provides a new level of security by restricting SWF files from manipulating data on different systems. With Local Access Only as the setting, the published SWF file can only copy or write data to files on the local system. With Network Access Only, the SWF file can copy or write data only to files on the network and not on the local system.

Advanced Sound Handling

The sound-compression settings in the Publish Settings dialog apply to all the sounds in your movie unless you've specified sound settings for individual sounds in the library of the Flash document. A more advanced method of dealing with sound compression is to set compression options and sample rates for sounds individually. Assigning the highest quality to selected sounds helps you keep file size reasonable but still have high-quality sound where you need it.

You set compression options for individual sounds via the Sound Properties dialog, which you access from the movie's Library panel. Control-click (Mac) or right-click (Windows) a sound name in the Library panel; then choose Properties from the contextual menu that appears. The Sound Properties dialog appears. Its Compression pop-up menu gives you access to the same sound-export settings as the Flash tab of the Publish Settings dialog.

If some sounds in a movie have individual sound-export settings, Flash uses those settings for those sounds when you choose Publish. Flash uses the sound options you set in the Publish Settings dialog for all other sounds in that movie.

If you've used individual compression methods for some sounds in your movie, you can force Flash to ignore them and publish all sounds with the sound options you've chosen in the Publish Settings dialog. In the Flash section of the Publish Settings dialog, choose Override Sound Settings. You might use this feature to make a lower-quality Web version of a movie you created for CD-ROM.

A Note about Flash Player 8's Security Settings

Flash 8 and Flash Player 8 allow you to create Flash content that uploads and/or downloads files at runtime; this capability gives Flash more power than in previous versions, but with that power comes the potential to do harm. A new security feature ensures that SWF files can't perform malicious deeds on the systems of your target audience. Flash's default local-security settings prohibit SWF files running locally (on a single computer) from communicating with files being served on the Internet (and vice versa); to allow such communication, you must give Flash Player specific permissions. If you test a movie published to Flash 8 locally, before deploying it to a server, and you use a button or link in the movie to connect to the Internet, you may receive a warning that Flash Player has stopped an operation that might be unsafe.

If the file you're testing doesn't need to communicate with both the local system and the Internet, you can solve the problem by changing your Publish Settings. (In the Flash section of the Publish Settings dialog, under Local Playback Security, choose Access Network Only.)

If, after changing the Local Playback Security setting, you still get the warning, you need to give your SWF file special permission to communicate with the Internet. When the Macromedia Flash Player Security dialog appears (**Figure 16.27**), click the Settings button. Flash opens a browser window and directs you to a page of the Flash Player documentation on the Macromedia site (http://www.macromedia.com/support/documentation/en/flashplayer/help/settings_manager04a.html). This page gives you access to the Settings Manager (**Figure 16.28**).

continues on next page

Figure 16.27 When a SWF file on a local computer attempts to access a file on the Internet, Flash Player 8 won't allow it to, unless you've set the proper security settings. You'll see a warning dialog to alert you to the fact that your settings don't allow this communication.

Global Security Settings tab

Click to add trusted files and/or folders

Figure 16.28 The Global Security Settings tab of Macromedia Flash Player Settings Manager lets you create a list of trusted files and/or folders for Flash Player 8 security. Any SWF files in locations covered by this list can communicate with Internet files.

A Note about Flash Player 8's Security Settings *continued*

Use the Global Security Settings tab of the manager to create a list of trusted items. Flash Player always allows SWF files from the Global Security Settings list to communicate with the Internet, even though they're being run locally. Use the Edit Locations pop-up menu to add individual SWF files or folders to the trusted list or remove them from the list (**Figure 16.29**).

If you'll be doing lots of this type of testing, it makes sense to set up a special trusted folder where you keep only your own SWF files you need to test. Don't allow Flash Player to trust folders on your system that might include SWF files downloaded from other sources. Such files have the potential to do something dangerous, such as copying information from your system and sending it to an outside location.

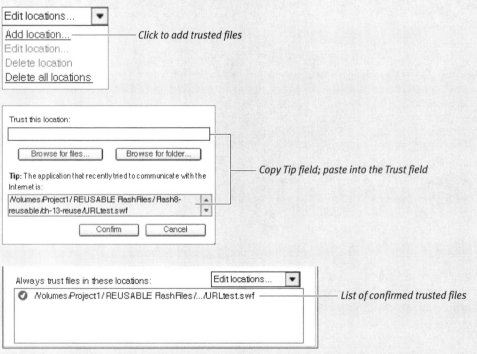

Figure 16.29 Click the Edit Locations pop-up menu to manage a list of trusted files (top). Click Add Location to open a window (middle) where you can add a new file or folder to a Trusted list. If you opened the Global Security Settings Manager by clicking the Settings button of the security warning dialog (Figure 16.27), the window's Tip field shows the path name for the file you were working on. Copy and paste that name to the Trusted field (or use one of the Browse buttons to navigate to the file or folder you want to add); click Confirm to add the trusted file to the Trust list (bottom).

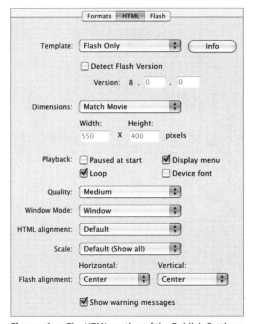

Figure 16.30 The HTML section of the Publish Settings dialog contains options for displaying your Flash movie in the browser window.

Publishing HTML for Flash Player Files

An *HTML document* is a master set of instructions that tells a browser how to display Web content. The Publish function of Flash creates an HTML document that tells the browser how to display the published files for your document (these files can be in Flash, GIF, JPEG, PNG, and/or QuickTime format, whatever you choose in the Formats tab of the Publish Settings dialog).

The Publish command creates the required HTML by filling in blanks in a template document. Flash comes with ten templates; you can also create your own.

To publish HTML for displaying a Flash file:

1. Open the Flash document you want to publish for the Web.

2. Choose File > Publish Settings.

   The Publish Settings dialog appears; choose a new publishing profile, or leave the current setting.

3. Click the Formats tab (Windows) or button (Mac).

4. In the Type section, choose HTML (.html).

   When you choose HTML, Flash automatically selects Flash (.swf) as well.

5. Select the HTML tab (Windows) or button (Mac) (**Figure 16.30**).

   The options for displaying your Flash movie in the browser window appear in the dialog. When you publish the current file, Flash feeds your choices into the appropriate HTML tags and parameters in the template of your choice.

To create HTML for Flash only:

◆ From the Template pop-up menu, choose Flash Only (**Figure 16.31**).

This template is the simplest one. It uses the HTML OBJECT and EMBED tags to display your Flash content for viewers who are properly equipped with the Flash Player version that you select in the Flash section of the Publish Settings dialog. Other viewers will be unable to see your content. (Other template choices create HTML that performs other tasks; for example, the Image Map template creates HTML that displays alternate images or files when the viewer lacks the proper plug-in.)

✔ Tip

■ If you can't remember what one of the included HTML templates does, select it from the Template pop-up menu in the HTML tab of the Publish Settings dialog, and then click the Info button next to the menu. Flash displays a brief description, including instructions about choosing alternate formats, if necessary.

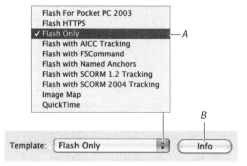

Figure 16.31 Choose Flash Only (A) as the template when you want to create HTML for displaying only a Flash movie with no other options for alternate images. Click the Info button (B) to see a description of what the template does (C).

The Mystery of HTML Templates

The HTML codes (called *tags*) required for displaying a SWF file in a browser window are `OBJECT` for Internet Explorer (Windows) and `EMBED` for other browsers. (In addition, Flash can use the `IMG` tag to display a file in another format, such as a JPEG image or an animated GIF. If you've created named anchors in your Flash movie and you choose the Flash with Named Anchors template, Flash can create anchor tags for browser navigation, as well.)

Flash's Publish command works hand in hand with HTML templates—which are fill-in-the-blank recipes—to define the parameters of those tags. These parameters include the width and height of the movie window, the quality of the images (the amount of antialiasing to provide), and the way the movie window aligns with the browser window.

Each option and parameter in the HTML section of the Publish Settings dialog has an equivalent template variable. The *template variable* is a code word that starts with the dollar sign (`$`). When you choose an option in the Publish Settings dialog, Flash enters your choice as an HTML tag that replaces the variable in the template document. If you set the width of your movie as 500 pixels in the Publish Settings dialog for HTML, for example, Flash replaces the template variable for width (`$WI`) with the proper coding to display the movie in a window 500 pixels wide.

Flash's HTML templates contain coding not only for displaying your Flash movie, but also for showing the JPEG, GIF, or PNG version of your movie that you want to make available to viewers who don't have the proper browser player to view Flash.

During the publishing process, Flash saves a copy of the HTML template for your movie, giving it the name of your movie file and adding whatever extension the template file has. (The template files that come with Flash use the extension .html, for example.) You can go into a template file as you would any other text file and modify the HTML coding.

You can extend the Publish command's capacity for creating HTML documents by setting up your own HTML templates. To be available to Flash's template menu, the HTML file must include a title (use the code `$TT`). The HTML file must be inside the HTML folder, which lives in the Configuration Folder. For more details on locating this folder, see the sidebar "The Mystery of the Configuration Folder" in Chapter 1.

To set the dimensions of the movie-display window:

◆ To set the width and height of the rectangle created by the OBJECT and EMBED tags for displaying your movie in the browser, from the Dimensions pop-up menu in the HTML section of the Publish Settings dialog (**Figure 16.32**), *choose one of the following options:*

Match Movie uses the movie's dimensions (specified in the Document Properties dialog).

Pixels lets you specify new dimensions. Type the new values in the Width and Height fields.

Percent lets you specify the dimensions as a percentage of the browser window's dimensions. Type a value between 1 and 100 in the Width and Height fields.

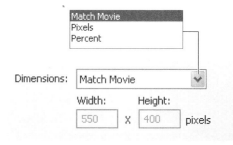

Figure 16.32 Choose a method for sizing the movie-display window (the window in which a browser displays your Flash movie).

Fitting Movies into Browser Windows

When you publish HTML for displaying movies in a Web page, think in terms of three windows:

◆ The *browser window* contains the entire Web page.

◆ Within the browser window is a *movie-display* window (created by the OBJECT, EMBED, and IMG tags) where the Flash plug-in displays a Flash movie.

◆ Inside the movie-display window is the actual *movie window*, which corresponds to the Stage of your Flash document.

Each of the three windows has its own dimensions, and you need to tell Flash where to put the windows and how to handle them if their aspect ratios differ, for example, or if a user resizes the browser window. To instruct browsers on how to deal with these three windows, choose settings in the HTML section of the Publish Settings dialog. When you define a movie-display window with a different width or height from the original Flash document, you must tell Flash how to scale the movie to fit in that window.

Scale: [Exact fit]

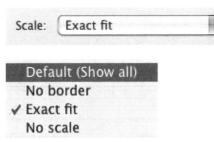

Default (Show all)
No border
✓ Exact fit
No scale

Figure 16.33 The scale method tells Flash how to fit the Flash movie inside the movie-display window that you define. You need to set the scale only if you define a movie-display window with different dimensions from those of the movie itself—as a percentage of the browser width and height, for example.

To scale the movie to fit a movie-display window:

◆ From the Scale pop-up menu (**Figure 16.33**), *choose one of the following options:*

Default (Show All) keeps the movie's original aspect ratio (width to height) and resizes the movie so that it fits completely within the newly specified rectangle (**Figure 16.34**). (Be aware that the resized movie may not fill the new rectangle: Gaps may appear on the sides or at the top and bottom.)

No Border keeps the movie's original aspect ratio and resizes the movie so the whole new rectangle is filled with it. (Some of the movie may slop over the edges and be cropped.)

continues on next page

Dimensions: Match Movie;
Scale: NA

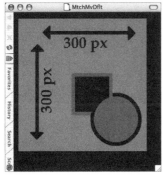

Dimensions: 100 by 50 pixels;
Scale: No Border

Dimensions: 100 by 50 pixels;
Scale: Exact Fit

Figure 16.34 This 300-by-300–pixel movie looks quite different in the different dimension-and-scale combinations. The movie-display window's dimensions and the scale setting are identified in the examples above. (Here the browser background has been set to black to make the movie display window visible.)

PUBLISHING HTML FOR FLASH PLAYER FILES

Exact Fit changes the movie's height and width to the new specifications, even if it involves changing the aspect ratio and distorting the image.

No Scale keeps the movie at a constant size. Resizing the browser window can crop the image.

✔ Tip

■ If you define the movie-display window as 100 percent of the width and height of the browser window, in some browser versions, no matter how large your viewer makes the browser window, a scroll bar always appears. Setting the width and height to 95 percent (or lower) ensures that all viewers will be able to enlarge the browser window enough to eliminate the scroll bar.

To control placement of the movie window in the movie-display window:

◆ To align the movie window within the movie-display window, in the Flash Alignment section of the HTML tab of the Publish Settings dialog, *do either of the following:*

▲ From the Horizontal pop-up menu, choose Left, Center, or Right.

▲ From the Vertical pop-up menu, choose Top, Center, or Bottom.

Flash positions the movie within the movie-display window (**Figure 16.35**).

Horizontal: Right; Vertical: Center

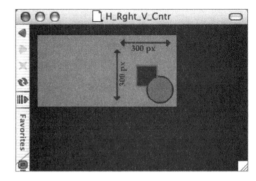

Horizontal: Left; Vertical: Center

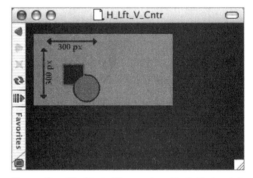

Figure 16.35 The Flash Alignment section's Horizontal and Vertical pop-up menus allow you to position your movie within the movie-display window when the dimensions of that window differ from those of the movie. Compare the results of two different settings for this 300-by-300–pixel movie set inside a 200-by-100–pixel display window. The light-gray rectangle is the display window, which automatically fills with the same color as your movie's background.

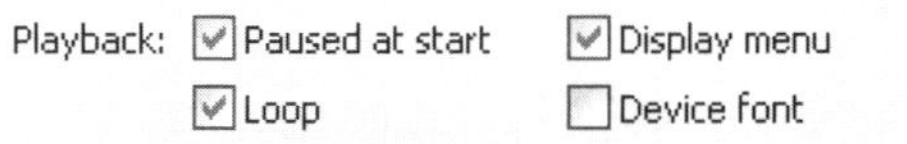

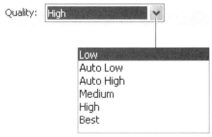

Figure 16.36 The HTML section of the Publish Settings dialog gives you options for controlling playback. You control whether the movie starts playing immediately in the browser window, or if it's in a paused state waiting for user input to start; whether the movie loops, or plays through just once; and whether users can control playback from the contextual menu. For Windows machines, you can improve speed playback by activating device fonts.

Figure 16.37 The Quality setting for publishing HTML balances image quality against playback speed in a published movie.

To set playback options:

◆ In the Playback section of the HTML section of the Publish Settings dialog (**Figure 16.36**), *choose any of the following options:*

Paused at start makes users begin the movie manually (by clicking a button or by choosing Play from the contextual menu).

Display menu creates a contextual menu with playback options available to users.

Loop makes the movie start over when it reaches the last frame.

Device font speeds playback on Windows systems. The Device Font option allows Windows systems to substitute aliased system fonts for fonts that aren't installed on the user's system. This substitution takes place only in static text blocks where you've enabled device fonts during the authoring phase.

To control antialiasing and smoothing:

◆ From the Quality pop-up menu in the HTML section of the Publish Settings dialog (**Figure 16.37**), *choose one of the following options:*

Low. Flash keeps antialiasing off.

Auto Low. Flash starts playback with antialiasing off; but if it finds that the viewer's computer and connection can handle antialiasing while keeping the movie's specified frame rate, Flash turns antialiasing on.

Auto High. Flash turns antialiasing on to start with and turns it off if playback drops below the movie's specified frame rate.

Medium. Taking the middle ground, Flash forgoes bitmap smoothing but does some antialiasing.

High. Flash uses antialiasing on everything but smooths bitmaps only if there is no animation.

Best. Flash keeps antialiasing on and smooths all bitmaps.

To control transparency:

◆ From the Window Mode pop-up menu
(**Figure 16.38**), *choose one of the following options:*

Window plays the Flash movie in a separate movie-display window within the Web page. Flash sets the background color of the Web page to be the same as your movie's background color. The movie-display window prevents the appearance of HTML elements that lie on layers below the Flash movie and often prevents (or interferes with) the appearance of elements above the movie-display window as well. Window mode gives Flash complete control of the window-display area of the screen and therefore results in the best performance.

Opaque Windowless plays the Flash movie window directly in the browser window. This setting allows elements of the Web page that lie above the Flash movie to appear. Elements of the Web page that lie below the Flash movie do not appear.

Transparent Windowless plays the Flash movie window directly in the browser window. This setting allows elements of the Web page to show through in any areas of your Flash movie that don't contain objects. Using this setting may slow the playback of your animation.

Only certain browsers (and certain versions of Flash Player) support the ability to create transparent backgrounds for your published SWF content. The earliest versions of Flash Player that support the transparent windowless setting are 6.0.65.0 (Windows) and 6.0.67.0 (Mac). In Mac OS X (browsers in Mac Classic mode don't support the transparent windowless setting), Internet Explorer (IE) 5.1 and 5.2 support this setting. In Windows, IE 3 or later supports it. Other browsers that support this setting, on both platforms, include Netscape 7.0 (or later), Mozilla 1.0 (or later), and AOL/CompuServe.

Figure 16.38 For viewers of your Flash movie who use qualified browsers, you can create a transparency effect that reveals Web-page elements beneath any transparent areas of the movie. In the HTML tab of the Publish Settings dialog, set Window Mode to Transparent Windowless.

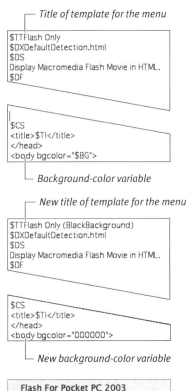

Title of template for the menu

```
$TTFlash Only
$DXDefaultDetection.html
$DS
Display Macromedia Flash Movie in HTML.
$DF
```

```
|
$CS
<title>$TI</title>
</head>
<body bgcolor="$BG">
```

Background-color variable

New title of template for the menu

```
$TTFlash Only (BlackBackground)
$DXDefaultDetection.html
$DS
Display Macromedia Flash Movie in HTML.
$DF
```

```
$CS
<title>$TI</title>
</head>
<body bgcolor="000000">
```

New background-color variable

```
Flash For Pocket PC 2003
Flash HTTPS
✓ Flash Only
  Flash Only (BlackBackground)
Flash with AICC Tracking
Flash with FSCommand
Flash with Named Anchors
Flash with SCORM 1.2 Tracking
Flash with SCORM 2004 Tracking
Image Map
QuickTime
```

Figure 16.39 The default HTML template picks up the movie's background color as the Web page's background color. You can modify a copy of the template (top). Change the Title tag, and set a specific background color (middle). The new title appears in the Template menu in the HTML tab of the Publish Settings dialog (bottom).

To see warnings about missing alternate content:

◆ At the bottom of the HTML section of the Publish Settings dialog, select the Show Warning Messages check box if you want Flash to notify you if the currently selected template creates tags to display alternate content—a GIF file, for example—but you've neglected to select the appropriate format in the Formats section of the Publish Settings dialog.

✔ Tip

■ The default HTML template automatically sets the background color of your Web page to the background color of your movie. If you want to use a different color, try creating a modified template (**Figure 16.39**). Open the default template, and save a copy with a new name. In the first line of code—$TTFlash Only—change the title to something like $TTFlash Only (BlackBackground), so Flash recognizes and adds the template to the Template menu. In the tag <BODY bgcolor="$BG">, replace $BG with the HTML code for a specific hex color (000000 for a black background, for example). Be sure to place the new template in Flash's HTML folder inside the Configuration folder (for more details, see the sidebar "The Mystery of the Configuration Folder," in Chapter 1). You will see the new template in the Template menu only after you restart Flash.

PUBLISHING HTML FOR FLASH PLAYER FILES

Using Alternate Image Formats

Although most viewers have access to the Flash Player plug-in required to view your Flash content, some may not. You can make at least some of your site available to them by providing alternate image files for their browsers to display. If you're using Flash animation for a simple Web banner, for example, you can use an animated GIF to re-create that banner for viewers who lack the Flash plug-in. Flash can publish alternate GIF, JPEG, PNG, and QuickTime files. Of course, you need a file with the proper HTML coding to direct the viewer's browser to display the alternate file. The HTML Templates named Image Map and QuickTime can assist you in creating the necessary HTML file, as can Flash's version-detection feature (see "Using Version Detection," later in this chapter).

Although each image format has its own set of publishing options, the basic methods for publishing all four alternate formats are the same. This task walks you though the settings for GIF files.

To publish GIF files:

1. Open the Flash document, and choose File > Publish Settings.

   The Publish Setting dialog appears; choose a new publishing profile, or leave the current setting.

2. In the Formats section of the dialog, choose GIF Image (.gif).

3. In the GIF section of the dialog (**Figure 16.40**), set GIF options as described in the following tasks.

4. Click Publish.

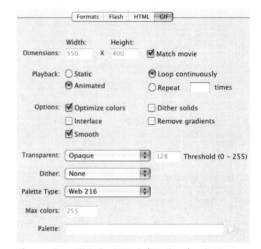

Figure 16.40 Click the GIF tab (Windows) or button (Mac) of the Publish Settings dialog to access the options for creating a static or animated GIF for your alternate image.

About the Image Map Template

If your Flash file contains button symbols linking to URLs, you can convert that content to an *image map*, a GIF (or PNG or JPEG) file containing hot spots that link to other sites. To have Flash create an image map whose hot spots coincide with your Flash button symbols, choose HTML as well as GIF (or PNG or JPEG) in the Formats section of the Publish Settings dialog. From the Template pop-up menu in the HTML section of the dialog, choose Image Map. Click Publish. Although Flash creates a SWF file whenever you publish HTML format files, the Image Map template creates an HTML file that tells browsers to display the GIF (or PNG or JPG) file and not the SWF. When the browser displays the image map, viewers see your graphic content, and the buttons seem live because they're active links. (Note that the Image Map template creates hot spots only from button symbols, not button components or movie clips acting as buttons).

Figure 16.41 Deselect Match Movie to enter the dimensions you want the published GIF image to be, or select Match Movie to use the movie's dimensions as the dimensions of your GIF image.

✔ Tip

■ The GIF section of the Publish Settings dialog contains a pop-up menu labeled Transparent, with choices of Opaque, Transparent, and Alpha. In previous versions of Flash, choosing Transparent created a GIF with a transparent background; choosing Alpha also created a GIF with a transparent background and allowed you to set a Threshold value for converting partly transparent Flash fills to completely transparent areas of the GIF (any fills with Alpha settings lower than the specified threshold became completely transparent in the published GIF). In Flash 8, however, the feature seems to be broken. No matter what settings you choose, the published GIF file always turns out to be fully opaque.

To set the dimensions of the GIF image:

◆ Under Dimensions in the GIF section of the Publish Settings dialog (**Figure 16.41**), *do either of the following:*

▲ To create a new size for the published GIF image, deselect Match Movie and enter values in the Width and Height fields.

▲ To keep the GIF images the same size as the original Flash movie, select Match Movie.

About the QuickTime Template

To convert your Flash content to a QuickTime movie, choose QuickTime and HTML in the Formats section of the Publish Settings dialog. From the Template pop-up menu in the HTML section of the dialog, choose QuickTime. Click Publish. The QuickTime template embeds the QuickTime version of your content within the HTML file. Note that currently, the QuickTime player can only handle playback of Flash Player 5 (or earlier) content.

To create static or animated GIFs:

♦ Under Playback in the GIF section of the Publish Settings dialog (**Figure 16.42**), *choose either of the following options:*

Static creates a static GIF.

Animated creates an animated GIF.

The animation settings become active. To make the animation run repeatedly, choose Loop Continuously. To repeat the animation a set number of times, choose Repeat and enter a number in the Repeat field. Flash exports all the frames of the movie as an animated GIF.

✔ Tips

■ By default, when creating a static GIF, Flash uses the first frame of your movie. To use another frame, create a keyframe at the desired frame number. Assign it the frame label #Static (**Figure 16.43**).

■ When creating animated GIFs, you can tell Flash to publish a subset of the movie's frames. Assign the label #First to the first keyframe of the subset; assign the label #Last to the keyframe that ends the subset. Flash creates an animated GIF from that range of frames (**Figure 16.44**).

Figure 16.42 To preserve the motion of your Flash movie (though not the sound or interactivity) for viewers who lack the Flash plug-in, choose Animated for Playback in the GIF section of the Publish Settings dialog.

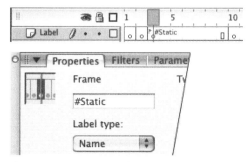

Figure 16.43 Assigning the frame label #Static tells Flash to use that frame for static GIF files.

Figure 16.44 Assigning the frame labels #First and #Last lets you limit the range of frames that Flash publishes as an animated GIF.

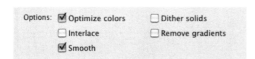

Figure 16.45 The Options settings in the GIF section of the Publish Settings dialog help you limit the amount of time that your viewers spend looking at a blank screen, waiting for an image to appear. (The Remove Gradients option is available only in the Publish Settings dialog, not in the Export GIF dialog.)

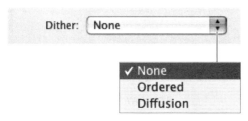

Figure 16.46 The GIF format has three options for dithering the colors that aren't included in the current color table.

To balance size, download speed, and appearance:

◆ Under Options in the GIF section of the Publish Settings dialog (**Figure 16.45**), *choose any of the following options:*

Optimize colors removes any unused colors from the GIF file's color table.

Interlace makes the GIF appear quickly at low resolution and come into focus as the download continues. (The Interlace option should be used only for static GIFs.)

Smooth makes Flash create smoothed bitmaps for your animated GIF. Deselecting Smooth reduces the size of the file.

Dither solids applies the dither method to solids as well as gradients and bitmapped images.

Remove gradients reduces file size by converting gradient fills to solid fills. (Flash uses the first color in the gradient as the solid fill color.)

To control colors that aren't in the current color palette:

1. From the Dither pop-up menu in the GIF section of the Publish Settings dialog (**Figure 16.46**), *choose one of the following options:*

None replaces the missing color with the closest match from the current palette.

Ordered simulates the missing color by applying a regular pattern of colors from the current palette.

Diffusion simulates the missing color by applying a random pattern of colors from the Web 216 palette. (You must also choose Web 216 as your Palette Type in step 2 for Diffusion to work.)

continues on next page

USING ALTERNATE IMAGE FORMATS

2. From the Palette Type pop-up menu, choose a color table for use with this GIF (**Figure 16.47**).

Your choices are Web 216 (the standard 216 Web-safe colors), Adaptive (only colors used in your document; 256 colors maximum), Web Snap Adaptive (a modified Adaptive palette, substituting Web-safe colors for any near matches to colors in the document that aren't Web safe), and Custom (the color table specified in step 4).

3. If you chose Adaptive or Web Snap Adaptive as the Palette Type, in the Max Colors field, type the number of colors you want to use.

This option lets you further limit the size of the color table available for the GIF and thus reduce file size.

4. If you chose Custom as the Palette Type, load the custom palette (**Figure 16.48**).

Click the Browse button (the folder icon). The file-import dialog appears; navigate to the custom palette file, select it, and click Open.

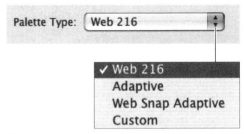

Figure 16.47 Choose a palette that optimizes colors for the published GIF image. You can create custom palettes or use the Web-safe or adaptive palettes provided by Flash.

Figure 16.48 When you choose Custom from the Palette Type pop-up menu, you must enter a filename in the Palette field. Click the Browse button (the folder icon) to open a dialog for locating the file.

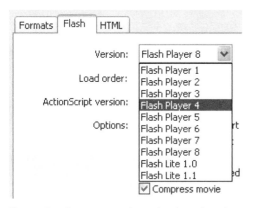

Figure 16.49 To get automatic version detection when you publish your Flash document, you must select version 4 or later in the Flash section of the Publish Settings dialog.

Using Version Detection

Version detection is the process of verifying what version of Flash Player is running on a viewer's system. Two of the HTML templates that come with Flash 8 create the coding necessary to carry out one form of version detection. If an end user is trying to view your Flash content from a system that has the required player, the browser displays your content. If Flash Player is missing or the version number is too low, the browser displays a Web page containing a link to Macromedia's Web site where the correct player can be downloaded.

To detect the viewer's Flash Player version:

1. Open your Flash document, and choose File > Publish Settings.

   The Publish Settings dialog appears; choose a new publishing profile, or leave the current setting.

2. Click the Flash tab (Windows) or button (Mac) in the dialog.

   The settings for Publishing SWF files appear.

3. From the Version pop-up menu, choose Flash version 4 or higher (**Figure 16.49**).

4. Click the HTML tab (Windows) or button (Mac) in the dialog.

continues on next page

5. From the Template menu, choose Flash Only or Flash HTTPS.

These are the only included templates that automatically create version-detection code for you.

6. Select the Detect Flash Version check box.

If you want to detect specific revisions to the Flash Player, enter them in the fields for minor and incremental revisions (**Figure 16.50**).

7. To confirm your settings, click OK.

When you publish a document using version detection, Flash creates an HTML file that displays the SWF file in a browser window; this HTML file also contains JavaScript coding for detecting the Flash Player version on the end user's system.

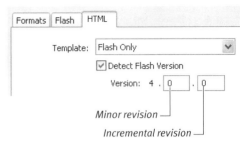

Figure 16.50 When you select the Detect Flash Version check box, the fields for minor and incremental revision numbers become active. Enter the precise version numbers that your end user will need to view your Flash content.

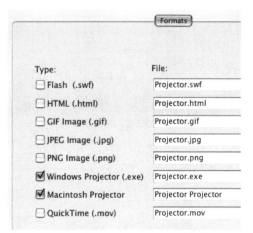

Figure 16.51 To create a stand-alone run-time version of your movie, choose Windows Projector or Macintosh Projector in the Formats tab of the Publish Settings dialog. You have no other options for formatting projectors.

Created on Mac

Created on Windows

Figure 16.52 The projector is a stand-alone run-time file with a special icon. When you create a Windows projector on a Mac, the icon looks like an ActionScript file's icon. When you view the file on Windows, the circular Flash icon appears. Double-click the icon to launch the projector.

Creating Projectors

Projectors are self-sufficient applications for playing Flash content. To play a projector file, the end user double-clicks the projector icon. Projectors are an excellent way to distribute movies directly to people; for example, you can e-mail a Flash-animated greeting card to a friend. Projectors are platform-specific, but you can make projectors for both the Mac and Windows platform from either platform.

To create a projector:

1. Open the Flash document from which you want to publish a projector.

2. Choose File > Publish Settings.

   The Publish Settings dialog appears; choose a new base publishing profile, or leave the current setting.

3. In the Formats section (**Figure 16.51**), *choose one of the following options:*

   Windows Projector (.exe) creates a projector that runs in Windows.

   Macintosh Projector creates a projector that runs on a Mac.

4. Click the Publish button.

   As it creates the projector files, Flash displays the Publishing dialog, which has a progress bar and a button for canceling the operation. Unless you choose a new location (via the file destination button), Flash places the projector files in the same location as the original Flash document. A projector has a distinctive icon (**Figure 16.52**).

Playing Macintosh Projectors Created in Windows

When you publish a Macintosh projector on a computer running the Windows operating system, Flash gives the projector the extension .hqx. That extension indicates a file encoded in binhex format. Macintosh users need to translate the file by using a program such as BinHex or StuffIt Deluxe to play the projector on the Mac OS.

Creating Publishing Profiles

Setting all the various publishing options can be tedious. If you use particular groups of settings repeatedly, you can save them as a publishing profile.

To save settings under a new profile name:

1. From an open Flash document, choose File > Publish Settings.

2. In the Publish Settings dialog, click the Create New Profile button—the plus sign to the right of the Current Profile menu (**Figure 16.53**).

   The Create New Profile dialog appears (**Figure 16.54**).

3. Type a name for your profile in the Profile Name field; for example, MyPubSettings.

4. Click OK to accept the name in the Create New Profile dialog.

   You return to the Publish Settings dialog, with your new profile selected in the Current Profile menu.

5. Set your desired publishing options using any techniques learned earlier in this chapter.

6. Click Publish or OK.

   Flash updates the current profile in the open document and publishes and/or closes the dialog. Flash incorporates the settings you made in step 5 into the profile named MyPubSettings and stores them with the current document. If you open a new document, that profile isn't available. To make the profile available to other documents, you must export it.

Delete current profile
Open the Profile Properties dialog
Duplicate an existing profile
Create a new profile
Import/export a custom profile

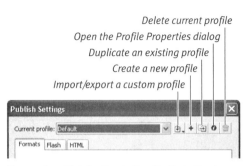

Figure 16.53 Click the Create New Profile button to begin the process of adding a new publishing profile to the current document.

Figure 16.54 Name your profile in the Create New Profile dialog.

CREATING PUBLISHING PROFILES

✔ Tips

■ To make small adjustments to an existing profile and save it as a new profile, start by duplicating the basic profile. Select the basic profile from the Current profile menu, and then click the Duplicate Profile button. The Duplicate Profile dialog appears for naming the new profile. Now follow steps 3–6 in the preceding task.

■ To delete a profile from the current Flash document, select the profile from the Current Profile menu and click the Delete Profile button (the Trash can icon). A warning dialog appears, asking you to verify the deletion. Click OK.

■ To rename a profile in the current Flash document, select the profile from the Current Profile menu and click the Rename Profile button (the *i* icon). The Profile Properties dialog appears. Type the profile's new name in the Profile Name field. Click OK.

More about Publishing Profiles

Publishing profile information is stored with each document. Unlike the case with HTML templates, no master menu of profiles is available each time you call up the Publish Settings dialog. You can, however, import and export profiles to make them available to other documents. Another important difference between publishing profiles and HTML templates is that a publishing profile isn't an immutable set of options that's the same each time you choose it. When you click OK or Publish in the Publish Settings dialog, all the current publishing options are incorporated into the profile that's selected in the Current Profile pop-up menu. Next time you open the Publish Settings dialog for that document, either in this work session or a later one, choosing a profile calls up the last settings you made with that profile selected in that document.

To export a profile:

1. Follow steps 1–5 in the preceding task.

2. From the Import/Export pop-up menu to the right of the Current Profile field, select Export (**Figure 16.55**).

   The Export Profile dialog appears (**Figure 16.56**). This is basically a Save As dialog, with a different name. By default, Profile (.xml) is selected in the Format (Mac) or Save as Type (Windows) menu.

3. Navigate to the location where you want to save the profile file.

4. Enter a name for the file.

5. Click Save.

   Flash saves the profile as an XML file in the specified location.

✔ Tip

■ The default location for storing profiles is a folder named Publish Profiles in the Configuration folder (see "The Mystery of the Configuration Folder," in Chapter 1). However, because the profiles aren't pulled into new Flash documents automatically, there is no reason you must store them there.

Figure 16.55 You can export publishing profiles to make use of them in other documents.

Figure 16.56 Store exported profiles in the Publishing Profiles folder in the Configuration folder, or store them with your Flash documents.

Figure 16.57 To use a saved profile in a different document, you must import it. Select Import from the Import/Export Profile menu in the Publish Settings dialog.

Figure 16.58 Navigate to the saved profile via the Import Profile dialog, and click Open to make the profile available from the Current Profile menu in the Publish Settings dialog.

To import a profile:

1. In a Flash document in which you want to use the saved profile, choose File > Publish Settings.

2. From the Import/Export pop-up menu, select Import (**Figure 16.57**).

   The Import Profile dialog appears. This is basically a normal file-import dialog (**Figure 16.58**). By default, Profile (.xml) is selected in the Enable (Mac) or Files of Type (Windows) menu.

3. Navigate to the saved the profile.

4. Click Open.

   The profile becomes available from the Current Profile menu in the Publish Settings dialog of the active Flash document.

Exporting Flash to Other Formats

When you export Flash movies, you can export the entire movie or just one frame. Flash exports to a variety of formats that aren't included in the Publish Settings dialog (see the sidebar "Flash Export Formats"). Although the options for the export formats differ, the basic process is always the same.

When Flash exports an entire movie, it outputs each frame of the movie to create frame-by-frame animation. Playing an exported movie works just like playing a movie in the authoring environment. The animation in movie clips doesn't play; there is no execution of ActionScript. This is true even when you export to AVI or QuickTime; Flash exports a sequence of bitmaps. (When you publish to QuickTime, Flash creates a Flash layer, using vectors, inside a QuickTime movie, thus preserving interactivity.)

The example used in the following sections exports to Illustrator format, which preserves the vector information from your Flash graphics.

To export a single frame to Illustrator format:

1. With your Flash document open, in the Timeline, move the playhead to the frame you want to export.

2. Choose File > Export > Export Image (**Figure 16.59**).

   The Export Image dialog appears (**Figure 16.60**).

3. Navigate to the location where you want to save the file.

4. Enter a name in the Save As (Mac) or File Name (Windows) field.

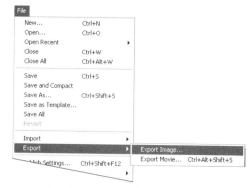

Figure 16.59 To export a single frame of your movie, choose File > Export > Export Image.

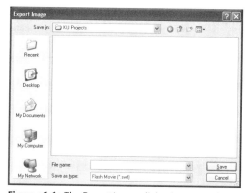

Figure 16.60 The Export Image dialog lets you select an export format, name your file, and navigate to the location where you want to save the file.

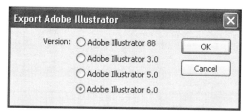

Figure 16.61 Whenever an export format requires additional settings, a dialog with format-specific options appears when you click Save in the Export Image dialog. You can export to four versions of Illustrator, for example.

EXPORTING FLASH TO OTHER FORMATS

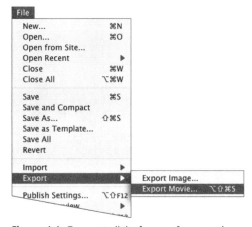

Figure 16.62 To export all the frames of your movie, choose File > Export> Export Movie.

Flash Export Formats

You can export a single image from your movie or export all the frames as separate images. On both Mac and Windows, you can export the following file formats: Adobe Illustrator (.ai); GIF image, animated GIF, and GIF sequence (.gif); DXF Sequence and AutoCAD DXF Image EPS (.eps), Flash player (.swf), Macromedia Flash Video (.flv), JPEG Sequence and JPEG Image (.jpg), PNG Image and PNG Sequence (.png); and QuickTime (.mov). On Windows systems, you can also export to Bitmap (.bmp), Enhanced Metafile (.emf), WAV audio (.wav), Windows AVI (.avi), and Windows Metafile (.wmf). On the Mac, you can also export to PICT (.pct) and QuickTime Video (.mov).

5. From the Format (Mac) or Save As Type (Windows) pop-up menu, choose Adobe Illustrator.

Flash adds the proper extension, .ai, to your filename.

6. Click Save.

The Export Adobe Illustrator dialog appears (**Figure 16.61**).

Whenever your chosen export format requires you to set further parameters, Flash displays those parameters in a dialog after you click Save. For Illustrator format, the additional parameter is a version number.

7. Choose the version to which you want to export.

8. Click OK.

Flash displays the Exporting dialog, which contains a progress bar and a button for canceling the export process.

To export the entire movie to Illustrator format:

◆ Follow the instructions in the preceding task; but in step 2, from the File menu, choose Export > Export Movie, or press Option-Shift-⌘-S (Mac) or Ctrl-Alt-Shift-S (Windows) (**Figure 16.62**); and in step 5, choose Adobe Illustrator Sequence.

When you choose Export Movie, Flash creates a separate Illustrator file for each frame of the movie and numbers the files sequentially.

Printing from Flash

When you're editing a Flash document, you can print frames as individual pages or print several frames per page in a storyboard layout. You choose how many frames each row in the storyboard contains. Flash sizes the frames accordingly. Use the Print Margins (Mac) or Page Setup (Windows) command to choose layout options.

To print one frame per page:

1. In your open Flash document, choose File > Print Margins (Mac) or Page Setup (Windows).

   The Print Margins or Page Setup dialog appears (**Figure 16.63**).

2. From the Frames pop-up menu, choose All Frames.

3. From the Layout pop-up menu, choose Fit on One Page.

4. Click OK.

5. Choose File > Print.

   The Print dialog appears.

6. Enter the desired frame numbers in the From and To fields.

7. Click Print.

✔ Tips

- If your Macintosh printer isn't capable of printing PostScript, be sure to select the Disable PostScript check box.

- To print just the first frame of each scene in your movie, in step 2, choose First Frame Only.

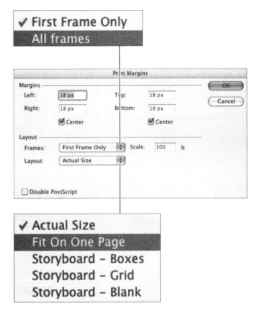

Figure 16.63 The options in the Print Margins (Mac, top) and Page Setup (Windows, bottom) dialogs enable you to print the frames of your movie as single pages or as storyboard layouts during authoring.

PRINTING FROM FLASH

Figure 16. 64 The Layout menu of the Print Margins (Mac) or Page Setup (Windows) dialog offers three storyboard options: Boxes, Grid, and Blank.

Storyboard boxes

Storyboard grid

Storyboard blank

Figure 16.65 When you print your Flash document in a storyboard layout, each movie frame is either outlined in a box, set inside a grid, or printed as just a frame.

To print storyboard thumbnails:

1. Follow steps 1 and 2 of the preceding task.

2. From the Layout pop-up menu (**Figure 16.64**), *choose one of the following options:*

   Storyboard - Boxes outlines each movie-frame rectangle.

   Storyboard - Grid prints the frames in a grid.

   Storyboard - Blank prints just the graphic elements of each movie frame. The layout parameters appear.

3. In the Frames (Mac) or Frames Across (Windows) field, enter the number of frames you want to print across the page.

   Flash prints as many as 128 frames in a single storyboard row.

4. In the Story Margin (Mac) or Frame Margin (Windows) field, enter the amount of space you want to use between frames in your layout.

5. Click OK.

6. Choose File > Print.

   The Print dialog appears.

7. If you want to print only some pages of your thumbnails, type those page numbers in the From and To fields.

8. Click OK.

   Flash creates the thumbnails, using the options you specified (**Figure 16.65**).

✔ Tip

■ To print the scene and frame number below each frame in the layout, select the Label Frames check box in the Page Setup (Windows) dialog. The check box appears in the Print Margins (Mac) dialog as well, but it doesn't actually create labels for your printed thumbnails.

PRINTING FROM FLASH

549

Printing from Flash Player

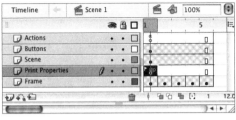

Flash gives you the option of letting your viewers print some or all of a movie directly from Flash Player's contextual menu. By default, the contextual menu's Print command prints every frame in the movie. You restrict printing to certain frames by labeling them as printable in the original Flash document. (Advanced ActionScripters can provide viewers with other options for printing Flash content.)

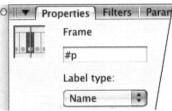

Figure 16.66 To define keyframes that print when viewers choose Print from Flash Player's contextual menu, select the keyframe and enter #p in the Label field of the Frame Properties tab of the Property inspector.

To set frames to print from the contextual menu:

1. To create a test document, open a new copy of the ObjectActionsTemplate you created in Chapter 13.

    This document has separate layers for Actions, Buttons, Scene, and Frame. Identifying text for each frame makes it easy to see what frames are printed in this task.

2. In the Timeline, insert a new layer; name it Print Properties.

    This layer will hold the frame labels that define a frame as printable. By default, frame 1 of the layer is a keyframe.

3. Select keyframe 1 of the Print Properties layer.

4. Access the Frame Properties tab of the Property inspector.

5. To define the selected frame as printable, in the Label field, enter #p (**Figure 16.66**).

    Note that the label must be a lowercase letter *p*.

6. In the Timeline, select frame 3 in the Print Properties layer, and choose Insert > Keyframe.

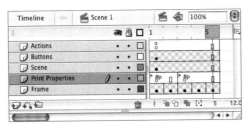

Figure 16.67 Create a keyframe with the frame label #p for each frame you would like to be printable.

Figure 16.68 In your browser, Control-click (Mac) or right-click (Windows) to access Flash Player's contextual menu. Choosing Print outputs all the pages defined as printable.

7. To define the selected keyframe as printable, in the Label field, enter #p (**Figure 16.67**).

8. Publish your Flash movie.

For the contextual menu to be available in the published movie, you need to set the playback options in the HTML section of the Publish Settings dialog to Display Menu (see "Publishing HTML for Flash Player Files," earlier in this chapter).

9. View the resulting Flash Player file in your browser.

10. To access the contextual menu, Control-click (Mac) or right-click (Windows) anywhere in the movie window.

The contextual menu appears (**Figure 16.68**).

11. Choose Print.

Flash prints the frames you labeled as printable (1 and 3) and skips the frames that don't contain the #p label (frames 2, 4, and 5).

✔ Tips

■ If there are no frames with the #p label in the movie, the contextual menu's Print command prints each frame in the movie.

■ If you define more than one frame as printable by labeling it #p, when you publish the movie, Flash displays a warning message in the Output window, letting you know that there are multiple frames with the same label name. If the only duplicates are #p labels, just ignore the warning.

To disable printing from Flash Player:

1. Open the Flash file for which you want to disable printing.

2. In the Timeline, select any keyframe.

3. Access the Frame Properties tab of the Property inspector.

4. In the Label field, enter !#p.

   When you publish the file, the Print option is unavailable from Flash Player's contextual menu (**Figure 16.69**).

✔ Tip

■ You can limit the options available from the contextual menu in a published Flash Player file by deselecting the Display Menu check box in the Playback section of the HTML tab of the Publish Settings dialog (**Figure 16.70**). (Note that the menu choices Debugger and Show Redraw Regions apppear only in the version of Flash Player that installs with the Flash authoring application. End users who don't have that version of the Player won't see those options.)

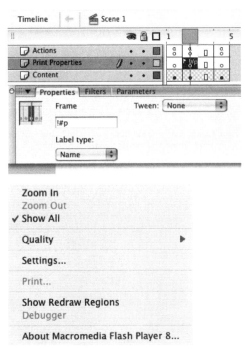

Figure 16.69 Attaching the label !#p to any frame in a movie (top) grays out the Print option in the contextual menu of Flash Player (bottom).

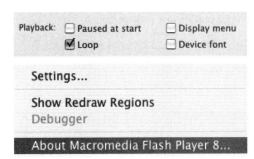

Figure 16.70 Deselecting the Display Menu check box in the HTML section of the Publish Settings dialog (top) limits the functions of the contextual menu for your published movie and is one way to disable printing from within your movie (bottom). The browser's print functions will still be available, however

INDEX

P

Page Setup dialog, 548
paint-bucket tool, 119
Paint Normal mode, 166–167
panels
    Actions, 390–395
    Behaviors, adding actions to buttons, 407–410
    documents, 28–30
    grouped
        creating tabbed, 33–34
        open default panel set, 35
        separating tabbed, 34
        separating vertical, 32
        vertically, 31–32
    Help, 510
    Scene, 320
    settings, 120
paragraph attributes
    alignment, 90
    first-line indent, 92
    line spacing, 92
    margins, 91
    selecting paragraph, 89
parameters, grid, 20
Parameters command (Window menu), 36, 377
parentheses syntax, 402
Paste command (Edit menu), 103, 463
Paste Frames command (Edit menu), 248, 324
Paste in Center command (Edit menu), 103
Paste in Place command (Edit menu), 103
Pasteboard, 16
pathnames, 408
paths, 68
pausing, movie-clip buttons, 433
PDF (Portable Document Format) files, importing, 460–461
pen tool, freeform shapes, 65–68
pencil tool
    freeform shapes, 64
    smoothing sketches, 129
pinned scripts, 454
Play command (Control menu), 482
Play Rhythm button, 495
Play Sound dialog, 495
playback
    delivery preparations, 506–509
    movie options, 531
    stopping sound, 489–490
Polygon mode, 100
Portable Document Format (PDF) files, importing, 460–461
positioning graphics
    bounding box, 110
    Property Inspector, 108

visually, 109
preferences
    launching Flash, 2–3
    new settings, 3
    selections, 94
Preferences command (Edit menu), 2, 463
Preferences dialog, 2, 19, 394
Press check box, 414
Press mouse event, 417
previewing actions, interactivity, 411–412
Print command (File menu), 548
Print dialog, 548
Print Margins command (File menu), 548
Print Margins dialog, 548
printing
    disabling, 552
    from Flash, 548–549
    from Flash Player, 550–552
    storyboard thumbnails, 549
projectors
    Macintosh, 541
    movie delivery, 541
Properties command (Window menu), 36
Properties tab (Property Inspector), 36
Property Inspector
    accessing Properties tab, 36
    assigning fill colors, 54
    entering values, 37
    hide/show information area, 37
    positioning graphics, 108
    power of, 38
Protect from Import check box, 518
Publish command (File menu), 513
Publish Preview command (File menu), 513
Publish Settings dialog, 509, 511
publishing
    versus exporting, 511
    GIF files, 534–535
    movie delivery, 511–514
    profiles, movie delivery, 542–545
    SWF files, 515
Publishing dialog, 513

Q–R

QuickTime template, 535

radial gradients
    creating, 48
    focal points, 123
raw shapes, 60
Rectangle Settings dialog, 61
registration marks, 211
relative pathnames, 408

INDEX

INDEX

The Learning Curve
Allan Glen's Building
Central College of Commerce
190 Cathedral Street
Glasgow
G4 0ND
Tel 0141 271 6240

Visit Peachpit on the Web at www.peachpit.com

- Read the latest articles and download timesaving tipsheets from best-selling authors such as Scott Kelby, Robin Williams, Lynda Weinman, Ted Landau, and more!

- Join the Peachpit Club and save 25% off all your online purchases at peachpit.com every time you shop—plus enjoy free UPS ground shipping within the United States.

- Search through our entire collection of new and upcoming titles by author, ISBN, title, or topic. There's no easier way to find just the book you need.

- Sign up for newsletters offering special Peachpit savings and new book announcements so you're always the first to know about our newest books and killer deals.

- Did you know that Peachpit also publishes books by Apple, New Riders, Adobe Press, Macromedia Press and palmOne Press? Swing by the Peachpit family section of the site and learn about all our partners and series.

- Got a great idea for a book? Check out our About section to find out how to submit a proposal. You could write our next best-seller!

You'll find all this and more at www.peachpit.com. Stop by and take a look today!